LANGUAGE ENDANGERMENT AND LANGUAGE MAINTENANCE

LANGUAGE ENDANGERMENT AND LANGUAGE MAINTENANCE

edited by

David Bradley
and
Maya Bradley

Routledge
Taylor & Francis Group

LONDON AND NEW YORK

First published 2002
by Routledge Curzon

Published 2013 by Routledge

2 Park Square, Milton Park, Abingdon, Oxfordshire OX14 4RN

Simultaneously published in the USA and Canada
by Routledge
711 Third Avenue, New York, NY, 10017

First issued in paperback 2014

Routledge is an imprint of the Taylor & Francis Group, an informa business

British Library Cataloguing in Publication Data
A catalogue record of this book is available from the British Library

Library of Congress Cataloguing in Publication Data
A catalogue record for this book has been requested

ISBN 978-0-700-71456-8 (hbk)
ISBN 978-1-138-87834-1 (pbk)

Table of Contents

Table of Figures, Maps and Tables

1. FIGURES

Bowden, The Impact of Malay on Taba

van Engelenhoven, Concealment, Maintenance and Renaissance

2. MAP

Bowden, The Impact of Malay on Taba

3.   TABLES

Mühlhäusler, A Language Plan for Norfolk Island

Hajek, Language Maintenance and Survival in East Timor

Burridge, Steel Tyres or Rubber Tyres

Eira, Language Maintenance at the Micro Level

Introduction
David Bradley & Maya Bradley

Until recently, most linguists appeared not to be concerned with the rapid disappearance of most of the languages of the world, and linguistics as a discipline also paid only limited attention. Those who did work in this area used terms such as language death and other lugubrious metaphors. More recently, this complacency about the human disaster of loss of language and culture has been replaced by concern and action, and many linguists are now working with communities in documentation, maintenance, salvage and revival programmes. We still must contend with community attitudes which do not value "small" languages and view the global spread of English and other dominant languages as progress.

The level of language endangerment is now much more extreme than that of other kinds of loss of biodiversity. Various scholars have estimated that up to 90 per cent of the world's languages will disappear during the 21st century unless — and many perhaps even if — we do something now. If 90 per cent of the world's animal or plant diversity were equally at risk, there would be an international outcry, David Suzuki would move into overdrive, and green politics would garner much greater support. Language is the richest part of our human diversity, yet we have not reached the public consciousness with this issue.

Why is work on endangered languages (ELs) important? There are at least four main types of reason: linguistic, ethical, scientific and symbolic.

1) From the point of view of linguistics, we must describe ELs. If languages disappear undescribed, we will never know whether they had otherwise unattested or rare structures. Also, it is clear that ELs change in different ways from other languages, and this has important implications for historical linguistic theory.

2) Ethical reasons: if languages disappear undescribed, future generations will not be able to learn the language of their ancestors and will not have access to various aspects of

traditional knowledge and culture. From an ethical point of view, we have no right to deprive them of the possibility of retaining or regaining their language and culture.

3) Scientific reasons: every society has different knowledge and encodes it using distinctive linguistic patterns, so each language categorises the world in a unique way which comprises a world view. Furthermore, each society lives in a different ecological system and has unique knowledge of its environment and the plants and animals in it; this would be lost if the language disappears. It may turn out that much of this knowledge has scientific value for the development of new drugs, foods and materials, all of which have practical and economic benefits too.

4) Symbolic reasons: group identity and self-esteem are of paramount importance. Language is a crucial element of this identity, even when speakers do not feel the need to attain fluency in the language.

Of course the first type of reason could be seen as primarily linguistic self-interest. But it and the third are exactly parallel to the biodiversity arguments which have gained so much public support for environmental activism. How would we ever know that the group whose language died did not know about a medicinal plant which can cure cancer or a cultivated plant which can resist pests without chemicals? But the fourth type of reason — the need for identity and a positive self-image — is the one which is crucial to so many communities and groups in this age of globalisation.

The globalisation of English and the spread of other national languages are not so different from the spread of new genetically modified plant varieties controlled by multinational companies. English is even being promoted by many governments in countries where English is nobody's first language, and nearly all nations promote their national language at the expense of minority and migrant languages. So, if anything, the language experiment now underway will lead to even greater homogeneity than the experiment with our food; and to even greater centralisation and control of knowledge than the commercial monopolies created by the sterile strains of genetically modified plants.

1. THIS VOLUME

This volume contains twenty chapters on many aspects of research on ELs in a wide range of settings. These are grouped into four sections: theoretical overview (Chapters 1 to 4), what happens to languages in various indigenous settings (Chapters 5 to 13), in migrant settings (Chapters 14 to 17), and practical strategies and resources for maintaining ELs (Chapters 18 to 20). Of course there are many theoretical and practical observations in the thirteen chapters on specific indigenous and migrant settings as well.[1]

The chapters represent long field experience with ELs, particularly those of Australia and its Pacific and Asian surroundings, and many years of working with speech communities to help them to keep and develop their languages.

Languages of Australia and its territories, Papua New Guinea, eastern Indonesia, mainland Southeast, South and East Asia, Europe, Canada and South America are represented. Since most previous work on ELs has concentrated on those of Europe and North America, the case studies here are novel in a variety of ways. For example, many of these languages are endangered by a non-European language — Chinese, Assamese, Indonesian/Malay, Tok Pisin and so on. There is also one discussion of an endangered creole, that of Norfolk Island; conversely, several Australian Aboriginal languages are being replaced by Kriol, the creole spoken across much of northern Australia.

A number of chapters discuss the distinctive nature of language change during language shift, and others raise a variety of additional theoretical issues which have arisen during research on language endangerment.

Practical issues including the development of dialect surveys, orthographies, fonts, dictionaries, procedures for recovery of recently extinct languages from imperfect written records and other

---

[1] The editors are most grateful to the anonymous referees and others who have provided comments on the chapters which follow; but of course only we are responsible for remaining shortcomings.

tools for language maintenance (LM) are outlined. Also, we are reminded again and again to listen to the speech community and not to presume that we know what LM strategy is best for them.

The authors are based at nine universities in Australia, Europe and the United States. Six of us have been working in a joint Australian Research Council project[2] with David Bradley as Team Leader since 1998, and nearly all authors participated in a symposium which we convened at La Trobe University in Melbourne, Australia in November 1999.

However this volume is not a conference proceedings. This introduction and several chapters included here were not presented at the conference, and most other chapters have undergone substantial refinement and expansion from the versions which were presented. Two papers presented at the symposium do not appear here.[3]

1.1   Theoretical issues

The four chapters in this section deal with four important issues often overlooked when considering ELs, and discuss their theoretical ramifications. These are:

1)   What people think about language is crucial

2)   Linguists have a variety of ways to change attitudes and maintain languages

3)   Multilingualism is normal in much of the world, and so it is not unreasonable or cognitively problematic to maintain ELs in addition to Languages of Wider Communication (LWC)

4)   However, languages exist as part of a total social system, and we cannot prevent that system from changing.

---

[2]   David Bradley, Blake, Maya Bradley, Burridge, van Engelenhoven and Florey most gratefully acknowledge the support of the Australian Research Council large grant (project A59803475) as well as additional support from the UNESCO Endangered Languages programme for this research.
[3]   These were by Michael Clyne on the situation of a variety of languages spoken by migrants in Australia, and by David Nash on computer and Internet resources for LM.

The discussion of attitudes to languages in Chapter 1 provides a sociolinguistic framework for issues which arise in all of the following chapters. Wurm's outline of LM strategies in Chapter 2 similarly foreshadows what is being done by the authors and other linguists to help many communities. Chapter 3 by Aikhenvald gives specific examples of exuberant multilingualism from South America and from Papua New Guinea; parallels are very widespread in the world. She notes that contact with an LWC may result in a breakdown of this stable multilingualism, so that people may lose not only their "own" language, but also their ability in those of many of their neighbours.

Chapter 4 discusses the development of an ecological linguistics, originating with Haugen (1972). Mühlhäusler outlines this model and its implications, referring to his own extended studies of the ecology of language and the development and spread of pidgins and creoles in the Pacific since the nineteenth century, as further exemplified and discussed in his Chapter 12.

1.2 Language in indigenous settings

Even in Europe there are quite a few languages which are not LWCs. Some which are national languages, such as Irish, are severely endangered. National languages spoken by groups outside the borders of the primary countries where they are used may also be in a similar situation, as Swedish is in Finland. Ahlqvist provides background on these two cases in Chapter 5. Of course there are also many regional languages of Europe which have become progressively more endangered by national languages over the last two centuries; but some of these, such as Catalan, Basque, Sami, Romansch and so on, have now become the focus of enthusiastic popular revitalisation movements and are receiving substantial government and European Community support; for some examples, see Dazzi Gross & Mondada (1999).

Countries mainly settled by Anglophone migrants in the initial stage of contact, like the United States, Canada and Australia, have until quite recently made it particularly difficult for indigenous groups to maintain their languages. Now this is changing, but for many communities it may be too late for normal transmission to resume. In the United States there are now many tribal colleges and other tribal organisations struggling to keep languages and cultures alive; their journal, *Tribal College*,[4] is compelling reading. Similar work is underway among the Original Nations in Canada and in many Australian Aboriginal communities. In Chapter 6 Stebbins discusses efforts to maintain the Sm'algyax language of the Tsimshian Nation in Canada, and her work with them to prepare a dictionary. Chapter 19 by Corris et al. also provides some suggestions about how to go about making dictionaries for practical use, with case studies from various Australian Aboriginal and Papua New Guinea settings. Blake has been working towards language revival for a number of Aboriginal communities in Victoria, Australia whose languages are extinct. He has been recovering data from early materials collected mainly by non-linguists. In Chapter 11 he outlines the procedures he has used and the quantity of available data for the 22 such languages. Blake's materials have been used by other linguists and by Blake himself to prepare teaching materials for a number of these groups. A revival of the Kaurna language in South Australia is also underway, using materials compiled by Amery and Mühlhäusler from similar old sources. Chapter 20 lists some of the other organisations doing Aboriginal language work in Australia.

Another outcome of colonial contact has been the development of pidgins and creoles. Many, including speakers of some such creoles, may regard them as just "broken" or debased versions of the lexical source language, as in the case of the Torres Strait creole, also known to its speakers just as "Broken". Mühlhäusler has conducted extensive research into the development of the English-lexicon pidgins and creoles in the Pacific region, and in Chapter 12 of this volume he reports on a project which has just started, to document and maintain the creole of Norfolk Island, an offshore territory of Australia. While other creoles, like Papua New Guinea Tok Pisin and Kriol of northern Australia, are endangering many indigenous languages in the region, such creoles are themselves in turn threatened by decreolisation towards or replacement by English, as is Norfolk creole.

Major political change due to non-Anglophone colonialism and conflict is another source of language endangerment; in Chapter 13 Hajek discusses the situation in East Timor, tracing changes in

---

[4]   Available from PO Box 720, Mancos CO 81328, USA, or <http://www.tribalcollegejournal.org>.

language use during the Portuguese colonial period and the period of Indonesian control from 1975 to 1999. While one indigenous language, Tetum, may have spread, others have declined or even become extinct during the violence of the last 25 years; but Indonesian, which expanded massively after 1975, has now contracted even more rapidly.

Chapters 7 to 10 detail various instances of endangerment and change due to contact between indigenous minority languages and other indigenous languages of Asia and South America. While this is an extremely common type of endangerment, there have been relatively few previous such studies. The linguists involved have also been working with the various communities in maintenance efforts.

Our Chapter 7 discusses minority language policy in China and a survey of a small area of Southwestern China. All minority languages of China are endangered by Chinese, especially those which have been politically lumped into a larger ethnic group. We located a surprising number of unreported and undescribed ELs just within one minority group, the Yi; extending the survey would certainly yield many more. As the government is now teaching literacy in Yi with a character script that, like Chinese, represents meaning but not sound, we have tried to help some communities to prepare materials using a romanised transcription of the local language so that children who do not speak the language of their family background will have a way to learn it and become literate in it at the same time.

Morey has been working in a number of Tai-language communities in northeastern India, each of which has a distinct literary tradition and manuscripts. However, many are losing or have lost the spoken language, which is largely replaced by Indic Assamese. In Chapter 8 he describes the situation and gives examples of the various fonts he has created for these scripts. He has also been printing small books in various of these languages, to assist in LM work.

Chapter 9 discusses a fascinating and very frequently encountered type of language contact: influence from a dominant language into a more localised language. Here, it is Malay into Taba; both are Austronesian languages. Contact between genetically related languages of course raises special problems: what is genetic, what is drift and what is contact-induced? Bowden observes that many complex syntactic constructions can only be expressed in Taba using Malay words and structures. Whether this is a stage on the way to total replacement of Taba by Malay is not yet clear; but Indonesian/Malay is now replacing many local languages in eastern Indonesia and elsewhere, as Florey and van Engelenhoven observe in Chapters 16 and 17.

In Chapter 10 Aikhenvald provides data on rapid morphosyntactic change and convergence among various Amazonian languages, concentrating on Tariana. In mid-2000 she conducted a workshop, teaching the EL Tariana to non-speakers and testing a new dictionary for the community.

1.3   Language in migrant settings

Another neglected issue in studies of endangered languages concerns dialect death and language loss among migrant communities. One might think that this is not likely to lead to language death, but paradoxically some Austronesian languages of the Moluccas in eastern Indonesia, represented in three chapters by Bowden, Florey and van Engelenhoven, may be less intact in their original homelands than elsewhere, though they are very severely endangered in the migrant setting in the Netherlands as well. Florey and van Engelenhoven discuss some of these using a variety of case study and other materials from the Netherlands in Chapters 16 and 17. Burridge also deals with another instance in Chapter 14: Anabaptist communities in Canada, some maintaining and some losing their distinctive variety of German while also using or losing standard written German as a diglossic High for liturgical purposes — though of course German in Europe is not endangered.

The importance of writing systems and their symbolic value for group identity is illustrated in Chapter 15 by Eira on the Hmong, a group who came after 1975 as refugees from Laos to various countries including Australia. The Hmong, like many groups in Southeast Asia and elsewhere, have cosmologised their former lack of writing in a traditional story. Now they closely associate the development of an orthography with progress and improved self-esteem; and some prefer a new writing system which is maximally distinctive, the *Phaj hauj* script discussed here.

The parallel with the situation of the various Tai groups in Northeastern India described in Chapter 8 by Morey is not exact, as those Tai scripts have a long history and in most cases a large quantity of manuscripts which can now hardly be read; but the focus on orthographies is similar. On the other hand, an EL may also be maintained in purely oral form; linguists should be the last people to confuse the existence of writing with the status and structural integrity of a language. In China, the minority leadership of some groups has decided that their group will use Chinese for written purposes, and the minority language only orally. This is of course a reasonable option given the need for knowledge and literacy in the national dominant language, but may eventually lead to language shift.

1.4 Practical issues

Thieberger's Chapter 18 provides a cautionary discussion: what exactly does a speech community mean when it says it wants to maintain its language, and does this mean that linguists and school systems should promote full knowledge and use of the traditional form of the language? His answer, based on extensive experience in Australia and the Pacific, is that language has a symbolic heritage value but the community sometimes does not want to go back to it other than to a limited degree — which an outside linguist might paternalistically regard as insufficient.

As we have seen, Chapter 19 by Corris et al. gives a variety of suggestions about how to make a dictionary accessible and useful for the community of speakers. In the conclusion, Chapter 20, we have outlined some other resources and general desiderata for work on ELs.

2. WHAT IS TO BE DONE?

Even if a community may now have other priorities, it is surely our duty as linguists to preserve what exists — oral and literary traditions of all kinds as well as descriptive materials on threatened languages. Our concern about language endangerment must now be channelled into this work. As Himmelmann (1998) suggests, such documentation research is really a separate subfield of linguistics which requires community involvement and preparation of suitable materials for community use. Linguists who do this will be producing some outputs which may seem less "theoretical", and therefore may be less able to draw on conventional forms of support for academic research. Their materials may also take longer to appear because of the need for community participation and approval.

This means that special kinds of funding may be needed, like what the European Community now provides for its regional languages, or what has been provided through various programmes to support Aboriginal language work in Australia. Economic rationalism is sweeping the globe, and it is linked with widespread elite attitudes in favour of English as the global language. Thus such programmes are increasingly vulnerable. Also, many major research funding bodies are still tied to rapidly disseminated theoretical outcomes. So we need to be creative and effective in our advocacy of documentation work and our feedback to communities where we work, and also provide the theoretical framework to account for what is going on.

It is extremely encouraging that most linguists are now aware of and concerned about language endangerment, and that many are now working with communities to provide documentation and help them in LM efforts. Further, many minority communities in the developed world are starting to insist on their linguistic rights. Our next task is to raise the consciousness of other speech communities, both minority and majority, about how precious and unique the resource of human linguistic diversity really is.

REFERENCES

Dazzi Gross, Anna-Alice & Lorenza Mondada (eds) 1999. _Les langues minoritaires en contexte/Minderheitensprachen im Kontext. Bulletin Suisse de linguistique appliquée_ 69/1-2. Neuchâtel: Institut de linguistique de l'université de Neuchâtel.

Haugen, Einar 1972. _The Ecology of Language_ (Anwar S. Dil, ed.). Stanford, CA: Stanford University Press.

Himmelmann, Nikolaus P. 1998. Documentary and descriptive linguistics. _Linguistics_ 36: 161-195.

Chapter 1

Language Attitudes:
the key factor in language maintenance[1]
David Bradley
La Trobe University

1. ATTITUDES CONCERNING LANGUAGE

Why is it that one minority group assimilates and its language dies, while another maintains its linguistic and cultural identity? Perhaps the crucial factor in language maintenance is the attitudes of the speech community concerning their language. Thus we need to know more about attitudinal factors which disfavour language maintenance (LM) and may lead to language endangerment.

Overall attitudes are extremely important. There is considerable discussion in the literature about ethnolinguistic vitality - the group's attitude about itself and its language, a concept discussed in Giles (1977). Equally crucial is whether language is regarded as a core cultural value (Smolicz 1981) — whether the group sees their language and its maintenance as a key aspect of the group's identity.

More specific minority and majority beliefs and preferences about the following are also highly relevant:

whether bilingualism is accepted and valued or even normal and expected

how public use of a minority language in the presence of monolingual majority speakers is viewed

whether minority group members view their language as 'difficult' or 'hard to maintain'

[1]   I am very pleased to acknowledge the support of the Australian Research Council (A59803475) and the comments of various colleagues, especially Maya Bradley; all errors are solely my reposnsibility.

1

the attitudes of the majority, the minority itself, and other minorities about the relative utility, importance and beauty of the majority and various minority languages

whether the society as a whole supports, tolerates or represses LM for minority languages

Another key issue is linguistic boundary maintenance, which ranges along a continuum from purism to acceptance. Maximal purism involves conservative attitudes to the minority language and rejection of any effect of language contact or other change; maximal acceptance naturally also leads to rapid internal change, as several other papers in this volume have indicated. This also determines the source of lexical enrichment — loanwords from a majority language, from a high culture language, or internal coinage of new words; likewise the likelihood of code switching and code mixing between minority and majority languages - do parents choose to speak only the majority language to their children, to 'help them get ahead' in the majority society, or do they support and approve of their children's minority language skills. Even some linguists who are native speakers of endangered languages feel entirely comfortable that their language is dying, because they share the attitudes within their own group that led to the breakdown of transmission.

A further important factor in determining attitudes is the historicity of the minority language. Does it have an orthography or orthographies? How long has it been written? How widespread is literacy? How much and what kind of literature exists? As linguists we know that written language is secondary and that many minority languages are spoken in viable nonliterate societies with a very rich oral tradition, but in contact with literary majority languages, many though of course not all minority groups have accepted the idea that a 'proper' language must be written. This may even lead to internal movements to create a new orthography, as in the case of the Hmong (Eira 2000).

Attitudes about a number of linguistic and sociolinguistic factors also have a bearing on the likelihood of LM, such as:

degree of internal difference within the minority language

existence of a traditional standard dialect

use as a local lingua franca

traditions concerning bilingualism

Many endangered languages (ELs) have undergone rapid and substantial internal diversification in the absence of a literary or spoken standard, and because speakers of some languages do not see a need for everyone to speak the same and are more willing and able to understand or even adjust towards a range of other subvarieties. For example, speakers of Lao are highly tolerant of local tonal differences and can readily comprehend them and even mimic them; while speakers of Thai are not, and do not feel that they can or should understand regional varieties.

Some groups with a more puristic attitude may even have a traditional internal standard dialect which speakers of other dialects are able to understand and willing to adjust their speech towards, as in the case of Lahu (Bradley 1979). While this may be negative for the continuation and development of internal dialect differences, it is clearly favourable for LM. In some cases, even out-group members may learn and use a local language as a lingua franca, again as in the case of Lahu (Bradley 1996b) or Bantawa Rai (Bradley 1996d); in this case the lingua franca may survive at the expense of the ELs of smaller groups, as Lahu is now replacing languages such as Bana in Laos, Pyen in Burma and Laomian in China. Small groups who are regarded, and may even regard themselves, as members of a larger minority group may be absorbed into that minority and their own language disappear; this is happening to Akeu which is disappearing into Akha in Thailand, Laos, Burma and China; and to various Kuki languages which are disappearing into Mizo in northeastern India. Small groups may even choose to fuse themselves into larger ethnicities, like the Zeliangrong which includes the former Zemi, Liangmei and Kabui/Pochuri groups in northeastern India (Bradley 1996c) or have this choice made for them, as within the numerous composite national minorities in China like the Yi (Bradley 1996e and Forthcoming).

In many societies, as noted in several other contributions to this volume, bilingualism or multilingualism is normal and traditional.

With language exogamy as among the Kachin (Bradley 1996a) or in the Amazon (Aikhenvald 2000), the family home will have at least two first languages, and there may be other minority or majority lingue franche in use, in addition to a national official language. In such cases there is often a hierarchy of languages or a domain-specific use of different languages for specific purposes, such as the use of Jinghpaw Kachin as an in-group lingua franca and literary language (Bradley 1996a). When a minority is transnational, the same group may use different national languages depending on which country they happen to be in. Reactions can go either way as societies develop: the minority languages lower in the status hierarchy may disappear, or they may seek to assert themselves and become separate literary languages and expand their domains of use, as is now happening for four of the languages within the Kachin group: Lacid, Lhaovo, Ngochang and Zaiwa.[2] The linguistic repertoire of groups lower in such hierarchies can be startling; I have met Kachin and Lisu who can converse happily in at least half a dozen languages, with native knowledge of three or more.

2.   SOCIAL FACTORS IN LANGUAGE ATTITUDES

Many characteristics of the social use of the language and beliefs concerning language use are also highly relevant. These concern domains of language use, networks for language use, and the degree of accommodation towards the speech of one's interlocutors.

Speakers may feel it is more or less appropriate to use their language in certain domains, depending on their attitudes. Some groups maintain their language in a wider range of domains; for others it retreats into the village and the home.

---

[2]   Lacid is better known as Lashi, its Burmese and Jinghpaw name. Lhaovo is known as Maru in Burmese and Jinghpaw, and as Langsu in China; it is also sometimes writtten as Lawngwaw. Ngochang is also known as Achang in China and as Maingtha in Burmese; it is also spoken by the Tai Sa blacksmiths among the northern Shan of Burma. Zaiwa is known as Atsi in Jinghpaw and as Zi in Burmese. The spelling of the Zaiwa autonym is derived from Chinese *pinyin* 'z' for [ts].

The social network, that is, the patterns of contact and interaction between people, is another major factor in LM. Some ethnic groups have more closed, in-group interaction patterns with a high density and multiplexity of network; that is, the same people talk to each other all the time, in a variety of domains. Others have a more open network; that is, greater contact with out-group members more of the time in more domains. Naturally as governments spread their reach and the network becomes more open, some new domains in which a minority language cannot be used come into existence, and some existing domains may shift to an outside language.

If the local network includes out-group members or younger non-speakers of the group language, this poses great difficulties for LM. Exogamy, in-migration and the extension of government and other services such as schools, medical services, agricultural technology and so on may gradually lead to a higher proportion of outsiders in a minority community. The earliest arrivals in a minority community, such as the first few Lao husbands in the Gong villages in Thailand (Bradley 1989: 37) or local shopkeepers, may learn the ethnic language; but as the proportion of out-group speakers increases, this becomes less necessary and thus less likely.

One of the basic principles of human interaction is that there is accommodation to the speech of the interlocutor; that is, one adjusts to the speech repertoire, abilities and preferences of the people one is speaking with. Thus, as more outsiders move in, more and more of the speech within a community with an increasingly open network will not be in the endangered minority language. Speakers may also begin to choose not to transmit their language to children. In societies where children are largely socialised and cared for by their elder siblings, minority language ability may begin by being restricted to the eldest children, with gradual or abrupt decline in knowledge among younger siblings within each family.

Many studies of language contraction and death have observed the same patterns of network effect: some communities, and families are more language-solidary, and a minority language may survive longer among them while disappearing from other households and villages. Thus at one time various stages of language loss can be observed. For example, the Bisu and Gong languages in Thailand are completely dead in many former villages; people may deny or even be unaware of their former language and ethnicity. In other villages there are elderly speakers or semispeakers but the language is not used or understood by the young. In some villages, the youngest community members are non-speakers or at best passive understanders of their traditional languages, with middle-aged semispeakers and elderly fluent speakers; but everyone, of whatever age, is fluent in the dominant language, in this case varieties of Thai. In some families the former language may still be known but not used much, and as the last fluent language-solidary elders die the language disappears from everyday use even in those homes.

Even such a bleak picture is not necessarily the end. I was delighted to discover recently that my main Bisu language co-worker, now a prosperous village leader, has been using the Thai-based script which I devised with him in 1976 to write ever since, and is now leading a revival movement with participation of relatively fluent semispeakers and assistance from Payap University. He doesn't want his language to die! But in the meantime it has disappeared from two other villages and has a precarious hold in only his and one other.

3.   PROBLEMS IN LANGUAGE ATTITUDES

Some specific attitudinal problems confront endangered languages. One noted in Schmidt (1990) for Australian Aboriginal languages is that recognition of language loss is often delayed; that is, speakers feel that their language is healthy enough within the in-group network until the remaining fluent speakers are all old; even if younger people are all semispeakers, passive understanders or have no knowledge of the traditional language, and normal transmission stopped long ago. By the time a community becomes aware of impending language loss, it may be very difficult to reverse.

Another kind of problem often confronts communities in which the younger speakers of the language speak something which is radically different from what is spoken by fluent elders. This results from the widely-observed phenomenon of extremely rapid change within an endangered language.   If the speech of the younger people is regarded by the elders as inadequate because of puristic attitudes, the younger people may be discouraged from continuing to speak, as Dorian (1994) has observed. Conversely, if the semispeaker version of the language is accepted within the community, even by the elders, the changed version may persist or rapid change may continue.

It is often suggested that such changed varieties have been simplified and have converged towards the structure of the replacing language, in which all or most speakers are likely to be bilingual. Also, loanwords may become very prevalent, spreading beyond nouns, verbs and discourse markers into all parts of the lexicon including closed classes of grammatical markers. This may lead speakers and outsiders to feel that the language is becoming impoverished. However, widely dispersed findings suggest that some structural changes in ELs may also lead to more complex structures, such as the complex tone sandhi and multiplication of vowels in Gong described in Bradley (1992).

4.   CHANGING LANGUAGE ATTITUDES

In many developed countries, indigenous groups are vigorously reasserting their linguistic rights. This major shift from acceptance of a dominant language and linguistic assimilation has taken place at different times in different places over the last century or so, and is a direct reflection of changing linguistic attitudes among the EL community. One spectacularly successful example of revival is Hebrew over the last century. Crystal (2000) traces the remarkable resurgence of Welsh in Wales over the last thirty years. Current efforts are underway among the Basque in Spain, various other small indigenous groups speaking 'regional languages' throughout Europe, with many Original Nations in different parts of North America, and in many Australian Aboriginal communities.

We need to look at the successful examples of language revival or reversal of language shift like Hebrew and Welsh, as well as the lessons to be learned from less successful efforts elsewhere. The basic question is: how do we change speakers' attitudes. A highly relevant but often neglected issue is whether we should do so, or whether communities should be left to make their own decisions.

A revival which is essentially a heritage activity aimed at building community self-esteem or which is based on efforts by an intellectual elite is inherently less likely to maintain a language than something which also changes attitudes and ultimately linguistic behaviour. This is not to belittle such efforts; Thieberger (2000) discusses why our preference as linguists for languages to be maintained intact at all costs is unrealistic, and provides a number of examples where LM activities have had less ambitious goals more in accord with what the community wants and what can realistically be achieved.

The outsider linguist who enters a community for research purposes can become a focus for LM activities, but unless the group itself choose to keep their language, we can do nothing but document the language and hope that the descendants may later find some use for our material. This is happening among various Original Nations in North America, where 19th century ethnographic materials are used in attempts to reclaim their languages and cultures. Some linguists, such as Blake (2000), are using archival materials to describe dead languages and then preparing materials for heritage language activities in various Koori (Australian Aboriginal) communities in Victoria. Even if such attempts may ultimately not succeed in recreating a speech community, they still contribute to a group's positive feelings and self-knowledge.

Sometimes, however, the linguist may encourage and energise indigenous co-workers who may change their attitudes and work for LM after the linguist goes away. To return to the Bisu in Thailand: I thought the language was well on its way to death in 1976, but more than twenty years later my former co-worker is leading a revival which is publishing textbooks, books of traditional stories and so on, and has recruited linguists from Payap University to assist. How did I help in the meantime? I sent tapes of closely related languages such as Phunoi in Laos and Laomian in China, which showed the Bisu that they are not alone. When they heard these tapes, they wanted to go off to Laos and China immediately to meet their long lost brothers. I also sent materials including notes, stories and so on in our Thai script for Bisu to the Bisu through the team at Payap. Now the Bisu have gone to Burma and found the Pyen, who also speak a very closely related EL. I thought Pyen was completely dead, and would not have been able to go and look for it; but the Bisu found it, and now the Pyen are talking about sending a group to Thailand for literacy work. Thus broken ethnic links can be re-established, and self-esteem enhanced.

In conclusion, I believe we can try to change attitudes, and we can help people to maintain their languages, but only if they want to. This also requires the training of community members, the provision of interesting materials such as traditional stories which people want to hear or read, helping the minority groups with whom we are associated in other ways, and even acting as advocates for them. So how many linguists does it take to save an EL? None, if the people have a positive attitude based on community needs and desires; but of course we should help them when we can and they want us to.

REFERENCES

Bradley, David 1979. *Lahu Dialects*. Canberra: Faculty of Asian Studies, Australian National University.

_____ 1989. The disappearance of the Ugong in Thailand. In Nancy C. Dorian (ed.) *Investigating Obsolescence: Studies in Language Contraction and Death*, 33-40. Cambridge: Cambridge University Press.

_____ 1992. Tone alternations in Ugong. In Carol J. Compton and John L. Hartmann (eds) *Tai Languages, Linguistics and Literatures in Honor of William J. Gedney on his 77th Birthday*, 55-64. DeKalb, IL: Center for Southeast Asian Studies, University of Northern Illinois.

_____ 1996a. Kachin. In Stephen A. Wurm et al. (eds), 749-751.

_____ 1996b. Lahu. In Stephen A. Wurm et al. (eds), 753-755.

_____ 1996c. Nagamese. In Stephen A. Wurm et al. (eds), 757-762.

_____ 1996d. Bantawa Rai. In Stephen A. Wurm et al. (eds), 772-773.

_____ 1996e. Yi. In Stephen A. Wurm et al. (eds), 841-844.

_____ Forthcoming. Language policy for the Yi. In Stevan Harrell (ed.) *Perspectives on the Yi of Southwest China*. Berkeley: University of California Press.

Crystal, David 2000. *Language Death.* Cambridge: Cambridge University Press.

Dorian, Nancy C. 1994. Purism versus compromise in language revitalization and language revival. *Language in Society* 23: 474-494.

Eira, Christina 2000. Language maintenance at the micro level: Hmong ex-refugee communities in Melbourne. In this volume.

Giles, Howard (ed.) 1977. *Language, Ethnicity and Intergroup Relations.* London and New York: Academic Press.

Schmidt, Annette 1990. *The Loss of Australia's Aboriginal Language Heritage.* Canberra: Aboriginal Studies Press.

Smolicz, Jerzy J. 1981. Core values and cultural identity. *Ethnic and Racial Studies* 4: 75-90.

Thieberger, Nicholas 2000. Extinction in whose terms? Which parts of a language constitute a target for language maintenance programmes? In this volume.

Wurm, Stephen A., Peter Mühlhäusler and Darrell T. Tryon (eds) 1996. *Atlas of Languages of Intercultural Communication in the Pacific, Asia and the Americas.* Berlin: de Gruyter.

Chapter 2

Strategies for Language Maintenance and Revival
Stephen A. Wurm
Australian National University

1. INTRODUCTORY REMARKS AND BACKGROUND

The present writer's many years' experience with speakers of a large
number of small to very small healthy or threatened languages in the
New Guinea area and Melanesia, Australia, Indonesia, South America
and Siberia, where languages with a hundred or a few hundred, or even
less than a hundred speakers, are very common, has acquainted him with
some facts which are essential to the maintenance or reinvigoration of
such languages. Similar facts do play a part in the maintenance of larger
languages, but because the communities speaking such languages are
less close-knit and more multi-facetted than very small speech
communities, these facts may not be as clear-cut with them as with very
small speech communities.

Especially in the New Guinea area and Melanesia, but also in some of
the other areas mentioned above, the speakers of small languages regard
them as the most important symbol of their identity. This need not be so
important with speakers of considerably larger languages with whom
other factors may be regarded more important symbols of group identity.
One of the reasons of this may be that with larger languages, variations
and dialectal differences are more in evidence than with very small
languages and therefore, such languages can be less of paramount
importance to the community as a whole than other cultural and social
characteristics. Languages fragmented into units of regional or group
importance while other factors are of importance for identifying the
speech community as a whole are less important for group identification
than monolithic small languages. In this connection, it is of interest to
mention that observations by the present writer have shown that
seriously endangered or moribund languages which had few to very few

11

speakers when they were healthy, are often less affected by reductions and changes in their grammatical and semantic setup when used by the surviving speakers, than this is the case with many languages which had a large number of speakers, when they were healthy, but are now seriously endangered or even only endangered or potentially endangered (Wurm Forthcoming a).

The great importance attached by speakers of small languages to their own languages allows them, in the areas mentioned above, to deal with other languages penetrating their orbits through resorting to bi- and multilingualism which in consequence, is, or was, very widespread especially in New Guinea, Melanesia, traditional Australia, parts of South America, and, largely as passive bi- and multilingualism in parts of Siberia (Wurm et al. 1996). In the Philippines there is a similar situation.

What has been said above is on the understanding that the members of speech communities remain together, that the impact of speakers of other languages is moderate, and that there is no major impact of a dominant language, which is accompanied and supported by negative attitudes and policies by its speakers aiming at the elimination, through suppression or other less direct means, of small languages in its orbit.

2.   RECENT DEVELOPMENTS

In some of the areas mentioned, especially in New Guinea, there has been a rapidly increasing mobility of the population in the last decade or so which lead to a fragmentation of speech communities through more and more frequent intermarriage between speakers of different languages. This resulted in a lowering of the value and importance of small languages to their speakers, and increased the importance of large languages which were more and more becoming family languages in mixed marriages. This in turn decreased the rate of transmission of small languages to the children, accompanied by a frequent and deliberate decision of parents not to teach their children a small language which they regarded to be of no further use and to encourage them to speak only a large language which they regarded as being of economic and social value to them. The traditional bi- and multilingualism declined in many areas as a result. Deliberate policies aiming at the suppression of small languages were not present in places like Papua New Guinea and much of Melanesia, but had been very much in evidence until some time ago in Australia, Siberia, parts of South America, and in Indonesia. In much of these areas, these negative attitudes and policies have given way to positive and supportive, or at least neutral ones, in recent decades and years, but are in an indirect way, still very much present in Indonesia through the exclusive use of Indonesian in all aspects of education, administration and all aspects of public life, with this being supported by policies of transmigrating, and also of splitting up whole speech communities.

3.   LANGUAGE ENDANGERMENT

The result of what has been said above, has, in recent years, been a rapid increase of language endangerment in the areas mentioned, though, apart from Australia, the percentage of extinct (mainly recently extinct) and threatened languages is still comparatively low by world standard in much of them. Language endangerment in this paper is to be understood in a sociolinguistic sense, i.e. the gradual disappearance of speakers of a language until they reach zero.

There is another phenomenon which is also referred to as language endangerment by linguists, and which manifests itself in a gradual change of the nature and structure of a language as a result of the loss of the original culture of its speakers, and the strong influence of another, usually dominant, language. This leads to the reduction of the number of registers in the languages to changes and simplifications of its grammar and the semantic composition of its vocabulary, as well as to the taking over of lexical items and structural features from the dominant language. The result of all this is a new altered form of the original language which often reflects some characteristics of the influencing dominant language. However, this new form of the language may continue to exist without suffering a progressive dwindling of its speakers leading to its eventual disappearance, though this may also occur. In some other extreme cases it may merge with the dominant language in losing all its original grammatical properties and becoming a language which is a structural copy of the dominant language, with a number of lexical elements with the semantic tags from the original language. An example of this is the present form of the Gamilaraay language in northern New South Wales (Austin 1992). The changed form of an original language may sometimes turn into the form spoken by speakers who have forgotten, or never learned, much of the language (so-called "semi-speakers"). Something similar, though more elaborate, could have been a simple, juvenile register of the former full language, but has become the standard form of it (e.g. Nganasan Samoyedic is on the way to this).

As has been pointed out above, any reference to language endangerment in this article is to be understood in the sociolinguistic sense, unless otherwise indicated. The hallmarks for the various levels of such an endangerment are: 1) decreasing use of the language by children (potentially endangered language); 2) the same by young adults, with very few or no children speakers left (endangered language); 3) the same by middle-aged adults, with the youngest good speakers about 50 years of age (seriously endangered language); 4) the same by the remaining aged speakers whose number is decreasing as they die one after the other (moribund language); and 5) there seems to be no speakers left (extinct language). This scale is not applicable in situations in which a healthy language (usually one with a small to very small number of speakers) is at any stage of endangerment by an approaching likely or imminent man-made or natural catastrophe affecting, damaging, or destroying and annihilating the speakers' environmental and other bases of existence. These can be for instance logging, mining, successful drilling for oil, local war, or genocide, an epidemic, earthquake, tsunami, volcanic eruption and upheaval etc. All these can lead to the breaking-up of the traditional speech community, the scattering of the speakers, and death and disappearance of most or all of the speakers, either gradually, or fast, or immediately.

4.   LANGUAGE MAINTENANCE AND REINVIGORATION

Turning to the question of the maintenance, reinvigoration and revival of a threatened small or minority language, it must first be pointed out that in any of the last mentioned cases involving man-made and material catastrophes, the question of saving the language is subordinate to saving its speakers and ensuring that the members of the speech community stay together at whatever place they may move or be moved to. The future of the language at such a new place will depend very much on the circumstances and conditions at such a place, i.e. whether or not it is adequate for them to continue a way of life comparable to their former existence, whether or not they find themselves in the middle of a large new speech community expecting them to assimilate to them and adopt their language, giving up their own in the process, etc. It may be mentioned that cases of threat to small speech communities through the various catastrophic events listed above are, or were, more common in New Guinea, Australia, Melanesia, South America, Siberia, Indonesia etc. than is generally believed to be the case.

It has been indicated at the beginning of this chapter that one of the most important factors for the maintenance and reinvigoration of a threatened language is the attitude of the speakers towards their own language and the importance which they attach to it as a major symbol of their identity. Another very important factor on which the maintenance and reinvigoration of threatened small or minority language very much depends, are the attitudes, policies and knowledge or ignorance of the speakers of the large or dominant language in whose orbit the threatened language is spoken or with which its speakers have close contacts. Negative attitudes and policies by the dominant language speakers which was the norm in many countries (e.g. Australia, Canada, USSR until the 1970s or later, and are still typical of several countries, such as Indonesia) augur badly for the maintenance of threatened languages. A change of negative attitudes and policies to positive ones often leads to the reinvigoration of a threatened language by itself, or to the re-emergence of an apparently disappeared (in fact, gone secret) threatened language, because of the disappearance of threatening attitudes by authorities. Such changes of attitudes and policies occurred since the

1970s and later, notably in Australia, Canada, Japan, Russia, Spain etc. and resulted in an increase of interest by speakers of threatened languages in these. In this connection, it may be said again that in much of the areas mentioned at the beginning of this article, stable bi- or multilingualism by considerable numbers of the speakers of individual small languages, if not of all their speakers, is (or in some areas, e.g. Australia, was) a characteristic feature. At the same time, the speakers of large languages with whom speakers of small or minority languages have had increasing contacts and have been influenced by their attitudes, beliefs and policies, are mostly monolingual. Moreover, they usually firmly believe that monolingualism is the natural state for a human being to be in, and cannot, or do not want to, understand that bi- and multilingualism is characteristic of the speakers, very many of small languages, and also of some quite large languages (i..e. in India). However, it is this bi- and multilingualism which has permitted the speakers of many small languages to maintain them. In situations of relative absence of negative language policies aiming at depriving speakers of small languages of their languages and making them adopt the dominant language instead, the bi- and multilingual speakers of small languages simply added the knowledge of the large or dominant language to their existing repertoire of languages, as was characteristically the case in Papua New Guinea with the speakers adding the major lingua franca and national language Tok Pisin to their existing language knowledge, with the same being the case with Solomon Pijin in the Solomon Islands and Bislama in Vanuatu in Island Melanesia, Tagalog and other very large lingue franche in the Philippines, large Amerindian lingue franche in South America, etc. In this, it may be remembered that bi- and multilingualism and the bi-culturalism that often goes with it, give speakers intellectual, emotional and social advantages over monolinguals, in addition to situational and sometimes economic advantages resulting from a knowledge of several languages. They are as follows (Wurm 1994, 1997, 1999a):

> Such individuals have access to a much wider volume of information and knowledge than monolinguals, have a larger volume of knowledge (both language-oriented and other) in their

minds, understand differing semantic associations better, and being used to switching languages and thought patterns, have more flexible minds, and as a result have greater applied intelligence than monolinguals;

They are less rigid in their attitudes and more tolerant of, i.e., less hostile and less on the defensive against, the unknown than monolinguals, more inclined to regard manifestations of other cultures by individuals as acceptable and to be respected, though they may be different from theirs; and are less single-minded and less culturally aggressive than monolinguals;

Their thought patterns and world view are more balanced because they are familiar with different, often somewhat contradictory concepts. They have better capabilities than monolinguals to learn something entirely new and to fit into novel situations without trauma, and to understand different sides of a problem.

Monolingual dominant language speakers, ignorant of what has been said above, unknowingly tend to deprive, through their attitudes and policies, speakers of small and minority languages in their orbit of the advantages of bi- and multilingualism, and to instil the belief in them that monolingualism is the 'normal' state to be in and is preferable to bi- and multilingualism.

In a situation in which small or minority language is getting threatened, with its speakers under pressure from the attitudes and policies of monolingual speakers of a large, usually dominant language (it being metropolitan or otherwise), the first step towards revitalising their flagging language is to make its speakers, or at least a few prominent members of the speech community aware of the advantage of bi- and multilingualism, and to point out to them that in knowing two or several languages, they possess something in their minds which the speakers of the large language, even the otherwise so clever speakers of a metropolitan dominant language do not have. In other words, speakers of a small or minority language, often of several of them, are in this respect superior to those monolingual speakers. This tends to bolster their fading self-respect and ethnic identity feeling and self-consciousness. It is quite interesting to see that among some bi- and multilingual Papua New Guineans, Australian Aborigines, Island Melanesians and other Pacific Islanders, South American Indians, Siberians, etc. it has become quite common to look down upon metropolitan and even other large language speakers because of their monolingualism which they equate with some shortcoming or stupidity in the brains of the monolinguals, at the same time boasting their own self-esteem thereby.

What has been said above, and also attempts at making speakers of a threatened small or minority language aware of the fact that their language can be a useful secret language to hide their thoughts from hostile authorities are the first steps to rekindle the flagging interest of the speakers in their own language, if necessary. (Aboriginal languages or at least fragments of them were effectively used in rural New South Wales in Australia in the 1950s to confuse police trying to stop trade in illicit alcoholic drinks, as the present writer was able to observe.) Another useful hint for stimulating interest in the speakers to maintain their small or minority language is to make them understand that acquiring a good knowledge of the dominant language does not mean that they have to abandon their own language, but be fully bilingual in both languages with all the intellectual, emotional and social advantages going with this, as has been outlined above. (With speakers who are bi- or multilingual in other languages, apart from the dominant language, this argument is usually readily understood.) Also, it has to be made clear to them that their own language and the dominant language have quite different functions and offer quite different advantages. An objection sometimes heard from speakers of small and minority languages encouraged to maintain their own languages is that their own language is of no use for getting any jobs in their present world which is dominated by the major language, and is therefore of no economic value. This has to be countered by pointing out to the speakers that the role of their own language is quite different from that of the dominant language with the economic benefits which its knowledge provides, and gives them spiritual benefits, the feeling and knowledge that they possess something additional to what the monolingual speakers of the dominant language have, together with the intellectual and other benefits their bilingualism gives to them, and of which they should be proud.

It is rarely the case that the entire speech community speaking a small or minority language is keen to maintain their language in the face of the pressure exerted upon them by the attitudes, and often policies, of the monolingual speakers of the dominant language. Especially members of the young generation are often quite unwilling to consider maintaining their small or minority language, and regard members of the older generation who want to maintain it, as old-fashioned fools. Also, some parents who are unaware that their children could easily be natural bilinguals in their own and the metropolitan language, tend to avoid teaching them their own language for fear that an imperfect knowledge of the dominant language would interfere with their economic chances in the future. The latter problem should be countered by making the parents aware of the possibility of full bilingualism of their children, and of the advantages of bilingualism. Members of the young generation should have it pointed out to them that they are not the same as the monolingual speakers of the dominant language, and that they can gain a lot from being bilingual and to some extent bicultural, and by being at home in two worlds. In some situations, this could even produce economic benefits for them, because they could work as interpreters, or in an administrative capacity employed by representatives of the dominant language and culture as experts in matters relating to their own people.

When efforts are to be made to maintain or reinvigorate a threatened small or minority language, it is, as has been said before, important to find one or several persons in the speech community who are interested and keen to see this happen. It is of advantage if such a person or persons are at least relatively young so as to have a link with the young generation and be respected by them. He or they are likely to have the support of the old generation who would like to see the language maintained or reinvigorated, and who, at the same time are good speakers of the language which the person or persons mentioned may not be.

At this stage, outside linguists usually come into the picture. Their taking up the study of an endangered language for research purposes, can by this activity rekindle the interest of its speakers in it, because they realise that their language, believed to be of no use to anyone except themselves, is not so useless after all. However, linguists can not by themselves maintain and reinvigorate a threatened language — this is up to the speakers of it who however usually lack the knowledge of how to do it. This is the point at which the linguists' task is to advise and help the speakers, and above all, to prepare materials for the speakers to use, under the guidance of the person or persons mentioned as being keen on seeing their language to be maintained or reinvigorated. The task of these people would, in the first instance, be to change the attitudes of members of the speech community who are not or not really interested in the maintenance and reinvigoration of their language, to more positive attitudes. They would then proceed to the actual reinvigorating of the language with the help of the materials prepared by the linguist(s) who has or have studied the language with the assistance of the old good speakers. These materials should be mainly textbooks and story books which by their contents, may also give an insight into some aspects of the probably decaying or decayed traditional culture of the speakers. If the language had no writing before the linguist took up its study, he would have to devise a practical alphabet for it with the help of those keen to reinvigorate the language and with whom the alphabet can be tested through their learning to read it. Such people, and probably others in the speech community, are likely to be familiar with writing and reading through having been exposed to a dominant language and some education. These key persons in the community would use these materials in their work aiming at the maintenance and reinvigoration of their threatened language. They would also bring the old good speakers into it who would speak to the younger members of the speech community in their language to steer them back into a fuller command of the language. This would also restore the respect for the old speakers in the eyes of the younger generation. At the same time, the language appearing in writing will contribute to its being maintained. As far as the children are concerned, who may have no or only a very rudimentary passive knowledge of the language, special playing situations should be devised by the old good speakers in which these participate with the children, using words from their language only, with explanations given in a language intelligible to the children, either by the old speakers themselves if they know that language, or by a bilingual member of the speech community standing by. The children should be encouraged to use words from the threatened language, and when they do, they should be rewarded with small gifts, e.g. sweets. This has been found to be highly successful, and permits proceeding to short phrases and sentences, also with rewards for the children. If regularly followed, a passable speaking knowledge of the children can be achieved. They should also be strongly encouraged to use the threatened language when speaking to each other, with this carrying special rewards.

A very important part of maintaining and reinvigorating a threatened language is to revive some aspects of the traditional culture of the speakers (Wurm 1997, 1999b), as far as they are compatible with the cultural ecological setting in which the speakers now live, i.e. feasts, dancing, singing, storytelling, the performing of mythological events, and also the re-enacting in playing or other performing situations, of former economic activities of the speakers such as hunting, fishing, gardening etc. Old members of the speech community who will remember at least some of the details of such activities, can act as advisers and instructors, and also as leading performers. The threatened language should be used in all these activities, with explanations in the dominant language for young participants who thereby learn something about their traditional culture, and acquire additional knowledge of their language. Again, increased mastery of the language by young speakers should be rewarded, at least in a symbolic form (e.g. a major part of the booty in the performance of a hunt, public praise etc.).

One problem for the maintenance of small languages in areas in which many small languages coexist, is the fact that electronic media, e.g. radio broadcasting, of necessity can use only a limited number of languages.

For instance, in Papua New Guinea which has around 800 languages, radio broadcasting is only in about 30 major languages (Mühlhäusler, Philpott and Trew 1996). This tends to give speakers of small languages the feeling that their languages are unimportant. This problem can be counteracted by a special oral part of elementary education which is under consideration as a desirable possibility (Wurm Forthcoming b). This takes into account that in every basic elementary education class in which the language of instruction is in a major language or lingua franca, intelligible to all the pupils because of widespread multilingualism, there are pupils from a number of different small language backgrounds. To give some oral education to the pupils with various local language affiliations, the class is to be split up into a number of groups for an hour or so every day according to the language backgrounds of the various groups. A well-informed elderly speaker of each of the local languages of the pupils will speak to his group in that language, be it in a corner of the classroom or outside, telling them about subjects of value to them in their lives, e.g. hygiene, plays, gardening, etc., telling them traditional stories, about their traditional culture, mythological beliefs etc. In this way, the pupils from the various language backgrounds learn something about their traditional culture and mythology and other matters useful for them, and at the same time, get a growing respect for their own language which will contribute to its maintenance and forestall and prevent it becoming endangered and eventually disappearing.

REFERENCES

Austin, Peter 1992. *Dictionary of Gamilaraay, Northern New South Wales*. Bundoora: Department of Linguistics, La Trobe University.

Mühlhäusler, Peter, Malcolm Philpott & Rachel Trew 1996. Modern media in the Pacific area and their role in intercultural communication. In Stephen A. Wurm, Peter Mühlhäusler and Darrell T. Tryon (eds), II.2: 1389-1454, also map no. 144 in vol. I.

Wurm, Stephen A. (ed.) 1994. World within words. *The UNESCO Courier*. Paris: UNESCO.

_____ 1997. Prospects of language preservation in the north. In Hiroshi Shoji and Juha Janhunen (eds) *Northern Minority Languages, Problems of Survival*, 35-53. Senri Ethnological Studies, no. 44. Suita, Osaka, Japan: National Ethnological Museum.

_____ 1999a. Endangered languages, multilingualism and linguistics. *Diogenes* (English edition), no. 185, vol. 47/1. Oxford: Blackwell.

_____ 1999b. Language revivalism and revitalization in Pacific and Asian areas. *International Journal of the Sociology of Language*, Small Languages and Small Language Communities issue, 29: 163-172.

_____ Forthcoming a. Threatened languages of the Western Pacific from Taiwan to Papua New Guinea. In Matthias Brenzinger (ed.) *Language Diversity Endangered*. Berlin: Mouton de Gruyter.

_____ Forthcoming b. Language endangerment in the Pacific, in particular in the New Guinea area. To appear in *Pacific Linguistics*. Canberra: Department of Linguistics RSPAS, ANU.

Wurm, Stephen A., Peter Mühlhäusler & Darrell T. Tryon (eds). 1996. *Atlas of Languages of Intercultural Communication in the Pacific, Asia, and the Americas*. 3 vols. Berlin: Mouton de Gruyter.

Chapter 3

Traditional Multilingualism and Language Endangerment

Alexandra Y. Aikhenvald
La Trobe University

1. THE PURPOSE

Most linguistic communities in the world are traditionally multilingual and/or polyglossic. Little, however, is known about the ways in which language endangerment and language shift affect traditionally multilingual communities.

The loss of multilingual patterns of communication and of corresponding social patterns has serious consequences for generational continuity and affects the languages involved.

Language obsolescence and subsequent endangerment inevitably lead to a breakdown in traditional transmission of communication patterns, that is, of languages themselves and of rules of code-switching. As a result, traditional patterns of multilingualism — which used to be based on economic and ritual necessities — collapse, and this results in drastic changes in language situations, numbers of speakers for each language and linguistic structure in terms of borrowing and areal diffusion.

Using examples from multilingual communities in Northwest Amazonia and the East Sepik, I will show how disintegration of traditional life and cultural practices and of traditional education trigger a major breakdown in multilingual interaction patterns. In a number of cases, when the spheres of multilingualism become reduced, speakers 'lose' their ethnic language in favour of another indigenous language which they are now eager to lose because they do not identify with it. This implies serious psychological and social consequences and creates difficulties for language maintenance.

Multilingual patterns can be of different kinds, accompanied by different language attitudes and different degree of traditional knowledge. I am not going to talk about how communities believed to have been traditionally monolingual become multilingual as the result of contact and then lose their own language(s) (cf. Nidue 1990, on the fate of the Northern Arapesh dialect in the newly triglossic village of Makopin of the East Sepik province, Papua New Guinea).

The general tendency appears to be a reduction of traditional multilingualism: first 'enriching' it with one (or more) newly introduced lingua franca(s); then losing some of the languages, and then perhaps losing all the traditional languages.

I hypothesise that multilingual societies — when they come in contact with Western civilisation — go through a stage of bilingualism, and then may become monolingual.

2. TRADITIONAL MULTILINGUALISM AND LANGUAGE ENDANGERMENT IN THE VAUPÉS AREA, NORTH-WEST AMAZONIA

The linguistic area of the Vaupés — where East-Tucano languages and Tariana, an Arawak language, are spoken — is known for its rampant multilingualism due to exogamy and the ensuing one-way diffusion of structural patterns from East-Tucano into other languages (Tariana and Makú — see, for instance, Aikhenvald 1996, 1999, Sorensen 1967/1972 and Jackson 1974). The region of the Brazilian Vaupés is a culturally homogenous area where multilingualism is the norm. However, this cultural norm is endangered, and it is in a rather advanced state of obsolescence, accompanied by language attrition. The traditional multilingualism in the Vaupés area is accompanied by a very strong inhibition against language mixing viewed in terms of lexical loans. Thus, in spite of striking structural similarity between Tariana and genetically unrelated East-Tucano languages, there are almost no lexical loans between them.

The basic rule of language choice throughout the Vaupés area is that one should speak the interlocutor's own language. Descent is strictly patrilineal, and consequently, one identifies with one's father's language. According to the language 'etiquette' of the area, one is supposed to speak the language one identifies with — that is, one's father's language — to one's siblings, father and all his relatives, and mother's language to one's mother and her relatives. However, during past decades the traditional language transmission in the Brazilian Vaupés has been affected by a number of factors. When Salesian missionaries established themselves in the area in the early 1920s, they imposed Western-style schooling on the Indians, forcing children into boarding schools where they were made to speak just one language of the area, Tucano. Salesians aimed at 'civilising' Indians. This implied not only making them into 'good Christians'. Salesians also considered the traditional multilingualism of the area a 'pagan' habit, and strived to make Indians monolingual 'like other civilised people in the world'. The Tucano language was chosen because it was, numerically, a majority language. Salesian missionaries also practiced forceful relocation of Indian settlements closer to mission centres — where the Indians could be more easily controlled — and amalgamation of different settlements, eliminating the traditional longhouse system and introducing European-style nuclear family houses. Another reason for the disintegration of traditional multilingualism was a breakdown of traditional father-child interaction; with the needs for cash-flow, all the able-bodied men would go off to work for Brazilians — undertaking such tasks as collecting rubber and gold mining — and as the result children would have a considerably reduced degree of exposure to their father's language. This resulted in the spread of Tucano, and, to a lesser extent, of other East-Tucano languages, to the detriment of Tariana.

What happened during the last 100 years is the following. All the groups in the Vaupés are hierarchically organised into 'sibs' (these differ from each other culturally — in their versions of origin myths — and linguistically — they speak somewhat different dialects). The sibs that were hierarchically 'higher' tended to get closer to powerful white people. Consequently, within the ethnic Tariana now only one, lowest-ranking sib called Wamiarikune has preserved their language.

Tariana is an obsolescent language. It is not being learnt by children. The younger generation of Tariana speakers prefer to use Tucano when speaking among themselves or to their wives. They consistently use Tariana only when speaking to the members of their father's families. Table 1 below illustrates these points, showing a gradual shift from multilingualism, among sixty to eighty year olds, to monolingualism, among young people, through a stage of bilingualism observed for those aged between 30 and 50. Basically the same situation has been observed in Piratapuya (for instance, the village of Uluri on the Vaupés River) and in Desano-speaking villages.

Table 1:   **Multilingualism in Northwest Amazonia: the Tariana community of Santa Rosa**

Older generation (60-80 years of age)
mother's tribe and language: Piratapuya, Tucano, Wanano
father's tribe and language: Tariana
languages spoken: Tariana, also Piratapuya, Tucano, Wanano
understand: Língua geral (an old língua franca, now extinct), little Portuguese, little Spanish
wives speak: Tariana, Piratapuya, Tucano, Wanano, Kubeo, some Baniwa

Younger generation (30-50 years of age)
mother's tribe and language: Piratapuya, Tucano, Wanano, Kubeo, Baniwa
father's tribe and language: Tariana
languages spoken: Tariana, also Piratapuya, Tucano, Wanano, some Kubeo, some Baniwa
good to passable Portuguese, some speak reasonable Spanish
wives speak: Tucano

Their children
mother's tribe: Piratapuya, Tucano, Wanano
mothers speak: mostly Tucano
father's tribe and language: Tariana
languages spoken: Tucano, some seem to understand some
Tariana
good Portuguese
wives speak: Tucano, Portuguese

Their grandchildren
mother's tribe: Piratapuya, Tucano, Wanano
father's tribe: Tariana
mothers speak Portuguese, some Tucano
languages spoken: Portuguese, some speak or understand Tucano
native-like regional Portuguese
wives speak: some Tucano, regional Portuguese

One can draw the following preliminary conclusion. A traditionally multilingual area becomes bilingual, with a strong tendency to becoming monolingual. The language that goes first is the language of 'identity' because it is the one that is most affected by the breakdown of language transmission and external pressure. What kind of knowledge remains? As demonstrated by Sorensen (1967/72), the traditional 'requirements' for counting as a real speaker are very high. Speakers won't open their mouths if they are not native-like (since inappropriate language use, including 'wrong names' and mistakes, are ridiculed). Most of those who do not speak Tariana (or any other indigenous language) have at least some lexical knowledge (basically of flora and fauna, and basic kinship terms), obviously acquired through contact with their fathers and fathers' relatives.

3.   TRADITIONAL MULTILINGUALISM AND LANGUAGE ENDANGERMENT IN THE EAST SEPIK: MANAMBU AREA

Traditionally, members of the Manambu tribe of the East Sepik had links with the Iatmul people (also speaking a language from the Ndu family). These links were based on (a) trade exchange, and (b) shared cultural practices. Within Manambu clans traditional initiation ceremonies and debates (thoroughly described by Harrison 1990) involved 'trading' incantations and spells in the closely related (but far from mutually intelligible) Iatmul. The traditional exchange of material and 'spiritual' goods involved magic spells and even myths and songs. This interaction accounts for a complicated network of mutual interdependencies and diffusion of cultural and linguistic features. Representatives of older generations — especially men who achieved high degrees of initiation — have a very good knowledge of this language. The older generation were fluent in Iatmul. A strong Iatmul influence is reflected in the 'foiled' marriage songs published by Harrison (1983) (these songs are written in a special 'spell', or 'shadowy' style).

Additional language knowledge involved traditional trade partners. Older people used to have basic knowledge of the languages of their neighbours and trade partners, such as Kwoma and Kaunga (also from the Ndu family) (also see Bowden 1997). Multilingualism patterns are drastically diminishing among the younger generation. This is shown in Table 2.

Among the younger generation (30-50 years of age), full bilingualism in Iatmul and Manambu is almost non-existent. However, people can understand and compose songs in both Manambu-based and Iatmul-based styles; they have residual understanding of Iatmul. But due to the fact that there are almost no fully initiated men in this generation, the traditional knowledge of Iatmul spells and so on is gone. Tok Pisin and English proficiency are growing. Their children have some knowledge of Manambu — but they have lost any knowledge of Iatmul-based styles, while their proficiency in Tok Pisin and English is high.

Table 2:   **Traditional multilingualism in the Manambu speaking areas (East Sepik)**

Older generation (60-80 years of age)
Manambu
Iatmul (for trade and ritual purposes)
Kwoma (good knowledge; trade purposes)
little Tok Pisin

Younger generation (30-50 years of age) (in the village)
Manambu (little Iatmul; little Kwoma)
good knowledge of Tok Pisin
some knowledge of English

Younger generation (20-50 years of age) (city dwellers)
Manambu (little Iatmul; little Kwoma)
good knowledge of Tok Pisin
good knowledge of English

Their children (in the village)
good knowledge of Tok Pisin
passable knowledge of Tok Pisin
some knowledge of Manambu

Their children (city dwellers)
good knowledge of English
passable knowledge of Tok Pisin
little knowledge of Manambu

Thus, in this area the patterns of traditional multilingualism are replaced by bilingual patterns; and the younger generation tends to become monolingual.

Disruption of traditional multilingual areas in a situation of 'advanced language death' (Larsen 1984: 210-5) has been described for a few other regions of the world, e.g. village of Rodenäs south of the Danish-German border in the extreme north-west of the Federal Republic of Germany (Kreis Nordfriesland), with five varieties: Standard German,

Standard Danish, North Frisian, Low German and South Jutlandish. There is a strong tendency towards Germanisation, which can be illustrated with the following:

> 1st phase (70-89 years of age): High German/Low German/Frisian/Jutlandish
> 2nd phase: (30-69 years of age): High German/Low German
> 3rd phase (3-29 years of age): High German

"A period of bilingualism seems to have intervened between the stage of extreme multilingualism and that of monolingualism" (Larsen 1984: 215). The actual situation also included some strengthening of Low German due to an influx of refugees speaking Low German.

4.   LINGUISTIC CONSEQUENCES OF LANGUAGE LOSS

We have seen that the loss of multilingualism in the situation of language endangerment goes through reduction to bilingualism and then to monolingualism, depending on age groups. The linguistic consequences are of two kinds.

4.1   language change and reduction of spheres of knowledge

In Amazonia this implies loss of cultural knowledge and attrition of certain archaic morphological patterns. The surviving languages tend to become structurally more similar to the dominant one. For instance, Tariana rapidly loses morphological structures that have no equivalents in Tucano, e.g. morphological reflexive-reciprocal, morphological causative of transitive verbs and irregular gender forms of demonstratives. These survive only in very archaic traditional stories which young people just do not know. Language obsolescence may, however, involve some grammatical enrichment rather than straightforward loss; obsolescent languages can be innovative in that they develop new categories and new terms within already existing categories (see Aikhenvald in this volume and Dorian 1999).

4.2   Simplification of areal diffusional patterns

Language loss in multilingual language areas results in disintegration of multilateral language contact. This is replaced with bilateral contact. There is also strong pressure for one language to override the other, and this results in intensive one-way diffusion. In the Vaupés area, this implies diffusion from Tucano into Tariana. This accounts for striking structural leveling between Tariana and Tucano (and not, for instance, between Tariana and Piratapuya, in spite of the fact that Piratapuya women are the preferred marriage partners of the Tariana).

Thus, multilateral diffusion, which is said to be 'notoriously messy' (cf. Thomason and Kaufman 1988: 95), gets replaced with just unilateral or bilateral contact. This is reminiscent of the general tendency towards regularisation and simplification which often accompanies language endangerment (Campbell and Muntzel 1989).

REFERENCES

Aikhenvald, Alexandra Y. 1996. Areal diffusion in North-West Amazonia: the case of Tariana. *Anthropological Linguistics* 38: 73-116.

_____ 1999. Areal diffusion and language contact in the Içana-Vaupés basin, North West Amazonia. In R.M.W. Dixon & Alexandra Y. Aikhenvald (eds) *The Amazonian Languages,* 385-415. Cambridge: Cambridge University Press.

_____ 2000. Language obsolescence: progress or decay? The emergence of new grammatical categories in 'language death'. In this volume.

Bowden, John 1997. *A Dictionary of Kwoma, A Papuan Language of North-East New Guinea.* Pacific Linguistics C-134. Canberra: Department of Linguistics, RSPAS, ANU.

Campbell, Lyle & Martha Muntzel. 1989. The structural consequences of language death. In Nancy C. Dorian (ed.), *Investigating Obsolescence. Studies in language contraction and death*, 181-196. Cambridge: Cambridge University Press.

Dorian, Nancy C. 1999. The study of language obsolescence: stages, surprises, challenges. *Languages and Linguistics* 3: 99-122.

Harrison, Simon J. 1983. *Laments for Foiled Marriages: Love-Songs from a Sepik River Village*. Port Moresby: Institute of Papua New Guinea Studies.

_____ 1990. *Stealing People's Names: history and politics in a Sepik River Cosmology*. Cambridge: Cambridge University Press.

Jackson, Jean 1974. Language identity of the Colombian Vaupés Indians. In Richard Bauman & Joel Sherzer (eds) *Explorations in the Ethnography of Speaking*, 50-64. Cambridge: Cambridge University Press.

Larsen, Nils-Erik 1984. Statistical investigations of language death in a North Frisian community. In P. Sture Ureland & Iain Clarkson (eds) *Scandinavian Language Contacts*, 191-220. Cambridge: Cambridge University Press.

Nidue, Joseph A. 1990. Language use in a New Guinea Village: a triglossic profile of Makopin I. *Language and Linguistics in Melanesia* 21: 47-69.

Sorensen, Arthur P. Jr. 1967 (1972). Multilingualism in the Northwest Amazon. *American Anthropologist,* 69: 670-684. (revised in 1972, in John B. Pride & Janet Holmes (eds) *Sociolinguistics*, 78-93. Harmondsworth: Penguin.)

Thomason, Sarah Grey & Terrence Kaufman. 1988. *Language Contact, Creolization and Genetic Linguistics*. Berkeley and Los Angeles: University of California Press.

Chapter 4

Why One Cannot Preserve Languages
(but can preserve language ecologies)

Peter Mühlhäusler

Adelaide University

The topic of this chapter is why one cannot preserve languages. There is much I would like to say and much I have said on this issue but I shall concentrate on one issue which I believe is crucial: Linguists have operated with a concept of language that is ill-suited to the business of reversing the decline of the world's linguistic diversity and indeed may be one of the causes that accelerates it.

More precisely - my point is that there are numerous diverse ways of speaking and that our concept of language reflects the operation of certain historical processes in our own culture rather than any natural principle. For a more detailed argument see Mühlhäusler (1992, 1996) and the debate these have engendered. I would like to point out a number of personal thoughts to begin with:

a) I regard the decline of linguistic diversity an extremely serious matter.

b) I have come to conclude that no discipline, and this includes linguistics, can provide much certainty and that the gap between what linguists can know and what they should know inevitably is considerable.

c) I do not see any virtue in defending a particular paradigm just because one has learnt to operate with it if one has compelling reasons for doubting its intellectual and social adequacy, though it might have saved me a great deal of hassle had I continued working on developmental aspects of derivational morphology - or some other aspect of descriptive Pidgin and Creole studies.

Let me now turn to more specific matters and ask what exactly is wrong with the linguists view of language. The Italian Renaissance philosopher Vico drew attention to the fact that members of a culture tend to get so habituated to their cultural practices as to regard them as natural. The subculture of linguistics is no exception as is evidenced by the widely used notion of 'a given natural language' and its defining characteristics which are:

a) being separate and distinct from culture, land and non-linguistic forms of communication,

b) "a rule governed system, definable in terms of a grammar which separates grammatical from ungrammatical sentences, assigning a pronunciation and a meaning to each grammatical sentence" (Smith & Wilson 1979: 31).

c) a system that is discontinuous and/or distinct from other language systems.

I am not alone in doubting the validity of such a characterisation of language, (cf. Toolan 1996) which corresponds moderately well to the 'cultural artefacts' (Haugen 1972) European National Standard Languages but not to any universal principle.

Another culture bounded notion that linguists have tended to get habituated to is that of communication in the sense of transforming messages into signals by means of a code, sending those speech signals via a channel to a hearer who decodes them by means of a shared code into the original message. This conduit, telegraphic or plumbing model of communication may be appropriate while talking about telegraphy but as a characterisation how humans communicate it leaves a great deal to be desired. That this view of communication is strongly supported by the discursive practices of certain Western languages has been documented in great detail by Reddy (1979) and explains why linguists from Saussure to Katz and beyond have subscribed to it. We note that the notion of shared grammatical codes in the sense found in Wilson & Smith is implicit in this view of communication.

That "most languages have been studied and described as if they are standard languages" (Coulmas 1994) may be a fact but I do not regard it as a virtue. It prevents linguists from seeing what the loss of linguistic diversity means, it encourages them to equate preservation with maintenance   and to be satisfied with the production of "artefacts reduced to academic grammars and collections of texts" (Thieberger 1990: 335). Such preservation, as Thieberger continues, "is usually only entered into because it is of more use to the expropriators, the dominant culture, than it is to the speech community it is abstracted from."

There will of course, be disclaimers and protests and some of those who have attacked me on this point to their own good intentions and the good work that many practicing linguists have produced in the language maintenance field.   My reply is that adopting the missionary position of having good intentions is not always matched by desirable outcomes and that such useful work that linguists have carried out typically was done not qua linguists but because of other factors - and one may wish to add that some impressive things have been achieved by members of endangered communities with little or no formal linguistic training.

Let me return to my observations about the views of language in the prevailing system linguistic and sociolinguistic paradigm:

a) The view that linguistic practices can be separated from cultural practice, land, kinship and so forth has turned out to be an inadequate characterisation of how indigenous (including Australian) communities   work and indeed how they conceptualise the process: There is, for instance a considerable difference between the traditional Javanese Basa 'language, civility, nationality and truth' and the colonial Bahasa, the translation equivalent of Dutch 'taal' language.

b) That Smith & Wilson's dictum (1979: 13) "there is no way of describing or defining a given language without invoking the notion of linguistic rule" has not only been shown to be erroneous by recent work in the cognitive sciences, it also has been shown to be highly suspect by those who study spontaneous discourses and the syntactic work by Grace and Pawley on prefabricated structures. I would like to add that language preservation is about keeping discourses alive and to enable people to continue producing connected speech.

c) The concept of 'given language' is equally problematic as it confuses the linguistic practices encountered within arbitrary boundaries established by politicians, missionaries and linguists with real object. I am at a total loss for an answer to the questions:

> How many Aboriginal languages are spoken in Australia?
>
> How many Pidgins are spoken in Melanesia?
>
> How many languages are spoken in the Black Forest?
>
> How many languages are spoken in Micronesia/New Caledonia?

In numerous traditional situations, lexical and grammatical variants (if you want these to be the defining features of a language) were located on a continuum or multidimensional network. The emergence of distinct named languages is a historically late phenomenon in many parts of the world resulting from an array of historical contingencies. It is difficult, for this reason, to give a reasonable answer to the questions: How many language are spoken in the world, how many are endangered, how many speakers do these language have and other questions which feature prominently in the language loss debate: Of course, as the example of the linguistic minorities of Europe shows, not playing the game, not wishing to have a well defined territory or a name disqualifies you for grants, recognition and status.

What I have tried to argue is that there is a mismatch between what conventional linguistics suggests is happening - one language after another is disappearing and what may actually be happening - traditional ways of communication in a complex cultural and natural ecology disappear because of habitat impoverishment and destruction. This includes the weakening of the languages continuum and networks, layered multilingualism, loss of cultural contexts for language use, loss of places where language can been spoken traditionally and numerous more.

I have tried to reframe the problem as one of preserving linguistic ecologies i.e. dynamically changing and adaptive ecologies whose inhabitants are linked to one another and their sustaining environment by numerous functional links. As in biological ecologies the majority of these links are mutually beneficial (90 per cent) and only a small number competitive or exploitative. My reframing also means abandoning the notion that languages are in competition - with the implicit belief that languages can be made to survive by making them more competitive, i.e. giving them grammars, dictionaries, literacy etc. Instead language maintenance should ask: How can we preserve or recreate the ecological conditions for linguistics diversity. Let me offer a practical suggestion. One could conceive of the development of Linguistic Impact Statements supplementing already widely used Environment Impact Statements: But my main concern is that linguists have to rethink their discipline radically if they wish for it to be relevant to the maintenance of linguistic diversity.

REFERENCES

Coulmas, Florian 1994. Protestant ethics and profane language: economic aspects of language standardization. In Georges Lüdi (ed.) *Sprachstandardisierung,* 161-177. Freiburg: Swiss Academy of Humanities and Social Science.

Haugen, Einar 1972. *The Ecology of Language: Essays by Einar Haugen.* (Anwar S. Dil ed.) Stanford, CA: Stanford University Press.

Mühlhäusler, Peter 1992. Preserving languages or language ecologies? A top down approach to language survival. *Oceanic Linguistics* 31/2: 163-180.

_____ 1996. *Linguistic Ecology. Language change and linguistic imperialism in the Pacific region.* London: Routledge.

Reddy, Michael J. 1979. The conduit metaphor — a case of frame conflict in our language about language. In Andrew Ortony (ed.) *Metaphor and Thought,* 284-324. Cambridge: Cambridge University Press.

Smith, Neil & Deirdre Wilson 1979. *Modern Linguistics.* Harmondsworth: Penguin.

Thieberger, Nicholas 1990. Language maintenance — why bother! *Multilingua* 9/4: 333-357.

Toolan, Michael 1996. *Total Speech.* Durham, NC: Duke University Press.

Chapter 5

Irish and Finland Swedish

Anders Ahlqvist

National University of Ireland, Galway

The linguistic ecology of Europe, just like that of the rest of the world, is changing very fast. This can be seen in many ways. This chapter looks at a few changes that are taking place in European countries, focusing on two languages that are of special interest to me, Irish because it is my working language and Swedish because it is native to me. Because of its rather more unique position among the languages of the world, Irish will receive more detailed treatment. Finland Swedish will thus mainly serve as a standard of comparison.

1. IRISH

For well-known historical reasons, Irish is the first official language in Ireland, whereas English is, according to the Constitution, 'accepted as another official language' (see Ó Máille 1990: 3-4, Ó Cearúil 1999: 82-83; see further below). Nevertheless, the vast majority of the Irish population speak English only, and the future of Irish as a genuine spoken language looks uncertain, even in the short term.

It is usually accepted, presumably mainly for lack of contrary evidence — more than because we know it to be a definite fact — that Irish was established as perhaps even the sole language of Ireland by historical times. In this context this refers to the time around the completion of the Roman invasion of those parts of Great Britain that were invaded by Rome. The first language to challenge Irish in its assumed complete domination of the island was Latin. It came into Ireland quite early, probably quite some time (Adams 1986: 16) before Christianity arrived.

An early grammatical text contains, among other interesting material, a short passage (Ahlqvist 1982: 47, see 40) which has the audacity to maintain that Irish as a language is not equal to Greek and Latin but even that it is superior to them. This kind of notion I believe to be unprecedented in medieval Europe. Moreover, it does not seem to reoccur until much later. Consciousness about language — of this sort, anyway — is usually associated with the doctrines of Herder and other nineteenth-century German thinkers (Colliander 1963).

After Latin, the main outside linguistic influence to be felt in Ireland has been that of the English language. At first it was rather slow in establishing itself. The process of assimilation to English did not really get going very significantly — outside the main settlement areas of Dublin and a few other urban centres — until perhaps some time in the fifteenth and sixteenth centuries, even if it was much later before it achieved any momentum (Adams 1986: 23–4).

A few very basic facts about the language itself may be presented here. The first one is that it is a verb-initial language, the basic word order in most stages of attested Irish being verb, subject, object (VSO). This is interesting, for typological reasons. Irish shares this feature with the other Insular Celtic languages. It also shares another feature with them, which is that it has initial mutations.[1] In other words, the beginning of a word may change under certain circumstances, either because the previous word influences the word coming after it, or for syntactic reasons. This also illustrates a salient fact about the spelling of Irish, which is that it is a morphophonemic one, unlike that of Welsh. If we look at the following example (which I have made up myself but which I believe would be acceptable to native speakers both of Irish and of Welsh), this becomes clear: Irish *i gCanberra* corresponds to Welsh *yn Nghanberra;* both mean 'in Canberra'. In Irish, the radical remains in the spelling when the initial mutation has been at work; in Welsh it does not: this means that — at least if one does not know the radical — the Irish spelling system is more practical. For a native speaker this usually does not matter, except possibly in cases like the

---

[1]   This is rare, but not unprecedented in the world's languages: see for instance Evans (1998).

one just cited. Irish has another feature, not shared by the other insular Celtic languages: all consonants may be either "slender" or "broad" — to use the terminology of native grammarians.[2] It corresponds roughly to the distinction we find in Russian between hard and soft consonants. Thus one finds a clear phonemic distinction between a word like *guí* /gàiː/ 'praying' and a word like *gí* /ɡiː/ 'although'.

One can put the year 1600 as a rough date for the dismemberment of the Gaelic order. Around that time Irish began to cease to be used as the normal vehicle for communication of all social classes. There are various events which mark this process. One is that known as the Flight of the Earls,[3] when most of the old native noblemen were forced to leave the country.

In 1800, the situation was roughly this: the whole western seaboard still had an undoubted Irish-speaking majority, whereas English was the majority language only in and around Belfast, Dublin and a small area in and around Wexford, in the far south-east corner of Ireland. A map, taken from a book with the rather sinister-sounding title *The Death of the Irish Language* (Hindley 1990: 9), shows this reasonably clearly.

The nineteenth-century erosion of Irish took place quite rapidly. By 1851 the situation had deteriorated considerably: as another map of Hindley's (1990: 16) shows, Irish was no longer the majority language of a contiguous area on the Western seaboard. Instead, it remained dominant only in a number of areas (mainly in Counties Donegal, Mayo, Galway and Kerry), separated from each other by areas which had become English-dominated in the previous years. Shortly before 1851, the Great Famine had taken place. It affected the Irish-speaking part of the country much more than the English-

---

2   These are equivalent to "palatalised" and "non-palatalised" in more standard linguistic terminology.

3   After the battle of Kinsale, in December 1601 (see Canny 1989: 130–1 and MacCurtain 1972: 140).

speaking one. 1851 was also the year of the first Census. The whole island had roughly 6.5 million inhabitants, out of whom 320,000 spoke Irish only and about 1.5 million both languages. Irish was thus no longer the majority language of the island. According to the Census of 1911 (Hindley 1990: 22–3), the situation had then deteriorated considerably further. The whole island had a population of about 4.4 million, of whom some 600,000 spoke Irish and most of them English too.

Important political events took place in the years following, so that the following Census (in 1926, Hindley 1990: 25) excludes Northern Ireland, which remained part of the United Kingdom after the early 1920s. In 1926 the new Government of the then Irish Free State established a Commission to look at the Irish-speaking area. The term *Gaeltacht* was introduced to cover all the Irish-speaking areas and boundaries established. These boundaries are still officially recognised. In 1926 the population of the 26 counties of the Irish Free State was estimated (Hindley 1990: 23) at some 3 million, of whom a little more than 0.5 million spoke Irish. By this time the distinction between native speakers and learners of Irish becomes significant, even though subsequent Censuses have been interestingly uninterested in it.

In 1981 the Gaeltacht is sadly shrunk (Hindley 1990: 31–2): only some very few quite small districts remain majority Irish-speaking, again in Counties Donegal, Mayo, Galway and Kerry. The Census figures on the other hand (Hindley 1990: 27) show that the Republic by then had 3.2 million inhabitants. Of these, more than one million declared, in answering their Census questions, that they spoke Irish. After a thorough and very interesting discussion of most relevant factors involved, Hindley (1990: 251) states:

> Budding linguistic statisticians should note that 8,751 is the figure finally preferred as the most likely residue of native Irish speakers living in communities with sufficient attachment to Irish to transmit it to a substantial majority of their children as language of the home and community. They alone are living in circumstances in which continued transmissions seems

possible or even probable in the light of experience. This is all
that close scrutiny leaves of the 1,000,413 persons aged 3 years
and over who were enumerated as Irish speakers in the Census
of 1981 and is reasonably proportionate to 1,473 number of
children in 70 per cent *deontas*[4] majority schools. I do not
suggest this dogmatically but feel it safe to set a 10,000 upper
limit to the current numbers of habitual native speakers while
admitting that many of them share grave doubts about the
advisability of continuing to speak Irish and may well end their
careers more fluent in English and in normal circumstances no
longer using Irish.

Naturally, these findings have not been universally popular in
Ireland. In a review[5] Deaglán de Bréadún (1990) makes the point
that Irish is used for many purposes outside the Gaeltacht, mainly by
people other than genuine native speakers, indicating that that might
be where the future of Irish is. He finishes his review with these
words:

> An honest appraisal of the language movement combined with
> Hindley's clear-eyed view of the Gaeltacht could be the basis
> for devising a strategy to ensure that Irish will survive and
> even prosper.

Emotionally speaking, one might wish that he were right, but at the
same time, trying to be truthful and scholarly about things, one has
to wonder. Moreover, very recently, another undoubtedly honest
commentator (Ó Muirthile 1999) has stated bluntly that there now

---

4   *Deontas* 'grant' refers to the government grant for Gaeltacht
families with Irish-speaking children (see Hindley 1990: 48–62).

5   For just one rather important rejoinder in English, see Ó Ciosáin
(1991) *Buried Alive,* which has a title just as throught-provoking as that of
Hindley's book. It contains (1991: 27) a useful short bibliography of some
of the most interesting other comments (in Irish and English) on Hindley's
book.

cannot be more than five hundred people who have a high standard in writing Irish.

The question of the political and constitutional status of Ireland before the English conquest is interesting. Whether Ireland ever was something that could be described as a nation seems debatable, although it seems reasonable to state that it certainly was not a state. However, the Irish language itself certainly had a fairly strong position during this period, for the simple reason that the legal system functioned in Irish and was codified in it. During the period of British rule, Irish did not have any particular legal status. However, the constitutional position of any language in the United Kingdom is in any case a fairly grey area.[6]

Probably the first manifestation of legal recognition to touch Irish — during British rule — took place in 1908, with the establishment of the National University of Ireland. The Irish Universities Act provided for Irish to be a compulsory matriculation subject for admission to the colleges of the University. This is still the case, but in the National University only. After 1916, the new Irish Free State — called *Saorstát Éireann* in Irish — was established. It provided for Irish to be official in at least part of the island of Ireland. In 1937 a new Constitution was enacted; it is still in force. Amongst other things it provided for the official name of the country to be *Éire*,[7] or in the English language *Ireland*. This constitution contains a paragraph dealing with languages:

> 1. Ós í an Ghaeilge an teanga náisiúnta, is í an phríomhtheanga oifigiúil í. 2. Glactar leis an Sacs-Bhéarla mar theanga oifigiúil eile 'The Irish language as the national language is the first official language. English is recognised as another official language' (Ó Máille 1990: 3–4, Ó Cearúil 1999: 82-83).

---

6   See for instance Price (1984: 66–7, 106–9, 213–19).

7   Note that the frequent misspelling *(Eire)* of this name without the length-mark means (pronounced /ˈeʒə/) 'burden' and is thus quite naturally rather offensive to some.

It goes on to state that provision may be made in relevant cases for the use of either one or the other language. This has much to do with the symbolic function of the Irish language in Ireland today (see further Bressan 1976 for a commendably detached view). However, when Ireland, together with the United Kingdom, became part of the then European Economic Community, Irish was accepted as one of the languages of the Community but not given the status of a 'working' language. It is thus unique amongst the official languages of the countries that make up the Community. Evidence[8] has now come to light that this happened, not because of opposition from Brussels, but because the Dublin authorities felt that it would be easier that way.

Irish is a compulsory subject in all primary and secondary schools. Some schools use it not only as a subject that the children are instructed in but also as the medium for all or part of whatever instruction is given in that particular school. Standards vary enormously. At university level, Irish is a compulsory matriculation subject in the National University of Ireland. Students must pass in Irish to get into any of the National University's four constituent universities: Cork, Dublin, Galway and Maynooth. The other universities, Trinity College, Dublin, the new University of Limerick and the new Dublin City University, on the other hand, do not require Irish as a matriculation subject. The National University of Ireland, Galway has a special position in this regard, in that it is, by an Act of Dáil Éireann (the Irish Parliament), dating from 1929, required to become eventually a college that conducts all its business in Irish only. At the moment, it is possible to have Irish as a medium of instruction there, in a number of subjects, including Irish itself, History, Geography and some areas of Chemistry.

The Roman Catholic Church abandoned Latin over twenty-five years ago. This has had one positive result in Ireland, as far as Irish is concerned: Irish is now used for liturgical purposes. Given the

---

8   Ó Ruairc (1989); see Mac Congáil (1990: 574) for a very brief English summary.

aestethic poverty of the new English Mass (at least as celebrated in Ireland), it is not entirely surprising that for some Irish people, Irish is now acquiring the force of a very welcome new liturgical language.

Moreover, there is no doubt that Irish retains an important symbolic value for many Irishmen, probably even a majority of them. A good example of how this works is provided by the announcements made by flight attendants on the national airline Aer Lingus. These usually start in Irish with polite phrases to welcome passengers, followed by the same phrases in English. The obviously much more important safety announcements are then given in English only. In other words, where a need for real communication is felt, English is used. Naturally, that is really not good enough to enable the language to survive as a genuine spoken language.

Geography must be the principal reason for the decline of Irish. When the competing language is — whether one likes it or not — the main world language and when that is the language of all neighbouring countries (not forgetting the United States), the odds are formidable indeed. However, there are probably other reasons too. A comparison with Welsh is instructive. In Wales today, there are about a quarter of a million quite genuine native speakers of Welsh. The Welsh Bible[9] was published in 1588. In Irish, the entire Bible[10] was published around 1690, but since it was a Protestant rather than a Roman Catholic translation, it was never widely read. In fact the Bible in Irish (*An Bíobla Naofa*) for the Catholic population was not made available until 1981. Thus, it may well be that differences in religion account for some differences in linguistic history, as regards Ireland and Wales.[11]

---

[9]   See *Y Beibl Cyssegr-Lan* (1588).

[10]   See *An Biobla Naomhtha* (1690).

[11]   However, see further Wall (1969) for a somewhat different view of the Church's role in this respect.

In a situation like that of Irish, language planning is obviously called for. As it happens, this has a long and distinguished history in Irish-speaking Ireland. During the period (1200–1600) of what is known as Classical Modern Irish, there was a regulating agency at work for the language standardised; collectively it may be described as the Bardic grammarians.[12] They established and kept alive a standard for the language, from Northern Scotland to South West Kerry. The motivation behind it was quite practical: these were professional poets who had to find employment all over the Gaelic area. Incidentally, their example should be quite interesting to people in other countries with "small" languages. Theirs was a flexible standard that in many cases allowed for acceptable by-forms from varying dialects. There is a fine gradation of linguistic acceptability on these lines: z is the correct form, y is an alternative correct form, x is acceptable as dialect, and w lastly is not acceptable at all. Given also the intricacies of Classical Modern Irish metre, it was very useful to have a large body of different choices so as to be able to make it easier to get the language into the straightjacket of the metre. In the 16th century, a very acceptable standard for prose was set by Geoffrey Keating who wrote an historical work, *Foras Feasa ar Éirinn*.[13] In different circumstances it might have helped towards forming a standard for a printed written language, but with the dismemberment of the old social order in Ireland, Irish did not become a printed language until the last century. Something fairly close to the Keating standard was adopted in 1927, when Fr. Dinneen's authoritative *Irish-English Dictionary* was published. This worked reasonably well for some time. Some influential users of Irish became unhappy about the language changing a great deal since Keating's time. Eventually, a movement was set up to start basing the language on the dialects. Gradually, this led to government action that was codified in a new 'Official Standard' (*An Caighdeán*

---

12   For an introduction to this topic, see Ó Cuív (1973).

13   It is important to note that although written in the sixteenth century, this work was not made available in printed form until the beginning of the twentieth century.

Oifigiúil).[14] It simplified a ·number of items of orthography and of grammar. To mention but one example, the word meaning 'pay' which used to be spelt *páighe* is now spelt *pá*. This is fine for Southern (Munster) Irish where the word is pronounced ['pɑː] but not for Western (Connaught) Irish ['paːɪ] or Northern (Donegal) ['paːjə] Obviously, (cf. Ó Siadhail 1981: 73) for those dialects the old spelling would have been more practical. Parallel situations exist elsewhere. Thus, it seems to me that the spelling reformers who established the new standard of Swedish in 1905 made a serious mistake in removing the *h* from the word *hvad* > *vad* 'what', ignoring the fact that the sound it represents actually survives in some Swedish dialects, notably in Finland.

In 1959 and 1977, respectively, Tomás de Bhaldraithe and Niall Ó Dónaill published an *English–Irish Dictionary* and an *Irish–English Dictionary*. These are now the "official" dictionaries, which currently set what effectively is the standard for people wishing to write in Irish, not only for official purposes, but also in schools and even for literary purposes. The numeral system has by some been seen as a problem. In this regard the official standard departs completely from all genuine dialects of Modern Irish. For instance '96' in traditional native speaker Irish is *sé déag is ceithre fichid*.[15] This was felt to be too complicated. Instead it was thought that it would be more rational to devise a completely new system, with

---

[14]   See *Gramadach na Gaeilge* (1958), Ó Baoill (1988) for a (somewhat uncritical) account of how it was established and Ó Siadhail (1981) for some trenchant comments of how better insights in modern linguistics could have saved the authors some of thier mistakes, as for instance (1981: 72), when he states: "Where the Official orthography does fall down is that it is a ragbag of half-systematic and half-random choice. It lacks the necessary overall theoretical framework to provide a system which would contain the required degree of abstraction thast might enable speakers of various dialects to see the regularity of their own pronunciation". Much as I agree with this in principle, I also, in practice, have to agree with Ó Siadhail (1981: 74) that it "is probably too late" now for making "a case for reforming the Official orthography".

[15]   I.e. '(6 + 10) + (4 x 20)'.

forms like *nócha sé*[16] '96'. It is quite clear that had the Irish language planners involved been French speakers used to forms like *quatre-vingt-seize,* results might have been different. These new numerals have been officially adopted and are now used by most Irish-speakers, especially younger ones, even among Hindley's (1990:251) less than 10,000 genuine native speakers.

Another thing that official terminologists have been overly keen on is compounds, even though they do not suit the language. A dictionary of computer terminology *(Téarmaí Ríomhaireachta* 1990) lists *bogearraí* as the translation of 'software'. *Bog* means 'soft', *earraí* means 'goods' (of the type purchased in shops). No attempt was made to look at the basic semantic content of the lexical item and to base anything better on that, rather than slavishly on the English term. If one disregards the not unserious problems posed by the pronunciation,[17] the compound itself feels less than native.[18] French language planning might in this case have provided a better model. In French 'software' is *logiciel,* which corresponds neatly to *matériel* 'hardware'.

2.   FINLAND SWEDISH

In Finland,[19] Finnish and Swedish are equally official. Finnish is spoken natively by well over 90 per cent of the population, whereas Swedish is the language of some 200,000 people. Official policy is for both language to be supported by the state. Thus, members of both language groups are taught the other language at school.

---

16   I.e. '90 + 6'.

17   [ˈbɔgˌæri] would seem to be a fairly plausible standard pronunciation, but I have also heard it pronounced [ˈbʌgəri].

18   See Ahlqvist (1985) for further comments regarding some of the typological implications.

19   McRae (1987) provides an excellent introduction to the entire history of the languages of Finland.

However, it is clear that the real second language of younger Finnish-speaking Finns is English.

Very briefly, the history of Finland may be summarised as follows. In the twelfth century, the country became part of Sweden, remaining so until 1809, when she was conquered by the Russians and made into an autonomous Grand Duchy. Finland became independent in 1917. Her very first language, Lappish (= Sami), was pushed northwards by Finnish around the eighth century. Swedish established itself on the South and the West coast at an early period, probably at least as early as the time when Finland became part of Sweden. Nowadays, Lappish is a minority language in the North, whereas Finnish and Swedish have equal legal status, according to the basic law currently in force. The paragraphs treating of linguistic matters in the constitution are as follows:

Section 14 (17 July 1995/969)
The national languages of Finland shall be Finnish and Swedish. The right of everyone to use his own language, whether Finnish or Swedish, as a party in proceedings before a court of law or other authority, and to obtain documents from them in that language, shall be guaranteed by Act of Parliament. Public authorities shall take care to provide for the educational, cultural and social needs of the Finnish-speaking and the Swedish-speaking populations of the country according to similar principles. The Sami as an indigenous people as well as the Romanis and other groups shall have the right to maintain and develop their own languages and cultures. Provisions governing the right of the Sami to use the Sami language before the public authorities shall be prescribed by Act of Parliament. The rights of those who use sign language and of those who require interpretation or translation

because of a disability shall be guaranteed by Act of
Parliament.[20]

This is a very well-meaning piece of legislation, but it has to be
admitted that it does not echo the reality of linguistic life in
contemporary Finland. On the one hand, many Swedish-speakers,
especially in the south, often find it difficult to do business through
Swedish with the authorities. Moreover, many whose families used
to be Swedish-speaking have become Finnish-speaking, either
because of marriages across the linguistic boundary or because of
similar reasons.[21] On the other hand, it must be also be noted that
Finnish-speakers are seriously disadvantaged in the Åland Islands,
which have a very special legal status as an unchangeably unilingual
Swedish-speaking territory, where only Swedish has legal validity.

The schools have changed enormously since my own schooldays in
the fifties and early sixties. Then, the situation was quite simply that
primary schools, whether Swedish- or Finnish-speaking, were
unilingual: no other languages were taught in them. Thus, those who
left school without partaking of secondary education generally
remained monolingual. Secondary schools, on the other hand, started
with the other language of the country before moving on to foreign
languages. Before World War II, this foreign language was often
German, but after that German was increasingly frequently replaced
by English. Moreover, many schools also taught a second and even a
third foreign language. This allowed some space for French, which
after World War I was rarely taught as first foreign language.
Furthermore, Latin was taught as first foreign language in a number
of special Classical Lyceums, which also taught Ancient Greek.

---

20   This unofficial translation of the equally valid Finnish and Swedish
originals emanates from a Finnish Government web site:
‹http://www.vn.fi/vn/suomi/vn5f.htm›.
21   Tandefelt (1988), which includes a summary in English, contains a
detailed scholarly examination of the processes involved.

In the early 1970s, Finland undertook a thorough overhaul of its educational system. The old primary school was abolished and replaced by a new so-called basic school. This begins at the same age of seven as the old primary school, but continues for several more years. This new school introduced the general principle that all pupils must learn other languages than only their native ones and that one of these must be the other native language, that is Swedish in Finnish-language schools, and Finnish in Swedish-language ones. On the other hand, and crucially, the order in which they are introduced may vary. This causes a significant lack of symmetry between the two linguistic groups. The reason for this is simply that Swedish-speakers nowadays need Finnish more than Finnish-speakers need Swedish. The result is that a vast majority of Finnish-language schools have English as their first other language and that Swedish is taught as a third language, rarely well learnt, whereas Swedish-language schools often do the opposite, taking Finnish before English. Thus English has become by far the best-known foreign language, almost to the total exclusion of other important European languages, like French and German. Now that Finland has become part of the European Union, this is incidentally changing somewhat, since the authorities are conscious of the need of people who can do business in Brussels in German and French.

3.   CONCLUSION

Trying to compare some trends in the linguistic situation of the two countries, I see a very strong contrast emerging between official policies and more popular perceptions of the proper role the respective languages ought to play in the two countries. In other words, it is clear that in Ireland Irish now has largely been reduced to the status of a symbolic language, the purpose of which is to affirm that Ireland is not England. Likewise, in Finland, a period of transition has come about, which sees the other national language strongly marginalised.

Ireland is undoubtedly a strong warning example to the rest of Europe. If people cease to transmit their languages to their children, these languages do not remain alive. They commit linguistic suicide.

In some cases (although I hesitate[22] to use such loaded terminology), one might even talk about linguicide or linguistic murder.

There are of course those who feel that what is happening is just good riddance to old rubbish and that it is much better for everybody everywhere to speak the same language, by which nowadays they usually mean English. As Trudgill (1991), Westcott (1994) and Hale (1998) have pointed out, the cultural, ecological and linguistic impoverishment involved would be quite dreadful. Nevertheless, it may rather paradoxically be the case that there is a certain bit of uncomfortable truth in a statement that was made by my former Galway colleague Gearóid Mac Eoin, in his concluding remarks, at the very end of the Third International Conference on Minority Languages in Galway in 1986.[23] On that occasion, he argued that what is good for a minority language as a language is not necessarily always very good for the speakers of these languages as individuals, especially in the context of their material welfare.

REFERENCES[24]

Adams, G. Brendan 1970. Language and Man in Ireland. *Ulster Folklife* 15/16: 140–171 (repr. 1986: 1–32).

_____ 1986. *The English Dialects of Ulster. An Anthology of Articles on Ulster Speech by G. B. Adams.* Holywood: Ulster Folk and Transport Museum.

Ahlqvist, Anders 1982. *The Early Irish Linguist: An Edition of the Canonical Part of the Auraicept na nÉces.* Helsingfors: Societas

---

22   Scholars, however emotionally committed to native minority languages and ones worked with, must in my view try to be balanced and objective.
23   See Ahlqvist et al. (1987a, 1987b).
24   This includes references mentioned in the text as well as some generally useful introductory items.

Scientiarum Fennica *(Commentationes Litterarum Humanarum LXXIII)*.

Ahlqvist, Anders 1985. The Ordering of Nominal Compounds in Irish. In Jacek Fisiak (ed.) *Proceedings of the 4th International Conference on Historical Linguistics: Historical Semantics/Historical Word-Formation*, 1–9. Berlin, The Hague, New York: Mouton de Gruyter.

Ahiqvist, Anders, Gearóid Mac Eoin & Donncha Ó hAodha (eds) 1987a *Third International Conference on Minority Languages: Celtic Papers.* Clevedon & Philadelphia: Multilingual Matters.

_____, _____ & _____ (eds) 1987b. *Third International Conference on Minority Languages: General Papers.* Clevedon & Philadelphia: Multilingual Matters.

De Bhaldraithe, Tomás 1959. *English–Irish Dictionary.* Dublin: Stationery Office.

An Bíobla Naofa [The Holy Bible] 1981. Edited by Pádraig Ó Fiannachta. Maynooth: An Sagart.

An Biobla Naomtha [The Holy Bible] 1690. Translated by Uilliam Bedel and Uilliam O Domhnuill. London: R. Ebheringtham.

De Bréadún, Deaglán 1990. Review of Hindley 1990, *The Irish Times* 23.6.1990, *Weekend,* 8.

Bressan, Dino 1976. *Bilinguismo ufficiale e bilinguismo effettivo nella Repubblica irlandese.* Brescia: C.L.A.Di.L.

Canny, Nicholas 1989. Early Modern Ireland, *c.* 1500–1700. In Roy E. Foster (ed.) *The Oxford Illustrated History of Ireland,* 104–160. Oxford: Oxford University Press.

Colliander, Börje 1963. *Modersmålet som massrörelse* [The Mother Tongue as Mass Movement]. Ekenäs: Tryckeri Aktiebolag.

Dinneen, Patrick S. 1927. *Foclóir Gaedhilge agus Béarla. An Irish–English Dictionary.* Dublin: The Educational Company of Ireland, for The Irish Texts Society.

Edwards, John 1984. Irish and English in Ireland. In Peter Trudgill (ed.) *Language in the British Isles*, 480–98. Cambridge: Cambridge University Press.

Evans, Nicholas 1998. Iwaidja Mutation and its Origins. In Anna Siewierska & Jae Jung Song (eds) *Case, Typology and Grammar*, 115–149. Amsterdam & Philadelphia: John Benjamins.

Gramadach na Gaeilge agus Litriú na Gaeilge. An Caighdeán Oifigiúil [The Grammar of Irish and the Spelling of Irish. The Official Standard] 1958. Dublin: Stationery Office.

Hale, Ken 1998. On Endangered Languages and the Importance of Linguistic Diversity. In Lenore A. Grenoble & Lindsay J. Whaley (eds) *Endangered Languages*, 192–216. Cambridge: Cambridge University Press.

Hindley, Reg 1990. *The Death of the Irish Language*. London and New York: Routledge.

Keating, Geoffrey 1902–14. *Foras Feasa ar Éirinn. The History of Ireland I–IV*, edited by David Comyn & Patrick S. Dinneen. London: Irish Texts Society [reprinted 1987].

Mac Congáil, Nollaig 1990. Modern Irish. In David A. Wells, Glanville Price & Peter J. Mayo, (eds) *The Year's Work in Modern Language Studies*, 570–83. London: The Modern Humanities Research Association.

Mac Curtain, Margaret 1972. *Tudor and Stuart England*. Dublin: Gill and Macillan

McRae, Kenneth D. 1997. *Conflict and compromise in multilingual societies, Vol. 3 Finland*. Ontario: Wilfrid Laurier University Press.

Ó Baoill, Dónall P. 1988. Language Planning in Ireland: the Standardization of Irish. *International Journal of the Sociology of Language* 70:109–126

Ó Cearúil, Micheál 1999. *Bunracht na hÉireann [Constitution of Ireland], a study of the Irish text*. Dublin: Stationery Office.

Ó Ciosáin, Éamon 1991. *Buried Alive*. Dublin: Dáil Uí Chadhain.

Ó Cuív, Brian 1973. The Linguistic Training of the Mediaeval Irish Poet, *Celtica* 10: 114–140.

_____ 1976. The Irish Language in the Early Modern Period. In T.W. Moody, F.X. Martin & Francis John Byrne (eds) *A New History of Ireland III: Early Modern Ireland 1534–1691*, 509–545. Oxford: Clarendon Press.

Ó Dónaill, Niall 1977. *Irish–English Dictionary*. Dublin: Stationery Office.

Ó Máille, Tomás. 1990. *The Status of the Irish Language. A Legal Perspective*. Dublin: Bord na Gaeilge.

Ó Muirthile, Liam 1999. An Peann Coitianta [The Common Pen]. *Irish Times* 25/9/1999: 28.

Ó Ruairc, Maolmhaodhóg 1989. Faillí an Rialtais agus Seasamh na Gaeilge i gComhphobal na hEorpa: Ceist Bhunúsach Bhunreachtúil [The Government's Negligence and the Standing of the Irish Language in the European Community: a Fundamental Constitutional Question], *Comhar* 48/10: 13–19.

Ó Siadhail, Mícheál 1980. *Learning Irish*. Dublin: Institute for Advanced Studies; London and New Haven 1988: Yale University Press.

_____ 1981. Standard Irish Orthography — An Assessment, *The Crane Bag* 5/2: 71–5.

_____ 1989. *Modern Irish: Grammatical Structure and Dialectal Variation*. Cambridge: University Press.

Price, Glanville 1984. *The Languages of Britain*. London: Edward Arnold.

Tandefelt, Marika 1988. *Mellan två språk* [Between two Languages]. Upsala: Almqvist & Wiksell.

Téarmaí Ríomhaireachta 1990. *Computer Terms*. Dublin: An Gúm.

Trudgill, Peter 1991. Language Maintenance and Language Shift: Preservation versus Extinction. *International Journal of Applied Linguistics* 1/1: 61–69.

Wall, Maureen 1969. The Decline of the Irish Language. In Brian Ó Cuív (ed.) *A View of the Irish Language,* 81–90. Dublin: Stationery Office.

Westcott, Geoffrey 1994. Endpiece. *Language International* 6/6: 48.

Y Beibl Cyssegr-Lan [The Holy and Pure Bible] 1588. Translated by William Morgan, William Salesbury, Richard Davies & Thomas Huet. London: Deputies of C. Barker.

Chapter 6

Working Together to Strengthen Sm'algyax (Tsimshian Nation, British Columbia, Canada)

Tonya Stebbins
University of Melbourne

1.   INTRODUCTION

The Tsimshian Nation has its territory on the Northwest coast of British Columbia, Canada. The town of Prince Rupert (population 17,000) is the main service town for the Northwest coast and is within Tsimshian territory. Many Tsimshian people live in Prince Rupert, while many more live on reserves or 'villages' along the coast. (Hartley Bay, Kitkatla, Metlakatla, Lax Kw'alaams, Kitsmkaalum, Kitsalaas, and New Metlakatla are the principal Tsimshian settlements. Most of these are located on traditional winter village sites. Kitkatla has been continuously occupied for 5,000 years.) Others live further afield in towns such as Prince George and Vancouver.

The Tsimshian language is called Sm'algyax. This language, also known as Coast Tsimshian in the linguistic and anthropological literature, is part of the Tsimshianic language family, supposedly a branch of the Penutian language family. At this time there are around 6,000 people affiliated with the Tsimshian Nation (generally by matrilineal descent). Fluent speakers of the language however number only around 400. Within this group, those fully fluent in all aspects of the language are typically over 70 years old, those over fifty are fluent but tend to have gaps in their knowledge of the language, and there are only a few speakers under fifty.

This paper provides an overview of the fortunes of Sm'algyax to date. It relates social and political changes in the community to language attitudes. The motivations behind current language revival activities in the community are also considered. One project, the development of a learners' dictionary is described in more detail. The dictionary project was a cooperative effort sponsored by the Ts'msyeen Sm'algyax Authority. It involved the author (as linguist and dictionary compiler), and many elders from the community (as contributors and editors). Although it was potentially a politically divisive activity, the dictionary has been widely welcomed by the Tsimshian community. Some reasons for the acceptance of the dictionary in the community are suggested.

2.   A BRIEF SOCIAL HISTORY OF THE TSIMSHIAN NATION AND SM'ALGYAX

This section provides a brief overview of the key historical phases that have been experienced by members of the Tsimshian Nation since contact. These phases are: the fur trade period (mid 1700s to late 1800s), the mission era (mid 1800s to early 1900s) and the rise and fall of the cannery industry (late 1800s to late 1900s). Parallel with these changes in the economy of the coast were changes in educational patterns for Tsimshian children. Western education was first made available to Tsimshian children at the beginning of the mission period. Residential schooling was quickly established as an option for some children. By the early 1900s this practice was developing into government policy. Virtually every Tsimshian person over thirty today was required to attend residential school as a child if their family lived on reserve. The practice of educating children away from their families in an English only environment and the increasing dependence of Tsimshian people on wage labour combined to reduce opportunities for learning and speaking Sm'algyax.

During early contact with Europeans in the fur trade period, the Tsimshian were independent players in relationships with Europeans. Because they controlled the fur trade on the Northwest Coast, some Tsimshian Chiefs became incredibly wealthy. The system of ceremonial feasting and gift-giving (potlatch) that is the cornerstone of Tsimshian law, history and identity,[1] was elaborated during this time using wealth generated by the fur trade. Ceremonial feasts are

---

[1]   Individuals on the Northwest coast acquire names, ratified through feasting, that carry with them certain rights and responsibilities relating to particular tracts of land. For more information on Tsimshian practices see Miller (1997).

associated with a special register of Sm'algyax, often referred to as the elaborate style. This register has different vocabulary (including the use of many otherwise archaic terms), and makes many more complex grammatical distinctions than the everyday style of the language.

Smallpox epidemics and a decline in the quality and numbers of furs available for trade ushered in a new period in Tsimshian history in which community life was centred around missions. Much has been written about the missionaries and their reception by the Tsimshian (see for example Usher 1974 and Bolt 1994). From the outset the goal of the missions was the Christianisation and assimilation of the Tsimshian and their neighbours on the coast. Benefits of mission life included the acquisition of literacy, an alternative to life at the trading fort, and (during the smallpox epidemics) vaccinations. In order to become part of a mission community and receive any of these benefits, one had to convert. A crucial part of this process was the undertaking that the convert would no longer participate in the ceremonial life of the Tsimshian community.

Potlatches were outlawed by the Canadian government in 1885 (Cole & Chaikin 1990: 1). Although First Nations people all along the coast resisted this policy (several served gaol sentences because they openly refused to comply (Cole & Chaikin 1990: 107ff)), the policy (and assimilationist policies more generally) wiped out the practice in many communities. In 1996 I was privileged to attend the first naming feast held in Lax Kw'alaams in over fifty years. The opportunities for people to learn the elaborate style of Sm'algyax have been very limited during the twentieth century as a consequence of these policies.

During the mission period (late 19th century) the practice of separating children from their parents for the purposes of education began. Although initially this was limited to day schooling, a boarding school was established in the late 1850s (Mulder 1994: 12). By the early twentieth century this had evolved into a government policy of requiring children to attend residential schools away from their families. As Mulder (1994: 13) has observed, this practice ensured that fluency in Sm'algyax was limited since children were away from fluent speakers during a critical period in their language development (children typically went to school from the age of six). For the next few years they were away from their families for ten months of the year and had no exposure to fluent adult speakers during that time. Furthermore, the schools had an explicit policy of insisting on English, and children were severely punished for using their language.

Many children fared badly in this system and resolved to teach their own children English in order to give them some protection when they, in turn, went away to school. For example, one woman told me that she had gone to school for the first time with her sister before either of them could speak any English. When her sister got a toothache they found it very difficult to get help from school staff as they could not communicate with anyone in authority. Their own language was prohibited and they were not able to speak any other.

The result of all this is that there are many families in which only the great-grandparents (if they are still alive) are able to speak the language. The residential school system, which operated until the early 1970s broke the intergenerational transmission of the language as early as the 1930s in some families. Many older people within the Tsimshian community today feel extremely ambivalent about the language. It has been the cause of their greatest humiliation as children, even as it again becomes a powerful symbol for Tsimshian identity and authority. For elders in the community who were never able to learn the language, the ambivalence can run even deeper. At a time when younger people are turning to them for knowledge about the language, many are saddened and even ashamed that they have no knowledge to share. They grew up in a time when the language was being abandoned only to become elders in a time when people have the freedom and resources to choose to learn it again.

From the late nineteenth century the cannery industry replaced the fur trade as the main economic activity on the coast. The demand for labour was so great during the summer months that immigrant workers from as far away as Japan, as well as First Nations people were employed catching and canning salmon. Participation in the cannery industry required some ability in English. This reinforced the relative desirability of English over Tsimshian.

Like the fur trade, the cannery industry has resulted in a critical decline in a traditional resource of the Tsimshian. Over the past few years, salmon stocks have been so low that third and fourth generation Tsimshian fishers have been giving up their licences. For many Tsimshian people involved in the industry there are few alternatives other than the welfare system.

3.   THE TSIMSHIAN NATION TODAY: REASSERTING AUTHORITY

Economic factors such as the rise and fall of the salmon cannery industry, the decline of natural resources, and assimilationist policies of successive Canadian governments, both provincial and national, undermined Tsimshian economic independence and political strength. Today many members of the Tsimshian Nation are dependent on the Canadian government for their livelihood (in the form of welfare payments). Beginning in the 1970s there has been increasing interest from within the Tsimshian Nation in reasserting Tsimshian authority over matters such as education, natural resource management, and representations of Tsimshian culture in the wider world, particularly in academia. The Tsimshian community has become increasingly organised in addressing these issues through a number of processes and structures. These range from dialogue with the Canadian government about issues such as fishing and land rights to community control over First Nations designated funding in the school district.

Like many First Nations in British Columbia, the Tsimshian are negotiating a treaty with the provincial and national governments. This process is expected to take a number of years. Amongst other things, the Tsimshian hope to gain economic independence, title to their traditional lands and resources, responsibility for heath and education services through this process. The Tsimshian Tribal Council is the representative body of the Tsimshian Nation in treaty negotiations. It also functions as an umbrella organisation for the Nation in other ways. For example, it convenes an Annual Assembly at which a broad range of issues are discussed. This provides an opportunity for Tsimshian people to convey their views on treaty negotiations. A wide range of current and ongoing issues are also addressed.

The Ts'msyeen Sm'algyax Authority (TSA) is the name of the language authority overseeing publications in and research on Sm'algyax. The TSA has been convened on an ad hoc basis for many years. Since late 1996 it has met regularly to oversee the activities of the Sm'algyax Language Program (described below). The First Nations Education Council oversees the expenditure of Education Department funds that have been allocated to special programmes for First Nations children in the school district. The council is a decision making body. The First Nations Educational Services office (FNES) of School District 52 is then responsible for carrying out the aims of the council. Together with the TSA, the FNES has been instrumental in developing the Sm'algyax Language Program and producing a growing list of high quality publications in the language.

4.   PROGRAMMES FOR TEACHING SM'ALGYAX

Over the past few years there has been a groundswell of interest in maintaining Sm'algyax as a community language. Younger adults in the community are showing increasing awareness and concern about their own inability to speak the language and the advanced age of the most fluent speakers. This has resulted in the expansion of language programmes run through the school district and a variety of other activities, some of which are aimed at adults.

A number of universities based in British Columbia have offered instruction about Sm'algyax at different times (see Stebbins 1999: 26). These courses have typically focussed on examining traditional narratives rather than on language learning per se. Community classes in Sm'algyax have run intermittently in Tsimshian communities for many years. These classes play an important role in providing adult learners with a safe environment in which to learn about Sm'algyax. For many adults, who cannot make a commitment to the university courses just mentioned, the flexibility of these classes is an important benefit.

The Sm'algyax Language Program has been running in Tsimshian village schools since 1979. Up until 1997 the only second language available in the town of Prince Rupert was French. In 1997 the British Columbia Ministry of Education made changes its policy on language learning in grades five through eight. All children in these grades were required to have language instruction in some language. The First Nations Education Council has taken this opportunity to introduce Sm'algyax into the town schools. This represents a significant expansion of the programme: for example number of staff has grown from four to ten.

At the time of writing, students in the town schools attended two one hour long classes each week. Classes are not in fact an hour long as this time includes moving students from their regular classrooms as well as settling them down. Also, classes are regularly missed when special programmes for the whole school clash with the language programme timetable. Under these conditions full fluency is not a realistic goal for the language programme. The short term goal of the programme is to give students a framework for learning Sm'algyax. This includes learning basic vocabulary, useful sentences or sentence frames, developing pronunciation and comprehension skills.

Clearly the programmes represent a valuable assertion of Tsimshian identity and Sm'algyax language in an historically hostile environment.

4.1 Respect: Tsimshian culture in the classroom

The elders involved in the language programme are motivated by a number of other factors clearly related to issues around Tsimshian identity and power. This section discusses the issue of discipline in the Sm'algyax Language Program. In seeking to teach Sm'algyax to students, the teachers also feel that they need to teach aspects of Tsimshian culture. Also, the presence of Tsimshian elders in the school is an assertion of Tsimshian authority over the education of Tsimshian children. At a practical level this involves teachers relating to students in culturally appropriate ways.

The teachers expect to be treated with the respect due to them as elders within the Tsimshian community. Not surprisingly, given the great cultural differences between the schools and the elders, there have been ongoing discussions within the group about discipline issues in the classroom.

The language teachers were not trained as educators in the Western sense at the time of their appointments. In other words, their own days at school long past, the teachers were not acculturated to school practices. In their first months as teachers they found classroom management challenging. The language teachers are determined that they will interact with students in ways that feel right to them. Particularly at the beginning of their employment, they found the school environment unwelcoming and the disciplinary practices of other teaching staff affronting.

The students taught by the language teachers are virtually all from one of the First Nations in the region and are predominantly Tsimshian. By the time they begin classes in Sm'algyax the children are in grade five and have adapted to school culture in various ways. The teachers have a model of Tsimshian education that they apply in the classroom. The language teachers described their model as follows:

> Each individual has certain strengths and talents.
>
> These strengths and talents are valuable. They are an expression of each person's individuality. They are potential resources that the individual may use to serve the community.
>
> As someone grows up his or her strengths are recognised and fostered by elders.
>
> Elders approach this task from a position of respect for the potential of the individual.
>
> Learners approach this task from a position of respect for the knowledge and experience of the elder.

As the language programme has continued, students have begun to adjust to these new expectations about their behaviour. The central position of respect and individuality in this model is not reflected in the school system in general. Although it may be referred to as a fundamental value motivating rules and sanctions in the wider school system, the actual practice of classroom discipline can involve strategies that humiliate and depersonalise students.

As this discussion shows, Tsimshian language teachers are doing a number of things besides teaching about Sm'algyax. They are providing alternative models of behaviour and alternative visions of Tsimshian identity for many Tsimshian students.

4.2 More than the ear can hear

One other area of Tsimshian culture that is highly relevant to an examination of the prospects of Sm'algyax are Tsimshian expectations about displaying and sharing knowledge. Through my own observations and through discussions with Tsimshian people I have developed the following model of knowledge management in the Tsimshian community:

> All though their lives people acquire knowledge and skills. Elders are identified as people who have acquired considerable knowledge and experience. Many elders are identified as having expertise in particular areas.

> The status of being an elder is somewhat relative. Some reasonably young people have the status of elders because of their leadership and / or their knowledge. All but the oldest people have elders to whom they can turn for advice.

> Elders make choices about what information they pass on to others. Maturity and the ability to handle knowledge responsibly are fairly typical criteria that people apply in deciding whether or not to share their knowledge.

> People who are not elders should not act as sources of information for others. This is an example of handling information irresponsibly.

In the opening paragraphs I claimed that there are few speakers of Sm'algyax under fifty years of age. This is based on the way Tsimshian people identify themselves and others as speakers. I have observed that a great number of younger people (particularly those in their thirties) actually have quite a good passive understanding of the language and also have some ability to speak. For example they may know the names of a variety of everyday items and a good number of common expressions. They are able to make the opening comments of a public speech in the language by using written notes. These people could be identified as semispeakers.

The expectations about gaining and sharing knowledge in the Tsimshian community go a long way towards explaining the invisibility of semispeakers in Tsimshian estimations of Sm'algyax speakers numbers. There will come a time when these speakers will act as elders with knowledge about Sm'algyax. They will eventually teach the language to others. However, they are not elders yet and it would be counter-productive for them to assert much knowledge at this stage. If semispeakers asserted that they had any fluency at this stage they could be sanctioned for behaving inappropriately. The sanction is most likely to be a withdrawal of cooperation from the elders who are teaching them. I have on occasions made faux pas in this regard. At the very least, showing off one's partial knowledge is likely to bring the conversation to an abrupt close.

5.   LANGUAGE, IDENTITY, AND SOCIAL JUSTICE

Edwards notes that it is very easy when speaking of language and identity to adopt a value-laden stance. He suggests that, while there is a place for advocacy, it is best if the facts can first be set out clearly.

My view is simply that, even if one is wholeheartedly and unashamedly committed to a particular ideological position on, say, language and pluralism, the only way to avoid endless and vacuous debate is to confront the issues as they exist, not as one would wish them to exist (Edwards 1985: ix).

He frames his discussion of language shift in terms of *choice*, reminding the reader that terms such as language murder and language suicide muddy the true nature of events. There are rarely single causes for this complex phenomenon (Edwards 1985: 52).

What the preceding brief outline of Tsimshian history shows, I suggest, is that individuals within the Tsimshian community at some time made a *forced choice* to begin to use English themselves and to teach English to their children. Once the choice to use English as the maternal language was made, the break in intergenerational transmission had occurred. Some Tsimshian families have now been monolingual for three generations. Tsimshian people, in shifting to English, were not making the *free choice* of economic opportunists or social climbers. They were compelled by Canadian law, and Department of Indian Affairs policy, and by schools, and individual teachers to acquire and use English and to give up Sm'algyax and the cultural practices such as feasting that provided occasions for skilled and elaborate public speaking.

These events and experiences affected language attitudes as well as language choices. There is now a strong current of interest and commitment within the Tsimshian community for strengthening Sm'algyax and teaching it to children. One Tsimshian person put it like this:

> Sm'algyax is the 'beat of the drums in our hearts'. Let it be the medicine that heals and makes us whole again, and to further strengthen the heritage left to us by our ancestors.

This quote is a clear expression of the link between language and social justice in the minds of Tsimshian people. From the Tsimshian point of view, to take an active approach to language endangerment in this community is to make a contribution to the struggle for social justice. This understanding has a profound effect on the range of roles possible for a language worker in the area. Purely academic language research is viewed as an insult to the community because it is considered to perpetuate the appropriation of Tsimshian knowledge begun with the removal of ceremonial objects for museum collections last century. On the other hand research that is seen as relevant and useful to the community (such as the learners' dictionary project) is given enormous support.

Many of the people currently involved in language related activities are non-speakers or semispeakers learning about the language. These people do not seem to have the resources or time to achieve full fluency in Sm'algyax. For some this is a point of frustration but for many others it is not especially troublesome. People within the Tsimshian community who attend adult language classes have a range of motivations and goals. Edwards' (1985: 17) distinction between the communicative and symbolic functions of language may usefully be invoked here. A few want to be able to use the language to communicate, but many more want to have some knowledge about the language and how it is used in the community. For the majority, the ability to use Sm'algyax in its symbolic function is both a realistic goal and a satisfactory outcome.

The focus on Sm'algyax as a source of strength for the community is not simply an issue of elaborating group boundaries for the purposes of strengthening ethnicity. Indigenous communities that have been the target of assimilationist policies in British Columbia are not in any danger of losing their status as distinct groups. The group boundaries that distinguish First Nations people from Euro-Canadians and others on the Northwest coast of British Columbia on economic grounds alone are far too well entrenched for that.

Within the Euro-Canadian community identifiable characteristics of First Nations people include: material poverty, poor nutrition, low educational achievement, alcoholism, and health problems. Even within the Tsimshian community there is a dearth of positive ways of expressing and elaborating on Tsimshian identity. For example, in making statements about themselves or their community to me, Tsimshian people regularly said things like: 'We like to argue,' 'There's a lot of jealousy in our community,' 'You won't want to come back to us dumb Indians.' I am unable to recall an example in which a Tsimshian person made a positive statement about their community. Like the disputes over language variation outlined in the following section, and the ambivalence of older speakers mentioned above, these statements seem to express a negative evaluation of First Nations identities that was explicit in assimilationist policies but has become increasingly veiled in modern Canadian society.

What many people do have are enormous hopes for their community and commitment to affecting change. People see the revival of Sm'algyax as a powerful way of reasserting their ancestral strength as a nation. The focus on language as a means of identification for many Tsimshian people no doubt results in part from the fact that language was for many years a locus of overt oppression. As the community seeks to strengthen and heal itself, language, with its symbolic function, seems like a fairly obvious place to start. Tsimshian people are defined by rather negative criteria according to others, and these criteria do them no service. They are now seeking to define themselves in their own way.

6. DIALECTAL DIFFERENCES AND TOWN SM'ALGYAX

The use of Sm'algyax in its symbolic function, as an identifier for members of the Tsimshian Nation is not without its tensions. The language is comprised of a number of dialects traditionally associated with different villages. Sm'algyax is also used by speakers as a way of asserting their connections to villages as distinct from the nation.

The dialects of Sm'algyax can be difficult to pin down. Variant word forms may be shared between communities according to fairly complex patterns. One difficulty with this type of distribution is that it is easy to make understatements about the distribution of forms. Most speakers have a variety of Sm'algyax influenced by the home villages of each of their parents, as well as the village in which they spent most of their lives (which may be the village of their spouse).

Speakers of Sm'algyax understand that language variation is understood to be a significant characteristic of the language, and it is expected (in theory) that the language of others should be treated with respect. In spite of this, there can be considerable antagonism between speakers of different dialects. This has typically revolved around debates about who speaks the language properly.

Linguistic variation arising from geographic associations is frequently confused with (and indeed is sometimes very difficult to distinguish from) variation arising through individual attrition or incomplete learning. The situation is signalled by the practice of using the term 'dialect' as face-saving device which validates language variety of all kinds. It is especially effective as a defensive device (my Sm'algyax is different because I speak a different dialect), and in this guise it can obscure the status of words and grammatical structures in the wider Sm'algyax language community.

Teachers in the Sm'algyax Language Program have been attempting to teach a unified form of Sm'algyax to students so that they can move between schools and classes without too much disruption to their learning. The resultant Sm'algyax is effectively a standardised version because the dialect differences between speakers are levelled out, at least to some extent. For some outside the language programme this is viewed as a misrepresentation of the language. The Sm'algyax which is taught in the programme is sometimes labelled 'town Sm'algyax' by other fluent elders who hear what the children have been taught. The language teachers are troubled by this label because it implies that they lack knowledge about any particular dialect of 'real Sm'algyax'.

The tension between unity and division reflecting approximately the distinction between village and nation is not limited to language issues. Language teachers in their decision to present Sm'algyax in a unified way to students are seeking to be inclusive. They associate Sm'algyax with the Tsimshian Nation. Others in the community are critical of the hybrid form of Sm'algyax that they consider results from this strategy. They consider that the form taught in schools is inauthentic because it does not accurately represent any one of the Sm'algyax dialects associated with particular villages. Nevertheless, dialect differences are treated as a legitimate and significant point of inclusion/exclusion within the community.

This tension between village and Nation is reflected in many other areas of community life. Many disagreements that occur in the community, while they may begin as issues for particular individuals, quickly escalate into debates about the autonomy and power of villages or communities within the Nation. Like the notion of dialects belonging to particular villages, the notion of nationhood is both a reflection of reality and a particular interpretation of the facts.

7.   WORKING COOPERATIVELY ON THE DICTIONARY

When I first appeared on the scene in Prince Rupert in the fall of 1996 I carried with me a draft of a dictionary I had prepared from archival sources. It was titled *Coast Tsimshian Learners' Dictionary.* The title alone marked me as an outsider and an academic. No one involved in the community calls the language Coast Tsimshian. And so my education in the sociolinguistics and politics surrounding Sm'algyax began.

In order to take an active approach to supporting efforts in the Tsimshian community to revitalise Sm'algyax, I have worked in cooperation with, and under the direction of the Ts'msyeen Sm'algyax Authority. Building a working relationship with the Authority has been a long term process and, I believe, a very rewarding one. The Tsimshian Nation assumed the role of peak stakeholder in my research (the development of the Sm'algyax Learners' Dictionary). This partnership has seen the development of linguistic materials that are accurate, comprehensive and relevant to language revitalisation efforts being carried out in the community today.

Over two field trips and the course of a year members of the Tsimshian community and I got to know each other. For me this was a process of gradually learning how to function in the community as well as establishing personal and working relationships with a variety of people. I have been told that for the Tsimshian people concerned the process involved getting to know me and developing some confidence in my ability to work respectfully with members of the community. Once these foundations were laid, we began to develop a shared vision of the learners' dictionary and a work plan for completing it. During this time, funding from within the Nation and the School District was sought and the project was discussed in a number of Tsimshian forums such as the Tsimshian Tribal Council.

Once the project had been approved by the nation at the annual Tsimshian Tribal Council Assembly in November 1997 and funding arrangements had been settled, work on the project began. I was hired as the project manager for the dictionary project with the title Technical Adviser. This title reflects the fact that I was the only person involved with a working knowledge of the dictionary database. A Dictionary Committee was appointed. Members of the committee were elders who were fluent in the language and understood the orthography.

At committee meetings the words included in the draft version of the dictionary were evaluated. The meetings made use of words listed by semantic domain. Missing words were included and corrections were made to the spellings and translations. My role in these meetings was to record the decisions of the committee and generally keep things moving along. I also spent a number of hours each week working with individual speakers and was involved in a range of more political activities. These included visiting villages in order to discuss the dictionary with elders to reporting on the project to groups such as the Ts'msyeen Sm'algyax Authority. These politically focussed activities were crucial to the acceptance of the dictionary by the wider Tsimshian community. As I noted above, village rivalry is sometimes expressed through disputes about dialect differences. It was important that the dictionary was seen to be broadly representative and that I was seen to consult widely.

In May 1998 a new full draft of the *Sm'algyax Learners' Dictionary* was completed. This draft included example sentences for about two thirds of the entries. The draft was received by the community with much interest. This ended my direct involvement in the project. At the time of writing the Dictionary Committee continues to meet, making final corrections to the draft and completing the task of writing example sentences for each entry.

One of the things that happened during the development of the dictionary project was that Tsimshian authority was established as primary. The authority of the university in relation to my research was not considered by the community at all. This impinged on my plan of study but the benefits far outweighed the costs.

From the community's point of view the project became a case in which Tsimshian ownership of Sm'algyax was respected (through the role of the Ts'msyeen Sm'algyax Authority in the project). The community had final say in the way their language was represented. They are currently making final revisions to the draft. Expending funds and effort on the dictionary was a way of reasserting Tsimshian authority over the language, as well as affirming its cultural value and promoting interest in and discussion about the language in the wider community.

From my point of view the support of the community transformed the project. It began as a somewhat dry task undertaken in isolation and relying on archival documents. After the Dictionary Committee was established, it became a dynamic activity involving a large number of colleagues. The data that was collected is much more representative of the community as a whole than anything I could have gathered using my own resources. And best of all the project has a far wider audience now than a solitary effort completed away from the community could have had.

8.   CONCLUSION

Language is intimately tied up with social, political and economic factors. It can both cause and be affected by wider events. For example, the banning of feasting (potlatching) lead to a loss of ceremonial language. Individuals who have not acquired Sm'algyax have additional barriers to mount in seeking to learn about their culture. Language is clearly tied to personal and group identity. The symbolic function of language makes it a point of potential oppression and / or pride. The highly politicised nature of language for the Tsimshian community is a reflection of the language oppression they have experienced in the past. In this context linguistic work is also politicised by the community.

Sm'algyax may never again be the language of daily communication for the majority of Tsimshian people. This seems likely since the vast majority of Tsimshian people are currently monolingual in English, and there are limited resources for language planning. However, there are other ways in which the language is beginning to regain its place at the centre of Tsimshian community life. More and more people are making an effort to learn about the language. Also, the language is once again being used at public meetings. Even people who are not fluent in the language now tend to chose to make their opening remarks in Sm'algyax. In this context, the dictionary that the community and I have developed will stand as a record of the cultural wealth and linguistic sophistication embodied by the language. In this way it is a social as well as an educational resource, allowing people without fluency to enjoy the language of their community.

REFERENCES

Bolt, Clarence 1992. *Thomas Crosby and the Tsimshian: small shoes for feet to large.* Vancouver: University of British Columbia Press.

Cole, D. & I. Chaikin 1990. *An Iron Hand upon the People: the law against the potlatch on the Northwest Coast.* Vancouver: Douglas & McIntyre.

Edwards, John 1985. *Language, Society and Identity.* Oxford: Blackwell.

Miller, Jay 1997. *Tsimshian culture: a light through the ages.* Lincon: University of Nebraska Press.

Mulder, Jean 1994. *Ergativity in Coast Tsimshian (Sm'algyax).* Berkeley: University of California Press.

Mulder, Jean, Doreen Robinson & Tonya Stebbins Forthcoming. *A Collection of Teaching Adawx.* Prince Rupert, B.C.: First Nations Educational Services.

Stebbins, Tonya, Compiler 1998. *Draft of the new Sm'algyax Learner's Dictionary* (5 vols). Prince Rupert: Tsimshian Tribal Council and School District 52.

Stebbins, Tonya & Jean Mulder Forthcoming. *Communicative Grammar of Sm'algyax.* Prince Rupert, B.C.: First Nations Educational Services.

Usher, Jean 1974. *William Duncan of Metlakatla: a Victorian Missionary in British Columbia.* Ottawa: National Museum of Man, Publications in History No. 5.

Chapter 7

**Language Policy and Language Maintenance:
Yi in China**[1]
David Bradley & Maya Bradley
La Trobe University

1. LANGUAGE POLICY IN CHINA

China is a multiethnic country with 55 national minorities and the Han
Chinese majority; the minorities are about nine per cent of the total
population. China's nationalities policy follows that of the former Soviet
Union: small tribes and groups are amalgamated into larger nationalities.
This process took place during the early 1950s, with one addition in the
late 1970s. There is an ongoing process of amalgamating small
'unclassified' minority groups into existing nationalities.

For each nationality, a 'standard' language variety is chosen.[2] The
choice is determined by numerical, geographical, intelligibility and
economic factors, and was made for most groups in the late 1950s.
Where the same nationality is numerous in more than one administrative
unit, a different 'standard' variety is sometimes chosen in different
areas.

Many resulting nationalities are composite groups including quite
diverse languages; if the same level of classification had been applied in
a unified Europe, there would be one Romance nationality, one Slavic
nationality, one Germanic nationality, and Basque, Celtic,

[1] Many thanks for their participation and help in our survey to villagers
and local government officials in the Kunming region, and to Yi and other
colleagues and students, and especially Li Yongxiang of the Yunnan Academy
of Social Sciences. We are glad to acknowledge the financial support of the
CIPSH Endangered Languages Program of UNESCO, of the Australian
Research Council (A59803475 Language Maintenance for Endangered
Languages), and of the Yunnan Academy of Social Sciences.
[2] The sole exception is the Hui nationality who are almost all Chinese-
speaking Muslims with no distinct language

Finnish/Estonian, Greek, Hungarian, Romani and possibly Baltic minorities; but maybe Baltic languages would be regarded as part of Slavic. To continue the analogy, imagine that for each of these composite nationalities, one variety was chosen as the standard; such as the Italian 'dialect' for the Romance nationality, the Russian 'dialect' for the Slavic nationality, the English 'dialect' for the Germanic nationality, and so on. The degree of lumping in nationality formation in China is this great, and much more than that applied in the former Soviet Union or in adjacent countries with similar systems, such as Vietnam and Laos; so curiously there are groups which are amalgamated into one nationality in China, but subgroups within this nationality are classified as two or more distinct nationalities in Russia, Vietnam or Laos.[3] Another neighboring country, India, has an extreme splitting policy following the model of its caste system; so for example over fifty distinct scheduled[4] tribes of northeastern India are all classified within the single Luoba nationality in the adjacent Tibetan Autonomous Region.

The 1982 Constitution of China (Article 4) states that 'The people of all nationalities have the freedom to use and develop their own spoken and written languages ...'. It provides for autonomous administrative units for national minorities at various levels (Article 30) within which education and culture are a local responsibility (Article 119) and the local languages can be used in administration (Article 121) and the courts (Article 134). However there is a national priority for the promotion of *putonghua* or standard Chinese throughout the country (Article 19), and the local autonomous governments are also able to choose not to use minority languages; in fact at various times of political crisis, such as the anti-rightist movement of the late 1950s[5] and the Cultural Revolution of the mid-1960s to early 1970s, official promotion

---

[3]   For example, the quite diverse Southern Yi subgroup within Yi includes, among various others, the Nisu and Pula; but in Vietnam these are recognised as separate nationalities, the Lôlô and Phula.

[4]   That is, listed in the official inventory of tribal groups.

[5]   One aspect of this movement was the military overthrow of local 'feudal' leaders such as the Dalai Lama in Tibet and the Yi nobles in southern Sichuan, as well as all those who had been **tusi** or traditional local minority rulers on behalf of the Chinese throughout the country.

and use of minority languages stopped in most areas. In the late 1950s there was a lot of linguistic work done, but little was implemented before the political ructions from 1958 and especially from 1964 to 1973. Minority language work and language education in minority languages restarted in the mid-1970s and flourished for about twenty years; but with 'the Chinese way to socialism' of the 1990s (free enterprise in competition with state enterprises), governments at all levels have been decreasing their support for minority language activities including education, publishing and research.

In principle, matters relating to minorities are controlled by the Nationality Affairs Commission, a ministry which exists at the national level, the province or autonomous region level, and at the prefecture and county level where there are substantial numbers of non-Han Chinese; it has substantial input on minority language issues, often through provincial, prefectural or county language offices or language sections of cultural offices; a provincial level nationalities publisher; provincial or more local radio and print media; and so on. However, education is controlled by the Education Commission, another ministry; curiously, even the main university-level education system intended for national minorities, the institutes of national minorities, is under the Education Commission. In practice, decisions about minority language education in primary school are made by local prefecture and county governments, under sometimes conflicting directives from Nationality Affairs and Education Commissions at the next level up. Teachers for minority language education as well as other kinds of language workers are trained in provincial, prefectural or county teacher institutes or in minority language departments of the institutes of nationalities.

2.   ADMINISTRATIVE FRAMEWORK IN YUNNAN

Yunnan Province has a high proportion of minorities among its population, but because there is no one preponderant national minority, it has not been designated as an Autonomous Region like Tibet, Xinjiang, Guangxi, Ningxia and Inner Mongolia. It contains 17 prefecture-level administrative units, eight of which are autonomous prefectures designated for one or two specific national minorities. Of its

127 county-level units, 59 are included within an autonomous prefecture and a further 27, including 9 within autonomous prefectures, are designated as autonomous counties for one or more different national minorities. Thus more than 60 per cent of the county-level units are under nominal minority control. The head of the government and the party secretary[6] as well as many lower-level officials in an autonomous administrative unit are usually members of one of the local minorities.

However, the elite of administration and the party are the most Sinicised of their nationality; many are now second generation cadres who have been educated, lived and worked mainly in Kunming, the capital of Yunnan, or other Chinese-speaking towns. Quite a few do not speak the language of their nationality; a surprising number are from mixed marriages - the ultimate form of nationalities unity[7] - and have a Han Chinese parent or a parent from some nationality other than the one which they have chosen from their other parent.[8] This elite makes the decisions about language education; in many cases they do not see the economic benefit of language maintenance, and so minority language education was not restarted in some areas in the 1970s, or has since been dropped.[9]

3.   THE YI NATIONALITY

The four million Yi[10] are the most numerous non-Han Chinese nationality in Yunnan; there are 2.6 million Yi in other provinces, mainly in Sichuan and Guizhou with a few in Guangxi. The name of this

---

[6]   Head of the local Communist Party.

[7]   Along with the indivisible nature of China, nationalities unity is a touchstone of China's national policy.

[8]   Children are assigned to one nationality by their parents, but may choose either of their parents' nationalities when they reach 18, or later by special request. Massive increases in the population of many national minorities between the 1982 and 1990 censuses are partly due to people with one non-Han Chinese parent or grandparent reclaiming their minority identity.

[9]   As an interesting contrast, the Yunnan Institute of Nationalities now has some special language courses for children of cadres who live in town and do not speak their nationality's language to learn it from scratch.

[10]   All population figures are from the 1990 census.

group is a post-1950 innovation, replacing the former term 'Lolo' which some regard as pejorative but others still use. In Yunnan the Yi are the sole nationality in the name of Chuxiong Yi Autonomous Prefecture, the second of two in Honghe Hani and Yi Autonomous Prefecture, and the sole or joint named nationality in 15 further counties in addition to the 20 county-level units within Chuxiong and Honghe not assigned to other nationalities. Apart from these 35 county-level units where they are particularly concentrated, there are substantial numbers of Yi in most other counties in the province, as well as in one autonomous prefecture in Sichuan and further autonomous counties in Sichuan, Guizhou and Guangxi to the north and east of Yunnan.

Linguists in China divide the Yi 'language' into six 'dialects', Northern, Eastern, Southeastern, Southern, Central and Western, each of which has a great deal of internal diversity. All six are spoken in Yunnan; in Sichuan most Yi speak Northern, with a few Central speakers; in Guizhou and Guangxi varieties of the Eastern dialect are spoken.

The issue of 'standard' choice is therefore less problematic outside Yunnan. In Sichuan the central and numerically largest variety of Northern Yi, Shengza (as also spoken in northwestern Yunnan) has been selected, standardised and widely disseminated. Speakers of other varieties of Northern Yi need to learn this 'standard' variety in order to become literate, as the orthography is a syllabary based on the sounds of this variety. In Guizhou the traditional Yi characters have been adapted for wider use, allowing people to use their local pronunciation. In Guangxi there are not enough Yi for the local government to use it in education.

The area of northwestern Yunnan where Northern Yi is spoken is mainly Ninglang County but also in other parts of Lijiang Prefecture.[11] One class of cadres for this area were trained at the Yunnan Institute of Nationalities in Kunming by Yi teachers sent from the Southwest Institute of Nationalities in Sichuan from 1983 to 1985, but since then

---

[11]   A Northern Yi village near Lijiang, including its school in session with its Yi teacher teaching Chinese, was shown in the British television documentary 'South of the Clouds'.

students have been sent to Chengdu to study Northern Yi at the Southwest Institute of Nationalities. This variety of Yi has over 2 million speakers, mainly in Sichuan. It has seen a real explosion of linguistic development since a new syllabic script was officially recognised in 1980. This is now taught to students in primary, secondary and three tertiary institutions (in Zhaojue, Xichang and Chengdu), has textbooks available up to university level (for science, mathematics, and other subject areas as well as language and history), is used for an impressive range of grammars, dictionaries, traditional and modern literature, adult literacy, medical and agricultural handbooks, political and other materials, and has a daily newspaper published at Xichang, the capital of the Liangshan Yi Autonomous Prefecture in Sichuan. It is widely used in local government, and can be seen alongside Chinese on government signs and notices. In more remote areas there are even some monolingual signs. Original linguistic research of all kinds by Yi linguists is published in this variety of Yi. 100 per cent literacy is claimed for some counties, mainly those where the 'standard' is the local type of Yi; fairly high literacy has been achieved even elsewhere, though mainly in Sichuan. Many local Chinese cadres and some foreigners have learned it.

In Guizhou trial versions of language teaching materials for children and for adult literacy started to appear in 1982. The first class of Yi language students entered the Guizhou Institute of Nationalities in 1983 and graduated in 1987; other main centres of linguistic research are the Guizhou Nationalities Press, the Guizhou Nationalities Research Institute and other units in Bijie Prefecture and in Weining Yi, Hui and Miao Autonomous County. Because local pronunciation of various places is indicated alongside Yi characters in teaching materials, the script is relatively easy to learn. However, Yi is endangered in Guizhou, despite a population of over 700,000, because the Yi live intermingled with other nationalities and many younger people do not speak it. Up to the early 1980s literacy was restricted to shamans and a few scholars; those who are less positive about traditional Yi religion may be less than enthusiastic about learning the script.

In Yunnan there is also a tradition of literacy among shamans of some subgroups of the Yi; however the Central and Western Yi have no internal tradition of writing. In fact, their speech is very different from that of the other four varieties of Yi, and much more similar to the speech of the Lisu nationality. Of the four Yi literary traditions in Yunnan, one is catered for by the Sichuan Northern Yi syllabary; but the other three are each quite distinct and even have substantial internal differences; each lineage of shamans had their own individual versions of many characters. Because of book-burning during the Cultural Revolution and a transmission breakdown starting more than a century ago but greatly increased since the 1950s when very few young people chose to learn from their shaman father or uncle, there are extremely few young shamans. Nearly all of those under 50 have learned at least partly through the education system, mainly at the Central Institute (now University) of Nationalities in Beijing, or more recently at the Southwest, Yunnan or Guizhou Institutes of Nationalities. To compound the problem, most shamans regard their books as private or even secret; and these are traditionally cremated with their corpse.

From 1982 to 1985 a committee of twelve Yi representing each of the four literary traditions worked together at the Yunnan Nationalities Language Commission, a part of the Yunnan Nationality Affairs Commission, to devise a unified script for the Yi in Yunnan. Like the similar procedure adopted for the new unified Romansch language in Switzerland, the result is an item-by-item compromise. By 1985 over 1,600 characters had been agreed. A smaller committee of six worked out a further 600 by 1987, and a set of phonetic characters combining an initial consonant and a vowel to represent Chinese loanwords was prepared by 1989.[12]

This *Yunnan guifan Yiwen* (restored Yunnan Yi orthography) was approved by the government in February 1987, and materials started to appear using hand-written characters; in 1997 a computer font was created. The idea is that a character represents the word with the same meaning but different pronunciation in every variety of Yi in Yunnan,

---

[12]   A detailed discussion of this process is beyond the scope of this paper; as usual in modern China, it involved provisional materials for each stage being prepared and circulated, then discussed and agreed at a series of conferences with fairly wide invited participation.

including Central and Western varieties without a tradition of writing and whose languages are more similar to Lisu than to the rest of Yi. From 1987 it was made the standard form of Yi writing to appear on government signs, letterheads, banners and so on throughout the province. However, some areas such as Shilin County,[13] where the Sani subvariety of Southeastern Yi is the main kind of Yi, continue to use their own traditional characters for this purpose.

It must be said that this script is quite unpopular with literate Yi intellectuals, including most of those who do language work. It is no one's own, there is no history or prestige associated with it, and even the committee who devised it and the colleague at the Yunnan Institute of Nationalities who is the main person teaching it had trouble reading it at first. Nevertheless, in 1996 the Yunnan Nationality Affairs Commission decreed that it should be taught to Yi children in schools throughout the province; they also provided financial incentives to areas which did so, and some did. This decree has since been withdrawn, but not before a number of schools started to teach the script to children, and some continue to do so.

The first book to appear in this script was a 1987 mimeographed textbook for adult education; this was revised and published in May 1990 (4,000 copies) and reprinted in December (6,000 copies). This textbook has been used at the Yunnan Institute of Nationalities in the first year of every Yi class since 1988. It has character-by-character translations into Chinese below each Yi character, and contains a number of short stories in Yi. It also has an explanation of the phonetic characters used to represent Chinese loanwords.

In August 1991 a primary school picture book to teach the script was published (6,000 copies), and in May 1997 a revised version (5,000 copies) in the computer font appeared. This has pictures of the items and activities above the Yunnan Yi and Chinese characters, but no indication of phonetic values. We have seen this primer in use in various schools and in the first year Yi class at the Yunnan Institute of Nationalities.

---

[13]   Formerly Lunan, renamed Shilin ('stone forest') County in late 1998, after the main tourist attraction in the county.

A further series of three primary school language textbooks was published recently: book 1 (August 1993, 1,500 copies, reprinted for the first time in July 1994), book 2 (February 1994, 2,000 copies) and book 3 (October 1994, 2,000 copies). These are now used in grades 1 to 3 of a few schools in the Southern Yi and Eastern Yi areas of central Yunnan, including some schools in Luquan and Eshan counties.

Other publications in this script have started to appear, including some health education and other practical literature. These are much less numerous than those in Sichuan and Guizhou, and appear in pitifully small press runs compared to the overall Yi population of Yunnan.

4. SURVEYING YI LANGUAGES IN YUNNAN

From 1996 to 1998, the authors carried out a survey of Yi languages spoken in two non-urban wards and three counties in Kunming City. These were Xishan Ward to the west of the urban area, Guandu Ward to the east, Fumin County to the northwest, Anning County to the southwest, and Jinning County to the south. In these five county-level units we found 211 Yi villages representing four of the six varieties: mainly Eastern, but also 36 Southern, nine Central and six Northern. Just one county further east the concentration of Southeastern speakers starts.

Kunming is the historical centre of the Yi; the Dian and Cuan kingdoms which ruled the area up to the 9th century AD had Yi rulers, and all four literary traditions of Yi have historical records which trace their migrations back to the Kunming area. Thus Kunming is a particularly important area to survey, even though the vast majority of the population is now Han Chinese. This is mainly the result of migration since the Yuan (Mongol) Dynasty took direct control of the area in the mid-13th century, but also doubtless due to assimilation of many descendants of local Yi people into the Han population.

Given such long-standing Chinese rule, it may seem surprising that eight distinct languages, five of them within Eastern Yi, one within Southern Yi, one within Central Yi and one within Northern Yi, are still spoken within less than a hundred kilometres of the provincial capital. Five of these languages are undescribed, of which three are not spoken elsewhere and are endangered to moribund. In this area all eight are disappearing, some more rapidly than others. The trigger for the current decline seems to have been the post-1950 increase in direct contact through administration and education by the new government of China. Indeed there are virtually no monolinguals in the area surveyed; even the oldest people in the most remote villages surveyed could speak and read Chinese.

Table 1:   Yi groups in five counties around Kunming

Subgroup	Language
Eastern	Nasu
	Sanie
	Samataw
	Samei
	Gepo
Southern	Nasu
Central	Miqie
Northern	Nisu

4.1   Eastern Yi

The Nasu language, known in Chinese as Hei Yi ('Black Yi') and as Nosu in Christian materials, is spoken by a large group mainly found in Luquan and Wuding counties to the north, but also in 41 villages in the northern and western parts of the area surveyed, and spreading as far south as Jinning County where there is one isolated village, Qinglong. It is the medium of a traditional writing system, but this died out completely from the area surveyed in the early 20th century.[14] The language is moribund in about half of these villages and endangered to varying degrees in the others, but is much less endangered elsewhere.

---

[14]   One enterprising shaman from northwestern Xishan went to Luquan County in the north of Yunnan to get, learn and bring back books, but no local tradition has survived.

It is fairly well described, especially the variety spoken in Luquan and Wuding counties for which there are dictionaries and many published translations of various inscriptions and traditional books. There is a published grammar of the Nasu speech of Hetaoqing village in Xishan Ward of the area surveyed, Gao (1958).

The Gepo language, also known as Köpu in Christian materials, is widely spoken in Xundian County, Dongchuan City and other areas to the northeast and east of Kunming; in the area surveyed there are six Gepo villages in the extreme northeast of Fumin County. This language is also not endangered everywhere, but in many villages it is moribund. It is virtually completely undescribed, apart from one or two vocabularies in internal Chinese sources.

Sanie, a language whose existence was not previously reported, is the main indigenous language in 70 villages, most in Xishan Ward but also 11 in southwestern Fumin County and 4 in northern Anning County. Its eastern Sa'nguie subvariety is moribund to severely endangered in ten villages around the western suburbs of Kunming City; in the closest villages the youngest fluent speakers are in their sixties, with few semispeakers as there was an abrupt transmission failure from the 1950s when schools were set up. Western Sanie is endangered to severely endangered everywhere it is spoken; few children are now acquiring it. There are four other villages where both Sanie and Nasu live together; in these villages the dominant language is Nasu. Sanie there and in nearby villages also use some Nasu loanwords in their Sanie, probably reflecting more extensive knowledge of Nasu at an earlier stage. Sanie are not aware of any previous tradition of literacy, and in Chinese they call themselves Bai Yi ('White Yi') which is a general cover term for many of the more Sinicised groups of Yi. Some Sanie believe that they were the traditional charcoal sellers of Kunming,[15] and most have traditions that trace them back to places which are now in the inner western suburbs of the city, considerably closer than they now are.

---

[15]   This may be based on a false etymology: in western Sanie the group's autonym and 'charcoal' are homophonous, but not in eastern Sa'nguie.

Samei (the Chinese name for this group) or Sani (the indigenous name) are found in 42 villages in Guandu Ward to the southeast of Kunming; unlike Sanie, which is only spoken within the area surveyed, there are also a few Samei villages in Yiliang County further east. This language is extinct in some villages, moribund in others, severely endangered or endangered in some, but still transmitted to children, though in fewer domains, in some remote villages and in a cluster of less remote villages around Ala, about 20 kilometres southeast of the centre of Kunming. Samei had an indigenous literary tradition similar to that of the Nasu, and some books still exist; but no one can read them as the last fully literate shaman died in the early 1990s. A few examples can be seen in Xie (1987) which is an ethnographic account of a village near Ala. The language is undescribed apart from a couple of short internally-published articles and a wordlist in a rather poor transcription.

One reason that the Sanie and Samei languages have not been described is that their autonyms are so similar to the Chinese name of the main Yi group in Shilin County, the Sani. However, that Sani is a Southeastern Yi language with a separate and rather different literary tradition. Apart from Na Jiankun, a semispeaker who spent her entire career teaching Chinese in Guizhou, no Sanie has ever had linguistic training.[16] The only linguistically-trained Samei person, Bao Wenfeng, is a semispeaker who studied Lisu at the Yunnan Institute of Nationalities, married a Lisu fellow student and works in a local museum.

Samataw, sometimes referred to in local Chinese administrative materials as Samaduo, is the language of one large village, Zijun or Da'er, about ten kilometres south of the centre of Kunming; it is also sometimes called Zijun speech. The language is undescribed and moribund. Fluent speakers are all over 60, with the youngest semispeakers in their forties. The local government has designated a local teacher who is a semispeaker to teach the language to children in the school, and when we visited he was using the 1991 picture primer to teach this class; but the children (and their parents) do not speak the language at all, despite these efforts. The village appears to have maintained its identity, though not its language, by growing flowers for

---

16   Unfortunately Prof Na recently passed away.

the Kunming market. They have no tradition of writing, and no history of migration from elsewhere.

Linguistically these five languages are quite close; a Nasu linguist colleague claims to understand a substantial part of the other four. However Sanie who also speak Nasu in the four mixed villages and elsewhere regard themselves as bilingual. Village people do not understand the language of other Eastern Yi groups; even within Sanie, differences are so substantial that intelligibility is far from complete. Separate Christian Scriptures were prepared for Nasu and Gepo, meaning that the missionaries and their local co-workers felt that these two, which are more similar to each other than to the other three, are nevertheless distinct languages. Despite the similarity of some names, all are very different from the Sani of Shilin County.

4.2   Southern Yi

The Southern Yi are very numerous and widespread in Yuxi Prefecture, Honghe Autonomous Prefecture, southeastern Chuxiong Autonomous Prefecture, and eastern Simao Prefecture to the south of Kunming. The northernmost of these Southern Yi are in 33 villages in southwestern Jinning County, south of Kunming. There they call themselves Nasu, which like the Hei Yi autonym Nasu means 'black people', the former Yi nobility. Further south most Southern Yi call themselves Nisu or Niesu, with a different pronunciation of 'black'. According to our colleague Li Yongxiang who is a speaker of a variety of Niesu, all the Nasu in Jinning speak something very close to his own speech, though probably a non-linguist from this area would have difficulty in understanding Nisu or Niesu from further south as there are substantial vocabulary and sound change differences. There are also three villages somewhat closer to the Jinning county town who do not speak any Yi or know what kind of Yi they are; these were most likely also Southern Yi. There is an indigenous tradition of writing among the Southern Yi, but it has not survived in this area. While the phonology and lexicon of one variety of Niesu from further south, that of Mr Li, is fairly well known, and some texts have been published, no widespread dialect survey or grammatical analysis has been done, and so much more work is needed here too.

4.3   Central Yi

Miqie is a Central Yi language very similar to Lipo and Lolopo, which are also classified as Yi; and almost as similar to Lisu, which is classified as a separate nationality. The Miqie are also known as Micha, Mincha and other alternative versions of their autonym, according to local dialect differences. They are sometimes known as Mielang in Chinese, and are the 'Basket Tribe' known to Christian missionaries working in this area in the first half of the twentieth century. A Nasu colleague reports that some Miqie use Nasu writing to represent their language phonetically, but we have not encountered Miqie who are literate in this way in the area surveyed.

A Lipo speaker from two counties westwards who visited a Miqie village with us in late 1998 said he found about 30 per cent intelligibility, but appeared to be able to communicate moderately well; while a Lisu speaker from western Yunnan who also went with us found it impossible despite very high cognacy of vocabulary. The Miqie are an extremely scattered group who can also be found across Chuxiong Autonomous Prefecture, Dali, Lincang and northern Simao prefectures in western central Yunnan. A few Miqie married into a Lahu community from Simao Prefecture which later moved into Burma after 1950 and to northern Thailand in 1971.

In the Kunming region, there are nine villages of Miqie: one in southeastern Anning and three nearby in southwestern Jinning where the language is moribund or dead, and five in northwestern Fumin where the language is surviving moderately well in reduced domains. The latter are adjacent to other Miqie-speaking villages in southern Luquan and southeastern Wuding counties. These Miqie believe that they migrated from Dali Prefecture, which makes linguistic and historical sense. The language is undescribed.

4.4   Northern Yi

The Nisu in five villages of northwestern Fumin County and one village in northwestern Anning County are known in Chinese as Huang Yi ('Yellow Yi'), and have a tradition that they came from Sichuan. Linguistically they are the southernmost extension of the Northern Yi, who are mainly in Sichuan and northwestern Yunnan. These Nisu speak a southern variety of Northern Yi similar to Adur as spoken in Puge, Huidong and Huili counties in Sichuan, and in the northernmost parts of Yuanmou, Wuding and Luquan counties just south of the Sichuan border.[17] Here, they have no recollection of writing, and their language is endangered to moribund though very much alive further north. Though their villlages are quite remote, here their language is much less healthy than that of nearby Nasu and Sanie villages.

The data from our survey includes a comparative vocabulary using the picture primer and supplementary materials from over 30 locations including a wide range of distinct subtypes of Sanie, Samei, Eastern Nasu and Southern Nasu as well as two Miqie, two Nisu, one Gepo and the only Samataw villages. We also elicited local history, toponyms, and surnames where possible. We have already reported to the provincial government and sent a briefer report with a letter of thanks and copies of pictures taken there to the officials of villages surveyed and to speakers interviewed. A non-technical summary of the results has also been published in a recent issue of *Shan Cha*, the popular magazine of the Institute of Nationality Literature, Yunnan Academy of Social Sciences. A more scholarly version is to appear in a volume soon to be published by the Central University of Nationalities in Beijing. All the above reports and publications are in Chinese, but an English version is also under preparation.

5.   LANGUAGE IN EDUCATION AND PUBLIC LIFE

Because everyone in this area speaks Chinese and all economic and political life is conducted in Chinese, it is unrealistic and undesirable to attempt a return to monolingual separateness among the Yi around Kunming. One of the triggers for the universal spread of Chinese has been the extension of schools into relatively remote minority areas since 1950. This has also led to more or less abrupt transmission breakdown in some areas, especially but not exclusively those which are less remote.

---

[17]   Adur is quite different from the 'standard' Northern Yi variety selected and disseminated through education in Sichuan. Nisu or Huang Yi is again somewhat different from Adur, though not as distinct as the various subvarieties of Sanie/Sa'nguie or of Nasu/Hei Yi are from each other.

National minorities in China have some privileges, including financial subsidies through local governments, designated positions in the government and the party, quotas or relaxed selection procedures for things such as university entry, and in rural areas the right to more children than Han Chinese people. They also have their own ministry-level organisation, the Nationalities Affairs Commission, in areas with substantial minority population.

Efforts to promote Yi identity have been somewhat tokenistic around Kunming. The main visible evidence is public signs and banners. At Chejiabi, a Sanie village on a main road next to the Kunming power station, a new village gate with the village name in Chinese and in Yunnan Yi characters was put up in 1994, and a refurbished park next to the village has wall paintings with captions in Yi characters. However, in this village the language is moribund. All speakers are over 60, the local government has made no effort to teach the language in the school, and the Yi characters had to be copied from materials supplied by the provincial Nationality Affairs Commission.

Similarly, at Zijun the local government has a few banners in its office using Yunnan Yi characters along with Chinese characters; these are used in parades. Children are dressed up in colorful costumes for such parades, but these appear to bear little relation to local traditional clothing; rather, they draw on Sani clothing styles from Shilin County, but in different colours. At least in Zijun village the government has taken advantage of subsidies available from the Nationality Affairs Commission and was teaching Yunnan Yi with local pronunciation in the primary school in 1995 and 1996.

The Yi section of the Department of Nationality Languages of the Yunnan Institute of Nationalities was established in 1982, and as noted above taught only Northern Yi from September 1983 to June 1985 when the first and only two-year class graduated and the cadres returned to Sichuan. In September 1985 the department started to teach local varieties of Yi including Sani (southeastern), Nasu (eastern) and Nisu (southern). Annual classes of about 20 have started a four-year course since then; from June 1989 to June 1995 graduates were placed in language-related government work around the province: provincial, prefectural and county nationality affairs, nationality languages, education, information, museum, radio, publishing, culture and other offices, and as local primary teachers. From 1996 students have been expected to find their own jobs, but since many are sponsored by local government, they return to their own area and may find language-related work there. Admission to the Yi class is by interview and examination conducted annually in July, and though in principle all students should already be able to speak their local variety of Yi before they start, quite a few can not.

From 1985 to 1987 materials from the Central Institute of Nationalities in Beijing, prepared by Ma Xueliang[18] and his colleagues, were used in this course. In September 1988 the department started to teach the new Yi script to all first year students, using the adult literacy book and later also the picture primer. The first author has given a class on comparative Yi linguistics to each group since 1992, and worked individually with some of the students. In addition, supported by UNESCO funds, a number of the students have collected additional materials on their own home varieties of Yi.

From 1994 to 1996, the Yunnan Nationalities Commission, the Yunnan Institute of Nationalities and the Southwest Institute of Nationalities co-operated to teach this script to a group of over 40 Yi students, mainly government employees working on language and culture in various parts of Yunnan but also one each from Sichuan, Guizhou and Guangxi. We observed some of the classes, worked with some of the participants on their own varieties of Yi, and the first author taught a class on the comparative linguistic techniques used to create the script and its historical basis to this group.

Primary education in and about Yi language is quite limited. We have seen the picture primer in use in Zijun, where children do not speak Yi at all, though their grandparents and some older teachers do. The teaching method is not very modern: a character which appears in the textbook is written on the board, its pronunciation is given by the teacher, and the

---

[18]   The authors express their deep regret at the passing of Prof Ma Xueliang, the leading scholar of Yi language studies in China, in early 1999.

students chant it back. Teachers and local government are reluctant to disadvantage Yi students in the standard provincial and national exams which determine educational progress. Also, due to lack of materials the amount of time devoted to the study of Yi is limited; mainly just in the first year of primary, though a few areas continue this for three years. Chinese educationalists have borrowed the catchphrases of bilingual education, mainly with a transitional goal of integrating minority students into the Chinese-medium mainstream, but this has not found its way into local primary schools for the Yi in Yunnan, as far as we have seen. At best, a local Yi teacher uses the local variety of Yi to explain Chinese material at the beginning, but otherwise the standard Chinese materials are in use.

In some areas, as a local initiative, the local traditional orthography is taught in primary school. Our colleague Li Yongxiang has arranged such classes in his own Southern Yi village in Xinping County, further south outside the surveyed area, along with classes in traditional music, dance and other aspects of culture.[19] However, in the area surveyed, traditional literacy disappeared among the Nasu by the 1960s or earlier, and the county Nationality Affairs Commissions of Jinning and Anning counties have not been able to find any local books. As we have seen, one Nasu shaman from northwestern Xishan Ward went to Luquan and came back with Nasu books from there; so these are not local. In Guandu Ward, as noted, some Samei books still exist, but since the early 1990s no one can read them. In any case these written varieties are not the same as the new Yunnan Yi writing, and there is little hope of disseminating them given their association with old religious practices that have virtually disappeared from this area.

In Qinghe District of southwestern Fumin County, where there are both Nasu and Sanie villages with some language transmission to children, we were encouraged by the local government and primary school to help with teaching materials, and we prepared and sent a version of the Yi picture primer in the local subvariety of Sanie and standard Chinese. The Chinese is in the *pinyin* romanised transcription. *Pinyin* is useful as the

---

[19]   Mr Li is pleased to acknowledge the support of the Ford Foundation for this work.

students and teachers speak Yunnan dialect of Chinese with somewhat different pronunciation; all students learn *pinyin* in their Chinese classes anyway, but this is not reinforced by other teaching materials to assist with standard pronunciation for a wider range of lexicon. The Sanie transcription we devised follows the same principles, to maximise transference from learning in the mother tongue to learning the national language. These materials were sent to the local school for use there; we do not know whether they were successful, but hope to return and investigate this in the near future. The intention is to reinforce and give linguistic self-esteem for Yi language, to use first language knowledge to facilitate national language learning, and to improve the standardness of Chinese pronunciation. Similar materials can also be prepared for any other area, but we prefer to wait until there is a local request for them, rather than trying to impose something from outside the community.

6. CONCLUSION

A great deal remains to be done. In these areas, Chinese-speaking linguists could readily carry out more extensive work on any of the moribund languages; most urgent is Samataw, but Sanie and Samei will probably soon reach the same stage and have a great deal of internal diversity which make a detailed dialect study highly desirable. Gepo and Miqie are languages with substantial speaker populations elsewhere in Yunnan, and these languages are also virtually undescribed. Eastern Nasu, Southern Nasu/Nisu/Niesu, and Northern Nisu/Adur and related Northern varieties in Sichuan all still require more dialect survey work and grammatical description.

In preliminary surveys of some other areas, we have continued to locate similar numbers of other unreported and undescribed endangered languages. Projecting from work so far, just within the Yi nationality, one might expect to find at least 50 more languages within Yunnan alone; considering that there are many other composite nationalities and many other provinces with substantial minority populations, endangered language work in China is very urgent and needs to be done on a large scale. Many of the endangered languages are more or less closely related, and also related to the languages which are replacing them; thus the sociolinguistic and historical linguistic situation of contact, multilingualism and change is also particularly fascinating.

The prognosis for the survival of moribund languages like Samataw is very poor, even with external assistance; but other communities in the area may still be encouraged to keep their languages. Perhaps our basic challenge is to raise the self-esteem of minority groups through work with them on their languages, and see whether they then decide to keep them alive. They of course need to make their own decisions about the importance of language maintenance; but if we do not do the descriptive work now, their grandchildren may reproach them, and us, the members of a discipline which is presiding over the demise of most of the objects of our study!

REFERENCES

Anonymous 1987. *Yi Writing Practical Textbook* [in Restored Yunnan Yi and Chinese]. Kunming: Yunnan Nationalities Press. Revised edition 1990, reprinted 1990.

_____ 1991. *Children Look at Characters and Remember Writing* [in Restored Yunnan Yi and Chinese]. Kunming: Yunnan Nationalities Press. Revised edition 1997.

_____ 1993. *Language* [in Restored Yunnan Yi and Chinese], book 1, 2 and 3. Kunming: Yunnan Nationalities Press. Reprinted 1994 (twice).

Bradley, David 1979. *Proto-Loloish.* London: Curzon Press.

_____ 1983. Identity: the persistence of minority groups. In John McKinnon & Wanat Bhruksasri (eds) *Highlanders of Thailand*, 46-55. Kuala Lumpur: Oxford University Press.

_____ 1985. Traditional minorities and language education in Thailand. In David Bradley (ed.) *Language Policy, Language Planning and Sociolinguistics in Southeast Asia*, 87-102. Canberra: Pacific Linguistics A-67. Canberra: Department of Linguistics RSPAS, ANU.

_____ 1987. Language planning for China's minorities: the Yi branch. In Don C. Laycock & Werner Winter (eds) *A World of Language: Papers presented to Professor S.A. Wurm on his 65th birthdy*, 81-89. Pacific Linguistics C-100. Canberra: Department of Linguistics RSPAS, ANU.

_____ 1994. Building identity and the modernisation of language: minority language policy in Thailand and China. In Alberto Gomes (ed.) *Modernity and Identity: Asian illustrations*, 192-205. Bundoora: Institute of Asian Studies, La Trobe University, for Asian Studies Association of Australia.

_____ 1996. Language policy and the typology of scripts.' In Suriya Ratanakul et al. (eds) *Pan Asiatic Linguistics. Proceedings of the fourth international symposium on languages and linguistics, January 8-10, 1996*, 1845-1856. Salaya: Institute of Language and Culture for Rural Development, Mahidol University.

_____1997. Onomastic, orthographic, dialectal and dialectical borders: the Lisu and the Lahu. *Asia Pacific Viewpoint* 38/2: 107-117.

_____ 1998. Minority language policy and endangered languages in China and Southeast Asia. In Kazuto Matsumura (ed.) *Studies in Endangered Languages. Papers from the International Symposium an Endangered Languages, Tokyo, November 18-20, 1995*, 49-83. Tokyo: Hituzi Syobo.

_____2000. Endangered Yi Group Languages of Kunming [in Chinese]. In Bamo Ayi & Huang Jianming (eds) *Collected Articles on Yi Studies*, 162-169. Kunming: Yunnan Agricultural Press.

Bradley, David Maya Bradley & Li Yongxiang 1998. Report to Yunnan Provincial Government on Endangered Languages in Central Yunnan [in Chinese]. Unpublished official report.

Gao Huanian 1958. *Yi Grammar* [in Chinese]. Beijing: Chinese Academy of Science.

Xie Jian 1987. *The Samei People from East of Kunming* [in Chinese]. Hong Kong: Chinese University of Hong Kong Press.

Chapter 8

Tai languages of Assam, a progress report — Does anything remain of the Tai Ahom language?[1]

Stephen Morey
Monash University

1.   THE CURRENT LINGUISTIC SITUATION

Seven languages of the Tai family have been spoken in Northeast India in historical times. Six, Ahom, Aiton, Khamti, Nora, Phake and Tairong were exemplified or mentioned by Grierson in the *Linguistic Survey of India* (1902). The seventh, Khamyang, which according to some may once have been the same as Nora, is still spoken by elderly people in a single village in Tinsukia District, Assam.

Each of Aiton, Khamti and Phake is still spoken by several thousand people, and each is still taught to children. They are thus not under immediate threat of extinction, and the use of some of these languages is even expanding into small communities of ex-tea garden labourers (originally brought by the British from the tribal districts of Orissa and Bihar) who now work as labourers for the Tai and live in their villages.

Although basically mutually intelligible, some groups of Tai have difficulty understanding others. In particular it is reported that the Aiton presents some difficulties for speakers of Khamti and Phake.

Both the Nora and Tairong languages are extinct. Nora people now speak Assamese, whereas the Tairong or Turung have developed an interesting, and as yet uninvestigated, mixture of Singpho (Tibeto-Burman), with some Tai words and a tonal system that may also be influenced by Tai.

Details of the current situation of the seven languages are as follows:

---

[1]   This chapter is based on a paper presented at the symposium in the author's absence and revised with findings from a field trip in November 1999 to February 2000.

Ahom: Word list, grammatical notes and texts in Grierson (1902). Other references include Terwiel and Ranoo (1992), Ranoo (1996), Barua & Phukan (1964) and Barua (1936). There are large collections of manuscripts, mostly unstudied, but Terwiel and Ranoo (1992) published one of these. Ahom is a dead language, claimed to be undergoing a revival, and elderly priests are claimed to have knowledge of the language and its literature.

Aiton was briefly mentioned by Grierson (1902) where there is a word list, grammatical notes and texts. It is also discussed by Diller (1992). There is a significant collection of manuscripts in several villages – uncatalogued and largely unstudied. There are probably over 1000 native speakers. The language is still learned by children and a small group of second language learners, former tea garden labourers now working for the Aitons, are also speaking the language.

Khamti was described in some detail by Grierson (1902) who presented grammatical notes, texts and a comparative word list. Grierson based his work on Needham (1894). Other references include Harris (1976), Weidert (1977), Chaw Khouk Manpoong (1993) and Robinson (1849). There are said to be large manuscript collections, particularly in Arunachal Pradesh. There are several thousand native speakers in India, and more in Burma. The language is still being passed on to children.

The word Khamyang is not used by Grierson. It is believed by some that Nora is an Assamese term which refers to the Khamyang. In the village of Pawaimukh, there is a large (100+) collection of manuscripts. Khamyang is only spoken in Pawaimukh, by around 50 adults over about 40 years of age.

Nora was briefly described by Grierson (1902), with brief grammatical notes and texts, and a comparative word list. It is not spoken today, and even in Grierson's time there were said to be only about 300 speakers.

Phake was only mentioned by Grierson (1902) without any data. More recently it has been referred to by Aimya Khang (1997),

Banchob (1987), Gogoi (1994), Diller (1992). There are large collections of manuscripts in several villages – some of which have been catalogued and studied. There are perhaps over 2000 native speakers and it is still passed on to children.

Tairong or Turung is discussed by Grierson (1902) with brief grammatical notes and text, and a comparative word list. There are said to be manuscript collections in at least one village in Assam, but these cannot be read by the Tairong. As a Tai language, Tairong is extinct, even in Grierson's time the number of speakers being very small. The Tairong now speak a form of Singpho with some Tai words and a unique tonal system.

2.　　THE STATUS OF THE AHOM LANGUAGE

The Ahom were a band of Tai who ruled a kingdom in the Brahmaputra valley for six centuries, until the British conquest in the 1820s. Today the Ahoms number around one million, consisting largely of rural landowners, and a significant proportion of the political, business and educational elite of Assam. Some Ahom are keenly involved in a cultural revival movement, which for some people is linked to a desire for political autonomy.

Of the linguistic situation of the Ahoms, Terwiel has written the following:

> Linguists and historians are generally united in the view that the Ahom language has been dead for about two hundred years, and that all Ahom use Assamese as their mother tongue.
> This view is hotly contested by the traditional Ahom priests and spokesmen of the revivalist movement, who have staunchely maintained that the Ahom language did not die out and that the traditional priests can decipher the Ahom script and always have been able to chant from ancient Ahom documents.　　　　　　　　　　(Terwiel 1996: 283)

I will be arguing here that whilst it is clearly true that the Ahom language is no longer a mother tongue, nevertheless it does appear that the Ahom priests do have some traditional knowledge of their language, that is knowledge passed down from parents and elders. Furthermore, at least some of the linguistic content of their rituals is based on traditional Ahom, and it is clear that amongst the Ahom community those who possess the greatest knowledge are the priests, mostly rural people from often very remote villages.

It is also important to add that those who have the greatest knowledge of the Tai languages in Assam, including the ability to understand traditional Ahom texts, are those who speak one of the other Tai languages as a mother tongue. In particular three pandits, the late Aimya Khang Gohain (Phake), Smti. Yehom Buragohain (Phake) and Sri Nabin Shyam Phalung (Aiton) have great expertise in reading the Ahom texts.

The claim is often made in Assam that the priests possess knowledge of the language and can read and understand the manuscripts. Terwiel has very thoroughly investigated this, and following a symposium where several priests were asked to assist with the translation of manuscripts, came to the conclusion that 'whereas they could readily decipher the script, ... they did so without assigning tones ... and without any idea of the meaning of the words, except for a few of the simplest expressions. I reluctantly drew the conclusion that ... Ahom really was a dead language.' (1996: 284)

During January 2000, I spent some time with some of the Ahom priests. I was shown a manuscript which had been prepared by another priest, Mileswar Phukan.[2] The manuscript is a vast dictionary from Ahom into Assamese. One section of this dictionary which was analysed was a list of the names of various birds, mostly words which are not present in any of the published Ahom word lists. Many of these names are similar to those of the Phakes, but many more are not. He also prepared translations into Assamese of several old Ahom manuscripts. One of these, a creation story, was briefly

---

[2]   It is believed by his family that he learned his Ahom language from his forebears. It is not known where he is at present. Several years ago, it is believed, he set out for Burma to find the original home of the Tai Ahoms. If still alive he would be well into his 80s.

examined by Aimya Khang Gohain who informed me that although the translation was correct in part, it showed too much Hindu influence for a pre-Hindu Ahom creation story.

Difficulty in reading and translating manuscripts is not confined to the Ahom. Even those who are native speakers of the Tai languages are not necessarily able to understand the manuscripts, even if they are literate. The writing systems of both Ahom and the other Tai languages do not mark tonal distinctions, nor vowel length, nor in some cases vowel quality.[3] In the Aiton and Phake villages there are well-educated people who cannot fully read old manuscript, because it is sometimes necessary to know the meaning of the book in order to be able to read it. Even the most educated of the Phake argue about the readings of certain words in the manuscripts. In example (1), from a book entitled "Grandfather teaches grandchildren", there is a debate about the meaning of the last word.

(1) ᩅᩪᩡ   ᩣ᩶   ᩣ   ᩁᩪ   ᩃᩳᩢ |
     khām³   nam⁴   haü³   nū²   khɔn⁶ / khɔn³
     cross   water   give   look   snag, log in water
     'When crossing the river, you should look out for logs.'

It is not surprising, therefore, that the Ahom priests cannot necessarily fully explain the old Ahom texts.

Terwiel (1996: 284) further claims that "There are marked differences between the Ahom of the old documents,... and what the revivalists call Ahom, which has totally abandoned the rules of Tai grammar and often uses Ahom words in a non-idiomatic sense." One of the examples of what he describes as the Ahom pseudo-language is used in the Ahom wedding ceremony (Chaklong) described by Gogoi (1976). Terwiel says:

> ... the sentence *khung lu mao cao kao di di si hap ao jao*, which is translated 'I respectfully accept your offer'. The

---

[3]   For example all three front vowels are written the same way in closed syllables!

most probable dictionary equivalents of these words are *khrueang lu* 'offering'; *mo chao* 'priest'; *kao* 'I', *di di* 'very good'; *sia* a suffix; *hap* 'to accept'; *ao* 'to take' and *jao* 'finished'. All these words can be found in *Ahom Lexicons* (Barua and Phukan 1964). To any Tai speaker, however, it is gibberish.   (Terwiel 1996: 284)

During December 1999 I attended a ceremony of the Chaklong wedding officiated over by one of the most senior Ahom priests and performed almost entirely in the Ahom language. The texts used in the ceremony are of two types. The first are prayers which are intoned by the priests. Whilst the priests were willing for me to take copies of some of these, they explained that the knowledge contained therein was sacred and could not at this time be made available. It is therefore impossible to examine the level of their knowledge. The second type of text includes short responses in the Ahom language which the participants in the ceremony – the bride, the bride's father and the bridegroom – are expected to repeat. The priest explains the meaning of the response first in Assamese, then asks the participant to repeat after him. The sentence discussed by Terwiel above is one in which the bridegroom "accepts" the bride who has been "given away" by her father.

Following the conclusion of the ceremony I discussed the text with several priests. They translated the words as follows:

khrung lu "offering"	mao chao "you"
kao "I"	di di "cordially (=good)"
si "PARTICLE"	hap ao "to accept (lit:accept-take)"
yao "PAST TENSE"	

Several Phake informants[4] indicated that this sentence would be acceptable in Phake, (spoken as three intonation units, here separated by |).

---

[4]   Yenow Than Gohain stated that this sentence was an acceptable sentence in Phake, a fact confirmed by her father Aithown Che Gohain and also by the late Aimya Khang Gohain.

(2)   ဥၟၚၠ   ၟၞ | ၟ   ၟ   ၟ |

khauŋ⁶ lū¹   maü² cau³ | kau¹   nī² nī² sī⁶ |

offering   you | I   good   PRT |

     ၟ   ၟ   ၟ

     hap⁴   au²   yau⁴

     accept   take   PAST

     "I cordially accept your offering"

The late Aimya Khang Gohain however stated that this sentence, although syntactically acceptable, was pragmatically unacceptable because in Phake khauŋ⁶ 'thing' could never refer to a person.

A brief examination of some other responses from the ceremony suggests that these also may be acceptable to speakers of the other Tai languages. The priests stated that the texts used in the Chaklong ceremony are ancient, and are based on old manuscripts which still exist.

In January 1999 I met one of the senior priests of the Ahom, Sri Junaram Sangbun Phukan and interviewed him about the Ahom language. He was able to give Ahom versions of a list of words he was given, although in some cases only after hesitation. He freely admitted that the tones of Ahom were lost, indicating that the problem of potential homophony would be overcome by compounding, as shown in Table 1.

The first two are examples of words which are compounds of a class term followed by a more specific term. The word tū is a common Tai word for 'animal' and 'body', whilst the word phā is the word for 'cloth'. This strategy would not work for the words for 'dog' and 'horse', so a further word has been added to the word for 'dog'. Several Ahom priests stated that the word mā teng for 'dog' is found in old Ahom manuscripts.

Table 1:   **"Modern" Ahom compound words[5]**

	"modern" Ahom	transcription (after Barua and Phukan (1964)	Phake	transcription of Phake (after Banchob 1987)
tiger	ꠡ ꠥꠡ	tū chu	ꠡꠥꠡ	sɔ̄[6]
shirt	ꠥꠡ ꠥꠡ	phā chu	ꠡꠥꠡ	sɔ̄[3]
dog	ꠡ ꠥ ꠡ	tū mā teng	ꠥ	mā[6]
horse	ꠡ ꠥ	tū mā	ꠥ	mā[4]

It is unclear whether the loss of tones and the consequent compounding of words is a modern phenomenon arising as a result of attempts at language revival or whether it was a natural process during the period of the decline of the Ahom language. A similar phenomenon of tone loss is occurring in the Aiton Language. Diller (1992: 18) reports two tonal systems for Aiton, a six-tone system, which he describes as 'undoubtedly more conservative' and a three-tone system. In recent investigations, I have heard several informants claim that there are six tones for Aiton, but they cannot consistently produce more than three.

François Jacquesson (personal communication) has reported tonal loss in Deori, a Tibeto-Burman language spoken in Assam. He states:

> Deori speakers know (especially when asked) that some pairs of words exist which are contrasted for tone, and will tell you that you must not get mixed up with *ko*, because there is a lower *ko* meaning 'come' and a higher *ko* meaning 'pick up'. Many speakers know that there are such pairs without knowing very well which in the pair is lower or higher: they just know that there were such pairs. And they deny the

---

[5]   Tone 3 in Phake is a low glottalised tone, Tone 4 a falling tone and Tone 5 a rising tone.

existing (quite rightly as far as the present speech is concerned) of tonal contrasts in words that do not fit in pairs.

It appears that in Aiton, there are also some pairs of words for which speakers know that there once was a tonal distinction, and for which they can sometimes produce some distinction. For example in Phake kā³ 'dance' and kā⁴ 'trade' are contrasted. In Aiton, for most speakers most of the time, there is no contrast between these words, although some speakers can sometimes provide a contrast between them, especially in citation forms. This contrast probably refers back to an earlier period in the history of the language when there was a consistent contrast, where the word for 'dance' was probably glottalised. The speakers do not always get the contrast right. Glottalisation of 'trade' and not 'dance' has been recorded.

Three tones in a Tai language would lead to a large amount of homophony. Possibly as a strategy to overcome this, the Aitons are beginning to compound words, particularly in their citation form, in a way analogous to that seen for Ahom in Table 1 above. It may be that what has happened in Ahom, both tonal loss and the strategy of compounding to overcome the homophony that occurs as a result of the tonal loss, are natural processes of change which we are also seeing in Aiton.

In addition to word lists, several short Ahom sentences were elicited from Junaram Sangbun Phukan, such as (3).

(3)   ꩵꩰ ꩮꩾ   ꩬꩲꩴ   ꩧ°   ꩩꩳ   ꩧ°   ꩰꩵ

cāng nāi   kāo   ti   pāi   ti   kāt

now   1Sg   FUT   go   to   market

"Now I am going to market."

This sentence is almost identical to (4), elicited from the late Aimya Khang Gohain, a Phake Tai of Namphakey village.

(4)   ꧡ꧆   ꩫꩳ   ꩢꩶꩳ   ꩬꩲꩽ   ꩢꩲ   ꩢꩲ꩷

mɔ⁵   nai⁴   kau²   ta¹   kā¹   kāt¹

time   this   1Sg   will   go   market

"Today I am going to the market."

Sri Junaram Sangbun Phukan claimed that the Ahom language was passed down to him by his family, although he admitted to having visited the Phake villages frequently, suggesting that there is a possibility of his knowledge of Ahom being influenced by the Phake.

During 1999, I received the following letter in Ahom from him.[6]

To revd. Stephen Morey

... (Photos)

... (Research)

One example from the letter is:

---

6   I am unclear what 'revd.' is an abbreviation for.

(5)   ᯀᯣᯰ ᯖᯫ   ᯑᯮ᯲   ᯎᯩ   ᯀᯪᯨ   ᯅᯭᯉ   ᯕᯮ᯲   ᯖᯫ   ᯖᯫ

cāng nāi   kāo   ju   ti   bān   rāo   di   di
now   1Sg   live   at   village 1Pl   good   good
"I am now in good health, at our village."[7]

Neither the word order nor the syntax is Assamese, a language which
is strongly verb-final, as in:

(6)   হৰি   এতিয়া   কলিকতাত   আছে
hɔri   etijaː   kɔlikɔtaː-t   aːse
Hari   now   Calcutta-LOC   is.3Sg.PRES
"Hari is now in Calcutta."

However a pandit of the Aiton language, Sri Nabin Shyam Phalung,
offered the following sentence which is structurally similar to (5).

(7)   ᯈᯬᯉᯩ   ᯎᯮ᯲   ᯔᯮ   ᯀᯮ   ᯅᯩ᯲   ᯔᯮ   ᯃᯮ

caŋ[1] nai[3] kau[2] uu[1] nauu[2] maan[3] uu[1] nii[2]
now   I   live at in   village   live at good

ᯆᯮᯭᯩᯉ   ᯎᯩ
khyaam[2] saa[1] yau[4]
good   PAST
"Now I am living in good health in the village."

Neither examples (3) nor (5) are "gibberish" to any Tai speaker, nor
do either of the sentences show strong Assamese influence. Rather,
these two examples (and the other sentences from this informant that
I have been able to analyse) show features which would be expected
in Tai.

During my travels in Assam I have never found any person who can
converse fluently in the Ahom language, although I have met some
Ahom people who have learned Aiton or Phake to some extent. It is
also very difficult to find any Ahom person who can read right

---

[7]   The romanisations are following Barua and Phukan (1964).

through the manuscripts and clearly explain the meaning of every word. Nevertheless some of the priests clearly do possess some knowledge of the language. This knowledge may have come from any of three sources, or a combination of all three:

> It is possible that some part of their knowledge has been passed down from generation to generation, as they claim.

> Some part of their knowledge may have come from the study of old texts, and from the many primers and other books published recently about the Ahom.

> Some part of their knowledge may have come from the speakers of other living Tai languages, the Phakes and Aitons, with whom they have some contact.

3. SOME THOUGHTS ON THE MAINTENANCE OF TAI LANGUAGES OF ASSAM

The Ahom community is a large and influential community in Assam. There is an increasing interest by the Ahom in their heritage. It is to be hoped that this interest in the existing Tai languages and cultures not yet fully Indianised can be chanelled to maintain the languages. In comparison to the Ahoms, the Phake and Aiton are much less well connected in Assamese society. The support of the Ahom elite would be of great benefit in linguistic maintenance.

Whilst the language of the Aiton and Phake may not be immediately threatened, knowledge of the traditional script certainly is. The number of young people that can read the script is very small, and there is almost no usage of the scripts outside of sacred literature which is often very old. As explained earlier, the script does not show tonal contrast at all, and some vowel contrasts are also not shown. This makes newer texts, such as letters, prone to misinterpretation. Various members of the Tai community have been exploring reforming the script in order to show tone. An attempt by Chaw Khouk Manpoong to revise the Khamti script commenced in the late 1980s, but has not been widely accepted.

Table 2: Comparison of consonants: Fonts produced for the Tai languages of Assam

Phake	Phake "new"	Phake MS	Aiton	Revised Khamti	Ahom	Ahom MS	Sound
က	က	ၮ	က	ၮ	ၮ	ၮ	ka
ၯ	ၯ	ၮ	ၯ	ၯ	ၮ	ၮ	kʰa (xa)
ၯ	ၯ	ၮ	ၯ	ၯ	ၮ	ၮ	ŋa
ၯ	ၯ	ၮ	ၯ	ၯ	ၮ	ၮ	tɕa, sa
ၯ	ၯ	ၮ	ၯ	ၯ	ၮ	ၮ	sa, ʃa
ၯ	ၯ	ၮ	ၯ	ၯ	ၮ	ၮ	ɲa
ၯ	ၯ	ၮ	ၯ	ၯ	ၮ	ၮ	ta
ၯ	ၯ	ၮ	ၯ	ၯ	ၮ	ၮ	tʰa
ၯ	ၯ	ၮ	ၯ	ၯ	ၮ	ၮ	na
ၯ	ၯ	ၮ	ၯ	ၯ	ၮ	ၮ	pa
ၯ	ၯ	ၮ	ၯ	ၯ	ၮ	ၮ	pʰa, ɸa
ၯ	ၯ	ၮ	ၯ	ၯ	ၮ	ၮ	ma
ၯ	ၯ	ၮ	ၯ	ၯ	ၮ	ၮ	ja / ʒa
ၯ	ၯ	ၮ	ၯ	ၯ	ၮ	ၮ	ra, la
ၯ	ၯ	ၮ	ၯ	ၯ	ၮ	ၮ	la
ၯ	ၯ	ၮ	ၯ	ၯ	ၮ	ၮ	wa
ၯ	ၯ	ၮ	ၯ	ၯ	ၮ	ၮ	ha
ၯ	ၯ	ၮ	ၯ	ၯ	ၮ	ၮ	ʔa

Furthermore, because the Tai of Assam have different scripts from both Assamese and Roman, they have until now been unable to print books. With the development of computer fonts, books can be easily printed. So far, I have produced seven fonts for different varieties in use amongst the Tai of Assam. Two of these fonts are based on particular manuscript traditions. The Phake Lama Mang is a famous manuscript, sometimes described as the Phake Ramayana, whilst Chicken Bone augury is an important traditional Ahom practice. Through the kindness of Shri Atul Borgohain of Dibrugarh, I was able to obtain copies of parts of these two important manuscripts. The other fonts were developed with the assistance of the communities concerned to reflect more contemporary usage. Table 2 illustrates these fonts.

In late 1999 we printed three books using these fonts:

A primer for the Phake language, and a primer for the Aiton language

An Aiton manuscript (history of the Aitons) with English and Assamese translation.

It is hoped that in early 2001 we will print two more books:

A Phake manuscript of proverbs (Grandfather teaches Grandchildren)

A Khamyang manuscript for calling up the Spirit (Khon) of a sick person).

In addition, a dictionary database has been prepared using previously published material such as Banchob (1987) and adding in the Tai scripts and Assamese translations. It is hoped that by early 2001 a draft Tai Aiton-English-Assamese dictionary will be made available for use in the various Aiton villages.

These, along with the recording and analysis of the many stories, songs, proverbs, prayers and other texts of the Aiton, Khamyang, Khamti and Phake, will hopefully document these languages and cultures and provide whatever help can be provided to ensure their survival for a little longer.

REFERENCES

Aimya Khang Gohain 1997. *Elementary Tai Primer* [in Phake]. Department of Assamese, Dibrugarh University.

Banchob Bandhumedha 1987. *Phake - Thai - English Dictionary* [in Thai]. Published by the Author.

Barua, Bimala Kanta & N.N. Deodhari Phukan 1964. *Ahom Lexicons, Based on Original Tai Manuscripts.* Guwahati: Department of Historical and Antiquarian Studies.

Barua, Ghan Kanta. 1936. Ahom Primer [in Ahom]. Guwahati: Department of Historical and Antiquarian Studies in Assam.

Diller, Anthony. 1992. Tai Languages in Assam: Daughters or Ghosts? In Carol J. Compton & John F. Hartmann (eds) *Papers on Tai Languages, Linguistics and Literatures*, 5-43. DeKalb, IL: Center for Southeast Asian Studies, Northern Illinois University.

Gedney, William J. 1972. A Checklist for Determining Tones in Tai Dialects. In E. Estelle Smith (ed.) *Studies in Linguistics in Honor of George L. Trager*, 423-37. The Hague: Mouton.

Gogoi, Nomal Chandra. 1994. *Morphological Study of the Tai Phake Language.* PhD Thesis, Dibrugarh University.

Gogoi, Padmeswar 1968. *The Tai and the Tai Kingdoms; with a Fuller Treatment of the Tai-Ahom Kingdom in the Brahmaputra Valley.* Gauhati: Department of Publication, Gauhati University.

_____ 1976. *Tai-Ahom Religion and Customs.* Gauhati: Publications Board, Assam. (cited in Terwiel 1996)

Grierson, Sir George 1966 (1902). *Linguistic Survey of India,* Vol. 2. *Mon-Khmer and Siamese-Chinese Families.* Reprinted Delhi: Motilal Banarsidass

Harris, Jimmy G. 1976. Notes on Khamti Shan. in Thomas W. Gething, Jimmy G. Harris & Pranee Kullavanijaya (eds) *Thai Linguistics in Honour of Fang Kuei Li*, 113-141. Bangkok: Chulalongkorn University.

Chau Khouk Manpoong. 1993. *New Tai Reader* [in Khamti]. 2 vol. Chongkham, Arunachal Pradesh: Tai Literature Committee.

Needham, J.F. 1894. *Outline Grammar of the Khâmtî Language - as spoken by the Khâmtîs residing in the neighbourhood of Sadiya*. Rangoon: Superintendent of Government Printing, Burma

Phukan, Punaram Mohan 1998. *Tai Ahom Vocabulary* [in Assamese]. Dibrugarh: Professor Girin Phukan.

Ranoo Wichasin 1996. *Tai-Ahom Chronicles* [in Thai]. Bangkok: Amarin Printing & Publishing.

Robinson, W. 1849. 'Notes on the Languages spoken by the various Tribes inhabiting the Valley of Asam and its mountain confines'. in *Journal of the Asiatic Society of Bengal*. Vol xviii, Part 1 311-318, 342-349.

Terwiel, Barend J. 1996. Recreating the Past: Revivalism in Northeastern India. *Bijdragen - Journal of the Royal Institute of Linguistics and Anthropology*, (Leiden) 152: 275-292.

Terwiel, Barend J. & Ranoo Wichasin (eds. and transls.). 1992. *Tai Ahoms and the Stars; Three Ritual Texts to Ward off Danger*. Ithaca: Southeast Asia Program, Cornell University.

Weidert, Alfons 1977. *Tai-Khamti Phonology and Vocabulary*. Wiesbaden: Franz Steiner Verlag.

Chapter 9

The Impact of Malay on Taba: a type of incipient language death or incipient death of a language type?

John Bowden
Australian National University

1. INTRODUCTION

This paper reviews some of the rather dramatic changes that are occurring in the vocabulary and grammatical structures of contemporary Taba, an indigenous language spoken on Makian island and in other parts of North Maluku province in Indonesia. The major source for the changes that are currently taking place is North Malukan Malay (NMM), the local lingua franca. The question I wish to answer in this paper is whether or not these changes can be seen as indicative of incipient language death. It is not possible to say whether or not Taba will continue to be spoken into the future for many more years: the speakers of the language will decide for themselves whether or not they continue to transmit the language to future generations. It is clear, though, that Taba discourse patterns are being remodelled to more closely parallel those found in NMM, and that other indigenous laguages of the area also seem to be refashioning themselves in a similar way.

In the first part of the paper I review work by Sasse (1992) which seeks to set out in general terms the kinds of processes that typically lead to language death, and in the following three sections I compare what is taking place in Taba with Sasse's general schema. While it is clear that Taba grammatical and discourse structures are in the process of a rather radical realignment towards the model provided by Malay, there is not really any clear evidence that Taba speakers are about to give up their language in favour of Malay in the near future. The realignment of discourse structures seen in progress here appears to be occurring as a component of a process of 'metatypy', defined by Ross (1999) as 'the change in morphosyntactic type which a language undergoes as a result of its speakers' bilingualism in another language'. The paper concludes by presenting a few more examples of what looks like the metatypical remodelling of indigenous eastern Indonesian languages in the direction of Malay. While it is still posssible that many of the small indigenous languages from eastern Indonesia will continue to be used well into the next century and beyond, it seems that virtually all of these languages will undergo dramatic changes in the direction of Malay. Although there may not be any language death in any sense that indigenous communities would recognise as such, there is undoubtedly going to be a great reduction in the typological variety of languages found in the region as linguists might recognise that concept. Although real language death is not very widespread in eastern Indonesia as yet, it is probably true to say that typological death is advancing at some speed.

2. PROCESSES LEADING TO LANGUAGE DEATH

When languages 'die', it is not usually the case that they just stop being spoken overnight. Language death is usually a gradual process brought about within the context of certain kinds of social situations. Through these situations, and usually over a course of a few generations, people gradually switch from speaking one language to speaking another language. Of course, the underlying reasons that people give up one language are never purely linguistic, but are primarily social. Sasse has provided a general overview of the kinds of processes that are typically seen in cases of language death (1992: 9-10). Sasse maintains that three sets of conditions are generally involved in the process of language death, and that these occur more or less sequentially. Only the last of his three factors is truly purely linguistic. Sasse lists these three factors as:

External setting:
> The external setting involves the extralinguistic factors which are present in situations of language death: 'cultural, sociological, ethnohistorical, economic, etc., processes, which create, in a certain speech community, a situation of pressure which forces the community to give up its language'

Speech behaviour:
> Such external settings, induce changes in people's 'speech behaviour'. This is characterised as 'the regular use of

variables, which in a given speech community, are bound with social parameters, e.g. the use of different languages in multilingual settings, he use of different styles of one language, domains of language and styles, attitudes towards variants of language, and so on'

Structural change:

This kind of speech behavior in turn results in certain structural consequences, i.e. 'the purely structural, substantial linguistic set of phenomena, e.g. changes in the phonology, morphology, syntax and lexicon of the language threatened by extinction'

These three processes are seen as occurring in a fixed temporal sequence, and Sasse illustrates this sequence as shown in Figure 1.

Figure 1:   Processes leading to language death
(after Sasse 1992: 13)

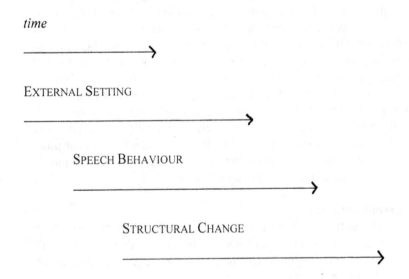

Map: Location of the Taba

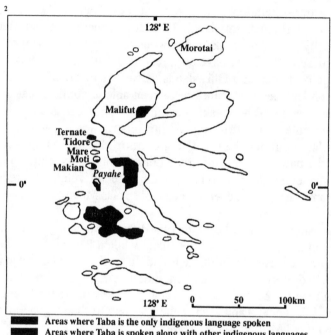

■■■ Areas where Taba is the only indigenous language spoken
■■■ Areas where Taba is spoken along with other indigenous languages

3.   THE EXTERNAL SETTING: A BRIEF HISTORY

As shown in the map above, Taba is spoken chiefly on the eastern side of Makian island, on parts of Moti and the Kayoa islands, as well as in a number of villages on adjacent parts of the South Halmahera coast. A sizeable community of Makianese people also live in a transmigration area in Malifut, near Kao on the northern peninsula of Halmahera island. In addition, there is a significant community of Taba speakers living in the regional metropolitan centre of Ternate. There have been reports of further speakers of the language on Bacan and Obi islands as well as in the hinterland of Jailolo on Halmahera. While I have been able to confirm that there exists at least one Taba speaking community on Bacan island, I have not been able to confirm any of the reports about communities around Jailolo. It may be true that groups of Makianese migrated to Obi in the past, but I am informed (Jim Collins, pers. comm.) that while the communities living on Obi are all relatively recent immigrants, these days, everyone on Obi speaks Malay.

Makian island itself is home to two different languages: Taba is spoken on the eastern side of the island while a Papuan language is spoken on the western half of the island. In English this language has been called West Makian and in Indonesian it is referred to as Makian Luar or 'Outer Makian'. Taba speakers refer to the language as Taba Lik 'Outer Taba', while the speakers of the language itself refer to it (and Makian island) as Moi.

Useful introductions to the history of North Maluku can be found in van Fraassen (1981) and Andaya (1993) from which most of the following notes, unless otherwise cited, have been culled. Makian, as well as Ternate, Tidore, Moti and Bacan islands are the islands to which cloves (*Eugenia aromatica*) are indigenous. From as early as the first century AD, there were reports of cloves in Chinese, Indian and Roman sources. Trade routes direct from Java to the North Malukan region were in existence from at least the fourteenth century, and it appears that Islam arrived in the region about this time. Before European contact, the people of these islands and the nearby region were to a large degree subject to the power of sultanates based in Ternate, Tidore, Jailolo and Bacan. Makianese oral tradition suggests that the sultanate of Bacan may originally have been Makianese. The sultanates acted as conduits for the trade and their rulers extracted tributes from the people living in the area. It appears that Malay has been spoken as a lingua franca in the region from about the 15th century. The language of the sultanates in Ternate and Tidore was also used as a lingua franca (although often labelled as distinct languages in the literature, Ternatan and Tidoran are mutually intelligible varieties of the same language). Given the fairly widely dispersed nature of power centres up to this time, it is unlikely that any particular lingua franca had any real dominance in the area until later historical events intervened.

In 1512 (just after Malacca's fall to the Portuguese in 1511) the Portuguese explorer Francisco Serrão first arrived in Ternate. Although the Portuguese did not immediately found any settlements in the area, Serrão remained in Ternate until his death early in 1521, and a number of Portuguese ships passed through the region over this period. Meanwhile, the Spanish had begun to take an interest in the region, and in late 1521, after Ferdinand Magellan's death in the Philippines, two ships from his fleet managed to reach Tidore where their crews were received hospitably. After staying in Tidore for about six weeks (and loading their vessels with a cargo of cloves) they returned to Spain as heroes and sparked off great interest in the region back in Europe.

The Portuguese returned to Ternate in 1522 and built a fort where they maintained a permanent settlement until 1574. They also established a presence in Ambon and a few other places. The Portuguese saw their role in Maluku as twofold: first, they wished to control the trade of cloves from the region, and second, they wanted to propagate Christianity. Both of these aims brought them into conflict with the Ternatans. After Sultan Hairun of Ternate was murdered in 1570, the Ternatans struck back. Assisted by Tidore and Bacan, they forced the Portuguese back to Ambon in 1574. At this stage, a number of loan words from Portuguese and/or Spanish entered the region, (probably through Malay or Ternatan / Tidoran) and are now widely used in Taba, e.g. *coklat* 'cocoa', *fer* 'iron', etc.

Tidore, fearful of the growing power of Ternate, invited the Portuguese back a few years later. They tried establishing a fort on Tidore in 1578, but Ternate remained the centre of the clove trade. A

succession of brief Dutch expeditions to Ternate around the turn of
the seventeenth century resulted in an alliance between the two
powers against the Portuguese who were finally expelled from
Tidore (and Ambon) in 1605.

However, the Dutch alliance with Ternate eventually secured control
of the region. The Spanish maintained a presence on Tidore and the
southwestern part of Ternate for a time, but the Dutch took control of
Moti, Bacan and also Makian islands and the western part of
Halmahera. During this period, Makian island was brought firmly
into the struggle between the colonial powers. The construction of
three forts on Makian took place after the Dutch expelled the
Spanish from the island during 1610 and 1611. By 1663 the Spanish
had given up any attempt at maintaining a presence in the region and
withdrew to Manila.

It was probably during this period that the use of both Malay and
Ternatan as lingue franche in the area began to emerge much more
strongly. However, once the Dutch had taken secure control, cloves
started being grown in a number of other places, most notably
Ambon, and the strategic significance of North Maluku declined.
The new lingue franche were not in a position to put any of the local
indigenous languages under any real threat yet, but the Dutch
language had left traces in many of the local languages by the time
the Dutch left. Taba has a number of Dutch loans, e.g. *bonci*
'peanuts' (< *boontje* 'small bean'), *fruk* 'early', *fis* 'bicycle' (< *fiets*),
etc.

The Dutch remained in control of what were the Dutch East Indies
and became Indonesia until World War II, when the Japanese
invaded. After Japan's eventual defeat, the Dutch attempted to
reassert control over their former colony but the attempt was
unsuccessful, and Indonesian independence was proclaimed on 17
August 1945. Makian has been a part of the Republic of Indonesia
since that time. National independence and economic development
have now brought a huge number of changes to Makian.

Most important of these changes as far as the language is concerned
is a huge growth in schooling. All schooling is conducted in
Indonesian, and this has contributed to the increasing

'Malayicisation' of Taba. Increased communications over this time, particularly radio, and to a lesser extent television, have also contributed to the increasing impact of Malay on the language.

Traditionally, society was organised into endogamous patrilineal clans or *soan*. Today, however, the traditional *soan* no longer plays a very important role in Taba society and the old rules of endogamy are no longer enforced. On Makian today, intervillage (and thus inter- *soan*) marriage is common. Marriage with people from other Islamic ethnic groups is also widespread.

Such social changes are not confined to Makian. Similar social trends are at work throughout Indonesia, and perhaps especially so amongst the small social groups typical of indigenous language communities in eastern Indonesia.

Makian island is an active volcano with a long history of devastating eruptions. Verbeek (1908: 14) reports that there were eruptions in 1646, 1760, 1861-64, and 1890. The most recent eruption in 1988 resulted in the temporary evacuation of all the island's inhabitants, and this evacuation has meant that all contemporary Taba speakers, no matter where they live today, have all experienced substantial portions of their lives living in locations which are predominantly non-Taba speaking. Over the years, eruptions have led to widespread migration both from and to Makian island. Although the propensity for eruptions has continued to provide a motivation for Makian's inhabitants to settle elsewhere a countervailing motivation to return to the island, or to occupy land left vacant by those who have fled, is provided by the island's rich volcanic soils. Lucardie (1980) discusses Makianese migratory traditions, and, in a paper published not long before the most recent eruption, Lucardie (1983) examines the Indonesian government's transmigration scheme which was designed to encourage the Makianese to settle in Malifut on Halmahera island. This scheme was motivated by geological reports which predicted that a further major eruption was imminent.

Before the advent of government sponsored transmigration in the twentieth century, large communities of Makianese people had already moved elsewhere. They set up villages on nearby islands where they maintained their native language. This occurred, for example, in the Bacan community referred to above, where Makianese people emigrated after the 1890 eruption.

Makian island itself has been less affected by modernisation than other parts of Indonesia, even other parts of its less developed eastern provinces such as Maluku. Inducements to the population designed to encourage their transmigration to Malifut have included the withdrawal of all government services from Makian island, including government health clinics, schools, and other government offices such as police and military posts. While the local population has found the resources to fund local schools (and pay their teachers), money is scarce on Makian, and the economy is to a fair degree still a subsistence one.

4.   SPEECH BEHAVIOUR: RECENT CHANGES

Any sensible discussion of recent changes in speech behaviour of the Makianese people must take into account where they are currently living. Although I do not have good information about Taba speakers in all of the areas they have settled over recent years, I can talk to some extent about the situation in Malifut, Ternate, and on Makian island itself.

In Malifut, the Makianese are giving up their language. The transmigration area is not just home to Taba speakers, but also to speakers of a number of other languages. Most significantly, there is a sizeable community of speakers of Makian Luar, or Moi, the language of the western side of Makian island. These people came to Malifut as a result of the same transmigration programme that brought Taba speakers to the area. There is also a sizeable community of Pagu speakers in the area who lived here before the advent of transmigration.[1] In addition, there are quite a number of

---

[1]   At the time of writing, relations between the original inhabitants of the Malifut area and the Makianese immigrants are in a parlous state. Interethnic violence between Muslim and Christian communities that started in Ambon has spread to North Maluku and a particularly virulent outbreak of violence between the Muslim Makianese and the Christian

migants from a number of different parts of Indonesia, most notably South Sulawesi and Java. In this environment, then, it is hardly surprising that Taba speakers are failing to pass on their language fully to their children. Although the younger Makianese who are being brought up here understand the language reasonably well, they are themselves imperfect speakers at best. While older Makianese often still do use their language amongst themselves, Taba is clearly dying in Malifut.

In Ternate, the situation is similar to that just outlined above for Malifut, except perhaps that the language is in an even more marked state of decline. Ternate is a fairly large regional centre with a population drawn from an even wider catchment than that of Malifut. With the splitting of the former Maluku province into two provinces in October 1999, and the installation of Ternate as the capital of the new province of Maluku Utara (North Maluku), there will probably be an even greater influx of people from outside the region into Ternate. Already, intermarriage with people from different ethnic groups is becoming the norm rather than the exception. Although there are suburbs of Ternate such as Kampung Pisang which have predominantly Makianese communities, those children who do learn anything of the language while living here are generally even more imperfect speakers than those from Malifut.

While Taba speakers are generally proud of their ethnic identity as Makianese, the conception of ethnicity they hold does not appear to be dependent on the language they use to any significant degree. Taba speakers refer to the whole of Makian island as *Taba*, whether the eastern side where their language is spoken, or the western side where the speakers of Makian Luar live. The label Taba is somewhat ambiguous as to whether or not it refers to the east or to the whole island. Speakers of Makian Luar are generally perceived as *manusia Taba* 'Taba people', although they can be further subclassified as manusia *Taba lik* if anyone feels a strong need to disambiguate. It is thus easy to maintain one's identity as *manusia Taba*, particularly in Malifut where such a large community of Taba people reside,

---

Pagu took place in October 1999, leaving several people dead and many houses in ruins.

without an overwhelming need to maintain the language.[2] In both Malifut and Ternate, then, the language is clearly on its last legs.

On Makian island itself, the situation is more complicated, and most of the rest of this paper will be devoted to discussing the situation on Makian. Children on Makian are still brought up speaking the language at the moment, but more and more, they are being taught Malay alongside Taba from an early age. When adults address very young children, in fact, they tend to use more Malay than Taba, especially when issuing orders. Baby talk, as I have heard it being used, tends to be Malay rather than Taba. Although as they get older, people start speaking to children in Taba rather than Malay, it is clear that at the moment, children on Makian are being brought up to speak both languages at the same time. How long this is likely to continue into the future is a moot point.

Other aspects of language use on Makian are also clearly changing. Formal speeches are not generally made in Taba any more. This is something which has largely come about since the eruption. The current *kepala desa* 'village head' in Ngofakiaha village, for instance, always uses Indonesian when making public addresses, whether the audience is a Taba speaking one or not, although his predecessor before the eruption used to use Taba. At weddings and other significant community feasts, etc., while Taba is used during informal conversation, Malay is invariably used for the formal parts of the occasion. Presumably this behaviour has emerged at least partially as a response to the fact that more and more people are marrying others from different ethnic groups, but Malay is still used even when both marriage partners and most of their respective families are Makianese. During my residence on Makian, I only saw

---

[2] It is interesting to note that Makianese people I have spoken to who live in Jakarta profess that their children are being brought up to speak Taba as a first language alongside Indonesian. Presumably, the great distance of these people from their homeland and from sizeable communities of other Makianese means that they see using the language as a more important prerequisite for maintaining their ethnicity than do the people living alongside many other Makianese. Of course, it is hardly conceivable that these children who appear to be learning Taba in Jakarta will go on to teach their own children the language.

Taba being used on an official occasion once. This occurred when the Sultan of Ternate made a brief visit to Makian island before returning to Ternate during the afternoon and leaving behind his deputy, the *Jogugu Moluku Kie Raha*, a Makianese man who now resides in Ternate, as the sultan's representative for further festivities in the evening. The Jogugu made his speech to the assembled crowd in Taba. I assume he did this for affective reasons, in order to show his identification with the Makianese, although his social standing was way beyond that of most of his village dwelling audience.

All of the population of Makian aged older than about ten years have now spent significant periods of their lives in residence somewhere other than Makian. After the last eruption, the whole population of the island was evacuated and resettlement did not start to take place until about a year after the event. It is perhaps not surprising, then, that significant changes in people's speech behaviour have taken place.

5.   THE LANGUAGE ITSELF: STRUCTURAL CHANGE

One of the most obvious ways of seeing linguistic change in progress is to examine the speech of older and younger cohorts of speakers and to plot the differences between the ways in which they speak. The speech of older people can be seen as representative of earlier stages of a language while that of younger people might be seen as representative of the way in which the language is headed. All languages change, whether they are 'healthy' or not. In Taba, as in all languages, there is evidence that linguistic change is afoot: there are many characteristics of younger Taba speakers' speech that differ from that of their elders. Many of these changes are clearly the result of influence from the regional lingua franca of North Malukan Malay which, as we have seen, all contemporay speakers of Taba are also fluent in Malay.

Change due to contact with other languages is one of the most common types of change found in any language, whether it is dying or not, and we need to be able to find ways of distinguishing between change in healthy languages and change in dying languages. While much of the change that occurs in healthy languages bears a close resemblance to change that occurs in dying languages, change in dying languages is generally much more drastic and faster occurring than in healthy languages (see, e.g. Dorian, 1981 and Schmidt, 1985).

In this section of the paper, I intend to review just a few aspects of language change in Taba, dealing with a selection of different changes that are presently under way, each of which I believe can be explained in different ways, not all of them by any means diagnostic of language death. We will discuss a variety of borrowed grammatical words, the use of numeral classifiers, and a decline in the use of speech levels.

5.1. Borrowed 'grammatical words'

It has long been argued that languages tend to be resistant to borrowing grammatical function words, e.g. prepositions or conjunctions, etc. from other languages (see, e.g. Weinreich 1953: 34). The existence of many such borrowed forms would appear on the face of it to be evidence of a language in trouble. In contemporary Taba usage, there are in fact quite a large number of such function words in common use and we will examine a few of them here: the existential verb *ada* 'to exist', the conjunctions *dadi* 'so' (< Malay *jadi* 'to become') and *karna* 'because', and the preposition *untuk* 'for'. All of the examples included below have been taken from natural speech and forms which have been borrowed from Malay are all presented in bold type.

ada 'to exist'

This form is very commonly used by younger Taba speakers. Older speakers also use it from time to time. Its use in Taba is exemplified in (1) below, which is taken from a conversation in which the protagonists are discussing some plastic fishing baits that I had brought with me from Australia as a present.

(1) **Yang model** *ine...*   ***suntung...*** *ine*   ***ada***
     yang model   i-ne   suntung   i-ne   ada
     REL model   DEM-PROX   squid   DEM-PROX exist
     'This type here, 'squid', this one exists.'

One of the first things that is remarkable about the example given above is the very large number of Malay loans found throughout what is otherwise a stretch of Taba discourse. The only 'pure' Taba forms found here are in fact the demonstratives. The relativiser *yang*, the nouns *model* and *suntung*, as well as the existential verb *ada* are all borrowed from Malay. While on the face of it, the existence of such utterances in 'Taba' speech is disturbing, none of the Malay forms seen above should be viewed with alarm on their own. Taba has no relativiser of its own and the use of Malay *yang* here simply serves to focus on *model ine* 'this type' more closely than would otherwise be the case (in much the same way as it would be used in North Malukan Malay). The words *model* and *suntung* are both common nouns, and as such, can be expected to be highly 'borrowable' in situations of language contact. In this case, although there is a perfectly acceptable Taba alternative for *suntung* 'squid' in *saisuak*, the Malay form is probably used here because the speaker is referring to the kinds of fishing baits that are available in Ternate shops. If he had been seeking to buy one in Ternate he would have used Malay rather than Taba. Finally, although *ada* is one of the function words which might normally cause alarm, there is no existential verb in 'pure Taba', and in many cases it is just simpler to use the Malay word rather than come up with the circumlocutions that would be required if the speaker was going to stick with pure Taba such as 'they sell these there'.

dadi 'so' and *karna* 'because'

These two conjunctions/discourse connectors were clearly borrowed into Taba at different times. The Taba conjunction *dadi* 'so, thus' is obviously a rather early borrowing from Malay *jadi* 'become, thus' since the Taba form reflects Malay /j/ as /d/. The Taba phonological inventory has 15 inherited consonant phonemes and four further phonemes which have ben borrowed. Amongst the borrowed phonemes in contemporary Taba is /j/ which can be seen in words such as *jeregen* 'jerry can' borrowed ultimately from English but via Malay. *Dadi* was clearly borrowed very early from Malay since the non-native /j/ was nativised as Taba /d/ at a time when /j/ was still not a productive phoneme in the language as it has since become. Further evidence for the rather fully nativised Taba status of *dadi* can be seen from the fact that it also occurs as a verb meaning 'to become' in which case its Actor is cross-referenced by the same

person and number marking proclitics as are other verbs. In example
(2), which illustrates the use of the verb *dadi* 'to become' we can
again see just how common Malay loans (again given in bold) are in
normal Taba speech.

(2) *Ni*   **suka**   **ndadi**   **guru**
     ni   suka   n=dadi   guru
     3sg.POSS   desire   3sg=become   guru
     'He wants to become a teacher.'

Although *dadi* is a conjunction/discourse connector borrowed from
Malay, it can hardly be seen as evidence of incipient language death
because it has been used in the language for a very long time without
any major decline in the use of the language.

The conjunction *karna* 'because' appears to be a much later loan
than *dadi*. While *dadi* is commonly heard being used by people of all
ages, *karna* is much more commonly used by younger, rather than
older speakers. Its use is illustrated in (3).

(3) *Lomosi*   *layok*   **karna**   *lkiu*   **kwat**
     lomo=si   l=ha-yok   karna   l=kiu   kwat
     other=PL   3pl=ACT-cry   because   3pl=be.frightened   EMPH
     'Others were crying because they were very scared.'

Taba clause sequences are noteworthy for the fact that there is a very
strong preference for iconic ordering. When two clauses encode
temporally sequential events, the event which occurred first must be
reported first, followed by the event which came second. There is no
Taba conjunction analogous to 'after' in English or *sesudah* in
Indonesian which allow non-iconic ordering of clauses as in 'I went
to the shop after I had eaten lunch'. In Taba, one would have to say
the equivalent of 'I ate my lunch and then I went to the shop.' Purely
indigenous Taba likewise provides no conjunction that would allow
us to express a cause after the clause expressing the result of that
causing event. Without using *karna* in example (3) above, the
speaker would have been forced to say something along the lines of
'others were very scared so they cried'.

Again, although *karna* appears on the surface to be a suspicious borrowing since it is a grammatical function word, I would argue that it should not really be seen as evidence for the decline of the language since it is a form which has had no ready equivalent in indigenous Taba. Speakers clearly find it very useful to be able to order their clauses in a non-iconic way and it is hardly surprising that they have adopted this Malay form to allow them to achieve this end.

untuk 'for'

The final 'grammatical word' I wish to examine here is the beneficiary marking *untuk* 'for'. Like *karna* 'because', *untuk* 'for' is not widely used by the oldest speakers of the language but it is common amongst younger speakers. It is illustrated in (4) and (5).

(4) **Untuk** yak... masure hasole   lao   ne
     for   me   good all   baits   PROX
     'For me, all these baits are good.'

(5) Ndadi... ayol   **untuk**   on   lo   imin.
     ndadi   a=yol   untuk   on   lo   imin
     so   1pl.excl=collect for   eat   and   drink
     'So... they took (things) for eating and drinking.'

As with the case of *karna* 'because' discussed above, although we might at first suspect that the adoption of a preposition from Malay could be rather alarming in that it may be diagnostic of the drastic changes that so often take place in a language on the verge of extinction, closer examination of the place of *untuk* within the Taba system suggests that the situation may not be as bad as it first appears. As was the case with *karna*, Taba has no indigenous form that allows the introduction of a purely beneficial argument as *untuk* allows in (4). Using purely indigenous Taba linguistic resources, the exact nature of the benefit bestowed on someone must be spelled out in some detail in a resultative/purposive clause. To translate something such as 'I sang a song for her', one would have to use something like the equivalent of 'I sang a song so she could listen to it'; to translate 'I cooked a meal for her' one would have to say 'I cooked a meal so that she could eat it'. In some cases, it is possible to license an argument that can be construed as a beneficiary by means of a possessive construction, as in (6).

(6) *Mina   npe   Mado   ni   woya   do*
    Mina   n=pe   Mado   ni   woya   do
    Mina   3sg=make Mado   3sg.POSS   water   REAL
    'Mina's made Mado's drink./Mina's made a drink for Mado.'

In a number of Oceanic languages such as Saliba (Margetts 1999: 324-329) possessive morphology as in example (6) has been extended in meaning so that it may mark a purely beneficial NP. In Taba, however, possessive morphology can only be used if the possessor NP actually does end up with something in his/her possession. If Taba speakers had not all known Malay and had access to the Malay preposition *untuk* it is highly likely that any method for introducing beneficiaries into Taba grammar would have involved the extension of possessive morphology to fill this function as has been the case in Saliba and other languages. However, given the fact that Taba speakers do all know *untuk* and its functions, it is not really surprising that younger speakers have found it useful to adopt the form into their native language and save themselves the trouble of having to spell out the benefits of actions in such detail as they wouild otherwise have to. So again, while they have indeed adopted another word from a closed class by using *untuk*, this should not really be taken as evidence of incipient language death any more than the adoption of forms like *ada* 'to exist', *karna* 'because' or the now rather ancient adoption of *dadi* 'so' should be.

The same kind of explanation can be advanced for the use of *untuk* in (5), although here it has a resultative meaning rather than a benefactive marking one. Although Taba has a conjunction *de* that is often used to mark resultative clauses, it can only be used to mark finite resultative clauses where Actor oriented intransitive verbs are cross-referenced by proclitics agreeing in person and number with the Actor argument of the verb involved. In the example given above, *untuk* seems to have been used because the speaker did not want to have to refer to any particular Actor argument, and it probably seemed more appropriate to use *untuk* with which this constraint didn't apply.

5.2. The loss of speech levels by younger speakers:
Taba has a system of speech levels, somewhat reminiscent of the better known systems found in languages such as Javanese and

Balinese, albeit rather less elaborated than in these languages. The speech levels are named by Taba speakers using labels which have been borrowed from Malay: *alus* 'refined', *biasa* 'normal' and *kasar* 'coarse'. *Alus* forms should be used when talking to people older than oneself or when talking to people who are owed special respect for some other reason. *Biasa* forms should generally be used when speaking to those of the same age or younger while *kasar* forms are only countenanced when speakers intend to be rude to their addressees as when perhaps an adult chides an errant child. Some illustrative examples are given in Table 1 below.

Table 1:   Taba speech levels

alus	biasa	kasar	
jou	ole	—	'yes'
maledi	hamolam	—	'hungry'
matutin	hacarita	—	'to chat'
palihara	toanam	—	'to bury'
pasiar	taggil	—	'to walk'
mul ni asal	mot	botang	'to die'
babas	babas	bor	'to bite'
haloin	ahon	hajaweda	'to eat'
		hatuto	
		matuto	
kuda	kuda	burat	'black'
		piés	
—	hagah	hanata	'to steal'
—	kabot	kaletaj	'dirty'

One of the most remarkable things about the *alus* forms shown in Table 1 is that while it was certainly easy to collect the *alus* forms — there were many people who knew them and who were eager to make sure that I knew them as well — it was a very rare occurrence when I actually heard young Taba speakers use them when addressing their elders. It seems fairly clear that while a number of people (mostly older) still have an extensive knowledge of the *alus* forms in Taba, the younger Makianese are not learning them any more and that they are falling out of use.

It appears that the reasons for the decline of speech levels are directly related to the fact that Taba is no longer used for formal addresses on ceremonial occasions. Since the *alus* forms are generally used only by younger people as they address their elders, most young Taba speakers are no longer being exposed to the *alus* speech level in such a way that they are able to master its use any more: older people do not use this level when addressing the younger people around them, and younger Taba speakers only seem to use the most common *alus* forms any more. From what I have seen of life on Makian, it appears that in the past, people gradually gained a command of *alus* speech by listening to formal speeches in which older speakers who had developed a command of the genre were forced to use it by reason of the fact that there might be older people in the audience. When I heard the *Jogugu* speak at the festivities occasioned by the arrival of the sultan of Ternate on Makian his speech contained an efflorescence of *alus* language such as I had never witnessed on any other occasion. Since such events happen much less frequently than they did in the past, it is no wonder that younger Taba speakers are not learning how to use the genre nearly as well as their parents did.

5.3. The loss of distinctions in numeral classification
Taba has a rather elaborate system of numeral classifiers. When one wishes to count something, different forms of numbers are required depending on the nature of the thing that is being counted. There is a set of numeral roots which require extra morphemes that 'classify' the things being counted in different ways. These 'classifiers' may take the form of prefixes, proclitics, or independent words that occur before the numeral root itself. A listing of the numeral classifiers I know about is given in Table 2. Although I tried to determine all of the classifiers that are used in the language it is quite likely that some less frequent forms have not yet been encountered.

Table 2:   Taba numeral classifiers

- *p-*   default
- *ha=*   intervals of measurement,
              ordinal numbers ('first', 'second', etc.)
- *i-*   single animate
- *mat=*   more than one human
- *sis=*   from 2-9 animals
- *beit=*   mutiples of 10 animals
- *mot=*   small square flat thin things
- *goha*   things assembled together
- *wato*   small oblong shaped things
- *hola*   piece of wood / stick
- *luklik*   rolled up things
- *ai*   trees
- *awa*   stalks
- *ising*   'hand' (of bananas, etc.)
- *kop*   grains
- *boka*   skewer
- *coat*   bundle
- *lof*   armspan
- *tonat*   ten armspans
- *odo*   joints (of bamboo)
- *opa*   days before
- *opo*   days ahead

Example (7) shows how classifier-numeral collocations are formed with the default classifier *p-*, and the animal classifiers *i-* and *si-*.

(7)

a	*pso*	*plu*	*ptol*
	p-so	p-lu	p-tol
	CLASS-one	CLASS-two	CLASS-three
	'one	two	three
	(pieces of fruit, etc.)'		

b	iso	silhu	sithol
	i=so	sis=lu	sis=tol
	CLASS=one	CLASS=two	CLASS=three
	'one (animal)	two (animals)	three (animals)'

c   *ai   so   ai   lu   ai   tol*
    CLASS (tree) one CLASS(tree) two CLASS(tree)three
    'one tree   two trees   three trees'

As I found when trying to learn *alus* forms in Taba, when it came to classifiers, I found that older people knew more of these forms than did younger people. Since people knew that I was trying to learn *Taba asli* 'authentic Taba' (ironically, *asli* 'authentic' is another Malay loan) I was sometimes coached by older Makianese people on what were the appropriate classifiers to be used when counting certain kinds of things, even when younger speakers were no longer using the forms. The system of Taba measurements *lof* 'armspan', etc. is giving way to modern metrical measurements; the traditional method for specifying ordinal numbers using the classifier *ha=* is being replaced by the Malay ordinals *pertama* 'first', *kedua* 'second', etc.; the less common classifiers such as *hola* 'long thin things' and *mot* 'small square flat thin things' have simply been replaced by the default classifier *p-*. On one occasion, for instance, when I was buying some envelopes in a local store and asked for *amplop mot oenam* 'envelopes - small flat thin things - six' I was corrected by the young woman working in the store and told to say *amplop p-oenam* 'envelopes - default - six'. An elderly Makianese man who witnessed the exchange in turn chided the young woman for not being able to speak Taba 'properly' any more and berated her for having less skills in the language than the *balanda-si* 'foreigner'.

6.   IS TABA THREATENED WITH EXTINCTION AND IN WHAT WAY?

The potential for the extinction of Taba is not evenly distributed amongst all the Taba speaking communities of North Maluku. It seems fairly clear that within a couple of generations, there will be hardly anyone speaking the language in places like Malifut or Ternate. The situation on Makian island itself is somewhat less clear. Assuming that there are no further earthquakes in the immediate future that will disrupt the community more than it has already been disrupted, however, the prognosis for the survival of the language many generations into the future in anything like its present form is not all that great, even if the language continues to be spoken in some altered form for some time to come.

If any one change in the grammars of younger Taba speakers is to be picked out as an example that might illustrate the potential for imminent language death in Taba, it would have to be the collapse of the classifier system which appears to be under way at present. Changes in the way classifier and counting systems are used in other eastern Indonesian languages have also been reported in the literature, although different languages systems seem to be afected in different ways. In Kambera (Klamer 1998:138), classifier use is obligatory when using lower numerals except when counting out *kilu*, a recent borrowing from Indonesian meaning 'kilogram' or 'kilometre'.

The loss of speech level distinctions which is also taking place, while cause for concern, is not quite so alarming. Other cases of the death of particular formal genres of what are otherwise quite healthy eastern Indonesian languages have been documented (see Kuiper's 1998 documentation of the loss of 'angry speech' genres from Wejewa, a language spoken in western Sumba, for example).

While changes such as those to the classifier system and in the use of speech levels are interesting in their own right, the changes I wish to spend some more time exploring here are those involving the adoption of grammatical words from Malay. I would contend that the changes mentioned above (as well as others that I have not yet addressed in detail) suggest that Taba is gradually remodelling itself to conform to discourse and grammatical structures found in Malay. Such typological remodelling has been discussed in more general terms in a recent paper by Ross (1999) on what he calls 'metatypy', and I would now like to review some of his findings.

Ross (1999) defines metatypy as follows:

> **Metatypy.** The change in morphosyntactic type which a language undergoes as a result of its speakers' bilingualism in another language. Usually, the language undergoing metatypy (the *modified language*) is *emblematic* of its speakers' identity, whilst the language which provides the *metatypic model* is an

inter-community language. Speakers of the modified language form a sufficiently tight-knit community to be well aware of their separate identity and of their language as a marker of that identity, but some bilingual speakers, at least, use the inter-community language so extensively that they are more at home in it than in the emblematic language of the community.

Metatypy, if taken to its extreme, results in emblematic languages completely adopting the grammatical structures of the languages supplying their metatypic models. Such extreme cases of metatypy are exceedingly rare. One possible example is the case of the Marathi dialect spoken in Kupwar village as reported by Gumperz and Wilson (1971). Marathi, an Indo-European language, appears to have remodelled its grammar to conform with the local variant of Kannada, a Dravidian language. This remodelling of Marathi has ben so spectacular that Gumperz and Wilson maintain that the grammars of the languages are identical, and that translation between the two languages need only involve substituting the particular forms of otherwise equivalent lexemes and grammatical formatives. At less extreme levels, though, metatypy is widespread. Ross gives seventeen examples of documented metatypy from all around the world. Many more examples could have been added to his list. While I would not want to argue that Taba is undergoing metatypy to anywhere near the extent that Kupwar Marathi has undergone it, (at least not yet), the Taba situation looks very similar to that encountered in languages where metatypy has not been so all encompassing.

Amongst Taba speakers who live on Makian island, the kinds of social conditions that give rise to metatypy are clearly in place. First, virtually all speakers of Taba are bilingual in both Taba and Malay. The Taba language is certainly emblematic of Makianese identity, and Malay is certainly the most important inter-community language spoken in the region. Furthermore, many Makianese do appear to be more at home in Malay, at least in certain contexts, than they are in Taba.

Ross describes what he sees as the typical sequence of changes which take place in languages undergoing metatypy. Such a sequence of changes is shown below.

Sequence of changes in metatypy:

lexical calquing
borrowing of discourse markers and conjunctions
metatypy and grammatical calquing

Alongside calquing, Ross also discusses literal translation of common idioms from the metatypic model language into the laguage undergoing metatypy. Examples of both these sorts are found in Taba, although perhaps to a lesser extent than Ross suggests they should be. A few examples are given in Table 3.

Table 3:   **Some lexical calques and common idioms from NMM found in Taba**

Taba	NMM	English
otik unak	*kasi tau*	'teach/tell' (lit. 'give know')
otik tongo	*kasi tinggal*	'leave behind' (lit. 'give stay')
pe moi	*bikin malu*	'make ashamed'
palo mot	*satenga mati*	exclamation of displeasure (lit. 'half dead')

While there may not be a huge number of lexical calques based on Malay in Taba, we have already seen a number of examples of borrowed discourse markers and conjunctions. We also saw one example of a borrowed preposition. The discourse markers and conjunctions discussed so far were only illustrative, since a number of other examples could have been given. Some more of these are listed, along with those already discussed, in Table 4.

Table 4:   **More discourse markers and conjunctions borrowed from NMM into Taba**

Taba	NMM	English	Word class
dadi	*jadi*	'so, thus'	discourse marker/conjunction
karna	*karna*	'because'	discourse marker/conjunction
turus	*turus*	'then'	discourse marker/conjunction
tapi	*tapi*	'but'	discourse marker/conjunction
supaya	*supaya*	'in order that/ eventually'	discourse marker/conjunction

Although Ross does not describe how a language might move from the borrowing of discourse markers and conjunctions to full scale metatypy in great detail, he does give some indications about how this process might come about. The basic idea he puts forward is that metatypic remodelling works its way from larger to smaller linguistic structures, so that characteristic discourse patterns would be the first to get affected, and that change would occur on successively smaller levels of organisation until eventually something like the Kupwar Marathi situation, where morpheme to morpheme intertranslatability is possible, might result.

The borrowing of a discourse connector or conjunction such as *karna* 'because' into Taba allowed a reordering of clauses within a discourse according to a model available to speakers of Malay but not previously available to Taba speakers. According to Ross, the way such forms would be adopted into the language would work roughly as follows. Taba speakers, having in mind the discourse structures available to them as speakers of Malay, would begin by expressing something that happened because of something else, intending to add a reference to the cause once they had finished expressing the result. Having expressed the result first, and lacking any indigenous Taba mechanism for explicitly relating this result to a following cause, they would then join the two clauses together with *karna*, knowing that their interlocutors would have no trouble understanding them because they too are presumed to be speakers of Malay. Although this might be the original motivation for using such forms when they first appear, this kind of usage would eventually become part of a new conventional discourse strategy in the target language. It is pretty clar that using *karna* has already become highly conventionalised in contemporary Taba.

A conjunction like *karna* 'because', then, which allows non-iconic ordering of result and cause clauses, might well be expected to have been borrowed into other Indonesian languages which lack any overt mechanism for conjoining clauses of these sorts. It is noteworthy that in fact the form *karena* in Malay was itself borrowed from Sanskrit around the seventh century AD (Adelaar 1998:17). As well as occurring in Taba, *karna* is also found in a variety of other languages from eastern Indonesia. It seems to be fairly widespread in languages of North Maluku and Sulawesi, e.g. Papuan Tidore from North

Maluku (van Staden 1998), Austronesian Pendau from North Central Sulawesi (Quick In preparation) and Austronesian Tukang Besi from southeast Sulawesi (Donohue 1995). It does not seem to occur as a borrowing in languages from the Sumba-Flores-Timor area or from Central Maluku very often, but all of the languages I have checked for information in this area already have indigenous conjunctions meaning 'because'.

It seems reasonable to suspect that once a language has borrowed a number of discourse connectors and conjunctions which then allow metatypic transference of characteristic discourse organisation, (or greater clause to clause intertranslatability), the next most vulnerable part of a language for metatypic remodelling might involve the outer parts of a clause, such as those concepts which are typically encoded in adjunct adpositional phrases. One would expect that these might be susceptible to metatypic influence before, for example, the core elements of a clause would be affected. This would seem particularly likely to occur, if, as we saw was the case with borrowed *untuk* 'for' in Taba, the concept encoded by the adposition concerned could not otherwise be encoded in the borrowing language. Borrowed adpositions, then, might be seen as one further step along Ross' progression towards full scale metatypy, which we might expect to occur after a stock of discourse connectors and conjunctions had been borrowed.

Like *karna* 'because', *untuk* 'for' has also been borrowed into a number of languages from eastern Indonesia. Again, it seems to have been mostly borrowed into languages which do not have an indigenous form that fulfils its function. The languages concerned are not always the same ones which have borrowed *karna*. For instance, although instances of *untuk* do turn up in Pendau texts, *untuk* seems to be used only with its purpose marking function. It is noteworthy that Pendau has productive applicativisation of verbs which can be used to mark beneficiaries. Keo, from Flores (Baird In preparation) has not borrowed *karna* from Malay, having an indigenous conjunction meaning 'beacause', but *utu* 'for' is used extensively to mark beneficiaries. Keo, unlike Pendau, has no way of marking beneficiaries using purely indigenous linguistic resources.

The sample of languages I looked at to find examples of borrowed *karna* and *untuk* is by no mean a scientificaly random one, consisting as it does basically of those eastern Indonesian languages for which I had a description sitting on my bookshelf, or languages which are known well by people I was able to discuss them with. There are some quite remarkable generalisations that can be made about this sample, however. Out of the sample, every single language which did not have an indigenous form meaning 'because' has borrowed *karna* from Malay, and every language which lacked an indigenous mechanism for marking beneficiaries has also borrowed *untuk*.

It seems that we have reasonably good evidence, then, that Taba is at present undergoing metatypy, redesigning parts of its discourse organisation and grammar so that it starts to take on more of the typological features that are characteristic of Malay. There is also evidence that this is a process being undergone not just by Taba, but also by a very large number of other languages in eastern Indonesia.

We have already noted that metatypy is widespread right across the world, so the final question I wish to ask here is: why should I be talking about metatypy in the context of a forum on language endangerment and language death?

I have for quite a while wondered whether or not the kind of evidence I have been presenting here is indicative of imminent language death for Taba. I believe that even though Taba is certainly a language under stress, there is still a reasonably good chance that there will be a community of Taba speakers for quite a while into the future. I think that this is probably also true of at least a large number of the other indigenous languages found across eastern Indonesia.

It doesn't seem to me that most of these languages are under immediate threat of extinction in any real sense that the speakers of these languages would recognise (although speakers do recognise that their languages are being 'corrupted' by the onslaught of Malay). While no-one can say with any certainty whether all of these languages are in the process of dying, it is absolutely clear that the typological variety that used to exist in eastern Indonesia is not just under threat, but that it is being rapidly killed off.

Metatypy has been well documented all over the world for a very long time. However, the kind of mass metatypy we have been looking at here, with hundreds of languages converging on the same metatypic model is probably unprecedented until recent times. Even if minority languages do not die out at the rates of the most alarming predictions that have sometimes been made, the typological variety found in languages around the world is certainly being rapidly diminished. Even if people continue to speak minority languages, the need to document them as soon as possible is undiminished as far as the linguistic typologist is concerned, if one of the aims of linguistic typology is to maintain a record of the variety of linguistic structures that exists in the languages of the world at present.

7. EPILOGUE

The fieldwork that was done to gather the data used in this paper was conducted over a period of about a year in 1993-1994 and in 1995. From about the beginning of 1998, the Malukus in Indonesia have been the scene of ongoing intercommunity violence. Christian and Muslim communities who used to happily coexist have started fighting each other; often these fights have been exacerbated by people from outside the region who have come to join in the fighting. Thousands of people have been killed in the violence and many more (over half a million by some estimates) have become refugees and fled their traditional homes.

While the situation with respect to language endangerment which has been outlined in this paper up until now reflects fairly closely what I believe the situation to have been until about the beginning of 1998, the prospects for the survival of local languages in much of Maluku have deteriorated quite sharply since then. The situation for Taba itself is probably not greatly changed from what I have outlined, since there is a relatively large community of Taba speakers who live on exclusively Muslim Makian island where there has been little or no fighting. However, the situation in other areas is far worse. In some cases it appears that entire comunities who once spoke some of the smaller languages from Halmahera such as Pagu, for example, have fled. Aside from the personal devastation suffered by the people involved, it looks like the prospects for any kind of survival for languages like Pagu are dim. The present situation in Maluku is probably far worse than it was when my research was done.

REFERENCES

Adelaar, K. Alexander 1998. Malay: a short history. *South Pacific Journal of Psychology*, 10/1, Asia-Pacific Language Research Special Issue, 14-24.

Andaya, Leonard Y. 1993. *The world of Maluku: Eastern Indonesia in the early modern period.* Honolulu: University of Hawaii Press.

Baird, Louise In preparation. *The Keo language of Flores.* PhD thesis: Austalian National University, Canberra.

Donohue, Mark 1995. *The Tukang Besi language of Southeast Sulawesi.* PhD thesis: Austalian National University, Canberra.

Dorian, Nancy C. 1981. *Language death. The life cycle of a Scottish Gaelic dialect.* Philadelphia: University of Pennsylvania Press.

Fraassen, Chris F. 1981. Historical introduction. In Katrien Polman, (ed.) *The North Moluccas: an annotated bibliography.* KITLV Bibliographic Series 11, 1-38. The Hague: Martinus Nijhoff.

Gumperz, John J. & Robert Wilson 1971. Convergence and creolization: a case from the Indo-Aryan/Dravidian border. In Dell Hymes (ed.) *Pidginization and Creolization of Languages*, 151-168. Cambridge: Cambridge University Press.

Klamer, Marian 1988. *A Grammar of Kambera.* Berlin & New York: Mouton de Gruyter.

Kuipers, Joel C. 1998. *Language, Identity, and Marginality in Indonesia: The changing nature of ritual speech on the island of Sumba.* Studies in the Social and Cultural Foundations of Language 18. Cambridge: Cambridge University Press

Lucardie, G.R.E. 1980. The Makianese: preliminary remarks on the anthropological study of migration-oriented people in the Moluccas. In E.K.M. Masinambow (ed.) *Halmahera dan Raja Ampat: Konsep dan strategi penelitan*, 347-374. Jakarta: LEKNAS LIPI.

_____ 1983. The geographical mobility of the Makianese: migratory traditions and resettlement problems. In E.K.M. Masinambow (ed.) *Halmahera dan Raja Ampat sebagai kesatuan mejemul: studi-studi terhadap suatu daerah transisi*, 333-345. Jakarta: LEKNAS LIPI.

Margetts, Anna 1999. *Valence and Transitivity in Saliba: An Oceanic language of Papua New Guinea.* PhD thesis: Katholieke Universiteit Njimegen.

Quick, Philip In preparation. *A grammar of the Pendau language.* PhD thesis. Austalian National University, Canberra.

Ross, Malcolm 1999. *Exploring metatypy: how does contact-induced typological change come about?* Paper presented to the Annual Meeting of the Australian Linguistics Society, Perth.

Sasse, Hans-Jürgen 1992. Theory of language death. In Matthias Brenzinger (ed.) *Language death: Factual and theoretical explorations with special reference to East Africa*, 7-30. Berlin & New York: Mouton de Gruyter.

Schmidt, Annette 1985. *Young people's Dyirbal: an example of language death from Australia.* Cambridge: Cambridge University Press.

Weinreich, Uriel 1953. *Languages in Contact: Findings and Problems.* The Hague: Mouton.

Chapter 10

Language Obsolescence: Progress or Decay?
The emergence of new grammatical categories in
'language death'

Alexandra Y. Aikhenvald
La Trobe University

1. THE PROBLEM

The difference between language change in 'healthy' and in endangered or obsolescent languages very often lies not in the *sorts* of change, which are typically the same (Campbell and Munztel 1989). Rather, it lies in the *quantity* of change, and in the *speed* with which the obsolescent language changes. As Schmidt (1985: 213) pointed out, "one distinguishing feature of the Dyirbal death situation is that vast amounts of change are compressed into a short timespan of about 25 years".

It is often taken for granted that change in an obsolescent language implies just loss or reduction of categories. There are, however, a number of important exceptions to these trends. Obsolescent languages can be innovative in that they develop new categories and new terms within already existing categories.

In my short case-study I show that an obsolescent language may enrich its morphology in a number of ways. These include loan-translation from another, dominant, language, or reanalysis of some already existing category. Examples from Tariana are discussed in Section 2. The last section contains a brief summary.

144

2.   MORPHOLOGICAL ENRICHMENT IN TARIANA

2.1 Tariana and the linguistic situation in the Vaupés area

Tariana is a highly endangered North Arawak language spoken in two villages by around 100 people in the linguistic area of the Vaupés, dominated by East-Tucano languages.[1] This linguistic area is known for its rampant multilingualism due to exogamy and the ensuing one-way diffusion of structural patterns from East-Tucano into other languages (Tariana and Makú — see Aikhenvald 1996, 1999a, Sorensen 1967/1972, Jackson 1974, 1983). The area of Brazilian Vaupés is a culturally homogenous area where multilingualism is a norm. However, this cultural norm is endangered, and it is in a rather advanced state of obsolescence, accompanied by language attrition. The traditional multilingualism in the Vaupés area is accompanied by a very strong inhibition against language mixing viewed in terms of lexical loans. Thus, in spite of striking structural similarity between Tariana and genetically unrelated East-Tucano languages, there are almost no lexical loans between these. Tariana is higly polysynthetic, and it combines head-marking properties inherited from the Arawak protolanguage and dependent-marking properties diffused through areal contacts with East-Tucano languages.

---

[1]   This paper is based on data obtained during fieldwork on North Arawak and East Tucano languages of the Upper Rio Negro, Brazil, in 1991-1999. My text corpus of Tariana consists of appr. 1200 pages (including 200 stories of different genres). I am grateful to all my teachers of Tariana — Cândido, Américo, Batista, Leonardo, José, Jovino, Graciliano, and Olívia Brito (Tariana), and all the inhabitants of the villages of Santa Rosa and Periquitos — and of East-Tucano languages — the late Tiago Cardoso (Desano, Piratapuya) and Alfredo Fontes (Tucano). I am very thankful to R. M.W. Dixon for useful discussion and comments. My warmest thanks go to Lenita and Elias Coelho without whose help this work would have been impossible.
Abbreviations: AFF - derivational affix; ANT - anterior; AUG - augmentative; COMPL - completive; EXIST - existential; INFR - inferred; LOC - locative; MASC - masculine; NEG - negative; nf - nonfeminine; NOM - nominaliser; OBJ - object case; PL - plural; PRES - present; REC.P. - recent past; REL - relative; REM.P. - remote past; REPR - reported; SG - singular; VIS - visual

The basic rule of language choice throughout the Vaupés area is that one should speak the interlocutor's own language. Descent is strictly patrilineal, and consequently, one identifies with one's father's language. According to the language 'etiquette' of the area, one is supposed to speak the language one identifies with — that is, one's father's language — to one's siblings, father and all his relatives, and mother's language to one's mother and her relatives. However, during past decades the traditional language transmission in the Brazilian Vaupés has been affected by a number of factors. When Salesian missionaries established in the area in the early 1920s, they imposed Western-style schooling on the Indians, forcing children into boarding schools where they were made to speak just one language of the area, Tucano. Salesians aimed at 'civilising' Indians. This implied not only making them into 'good Christians'. Salesians also used to consider traditional multilingualism of the area a 'pagan' habit, and strived to make Indians monolingual 'like other civilised people in the world'. The Tucano language was chosen because it was, numerically, the majority language. Salesian missionaries also practiced forcible relocation of Indian settlements closer to mission centres — where the Indians could be more easily controlled — and amalgamation of different settlements, eliminating the traditional longhouse system and introducing European-style nuclear family houses. Another reason for the disintegration of traditional multilingualism was a break-down of traditional father-child interaction: with the need for cash-flow, all the able-bodied men would go off to work for Brazilians — such as rubber, tree-sap ('sorva'), and gold-mining — and as the result children would have a considerably reduced degree of exposure to their father's language. This resulted in the spread of Tucano, and, to a lesser extent, of other East-Tucano languages, to the detriment of Tariana.

Tariana is an obsolescent language. It is not being learnt by children. The younger generation of Tariana speakers prefer to use Tucano when speaking among themselves or to their wives. They consistently use Tariana only when speaking to the members of their father's families. A number of phenomena discernible as due to language attrition can be pointed out (see the list in Aikhenvald 1996). These include obsolescence of grammatical categories not found in Tucano, e.g. morphological reflexive-reciprocal derivation, aspect markers, and spread of Tucano-like syntactic devices, e.g. discourse organisation, introductory and resumptive phrases, and clause chaining strategies (with the predicate of subordinate clause in participle form). Lexical obsolescence and loss differ from one speaker to another. Younger speakers have difficulties in remembering kinship terms, especially the suppletive and semi-suppletive vocative forms

Morphological enrichment of the obsolescent Tariana spoken by younger generation goes along two lines. Creation of new morphemes by loan-translation from Tucano, now a dominant language, is discussed in section 2.2. In section 2.3 I discuss the process of 'grammatical accommodation'. The creation of new terms in an already existing system of evidentials is dealt with in section 2.4.

2.2   Loan translation from Tucano as a source of morphological enrichment

Similarly to other genetically related North Arawak languages of the area, Tariana has productive verb serialisation (Aikhenvald 1999b) and incipient verb compounding. In contrast, verb compounding is very productive in East-Tucano languages — where it yields aspect markers, valency changing markers and markers of Aktionsart — whereas verb serialisation is almost nonexistent. Verb compounds in Tariana and in East-Tucano languages show striking similarity in all respects but productivity.

Verb compounding in Tariana appears to be expanding, and to involve more and more verbs as the result of grammatical calquing (loan translations). Verb roots get spontaneously used as second components of verb compounds where they follow the fully inflected verb; they subsequently acquire Aktionsart meanings. The loss of prefixes follows the general tendency to lose non-Tucano categories from Tariana and to conform to a general suffixing tendency of the Tucano type.

An example of such creation is the way *-yena* 'little by little' was spontaneously used by my consultants, as a loan translation of Tucano - *tiha* 'do little by little'. Compare (1) and (2).

Tariana
(1)   emite   di-hɲa-yena-naka
      child   3sgnf-eat-LITTLE.BY.LITTLE-PRES.VIS
      'The child is eating little by little.'

Tucano
(2)   ba'ã tiha-mi
      eat-DO.LITTLE.BY.LITTLE-3sg:masc:PRES.VIS
      '(The child) is eating little by little.'

After this enclitic was used once, it was picked up by other speakers, and started being used by most of them[2] in a way completely parallel to Tucano *-tiha* as a marker of small extent of action. The corresponding verb *-yena* 'pass, go by' is used by all generations. Parallel grammaticalisation patterns for the development of this marker are not found in other Arawak languages of the region.

It should be noted that the process of creating new morphemes via calquing must have been taking place long before Tariana became obsolescent. The Tariana spoken by less innovative representatives of the older generation contains a number of morphemes which arose as the result of reanalysis of verb sequences containing verbs such as *-sita* 'manage; be able to' and *whyume* 'be last' — this reanalysis resulted in the creation of aspect (*-sita* 'completive'*)* and switch-reference *(- whyume* 'after: same.subject') markers. This process is a part of the convergence of Tariana towards East-Tucano structures, a process which is typical of intensive areal diffusion, thus helping to fill in the gaps arising from structural differences between Tariana and East-Tucano

---

[2]   Some younger speakers tend to be more traditional than others; in this case the term 'younger speakers' is an approximation. Similarly, representatives of the older generation differ in how archaic their Tariana is.

verb structure and to express categories absent from Arawak but important in Tucano — e.g. aspect and switch-reference.

However, the process of obsolescence — whereby Tucano, and not Tariana, is in actual fact the main everyday language for younger people — has led to 'speeding up' of calquing and thus creating 'new morphemes'. This spontaneous process of creating new verbal Aktionsart-like morphemes as the result of loan translations makes these into what is virtually an open class, thus making Tariana verbal morphology more and more complex.

2.3 Grammatical accommodation

It would be wrong to say that Tariana has absolutely no loans from Tucano or any other neighbouring language (see discussion and some examples in Aikhenvald 1999c). Tucano influence on Tariana involves mostly calquing of patterns, sometimes accompanied by grammatical accommodation, that is, morphosyntactic 'deployment of a native morpheme on the model of the syntactic function of a phonetically similar morpheme in the diffusing language' (Watkins Forthcoming) (that is, the language which is the source of diffusion). This was illustrated by Watkins for the possible extension of the native morpheme -ske- in Ionic Greek to mark iterative imperfective under the influence of the morpheme with the same shape in Hittite and Luvian.

Tucano and other East-Tucano languages use -ya as a marker of imperative. Tariana has a phonologically similar morpheme -ya 'emphatic' which is used on imperative verbs. Similarly, Tucano has the marker -ri used for commands with a tinge of a 'warning' (e.g. 'Make sure you don't fall!'). Tariana has a relativiser ri used in a wide-variety of functions which is also used in commands, with a similar meaning; this morpheme goes back to Proto-Arawak.

'Grammatical accommodation' of this sort can be explained by the fact that the native morphemes which undergo extension under Tucano influence do not sound as foreign, and so their existence does not go against the prohibition against borrowing and 'language mixing'.

2.4   Reanalysis and creation of a series of new evidentials

Tariana has a fully grammatical system of evidentials. (cf. discussion of Tuyuca by Barnes 1984 and Malone 1988); similar to Tucano, there are visual, nonvisual sensory, inferred and reported evidentials. The situation 'The dog bit a man' can be described in the following four ways depending on how the speaker learnt about this. (3) will be used if they saw this happen. If they just heard a noise, (4) would be used, while (5) would be appropriate if all they had seen was a man with a wound (inferring that he must have been bitten); (6) would be used if they got the information from somebody else. Omitting an evidential results in an ungrammatical sentence.

(3)   tʃinu   nihwã-ka   di-na
      dog   3sgnf+bite-REC.P.VIS 3sgnf-OBJ
      'The dog bit him (we have seen it).'

4)   tʃinu   nihwã-mahka   di-na
      dog   3sgnf+bite-REC.P.NON.VIS 3sgnf-OBJ
      'The dog bit him (we have heard the noise).'

(5)   tʃinu   nihwã-sika   di-na
      dog   3sgnf+bite-REC.P.INFR 3sgnf-OBJ
      'The dog (apparently) bit him (he has a wound).'

(6)   tʃinu   nihwã-pidaka   di-na
      dog   3sgnf+bite-REC.P.REPR 3sgnf-OBJ
      'The dog bit him' (someone has told me).'

Visual, nonvisual and reported evidentials distinguish present, recent past and remote past, while inferred does not have a present specification. This is perfectly understandable: an inference has to be made post factum, based on something that has occurred previously, and thus is not compatible with present. Tucano has the same restriction. Both in Tucano and in Tariana the inferred evidential is used when inference is based on the direct observation of the results and/or on a common sense assumption.

A new series of evidential markers is also being developed in Tariana as the result of reanalysis of an erstwhile combination of the anterior aspect marker -*nhi* and visual evidentials.

The anterior aspect marker -*nhi* described an action (a process or a state) which started before the time-frame of the narrative, or the speech act, and continues to be relevant, thus setting the scene for the narrative. In (7) — the beginning of a story about the origins of the night — -*nhi* is used to set the scene. Previously, before the story started, there was no night; and as the result of this — within the time-frame of the story established by the remote past reported — people could not get any rest.

(7) ehkwapi   di-keɲá-ɾi-se   de:pi sede-pidana
     day,world 3sgnf-start-REL-LOC night NEG.EXIST-REM.P.REP

    <u>di-yã-nhi</u>   ke: ɾi-mia-pidana   aɾia
    3sgnf-stay-ANT   moon/sun-ONLY-REM.P.REP   EXIST

    <u>di-ɲa-nhi</u>   kayu-maka   ãtʃa   ka:-pidana
    3sgnf-stay-ANT   thus-AFF   man:PL like.that-REM.P.REP

    nehpani   nema-niki
    3pl-work   3pl+stay-COMPL

'In the beginning of the world there had been no night, there had been only moon/sun, and thus people stayed working just like that.'

Unlike other aspectual markers, when -*nhi* does cooccur with recent past and remote past visual evidentials, it forms non-compositional combinations -*nihka* (from -*nhi-ka*) and -*nhina* or -*nihna* (from -*nhi-na*). These are used to confirm the action, process or state for which 'visual' evidence is available, as in (8), from a story about a man who went fishing and saw a huge catfish enter the weir. He has seen the fish, and reported this to his wife as (8).

(8) katu-nihka   dihe-niki   me:puku-se
     piraiba-ANT+REC.P.VIS   3sgnf-enter-COMPL weir-LOC
     'A catfish has indeed entered the weir.'

There is evidence in favour of *-nhi* 'anterior' and *-nhi-* in *-nhina* and in *-nihka* becoming different morphemes. In some narratives, usually produced by younger speakers, *-nhi* and *-nhina* can cooccur in one clause with their different meanings. Example (9) comes from a story about a man who did not come back from the jungle; his children went to look for him and found his gun and his faeces. This was enough for them to confirm that somebody had previosly done something bad to him (this is why anterior is used). The marker *-nihka* goes onto the first component of a serial verb construction (in square brackets), while the anterior *-nhi* goes onto the last component.

(9)   wha-niri-nuku   [ma:tʃi-pu-nihka
      1pl+parent-MASC-REM.P.REP   bad-AUG-ANT+REC.P.VIS

      na-ni-nhi]
      2pl-do-ANT
      'They have indeed done something bad to our father (and we will do something about it).'

Anterior *-nhi* and *-nhina* or *-nihka* can never cooccur on one simple predicate; this shows that their 'split' as different morphemes is an incipient phenomenon. Thus, *-nihka* and *-nhina* have started to be used as a separate set of 'inferred evidentials', whereby the source of statement is based on the visually acquired results of an action. The other inferred term then tends to be employed to refer to inference based on information acquired otherwise than visually and/or by common sense. Similarly to the other inferred term — illustrated in (5) — the second inferred term has no present tense.

The 'second inferred' *-nihka* (anterior+recent past visual) and *-nhina* (anterior+remote past visual) in Tariana display a semantic similarity to the analytic 'confirmation construction' in Tucano languages (as my consultants pointed out to me). In Tucano, this construction involves a nominalisation (often marked with Ø or by a suprasegmental) and the auxiliary *nií* 'do' with any visual evidential specification (see West 1980: 75-76; Ramirez 1997: 140-1; 291-2), and is used when the speaker's statement is based on having seen the result of the action and not necessarily the actual thing happening, as in (10).

(10) Peduru   uí   niî-mi
      Pedro   be.afraid+NOM   be-PRES.VIS
      'Pedro is scared (I can see he is pale because he is afraid).'

Unlike Tariana, the Tucano *niî* construction does not have any restriction on tense — as shown in (10). It is possible that Tariana is developing a new inferred evidential specification with no present tense as a result of partial grammatical accommodation — that is, that *-nhi* in Tariana - *nihka* and *-nhina* develops some functional similarity with the Tucano *niî* due to their phonetic similarity (see section 2.3).

3. SUMMARY

In the discussion above I showed (a) how grammaticalisation can be 'sped up' by calquing as the result of intensive language contact and language obsolescence (section 2.2), (b) how 'grammatical accommodation' can be an alternative to borrowing a morpheme in a situation where lexical borrowings are not acceptable, and (c) how reanalysis — possibly accompanied by 'grammatical accommodation' — may result in the creation of a new term in an already existing grammatical system.

That is, in the case of intensive areal diffusion language obsolescence may go together with some gain, rather than with uniform loss, of grammatical categories and mechanisms — cf. the discussion in Dorian (1999). Similar phenomena of grammatical enrichment due to reanalysis have been described for other parts of the world. Dal Negro (1998) described how in a Walser German dialect in Italy an entirely new set of verbal cross-referencing emerged as the result of the reanalysis of post-verbal clitic pronouns within the verb paradigm. Young people's Dyirbal developed a new morpheme out of a combination of the antipassive allomorph *-lay* with purposive *-gu,* with a new function of purposive clause conjunction (Schmidt 1985: 116). Along similar lines, Pensalifini

(1999) demonstrated how speakers of Jingulu, an Australian language, appear to have developed focus-marking functions for erstwhile nominal case markers.

These facts provide new insights into the fate of morphological complexity in language attrition. Different processes are expected to operate depending on language attitudes — such as a cultural inhibition against lexical loans in the Vaupés area, areal diffusion, and the degree of language attrition itself.

REFERENCES

Aikhenvald, Alexandra Y. 1996. Areal diffusion in North-West Amazonia: the case of Tariana. *Anthropological Linguistics* 38: 73-116.

_____ 1999a. Areal diffusion and language contact in the Içana-Vaupés basin, North West Amazonia. In R.M.W. Dixon & Alexandra Y. Aikhenvald (eds) *The Amazonian Languages,* 385-415. Cambridge: Cambridge University Press.

_____ 1999b. Serial verb constructions and verb compounding: evidence from Tariana (North Arawak). *Studies in Language* 23/3. 479-508.

_____ 1999c. *Tariana Texts and Cultural Context.* Munich: Lincom Europa.

Barnes, Jean 1984. Evidentials in the Tuyuca Verb. *International Journal of American Linguistics* 50: 255-271.

Campbell, Lyle & Martha Muntzel 1989. The structural consequences of language death. In Nancy C. Dorian (ed.) *Investigating Obsolescence. Studies in language contraction and death,* 181-196. Cambridge: Cambridge University Press.

Dal Negro, S. 1998. Spracherhaltung in der Beiz — das Überleben von der Walsersprache zu Pomatt/Formazza. *Wir Walser* 36: 13-16.

Dorian, Nancy C. 1999. The study of language obsolescence: stages, surprises, challenges. *Languages and Linguistics* 3: 99-122.

Jackson, Jean 1974. Language identity of the Colombian Vaupés Indians. In Richard Bauman & Joel Sherzer (eds) *Explorations in the Ethnography of Speaking*, 50-64. Cambridge: Cambridge University Press.

_____ 1983. *Fish People*. Cambridge: Cambridge University Press.

Malone, Terrell 1988. The Origin and Development of Tuyuca Evidentials. *International Journal of American Linguistics* 54: 119-140.

Pensalfini, Rob 1999. The rise of case-suffixes as discourse markers in Jingulu — a case study of innovation in an obsolescent language. *Australian Journal of Linguistics* 19/2: 225-40.

Ramirez, H. 1997. *A fala Tukano dos Yepâ-masa. Tomo 1: Gramática*. Manaus: Inspetoria Salesiana.

Schmidt, Annette 1985. *Young People's Dyirbal. An example of language death from Australia*. Cambridge: Cambridge University Press.

Sorensen, Arthur P. Jr. 1967 (1972). Multilingualism in the Northwest Amazon. *American Anthropologist* 69: 670-684. Revised 1972, in John B. Pride & Janet Holmes (eds) *Sociolinguistics*, 78-93. Harmondsworth: Penguin.

Watkins, Calvert Forthcoming. An Indo-European linguistic area and its characteristics: ancient Anatolia. Areal diffusion as a challenge to the comparative method? In Alexandra Y. Aikhenvald & R.M.W. Dixon (eds) *Areal Diffusion And Genetic Inheritance: Problems In Comparatve Linguistics*. Oxford: Clarendon Press.

West, Birdie 1980. *Gramática popular del tucano*. Bogotá: Instituto Linguistico de Verano.

Chapter 11

Reclaiming Languages in Aboriginal Victoria[1]
Barry J. Blake
La Trobe University

1.   INTRODUCTION

Melbourne was founded in 1835 and what is now the state of Victoria was occupied within a decade. After a generation or so, the Aboriginal population had been reduced to a few thousand, most of whom were herded into reserves. These reserves were remote from centres of European population, and the Aboriginal people had no voice. They were largely forgotten, and it was expected that they would die out. A very different picture presents itself today. Aboriginal people in Victoria, as in other parts of Australia, are now seeking to establish their identity. They are taking a great interest in their traditional culture and are keen to revive their traditional languages.

However, this presents considerable difficulties. No indigenous language is still spoken in Victoria. For the most part the only source of information is in the form of amateur accounts from nineteenth century, but we are fortunate that Luise Hercus made an exhaustive survey of the last speakers in the 1960s. Significantly, she was able to record substantial amounts of grammar and vocabulary only in north-western Victoria; in other areas she could only record small amounts of vocabulary (Hercus 1986).

Although the general thrust of the white incursion into Victoria was to take over the land and to kill as many Aborigines as was necessary to achieve this aim, there were a few who took an interest in Aboriginal culture. These included George Augustus Robinson, who had previously been in charge of rounding up the last remnants of the Tasmanian Aboriginal population. He was a keen observer and diarist who travelled extensively in Victoria. His journals contain

[1]   I am pleased to acknowledge the suppport of the Australian Research Council (A59803475).

numerous word lists from various languages, though no grammatical information. Another was William Thomas, who served first as one of the one of the Assistant Protectors of the Aborigines and then later as Guardian of the Aborigines. He has left extensive materials in Woiwurrung, the language of the Melbourne area, plus a large vocabulary and a set of sentences translated into six Victorian languages.

The last and certainly the best of these early recorders was Robert Hamilton Mathews (1841-1918). Mathews was a surveyor who spent his retirement in collecting information about the Aboriginal people of south-eastern Australia and their languages. Between 1895 and 1917 he published 185 papers in Australian and overseas journals, some in French and some in German. He gathered material on 28 languages, though it is likely that he had just a few sessions with the one or two people for a particular language.[2] He seems to have had a questionnaire which involved asking his informants to translate a few sentences such as 'A man killed a possum' and 'A woman caught an eel' and a few phrases such as 'the man's boomerang'. The questionnaire also required a set of pronouns and some verb paradigms showing tense and person and number marking for the subject. He collected some general vocabulary. His phonetic notation was superior to that of his contemporaries.

2. CLASSIFYING VICTORIAN LANGUAGES

For anyone interested in finding out about the traditional languages of Victoria a confusing array of sources presents itself scattered in a variety of publications and manuscripts. There are well over 200 source materials, mostly short vocabularies. These bear a variety of labels. Some lists bear a language name such as *Laitji-Laitji* or *Wotti-Wotti*. These two names represent a common naming pattern for languages in Victoria, that of reduplicating the word for 'no'. Thus *Laitji-Laitji* refers to a language in which the word for 'no' is **laitji**. But even where language names appear with the sources, there are traps for the unwary. The name *wotti-wotti* (also *watty-watty*,

---

[2] The information on Mathews is based on unpublished notes of R.M.W. Dixon.

etc.) applies to two different, but adjacent, tongues. Another problem with the names is that of recognising different spellings as reflecting the same name. In north-eastern Victoria, for instance, the spellings *Dhudhuroa* and *Theddora* relate to the same language despite their dissimilarity. The correct form is probably **Dhudhuwurru**.[3] In many instances there is a clan name, a place name or just the name of the Aboriginal person from whom the information was collected. This means that a variety of sources with different names can reflect the same tongue.

The only way to sort this large collection of data is to count percentages of common vocabulary. Extensive comparison of variously named lists enables us to see that the 200-plus sources represent over a score of different tongues (see Table 2). In most cases one name emerges as appropriate as with Wemba-Wemba, Djadjawurrung, Wathawurrung, Woiwurrung, Yorta-Yorta and Dhudhuroa. In the case of the Warrnambool area there are a number of closely related tongues, each with its own name. These might be considered dialects of a single language for which there is no vernacular name.The people of the area have chosen one of the dialect names, **Keeraywoorroong**, and a recent publication is entitled *Dictionary of Keeraywoorroong and Related Dialects* (Krishna-Pillay 1996).

In a number of other cases tongues can be grouped on the basis of various degrees of similarity and my practice is to use English names for the groupings since the groupings are largely European concepts. These similarities are of some practical importance given the paucity of our sources. Where tongues are quite similar it is possible to fill in gaps from a related tongue.

3. PHONETICS

When the sources for a particular tongue have been identified on the basis of lexicostatistics, they need to be interpreted. The major problem lies in working out the pronunciation from various amateur

---

[3]   The convention adopted here is to use italics for the original notation and bold for a modern transcription.

notations. As might be expected, these early notations are phonemically under-differentiated. On the basis of what we know from other parts of Australia where Aboriginal languages are still spoken or where at least we have professional notations we expect dental and retroflex consonants as well as alveolar ones. The early observers were oblivious to dental n and l. They notated dental t as *th* or *dh*, but they did not pick it consistently. They did not hear retroflexes consistently, and even if they did, there remained the problem of how to notate them in English orthography. It is unfortunate that the notations are virtually all made by speakers of English, the language with the worst relationship between sound and spelling. English lacks a consistent way of representing vowels, and worst of all letter **u** is ambiguous between [ʊ] as in *put*, [ʌ] as in *but* and [ju:] as in *use*. Worse still, the notations are mostly made by speakers of the variety of English emanating from south-eastern England where r is silent in words like 'car' and 'card'. When one encounters *r* in an early notation in forms such as *kork* 'blood', one is left uncertain whether the *r* represents a rhotic or whether the combination of vowel letter and *r* represents a long vowel. In a notation such as *darti* 'later', it is uncertain whether *ar* represents a long vowel or whether *r* represents the r-colouring associated with a retroflex. On the basis of what we know of well recorded languages we expect two rhotics, a flapped or trilled r (as in Scottish English)and a glide r (as in mainstream English). However, no source makes such a distinction.

Despite these difficulties one can establish the pronunciation of most words fairly confidently if one has several tokens. Consider the following spellings for the word for 'father' in Wathawurrung. They have been aligned to facilitate comparison. A full guide to the sources can be found in Blake (ed. 1998).

(1)	*p*	*ee*	*ty*	*e*	*r*		*i*	*k*	'my father'
	p	*ee*	*ty*	*a*	*r*		*i*	*k*	'my father'
	p	*e*	*d*	*o*		*ng*			
	p	*i*	*tt*	*o*		*ng*			
	p	*e*	*tty*	*a*		*ng*			
	b	*i*	*tj*	*u*		*ng*			
	b	*i*	*t*	*a*		*ng*			
	p	*i*	*dj*	*a*	*r*	*o*	*ng*		

Looking first at the consonants we see the initial consonant has been notated *p* or *b*. Clearly we have a bilabial stop. In general, Australian languages do not distinguish voiced and voiceless stops, but English speakers do and notate accordingly. From some notations it is clear that the next consonant is a palatal stop. In many Australian languages, including those of Victoria it would appear, there is a laminal stop, nasal and lateral, and the pronunciation varies between dental and palatal. The notations *t* and *d* probably reflect a dental variant that has been heard as alveolar. Moving to the next consonant position we see that a rhotic appears in the first two entries before the suffix *-ik*, but is absent before the nominative *-ng*. It is likely that the rhotic has been missed before **ng** except in the last alternative where an epenthetic vowel has been inserted to break up a sequence unfamiliar to English speakers. The most probable form of this word is **pitjarng** or **bidjarng** depending whether one prefers voiceless or voiced symbols in the transcription.

4.   SEMANTICS

One cannot always accept the glosses of Aboriginal words at face value. In some semantic fields there is under-differentiation parallelling the under-differentiation we observe in phonetics. With kinship one finds glosses for 'brother' and 'sister' rather than 'older brother' and 'younger brother' and 'older sister' and 'younger sister'. Similarly old sources often record 'grandmother' and 'grandfather' rather than distinguishing 'mother's mother' and 'father's mother', 'mother's father' and 'father's father'. With fauna and flora there is often some uncertainty about the degree of specificity. A word may be recorded for both 'snake' and 'tiger snake' or both 'fish' and 'blackfish'. It could be that the generic gloss is inaccurate or it could be that the more specific term also served as the generic one.

Another problem lies in differences between colonial English and present-day English. In some instances the differences are transparent as with 'native bear' for koala and 'porcupine' for echidna, but not all cases are so obvious. They include 'gammon' (pretend), 'myall/bush' (uncivilised, untamed), 'warrigul' (wild dog, uncivilised), 'honeysuckle' (Banksia), 'iguana' (goanna), 'manna' (lerp), 'laughing jackass' (kookaburra), 'native companion' (brolga), 'to plant' (to hide), 'sloth' (koala), 'spear lever' (woomera) and 'water mole' (platypus).

There are sometimes big errors in the meanings attributed to words in the sources arising from eliciting words in isolation and confusing homophones such as 'son' and 'sun'. One source confuses 'today' and 'to die', which, though not homophonous in a particular variety of English, are confusible between accents. In some instances one-word glosses such as 'bark' or 'tear' are simply ambiguous unless other information is available.

Another problem stems from the fact that words of Aboriginal origin often circulated in English or Pidgin English and found their way into other languages. The words 'gibba/gibber' (stone), 'gunya(h)' (hut, camp), 'hielaman' (shield) and 'budgeree/budjeri' (good), for instance, spread from the Sydney area and were sometimes offered by Aboriginal people in other parts of the country as the local word. Similarly the words 'borack' (no) and 'merrijig' (good) passed into wider circulation from the Wathawurrung language of the Geelong-Ballarat area. The most interesting example is the well known word 'mia-mia/mi-mi' (hut, camp), which comes from the Nyungar language of Western Australia, but which was circulating in Victoria as early as 1839 and was sometimes offered as local (Dixon et al. 1990: 201). This word is still in general circulation.

In providing a glossary from a variety of word lists it is necessary to group words such as 'earth', 'ground' and 'country', which usually correspond with one particular vernacular term, even if only to bring the tokens together to improve the transcription. Other cases where words need to be considered together because there is one vernacular term for the set include: 'air', 'breath'; 'all', 'plenty', 'many', 'mob'; 'acid', 'bitter', 'salt'; 'die', 'hungry'; 'cold', 'wind'; 'dark', 'night'; 'sore', 'pain'; 'bone', 'stick', 'branch', 'tree'; and 'arm', 'branch'.

5.   GRAMMAR

Information on word formation and sentence formation is skimpy in the early sources. Some early observers simply chose to confine themselves to vocabulary; others provided only meagre data. For many languages the main source of information on grammar is R.H. Mathews. Mathews normally gives a few sentences to illustrate the 'causative' (ergative) case and the genitive. For Wathawurrung, for instance, he gives *Guliar goeng   bakkurnirring* and *Gulia bakunirring gōang* for 'a man caught an eel.' This we might transcribe as in (2). The original reference, the original notation and a modern transcription for Mathews' examples is to be found in Blake (1998: 65, 73, 77).

(2) **Guli-a**   **bakunirring**   **gowayn**
     man.ERG   catch   eel
     A man caught an eel.

However, we are left uncertain whether **-a** (or **-ya**) was the only marker for the ergative case, and we are not given data on the full set of cases. There is likely to have been half a dozen or so and Mathews has the annoying habit of mentioning cases such as locative and ablative without exemplifying them.

Mathews and other early writers present paradigms showing person/number marking for subject on the verb. Mathews, for instance, gives the following singular forms in Wathawurrung:

Table 1:   Wathawurrung verb inflection

		present	*past*	*future*
singular	1	**kilan**	**kilikan**	**kilinyan**
	2	**kilarr**	**kilikarr**	**kilinyarr**
	3	**kila**	**kilik**	**kiliya**

However, the apparent suffixes are actually clitics and do not attach only to verbs. They are frequently found attached to interrogative and negative phrases in clause-initial position as in **Kun=arr ngalbaliyn** 'Are you frightened?' where the second person clitic **=arr** is attached to the interrogative particle **kun**. Nevertheless they represent a substantial part of the meagre material available to us.

Some sources give examples of derivational suffixes and other examples can be found in the word lists. In this way we get some information on suffixes such as the following (Wathawurrung examples): suffixes that form agent nouns **moyu-gunang** (lie-AGENT) 'liar', the 'having' suffix **kurn-mil** (neck-HAVING) 'snake' and reciprocals **wa-tjarra** (give-RECIPROCAL) 'barter'.

6.   THE FUTURE

At the present time Aboriginal people in Victoria, like their counterparts in other states, are becoming very keen to learn what they can of their traditional culture and to revive aspects of it, including language. As mentioned earlier, the languages of Victoria are no longer spoken, though some people retain some vocabulary and a few phrases. This means that people have to rely on the amateur accounts of early observers except in the cases of Wemba-Wemba, Wergaya and Madhi-Madhi, where we have professional accounts from Hercus. As will be clear from the preceding sections, the amateur accounts need to be processed and consolidated into a single account for each tongue. So far we have consolidated accounts of Woiwurrung (Blake 1991), Wathawurrung and the Colac language (Blake (ed.) 1998), and dictionaries with notes on grammar have been produced with community consultation for the Keeraywoorroong people of the Warrnambool area (Krishna-Pillay (ed.) 1996) and the Yorta-Yorta people of northern Victoria (Bowe, Peeler and Atkinson 1997). A language learning programme was established in Warrnambool and the people of Gippsland have a language programme running. Feasibility studies have been undertaken for six other languages under the aegis of The Victorian Aboriginal Corporation for Languages.

Over the next five years we can expect to see the production of language materials for most Victorian languages. There is a good deal of optimism and some Aboriginal people are thinking in terms of speaking their traditional language in the next few years. However, it must be emphasised that the materials available are largely lexical. For most languages the grammatical information consists of only a half dozen or so pages, and even in the areas covered there are gaps.

Table 2:   **Languages and the extent of their sources**

Language	Vocabulary	Grammar (pages)	Relatives
Yitha-Yitha/Dadi-Dadi	150	5	60% with Keramin to W.
Bunganditj (Mt Gambier)	1000	18	35% with Warrnambool
Warrnambool	2000	10	42% with Tjapwurrung etc.
Colac	250	1	30% with neighbors
Mathi-Mathi	400	34	80% within group
Ledji-Ledji	150	3	80% within group
Wadi-Wadi (SH)	600	8	80% within group
Wadi-Wadi (P)	200	-	55% within group
Wemba-Wemba	1200	35	over 80% within group
Wergaya	1000	20	over 80% within group
Tjapwurrung (Hamilton)	2000	3	over 80% within group
Djadjawurrung[4]	1000	9	over 80% within group
Wathawurrung[5]	1200	20	45% with other Kulin
Woiwurrung (Melbourne)	1000+	14	over 80% within group
Thagungwurrung[6]			over 80% within group
Yorta-Yorta (Echuca)	1000	23	40% with Yabula
Yabula-Yabula (Echuca)	150	5	40% with Yorta
Dhudhuroa (Corryong)	300	9	20% with neighbors
Pallanganmiddang[7]	300	1	20% with neighbors
Ngarigu (Omeo)	200	-	20% with neighbors
Gippsland/Bidawal	1000	30	20% with neighbors
Thawa	100	-	37% with Dhurga to N.

Table 2 provides a summary of the amount of lexical and grammatical data that is available. All but the first four languages and the last six languages form a related group collectively known as

---

[4]   W. Bendigo area.

[5]   Geelong/Ballarat area.

[6]   Goulburn River area; for linguistic data compare Woiwurrung.

[7]   Wodonga area.

the Kulin languages (Schmidt 1919); there are four subgroups within Kulin which are separated in Table 2: two subgroups of four, a single language, and a subgroup of two.

It is obvious from the table that there is insufficient data available to give a full picture of any language. In the extreme case there is only a few hundred words and virtually no grammatical information. In some instances deficiencies could be made good by adopting vocabulary and grammatical forms from a related tongue that is better recorded. In the right-hand column of Table 2, I have indicated degrees of similarity in vocabulary between related tongues and this can be taken as a rough guide to similarity in grammatical forms. The Djadjawurrung of the Bendigo area or the Tjapwurrung of the Hamilton area, for instance, could make use of the Wemba-Wemba or Wergaya material recorded by Hercus. In some instances gaps can be filled in by comparative reconstruction. This is feasible for some of the Kulin languages. If any serious attempt is made to speak these languages, then syntax will be calqued subconsciously from English; alternatively it could be developed by looking at better recorded languages from elsewhere. Given that morpho-syntactic patterns are widespread, this would not do violence to the target language.

Some people will have a choice as to which group they can identify with, and it is common practice among Aboriginal people in the southeast of the continent to identify with a group in whose country they reside. Some may find the alternatives available to them include one of the better recorded languages.

If a critical mass of zealots gather, they could develop a full, spoken language by the natural processes of creolisation and by conscious borrowing and planning. However, this is unlikely to happen. The numbers are small and scattered. What can be realistically achieved is learning something of a language through a programme involving the production of a kit of learning materials and the running of classes. This will give people some language knowledge, something with which they can identify. Whether people manage to speak a language is not the only criterion by which the enterprise of language reclamation should be judged. Language can be a powerful marker of identity and even some knowledge of a language can serve that function and be a source of pride.

The Aboriginal languages of the mainland all appear to be related. Certainly many languages share vocabulary and grammatical forms. As Aboriginal people came to learn something of their own particular language, they will not only find satisfaction in knowing the language or languages with which they identify, they will find added satisfaction in discovering these common strands, words shared over particular areas and words shared between distant areas.

REFERENCES

Blake, Barry J. 1991. Woiwurrung: The Melbourne language. In R.M.W. Dixon & Barry J. Blake (eds) *Handbook of Australian Languages* 4: 30-122. Melbourne: Oxford University Press, Australia.

Blake, Barry J. (ed.) 1998. *Wathawurrung and the Colac Language of Southern Victoria.* Canberra: Pacific Linguistics C-149. Canberra: Department of Linguistics, RSPAS, ANU.

Bowe, Heather., Lois Peeler & Sharon Atkinson 1997. *Yorta-Yorta Language Heritage.* Clayton: Monash University, Department of Linguistics.

Dixon, R.M.W., William S. Ramson & Mandy Thomas. 1990. *Australian Aboriginal Words in English.* Melbourne: Oxford University Press.

Hercus, Luise A. 1986. *Victorian languages: a late survey.* Pacific Linguistics B-77. Canberra: Department of Linguistics, RSPAS, ANU. Revision of 1969 edition published by Australian Institute of Aboriginal Studies.

Krishna-Pillay, Sharnthi (ed.) 1996. *Dictionary of Keeraywoorroong and Related Dialects.* Warrnambool: Gunditjmara Aboriginal Co-operative.

Schmidt, Wilhelm 1919. *Die Gliederung der australischen Sprachen.* Vienna.

Chapter 12

A Language Plan for Norfolk Island

Peter Mühlhäusler

University of Adelaide

1. INTRODUCTION

This chapter is concerned with my practical experience with one language community, that of Norfolk Island, where I have been carrying out field work for the last four years and with the help of a large Australian Research Council grant hope to carry out considerably more work, particularly in the area of language revival and maintenance over the next four years.

In the history of ecological and environmental issues, islands have played a particularly significant role: Not only was environmental degradation first detected and investigated on islands such as St. Helena, St. Kitts and Pitcairn, which also continue to have a longitudinal body of studies, far bigger than their land mass or population size would suggest and we arguably have qualitatively better information about island situations than for large land masses.

It is my view that islands lend themselves particularly well to understanding processes of language change, decline and revival because the number of parameters involved is much smaller than in most other situations of language change. I have chosen Norfolk Island for a number of reasons which I have spelled out elsewhere (Mühlhäusler 1998, Mühlhäusler 1999): Some of these reasons are quite different from the popular perceptions and expectations of what to find on Norfolk Island.

a)   First, Norfolk Island does not offer a test case for the development of a single language (Pitcairn - Norfolk, Norfolk, Norfolkese or whatever) but a test case for the effects of rapid changes in the composition of the language repertoire of its inhabitants. English, Norfolk , Mota and up to twenty other mainly Melanesian languages, Whalers' Pidgin English,

N.S.W. Pidgin English, all of them 'exotic' to the island in a technical sense. The island thus is primarily a test case for the effects of contact.

b)   There is a common perception that Pitcairn Island by contrast is indeed a test case for isolation which again is quite fallacious. Contact between different language groups (Tahitian, West Indian Creole, English and others) dominates the first 25 years of its history and after 1820, contacts with the wider world were quite significant. There is little to recommend the view that Pitcairn is a laboratory test case for creolisation of children growing up in an isolated location in spite of what textbooks suggest (Sebba 1997). What is important is that the makeup of the language community of Pitcairn was quite different from that of Norfolk - it does offer a comparative test case for the effects of contact and change in different environmental conditions.

c)   Isolation in the history of Pitcairn - Norfolk occurred probably only once, and that quite late, around 1900 when some families on Norfolk Island lived cut off from the rest of the island and began to creolise Pitcairn - Norfolk which prior to that date had been a second language. One of the principal tasks for future years is to document the social history of the language of Norfolk.

I shall not say more about this topic here but I shall start at the end of this history, the year 1997 when I first visited Norfolk Island. By then the language had become greatly endangered. Only a small number of the Pitcairn descendants (900+ out of a total population of about 2,500) speak the traditional form of the language with any fluency, many young and middle aged islanders with little or no pretence in the language at all and the language together with many other cultural practices (cooking, dancing etc.) is likely to disappear within a generation, unless steps are taken to reverse current trends.

2.   THE DISCUSSION PAPER

After three years of discussions with a large number of stakeholders I have come up with a document whose key features I want to lay before you today - the draft Language Plan for Norfolk Island. The function of this plan is that of a discussion document for the islanders, who, like other communities affected by language loss, are not fully aware of either the problems, the processes involved, the issues or the remedies. The primary function of this plan is to create awareness of the issues, thus opening up a more informed debate as to how to deal with them. The document begins with a general discussion of the language planning processes, distinguishing between the well-known status planning and corpus planning and by laying before the community the processes that are involved in both areas:

a) recognition of issues and problems
b) observation and evaluation of the linguistic situation
c) developing language management strategies
d) implementation
e) monitoring ongoing programmes

One of the most important issues is the extent to which language problems can be separated from other issues. Because of the prevailing ideology of modern linguistics, most language planners have tended to subscribe to the view that language is a distinct phenomenon which can be planned in isolation from other phenomena. More recently, the importance of social and ecological factors have been given recognition and it is now widely agreed that language planning can not be isolated from social, economic and political planning.

The success or failure of deliberate interference with language thus would seem to depend on a complex array of factors and it is unsurprising that the success rate of language planning activities has not been very high: Like other areas of social policy making one can note a significant gap between policies and plans on the one hand and practical results on the other. It is important to learn from the mistakes that have been made.

The document continues by commenting on Amery's classification of language planning programmes for endangered languages developed in the Australian Indigenous Languages Framework (AILF) (Senior Secondary Assessment Board 1996), Table 1.

Table 1: Australian Indigenous Languages Framework

AILF Categories	Defining Characteristics
Language Maintenance (First Language Maintenance)	*All generations full speakers*
Language Revival/Language Revitalisation (3 subcategories, all involve children learning the language of their own heritage)	*Generation of (older) speakers left; children likely to have good passive knowledge.*
Language Renewal	*Oral tradition but no full speakers; children likely to have little or no passive knowledge.*
Language Reclamation	*No speakers or partial speakers; relying on historical sources to provide knowledge of the language.*
Language Awareness	*Non-speakers learning about the languages where it is not possible to learn and use the language; vestiges only, documentation poor.*
Language Learning (Second Language Learning)	*Non-speakers learning as L_2*

It is tentatively concluded that what we are dealing with on Norfolk is something between revitalisation and renewal.

It is important to ask why in fact is language revival desirable. In my view the arguments can be put forward in three discourses in support of taking active steps rather than adopting a free market rationalist or laissez faire approach. These are:

1) the *scientific* argument (also emphasised at the conference by Wurm) that bi- and multilingual abilities enhance greater intellectual achievement in all other areas.

2) the *economic* argument that greater intellectual abilities and the reduction of social conflict can have economic spin-offs and in the case of Norfolk Island cultural tourism could provide additional income,

3) and the *moral* argument that the loss of linguistic diversity indeed all diversity (cultural, ecological) means depriving future generations of choices, resources and their spiritual home. I share Fishman's view (1991) that the wish to maintain linguistic diversity is a rational one not a case of sentimentality or irrational nostalgia.

My next step has been to advocate an audit that makes explicit and conscious the parameters involved i.e.:

   i) issues
   ii) stakeholders
   iii) perceived solutions and
   iv) constraints.

Unless these matters are addressed (and some of them do not make pleasant reading for the community), the chance of getting anywhere with revitalisation is minimal.

3.   THE ISSUES

The principal issue is that the language of Norfolk is perceived to be declining in a number of senses:

a)   structurally - traditional ways of speaking are disappearing and are being replaced by modified Anglicised Norfolk

b)   the percentage of fluent Norfolk speakers in the total population is declining

c)   the absolute number of fluent Norfolk speakers is shrinking

d)   Norfolk is rarely passed on in its entirety to the next generation

e)   the decline of Norfolk is against the wishes of a very large proportion of the Norfolk islanders

Language loss is an experience Norfolk Islanders share with many people elsewhere - it is a world wide phenomenon. The next issue is how can we arrest the decline of the Norfolk language? Before addressing this point a number of other issues need to be faced:

a)   The relationship with Pitkern:[1] Is Pitcairn-Norfolk one language or two? Should they be one? Are they dialects of the same language? Should there be a single norm for spelling and grammar? Opinions on this point appear to vary considerably.

b)   What should the name of the language be? Should it be Norfolk, Norfolkese, Norfolk-English, Pitcairn-Norfolk or something else?

c)   Should Norfolk be a written language or simply an oral one? It should be noted that a number of Pacific communities have opted to keep their language oral and perceive this to be a way of keeping them strong but it should also be noted that the absence of a written form of the language in the past has not affected its viability. Will introducing a written standard strengthen it now? What do islanders want: For the next

---

[1] This is the agreed spelling for the variety of present day Pitcairn Island.

generation to speak the language in everyday communication or to have a body of written documents?

d)   If Norfolk is to be a written language, which writing system should be adopted? There are a number of competing writing systems and varying opinions about their relative strength and weaknesses.   Questions about writing systems can be particularly divisive issues - not all societies are ready to opt for a single system.

e)   Is the language going to be reserved for insiders (Pitcairn descendants) or should anyone residing on Norfolk be encouraged to speak it? The fact that even quite a few long-term residence married to Norfolk Islanders do not speak the language suggests that there is considerable pressure against its use by outsiders. Given a long history of being an insider (esoteric) language, much work will need to be done to make it a more accessible language for all. Regarding the question whether Norfolk should be a private or public language, its present visibility is rather low: Use of Norfolk for public signing, street names, place names, radio, television and newspapers would make it more visible. One could consider to what extent public signs on Norfolk should be bilingual.

f)   What is the relationship with English? This question can be approached from two angles: i) One can ask about the linguistic relationship: Is Norfolk a dialect of English, a broken English, an English Creole, or a related language? In the course of researching the history of this language all of the above have been stated and a satisfactory answer is still forth coming. What is certain is that its linguistic history has been very complex. An answer to this question is desirable for a special reason: If Norfolk is to be taught to English speakers there are different methods for teaching it as a foreign language, a dialect or a related Creole.
ii) The question can also be taken to mean: How are English and Norfolk used? Are we dealing with a clear cut high-low, public-private division or are the conventions for the use of English and Norfolk more complex, overlapping or a matter of

individual taste?   Research by Shirley Harrison (1985) suggests that the social rules for its use are very complex.

Status planning can only be done when the answer to this question is known but it seems clear that both English and Norfolk will remain the island's languages and that the importance of English is unlikely to decline.

g)   Is there one Norfolk language or many? Do the islanders agree on standards of pronunciation, lexicon and grammar or is it up to individuals and families? Linguists distinguish between focussed and unfocussed languages - and languages such as Belizian Creole for instance were unfocussed for most of its history but after independence of Belize in the 1970s acquired agreed norms (Le Page & Tabouret-Keller 1985). If Norfolk is relatively unfocussed, should it be more focussed? In other words, is standardisation desirable? What standards should prevail?

h)   What is the relationship with Tahitian? The impression one gains from the study of old documents is that Tahitian contribution to the Norfolk language and culture has tended to be under-emphasised until very recently. Most noticeable is the absence of Tahitian women in practices such as naming places and events.

With renewed interest in the Polynesian contribution to Pitcairn-Norfolk the view that we are dealing with a Polynesian-English indigenous language has gained strength. There is not much reliable linguistic knowledge at this point and any claim as to the status of Norfolk as an indigenous language will require very careful documentation.

The history of the views of Afrikaans offers a parallel. Up to the 1970s it was interpreted as a development from a dialect of Dutch.   Detailed linguistic analysis in recent years has uncovered a great deal of Hottentot and Cape Malay influence.

i)   Change and the role of children: All languages are changing. Language planning can at best decelerate or accelerate change but never arrest it. The issue then is to find a balance between preservation of older forms and change. Crucial in language change is the role of children. It would be useful to know how tolerant of children's innovations Norfolk Islanders have been in the past, and how much change they are prepared to accept for the future.

A number of islanders fear that leaving the language to the children will lead to it merging with English, but at present there is no reliable data on the attitude and practices of young islanders.

It needs to be mentioned that attempts to preserve languages that ignore the practice of young speakers have shown to do little to arrest their decline (e.g. Irish, Gaelic).

j) What should Norfolk's official classification be? Languages can differ considerably in their official status. In the past Norfolk has had no official recognition and for a considerable time was suppressed and denigrated. There is widespread agreement that Norfolk deserves to be given official recognition now. What forms this recognition might take, and what status Norfolk might eventually have, depends on the answers to questions (a) - (i): These include:
    i)   an indigenous language
    ii) a heritage language
    iii) a community language other than English
    iv) a co-official language
    v)   an official language

Its future status will be determined by a number of factors, most importantly Norfolk's relationship with Australia, Pitcairn and neighbouring islands.

k) the role of Norfolk in education. A number of issues remain to be resolved including:
    i)   the most adequate methods for ensuring good proficiency in both Norfolk and English
    ii) the need for materials for increased motivation for learning Norfolk
    iii) the best age at which Norfolk should be taught
    iv) the relative importance of old and written versions of Norfolk
    v)   the development of greater language awareness among both students and teacher

vi)   the role that other languages will have (e.g. French, Spanish)

vii)   the involvement of parents and other community members in teaching Norfolk

viii)   the question of continuity of teachers learning Norfolk language

ix)   technical support (e.g. computers, language laboratories etc.).

4.   STAKEHOLDERS

It is important to recognise that all stakeholders need to be involved - this is the bottom up aspect of ecological planning. Successful language planning depends on a balanced consultative process, involving a representative sample of all kinds of stakeholders. These would include, (in random order):

i) politicians representing different political views
ii) concerned individuals, particularly those who have been active in language matters
iii) educationists
iv) church and community groups
v) Australian government representatives
vi) children and adolescents
vii) writers
viii) tourist industry representatives

As all planning takes place under financial constraints it is important to include:

ix) finance experts advising on costs and benefits
x) representatives of industry and commerce
xi) outside experts, linguists, language planners and economists.

The role of outside experts should be an advisory one - it is important to train local language experts as soon as possible to diminish dependency on outside expertise. In case it is anticipated to coordinate language planning with Pitcairn Islanders it is also important to involve first:

xii) Pitcairn Islanders and possibly representatives of other Pacific Islands (e.g. South Pacific Commission)

Bringing together stakeholders will in the first instance be informal and ad hoc. However, since language planning is a long term process, more permanent bodies (with elected and appointed people) need to be selected, possibly following a public debate. Such a body would ensure:

a) continuity of planning
b) implementation and monitoring of implemented solutions
c) liaison with stakeholders
d) setting up a reference library/collection of language related materials
e) dissemination of materials and ideas
f) recommending policy and practices .
g) various other matters
h) training of experts

There are many models to choose from e.g. national language academies, Aboriginal Language Centres, Language Societies etc. It is important that the bodies should have a physical presence (a large building with library, archives and other facilities) and be financially secure on a long term basis.

The solution perceived by most concerned islanders is that the education system should take care of language matters - this I fear, is as problematic as leaving it to an academy or to the politicians. I strongly argue that language revitalisation is a matter for all islanders and that the contribution that schools can make is supplementary to this.

5.   SOLUTIONS

After lengthy discussions with stakeholders we came up with a tentative list of long and short term measures.

Short term measures:

a) setting up a central and accessible collection of language related materials (e.g. in the Public Library, Pitcairn Museum or Government Offices) and encouraging the population to contribute to this collection,

b) collecting texts from older speakers using up-to-date recording equipment (video, tapes, written texts),

c) giving the language greater visibility by increasing its use in public signing: One might consider, for instance, bilingual road signs, street and place names on maps and the use of Norfolk on postage stamps,

d) encouraging newspaper items in and about the Norfolk language,

e) increasing its oral use on radio and television,

f) reviving the Norfolk language experience in Norfolk studies concentrating on oral language in the first instance,

g) developing language camps where children can have an immersion experience in Norfolk language and culture,

h) having a competition for poetry and short stories written in Norfolk,

i) encouraging islanders to collect words and expressions, place names etc.

j) developing an extended website on Norfolk language and language issues and inviting public debate,

k) collecting names of stakeholders, relevant organisations and experts,

l) encouraging tourists and resident non-islanders to learn the language and setting up courses for other education on Norfolk,

m) strengthening the language content in Norfolk Island studies and preparing a series of public meetings with the aim of setting up a permanent body

The main long-term measure to be taken will include:

a) appropriate legislation determining the status of the Norfolk language

b) to appoint a permanent body of stakeholders and experts (e.g. a language academy) to look after language matters; an early matter to be addressed will be that of the implementation of a writing system

c) to design school syllabuses for a continued pathway of learning and teaching

d) to set up a permanent physical location for all language resources and materials

e) to budget for the long term implementation of a language plan

f) to identify outside organisations that can train teachers, language managers and planners and enter into long-term partnerships.

I shall conclude my report by mentioning briefly what has happened thus far and what is likely to happen in the future:

i) There is a growing awareness of the issues; whilst the local paper, the *Norfolk Islander* contains practically no reference to language matters up to 1995, there are now a growing number of readers letters and editorials.

ii) The Norfolk Island Government is about to appoint a cultural adviser whose principal duty will include advising on language revitalisation - a seeding grant has been received from the South Pacific Commission for this purpose.

iii) A decision was made to include Norfolk language in the primary syllabus of the island's schools - but there remains a lack of trained language teachers.

iv) On my last visit I held discussions to have all materials relating to language and culture on Norfolk Island to be located in the library at the Island Central School. This has now happened and the librarian has begun to organise the collection and make it available for public access.

v)   Alice Buffett has supplemented her grammar of Norfolk with Don Laycock with a 1,000+ word dictionary and she is in the process of further upgrading this booklet (Buffett, 1999).

vi) A body of islanders has adopted Buffett's suggested spelling as their preferred official spelling but universal acceptance is still forthcoming.

vii) The producers of the local TV and radio stations have increased the contents of programmes in Norfolk e.g. a TV series featuring older speakers and a brief radio programme on Saturday mornings by a young speaker. Both contain a significant amount of Norfolk language.

viii) The Minister for Culture and Education has been involved in these language maintenance issues as have a number of other government bodies.

ix) Norfolk is used in cultural tourism both in the form of language lessons and poetry readings.

x)   My draft for a language plan for Norfolk Island has been sent to a number of official and private bodies and individuals on Norfolk Island.

xi) The collection by Flint of Norfolk texts collected in the 1960s is currently being catalogued and digitised at the University of Queensland and will be made available to islanders.

6.   CONCLUSIONS

The survival of the Norfolk language is not a guaranteed thing but there are a number of positive signs in particular the greater public awareness of language issues, the revaluation of the language and greater involvement by a number of islanders. I hope that my new large Australian Research Council grant will enable Islanders to study language maintenance and language planning at Adelaide and return to the island with the skills necessary to make a significant contribution to the revival of the Norfolk language.

REFERENCES

Senior Secondary Assessment Board 1996. *Australia's Indigenous Language Framework.* Adelaide: Senior Secondary Assessment Board of South Australia.

Buffett, Alice 1999. *Speak Norfolk Today: An Encyclopaedia of the Norfolk Island Language.* Norfolk Island: Himii Publishing Company.

Fishman, Joshua A. 1991. *Reversing Language Shift.* Clevedon: Multilingual Matters.

Harrison, Shirley 1985. The Social Setting of Norfolk Speech. *English World-Wide, 6/1:* 131-153.

Le Page, Robert B. & Andrée Tabouret-Keller 1985. *Acts of Identity: Creole-based approaches to language and ethnicity.* Cambridge: Cambridge University Press.

Mühlhäusler, Peter 1998. How Creoloid can you get? *Journal of Pidgin and Creole Languages* 13/2: 121-130.

_____ 1999. More on Non-canonical Creoles *Journal of Pidgin and Creole Languages* 14/1: 355-371.

Sebba, Mark. 1997. *Contact languages. Pidgins and Creoles.* Basingstoke: Macmillan.

Chapter 13

Language Maintenance and Survival in East Timor: all change now? Winners and losers

John Hajek
University of Melbourne

Patterns of language maintenance and survival over time in East Timor are closely linked to the country's complex historico-political circumstances. At least three very different historical phases – political and linguistic – can be identified: each new one in turn radically shorter and more overwhelming than its predecessor, and each with very different linguistic consequences:

(1) Portuguese contact and colonisation (1500s-1975)
(2) Indonesian occupation (1975-1999)
(3) Post-Referendum/Independence (1999-)

1. OVERVIEW OF THE INDIGENOUS LANGUAGE SITUATION

In any discussion of the linguistic situation in East Timor – past or present – a clear distinction needs to be made between indigenous and non-indigenous languages of East Timor. From a historical, linguistic and cultural perspective, the most important non-indigenous languages of East Timor are Portuguese, and Malay/Indonesian, the languages of the two colonising powers in East Timor. To this list of non-indigenous languages can be added English, Portuguese Creole, varieties of Chinese and the many languages of Indonesian transmigrants entering East Timor after Indonesian occupation of East Timor began in 1975. Each of these, with the exception of specific transmigrant languages, will be referred to in the sections that follow.

With respect to the indigenous languages of East Timor, their precise number and classification remain in dispute. The estimated number of languages varies greatly from a low 10 to a very high 40, although the real number is likely to be in the range of 15-20. Despite centuries of contact, the Portuguese took relatively little interest in the linguistic make-up of East Timor. The little and sometimes unreliable linguistic information available was collected by priests or anthropologists in the region for other reasons. More recent Indonesian sources are also inconsistent and unreliable, with estimates of indigenous languages generally very low. The most recent edition of *Ethnologue* (Grimes 1996) lists the following seventeen languages as being spoken in East Timor, along with estimated numbers of speakers:

Table 1: **Languages of East Timor (Grimes 1996)**

size of ethnic group

Non-Austronesian

Adabe	1,000 (?)	
Bunak	50,000	(some speakers also in West Timor)
Fataluku	30,000	
Makasai	70,000	
Maku'a	50	

Austronesian

Atoni	650, 000	(14,000 in Ambeno/Oe Cusse, rest in West Timor)
Galoli	50,000 (?)	
Idate	5,000 (?)	
Kairui-Midiki	2,000 (?)	
Kemak	50,000	
Lakalei	5,000 (?)	
Mambai	80,000	
Naueti	1,000 (?)	
Tetun[1]	300,000+	(many in West Timor)
Tetun Dili	50,000 (?)	(also known as Tetum Praça)
Tukudede	50,000	
Waima'a	3,000 (?)	

Three of the listed languages (Atoni, Bunak and Tetun) are spoken in both East and West Timor. Of the seventeen languages listed by

---

[1]   Spelled Tetum in Portuguese and most East Timorese sources.

Ethnologue, at least nine appear to have relatively associated ethnic groups (30,000+ speakers). The actual size of the each ethnic group associated with the listed languages is open to debate: some sources (eg Fox 1997) report Mambai to be by far the largest group in East Timor, with up to three times as many speakers as listed by *Ethnologue.*

The distinction made by *Ethnologue* between Tetum/Tetun and Tetum/Tetun Dili is somewhat controversial, since Portuguese, Indonesian and most English-language sources, as well as the East Timorese themselves, tend to group all varieties of Tetum/Tetun under the single heading of Tetum/Tetun. The reasons for the distinction made by *Ethnologue* are made clear in the entry for Tetun Dili:

> Speakers of ...Tetun have significant difficulty understanding [Tetun Dili] in many   speech domains and vice versa. Some first language speakers of Tetun Dili consider themselves to be bilingual in Tetun because of contact, but when pressed, admit there   are domains in which communication is completely blocked.   (Grimes 1996: 654-655)

The accuracy of *Ethnologue's*   assessment about intelligibility problems across varieties of Tetum has been confirmed by Hajek (1999). That such problems should arise is not surprising: there is for instance substantial regional variation in the extent of adstratum influence. Tetum spoken in West Timor has long shown greater Malay/Indonesian influence with relatively little historical contact with Portuguese. At the other extreme, Tetum Dili has had long and intensive contact with Portuguese followed by intensive contact with Indonesian after 1975. Intercommunication is also hampered by the unusual geographical dispersion of the Tetum-speaking area into three physically separated zones: (1) Dili, the capital; (2) the Soibada-Viqueque area; and (3) a long strip which extends from Suai on the southern coast to Balibo on the north coast, straddling the East-West Timor border. Tetum (mainly Tetun Dili) has for some time been the lingua franca of East Timor, and it is estimated that some form of Tetum is spoken by 60-80 per cent of the local population.

The current classification of East Timorese languages is also incomplete – mainly due to the absence of sufficient information to allow for a proper assessment. Misclassification of Timorese languages has always been a problem as a result, e.g Capell (1944) and (1972) for examples. With respect to the five listed non-Austronesian languages, Maku'a is in fact an Austronesian language related to languages spoken on neighbouring islands. Its aberrant phonological shape was sufficient to have put Capell (1972), a very experienced Austronesianist, off the track completely. Although Adabe is listed as spoken on Atauro, there is no evidence that this is really the case.

2.   PORTUGUESE CONTACT AND COLONISATION (1500s-1975)

The first linguistic phase refers to the lengthy period of Portuguese contact and colonisation that lasted some five centuries. During this whole period there was little negative impact on indigenous languages of East Timor with the linguistic heterogeneity of East Timor well preserved. Only one indigenous language, tiny Maku'a, was threatened with loss – with as few as 50 speakers, in the 1970s. The threat to Maku'a came not from Portuguese, but from Fataluku, the surrounding indigenous language which had completely enveloped the eastern tip of the island.   The relative linguistic stability of East Timor during this period was in sharp contrast to what appears to have occurred in the other half of the island during much the same period. In West Timor, formerly under Dutch control, the number of local languages today is dramatically smaller, Helong which survives in a small area near Kupang, Tetum on the East-West Timor border and Atoni spoken in most of West Timor. Kupang Malay and Rotinese are relatively recent imports. It is believed that a range of interrelated factors such as sandalwood trade, continuing conflict and Dutch policies in favour of a new socio-political order more amenable to their control all conspired to shift local populations to Atoni (Fox 1997).

Whilst the Portuguese contact with East Timor goes back to the 1500s, it is important to realise how tenuous Portuguese influence in the region was for much of this period. In 1511 the Portuguese seized Malacca intent on expanding into the famous Spice Islands of eastern Indonesia. Their first written report on Timor is from 1517, although they appear to have visited the island in 1511. In 1566 the Dominicans established a fort in nearby Solor, and Portuguese interests began to expand in the region – including regular trade links with coastal Timor. In 1613 in the face of Dutch attacks, the Portuguese garrison was moved from Solor to nearby Larantuka. In 1642 the Portuguese and their allies entered Timor in large numbers to crush the most powerful kingdoms, in particular Tetum-speaking Wehale. Meantime Dutch-Portuguese rivalry continued —complicated by the increasing power of the Topasses, a Portuguese-speaking mixed-race force and Portugal's ostensible blood brothers and allies in the region. In 1653 the Dutch defeated the Portuguese at Kupang and entered West Timor, only to be defeated by the Topasses who were now to control most of the island. Victory of the Dutch at the battle of Penfui in 1749 was to guarantee Dutch control of West Timor until the twentieth century. Attempts by the Portuguese crown to take control of the rest of the island were long thwarted by the Topasses and their Timorese allies. The original capital of Lifao (today in the Oe-Cusse enclave) was abandoned in 1769 by the Portuguese governor who, besieged by the Topasses, was forced to transfer his army and administration to Dili. It was not until the late 1800s that Portuguese really began to establish control of their territory. But indigenous resistance was strong: between 1847 and 1912 the Portuguese conducted sixty military campaigns in an effort to pacify the colony. Full Portuguese rule was not achieved until 1912 with the crushing of the Boaventura uprising.

The lack of Portuguese control coupled with Portugal's lack of interest in East Timor until the twentieth century meant that the indigenous linguistic ecology of East Timor was for the most part relatively little affected by Portuguese. There is no evidence of any indigenous language being put in direct peril by the Portuguese language. A long tradition of stable indigenous multilingualism amongst the local population helped to maintain local language vitality. It was for instance quite common, at least until 1975, for villagers (especially males) to speak the language(s) of neighbouring villages. The introduction and use of Portuguese in these circumstances was dealt with as an expansion of the multilingual repertoire, rather than as a disruption to it.

Portuguese was, not surprisingly, well established in Dili, the colonial capital, but even here it was used alongside Tetum, not native to the area but implanted in the nineteenth century. Tetum benefited in Dili from its pre-existing use as a lingua franca in parts of East Timor and from the historical prestige of the Tetum-speaking kingdoms on the island. Outside of Dili, Portuguese seems to have been spoken by relatively few people until after World War II – although a report by a French explorer (Rosilly) in the eighteenth century suggests that all the local kings (liurais) were already fluent in Portuguese. Catholic missionaries in the nineteenth and twentieth centuries were also required to use indigenous languages - local languages in some places (e.g. Galoli) but Tetum in particular – in order to spread the Catholic faith.

Only in the Fataluku-speaking area, where Tetum was unknown, was Portuguese used as a lingua franca by the local population to communicate with other Timorese.

The numbers of Portuguese resident in East Timor were always tiny. As the table below shows, even as late as 1970, only 0.2 per cent of the resident population was Portuguese – and of this number, most, soldiers and administrators, were born in Portugal. The Portuguese instead relied mainly on the Timorese population with respect to local administration and military affairs. On both counts, the difference could not be starker when one compares these facts and figures with what occurred during the period of Indonesian control (1975-1999) – as discussed below.

Table 2: Population of Portuguese East Timor by Ethnic Group (1970)

	Number	Per cent
Portuguese	1463	0.2
Chinese	6120	1.0
Mestizo	1939	0.3
Goanese	42	
Negroes	22	
Timorese	599891	98.4
Total Pop.	609477	

Source: Recenseamento Geral da População e da Habitação 1970

Long accused of neglecting East Timor, Portugal began finally in the 1960s to turn its attention to the social development of East Timor through the closely intertwined mechanisms of expanding provision of education and the religious activities of the Roman Catholic Church. A principal objective of education and religious conversion - in the eyes of Portuguese authorities - was to 'civilise' the local population, so that, under Portuguese law, they would become true Portuguese citizens with full civil rights. To achieve this goal, an individual East Timorese had to accept fully the Portuguese way of life including profession of the Catholic faith, and proper command of Portuguese. The provision of mass education as a way of achieving linguistic acculturation in favour of Portuguese in all contexts was to become an explicit objective of the Portuguese administration:

> The second fundamental goal of our struggle in education is: that everyone has to speak Portuguese! If there are prayers? Pray in Portuguese. If there is discussion, discuss in Portuguese. If there is a real need to curse, then curse in Portuguese! If we need to understand each other, then let's understand each other in Portuguese!
>
> (translation of Grade 1973: 219)

In the period 1953-1974, the numbers of children attending primary school expanded, according to one estimate, from 8000 to 95,000 throughout East Timor, with a 77 per cent participation rate. The numbers receiving secondary education were of course much smaller. The learning of Portuguese was rigorously enforced in the classroom: Pinto & Jardine (1997: 35) report the use of the *palmatoria* (a type of rounded bat) used to beat children caught speaking Tetum. Despite belated Portuguese efforts, most students only received a few years schooling and the quality of learning was often poor. By 1975 it is generally believed that 90-95 per cent of the local population was illiterate (Pinto 1997). But it remains true that by the 1960s and 1970s many Timorese, through schooling (however limited), had some knowledge, rudimentary or otherwise, of Portuguese.

The local East Timorese also had increasing contact with Portuguese through the activities of the Church. Although Tetum (and other local languages) was widely used in missionary work, the Church and its structures, in particular its education system, operated in Portuguese. The process of conversion in East Timor was a slow one for most of the period of Portuguese control, but gained substantial momentum in the late 1960s and early 1970s. By 1975 one quarter of the population had become Catholic.

There was also in East Timor before 1975 a relatively large Chinese community – mostly Hakka but also some Cantonese from Southern China (Thomaz 1974). The Chinese first entered in substantial numbers in the nineteenth century – via Macao and came to dominate the retailing and import/export sector - by the 1960s 397 of the 400 retail outlets in East Timor were Chinese-owned (Taylor 1991). Although the Chinese community was concentrated in Dili and other large centres, such as Baucau, few areas of East Timor did not have at least one Chinese shopkeeper. They tended to live separately from the rest of the population, and were Taiwanese citizens like most other overseas Chinese after 1949. They spoke Hakka (and/or Cantonese), as well as Portuguese and Tetum (and sometimes other languages according to the locality). They also learnt Mandarin Chinese in their own separate Taiwanese-style school system, where by law they were also required to learn Portuguese. Although the 1970 census gives a figure of 6120 Chinese residents in East Timor, many sources cite much higher figures: Thomaz (1974) thought the Chinese community to be as large as 18,000, whilst Carey & Carter Bentley (1995) give a figure of 20,000 Chinese residents in 1975.

In addition to varieties of Chinese and Standard Portuguese there were during this phase three other non-indigenous languages spoken in East Timor and it is these which appear to have suffered most during the period of Portuguese control. Macau Creole Portuguese was spoken in Dili in the nineteenth century by incomers from Macau, a Portuguese outpost in South China. Little more can be said about it. More interesting is Bidau Creole Portuguese formerly spoken in a suburb of Dili. It is generally believed to have died out in the 1960s. Baxter (1990) examined tape recordings made in the 1950s and found close links with other varieties of Creole Portuguese, in particular the Malaccan Creole, as well as clear evidence of Tetum influence. Speakers of Bidau and Macau Portuguese Creole are presumed to have shifted to Standard Portuguese. Of special significance is the fate of Malay during the Portuguese era. Malay was once a widely spoken trade language throughout Timor, as elsewhere in the Eastern Indonesian region. Used for centuries even by the Portuguese-speaking Topasses it was still widely known in the early part of the nineteenth century in East Timor. But by the latter part of the century, Malay seems to have fallen off the map in Dili and most of East Timor. It appears that efforts by Portuguese authorities to eliminate it after 1870 (Fox 1997) were very effective, although how precisely this objective was achieved remains a mystery. Where Malay gave way, its functions, especially in Dili, were taken over by creolised Tetum-Dili and by Portuguese. Malay survived in Dili only as the language of the tiny 'Arab' community – 400 Moslems resident in one suburb. Elsewhere, Thomaz (1974) reported that there was some use of Malay/Indonesia as a second language in the Oe-Cusse enclave – this is hardly surprising given that this small piece of land is completely surrounded by Indonesian West Timor. But Thomaz's observation sits poorly with 1991 census figures (presented below) which show that some twenty years after Indonesian occupation of East Timor it is precisely this area (also known as Ambeno) with the lowest proportion of Indonesian speakers.

3. INDONESIAN OCCUPATION OF EAST TIMOR AND RAPID INDONESIANISATION

The brutal and cruel history of Indonesian occupation of East Timor (1975-1999) has been widely reported in print (e.g. Aubrey 1998, Carey & Carter 1995, Gunn 1995, Pinto 7 Jardine 1997) and, after the events of August-October 1999, is now well-known to the world public.

The consequences of 24 years of Indonesian occupation for the local linguistic ecology were in most respects very negative – in sharp contrast to what had happened during the Portuguese era. Military activity during this period led to massive population displacement, and to the death of 200,000 Timorese (a figure cited even by Indonesian sources) out of a population of little more than 600,000 at the time of the Indonesian invasion. East Timor, previously a Portuguese colony, was fully integrated into the Republic of Indonesia in September 1976 as the nation's 27th province. Despite Indonesian claims to having pumped hundreds of millions of development aid into East Timor, it remained during this whole period the country's poorest province.

Rapid Indonesianisation – cultural, political and linguistic – was at all times a paramount government objective. It was to be achieved as quickly as possible through a range of measures such as control of mass media, ideologisation through education, military and economic implantation, transmigration, and elimination of Portuguese (openly stigmatised as a 'colonial language'). Insistence on acceptance of the notion of *pancasila* (the 5 governing principles of the Indonesian state) as an aid to promote full integration resulted in the almost total conversion of the remaining animist East Timorese (75 per cent) to the Roman Catholic faith.

The use and knowledge of Indonesian has always been recognized by Indonesian authorities and experts (e.g. Dardjowidjojo 1998) as fundamental to the unity and development of the Republic of Indonesia. As a result, Indonesian authorities closely monitored the spread of Indonesian throughout East Timor, as a measure of East Timor's relative integration into Indonesia. The most recent census figures given below provide a snapshot of knowledge of Indonesian in East Timor in the early 1990s. Overall, the proportion of the resident population able to speak Indonesian had almost doubled in 10 years: from approximately 30 per cent in 1981 to 60 per cent in 1991. It appears at first glance that the intensive Indonesianisation of the East Timorese population was increasingly very successful. However, the 1991 census result masks a number of important issues that cast doubt on the accuracy of the figures presented in Table 3. In the first instance, the late 1980s and 1990s saw an exponential increase in the numbers of non-East Timorese resident in East Timor. Large numbers of Indonesian-speaking military personnel, bureaucrats and their families settling in East Timor were also accompanied by ever increasing waves of Indonesian-speakers – mainly Moslems, coming in primarily from provinces to the west and north of East Timor.

Table 3:   **Percentage of residents of East Timor who speak Indonesian, 1991 Census**

Local Area	Men	Women	Total
Aileu	68.69	58.11	63.81
Ainaro	57.36	42.20	49.81
Ambeno	46.52	38.32	42.46
Baucau	62.43	49.00	55.91
Bobonaro	64.90	49.18	56.88
Covalima	62.88	50.20	56.53
Dili	88.14	79.35	84.00
Ermera	58.37	51.78	55.30
Lautém	70.02	50.09	59.97
Liquiça	60.09	48.41	54.33
Manatuto	74.17	61.75	68.05
Manufahi	68.94	54.08	61.61
Viqueque	48.89	39.23	43.98
East Timor	66.30	54.10	60.34

Source: Statistik Kesejahteraan Rakyat Timor Timur 1995,
Hasil Survei Sosial Ekonomi Nasional 1995

By 1997, less than 10 years after East Timor was made an open province in 1989, of a population estimated to be 867,000, at least 250,000 were non-East Timorese newcomers (Carey 1999). The size of the Indonesian-speaking influx can be further confirmed by the religious affiliation of resident population in the 1990s: although the proportion of indigenous East Timorese professing to be Catholic was 97 per cent, the figure dropped to only 79 per cent of the total resident population of East Timor. The remainder at the time was mostly Moslem. Where once there were 400 Moslems resident in East Timor (in Dili) in the early 1970s, this number had increased 400-fold in less than twenty years. Although the province was by no means pacified at the time, on 16 January 1980, the Indonesian government made it a designated transmigration area. By May 1980, press reports from Dili spoke already of 150 transmigration sites in East Timor – for incoming Javanese and Balinese.

That Dili reports the highest proportion of residents able to speak Indonesian is hardly surprising – given its status as provincial centre of Indonesian administrative and military control. It also acted as the principal entry point for Indonesian transmigrants. The most surprising census result comes from Ambeno (also known as Oe Cusse) – with the lowest figure for Indonesian given. Before the Indonesian invasion of 1975, this was the one area, according to Thomaz (1974) where Malay was still used as a second language (see above). It is possible that local residents are under-reporting their knowledge of Indonesian – much as Estonians under-reported their knowledge of Russian during the Soviet era (Laitin 1996). Alternatively, it is possible that residents of Oe Cusse are carefully distinguishing between the local Malay variety used as a lingua franca in their area and Standard Indonesian. The whole issue of how language census data were collected in East Timor and what their real significance is deserves further investigation.

The two main non-indigenous languages of East Timor – Portuguese and Chinese – were targeted by Indonesian authorities for elimination. Portuguese was replaced in schools, administration and the media. In 1980-1981 Indonesian authorities banned the use of Portuguese by the Church as its liturgical language – in the hope that it would be forced to adopt Indonesian. Church authorities, with

Vatican approval, instead replaced Portuguese with Tetum (see below). Indonesian efforts to eliminate Portuguese appeared to have their desired effect: no longer openly spoken, nor taught in the schools, transmission of Portuguese to new generations of East Timorese became almost impossible – especially when everyone was required to learn Indonesian. Indonesian authorities also encouraged the study of English in local tertiary institutes, in the hope that this would further weaken the position of Portuguese amongst the educated elite. Somewhat paradoxically, Portuguese, the original colonising language, came instead to be the language of East Timorese resistance, used in particular by FRETILIN (*Frente Revolutionária de Timor-Leste Independente*), and by FALINTIL (*Forças Armadas de Libertação de Timor-Leste Independente*). Pictures and film footage from East Timor in the 1980s and 1990s show quite clearly the use of perfect Portuguese in banners held up in mass demonstrations organised by students in Dili. For many East Timorese, use of Portuguese was merely symbolic – they could not speak it. Yet despite Portuguese's clandestine prestige, by the 1990s observers such as Gunn (1995) and Carey (1997) were drawn to reflect in a concerned fashion about the much weakened position of Portuguese as an everyday language of communication.

During this same period of intense pressure in favour of Indonesianisation, the Chinese community also saw its position drastically undermined with its numbers reduced to a mere fraction of former levels. Most fled the country – with a large community resident in Melbourne. Their special status and privileges – including separate school system - were terminated and their dominant position in the local economy dismantled in favour of interests closely associated with the central government in Jakarta.

With respect to local languages, the predominant position of Tetum in East Timor was confirmed – it gained favour through the activities of the Church (and grudging acquiescence of authorities). A full liturgical language from 1981, it was also eventually being introduced gradually into the Catholic primary school sector in the Dili diocese as a medium of instruction in lower grades. Observers (eg Carey 1997) report that during the period of Indonesian occupation the use of Tetum spread substantially amongst East

Timorese – as a result of Church activities and as a symbol of resistance. On the other hand, the spread of Tetum may also have been exaggerated: Gunn (1995) reporting on his travels around East Timor notes very clearly the frequent use of Indonesian, not Tetum, as a lingua franca – a process aided by the spread of transmigrants throughout the country. In any case, it remains unclear to what degree Tetum had come to be used between 1975 and 1999 in formerly non-Tetum-speaking areas such as Fataluku and Oe Cusse. Unconfirmed reports suggest, for instance, that Indonesian replaced Portuguese as the lingua franca in Fataluku areas after 1975. The notion that knowledge of Tetum may have spread to the enclave of Oe Cusse can now also be rejected: Australian military officials in the enclave since the end of 1999 are reported to have found themselves unable to communicate to locals in Tetum.

The other indigenous languages of East Timor fared much less well during 1975-1999. They seem to have suffered from total neglect – from both Church and the Indonesian State. Whereas missionary work before 1975 was often conducted in the local language, and the preparation of language materials and grammars in conjunction with Church activities were becoming increasingly common, all of these activities in favour of local languages other than Tetum appeared to have ceased after 1975. The Indonesian State certainly had no interest in the preservation and/or promotion of East Timorese languages (other than the small space left to Tetum in Church-controlled activities). Although by the late 1980s official Indonesian policy had supposedly become more flexible on the teaching of local languages in schools throughout the archipelago state (see Dardjowidjojo 1998), the failure to provide any resources meant that nothing was done in their favour in the government-controlled education sector in East Timor. With respect to the Church-run school sector, Church resources, already meagre, were stretched to cover the use of Tetum, with nothing left for any other languages.

Military activity during this whole period must be viewed as the greatest threat to the linguistic ecology of East Timor because of the intense physical disruption it provoked. Indonesian occupation was characterised by periods of enormous dislocation (in particular forced mass resettlement at the behest of the Indonesian military in

1977 and 1978), and massive loss of life. When coupled with promotion of Indonesian by the State and of Tetum by the Church, these factors are sufficient to put the survival of other East Timorese languages at risk. Carey (1997) was convinced enough of the damage to report the 'virtual extinction' of East Timor's other indigenous languages. Fortunately, such a negative assessment is not borne out by other reports from East Timorese on the ground for the same period: these indicate that Carey was mistaken, since local languages had, at least until the events of 1999, shown remarkable resilience. It is true, however, that the long-term future of many of these languages could not be guaranteed – especially if Indonesian social and military policies continued unabated. There is no doubt however that one local language continued to fade – by the early 1990s one Indonesian source (Sudiartha et al. 1994) claimed tiny Maku'a was dead. However, such an announcement appears to have been premature: an East Timorese report confirmed that three elderly speakers of Maku'a were still alive in the late 1990s (G. Hull, pers. comm.).

4. EAST TIMOR POST-REFERENDUM (30 AUGUST 1999)

The third phase in East Timor's linguistic history is centred on events immediately before, during and after the internationally sanctioned referendum on self-determination held on 30 August 1999. This phase, although only months old at time of writing is the most radical and dramatic of all: the indigenous linguistic ecology appears to have been overwhelmed – at least for the present - by total population dislocation and the consequences of large-scale violence and destruction. The long-term consequences of events during this period for the survival of local languages, other than Tetum, remain unknown for both medium- and long- terms.

The behaviour of Indonesian authorities before and after the referendum in East Timor received worldwide media coverage and led finally to international military intervention.[2] The level of mass destruction and dislocation was unparalleled in the history of East Timor. All evidence, including secret Australian & Indonesian documents leaked to the media as well as United Nation reports, points to the chain of disastrous events as having been planned well in advance and fully orchestrated by Indonesian military officials.

Despite often violent intimidation orchestrated by the Indonesian military during the campaign period, the offer of autonomous status within the Republic of Indonesia was rejected by 78.5 per cent of the voting population. The incoming Indonesian president, B.J. Habibie, had previously announced in January 1999 that in case of such an outcome Indonesia would accept independence for East Timor.

Immediately after the vote was held and before the outcome of the vote was announced on 4 September, the security situation began to deteriorate rapidly throughout East Timor. By the time United Nations troops under Australian command began deployment on 20 September, at least 80 per cent of existing infrastructure had been destroyed and a similar percentage of the East Timorese population displaced from their homes. Approximately 200,000-250,000 East Timorese (30 per cent of the local population) left the region entirely, most forced by pro-Indonesian militia across the land border into Indonesian West Timor, but with substantial numbers also forcibly dispersed around the Indonesian archipelago. Most serious destruction and displacement occurred in four areas: (1) Dili and its environs; (2) the region adjacent to the border with West Timor; (3) the Fataluku-speaking eastern tip of East Timor, around Lospalos; and (4) the isolated enclave of Oe Cusse. Despite international pressure to allow the return of refugees to East Timor, by mid-January 2000 more than 100,000-150,000 people, according to press reports, were still to be living in militia-controlled camps in West Timor. In many cases, according to reliable press reports, whole communities were bussed en masse across the border. These include entire Fataluku-speaking villages from easternmost Lospalos

---

[2]   See Progress Report of the Secretary-General to the United Nations, 13 December1999, for details of events before, during and after the referendum.

transported to closed camps hundreds of kilometres away in West Timor. It is not known what the long-term future of these East Timorese refugees is, with some reports suggesting they may be settled permanently – at the behest of the militia and Indonesian military - in West Timor. Another 50,000-60,000 East Timorese were reported to be missing, months after the referendum, with humanitarian organisations unable to account for them.

Reconstruction of East Timor, under United Nations supervision, began in earnest in early 2000, coupled with the slow and very incomplete repatriation of externally displaced refugees to East Timor. It is not clear, however, to what extent internally and externally displaced persons have returned to their own villages or towns. If instead they have simply gathered in larger centres, then the chances of permanent disruption to indigenous languages is increased – as these newly mixed communities are more likely to shift to a shared common lingua franca, such as Tetum.

Whilst the Indonesian government in Jakarta appears to have been genuinely surprised by the East Timorese rejection of its offer of autonomy in 1999, supporters of East Timorese independence had already begun formal open planning for separation as early as 1997, long before Indonesia agreed to a referendum. A series of intra-party talks, which included pro-independence and pro-Indonesian supporters, were held in Europe. In 1998 the CNRT (Timorese National Resistance Council), the umbrella organisation of pro-independence groups, headed by imprisoned leader, Xanana Gusmão, adopted the so-called Magna Carta – an agreed document to serve as the basis for a future post-independence Constitution. The Magna Carta formally pronounced Portuguese as East Timor's 'official language' with Tetum as its 'national language'. Neither this document, nor subsequent pronouncements or documents give any explicit recognition to other indigenous languages. Language policy issues were also considered during the CNRT's Strategic Planning Conference held in Melbourne in April 1999 to develop formal policies for post-independence administration and development in East Timor. As part of the gradual transformation of the education sector, for instance, it was anticipated that the use of Indonesian as medium of instruction would be phased out over 10 years. Portuguese and Tetum would take its place, and some space (still to be finalised at the time) would also be given to English. The 10 year timeframe was intended to allow for the orderly replacement and retraining of Indonesian-speaking teachers (the overwhelming bulk of whom were Indonesian transmigrants). Whilst never explicit, there is little doubt that the progressive elimination of Indonesian from all public spheres was a long-term objective. Transmigrants, who were officially welcomed to remain in East Timor after independence, would, it was hoped, adapt to the new linguistic situation by learning Tetum and/or Portuguese.

Events since the referendum have overtaken CNRT's vision of orderly language planning for East Timor. Whilst it remains to be seen quite how much Indonesian will be used in East Timor in coming years, it is plausible to argue that the language may well have self-destructed – much faster than anyone might have otherwise envisaged in different circumstances. If this is indeed the case, then Indonesian/Malay may well have been effectively eliminated – for the second time in little more than 100 years. Such a scenario is assisted by the almost complete departure of non-East Timorese residents, i.e. Indonesian administrators, military and transmigrants. The disappearance overnight of Indonesian teachers also means that the education system can now be rebuilt from scratch – with new language medium policies effective immediately.[3] Many pro-Indonesian supporters ('pro-integrationists') – including their leadership - also remain outside East Timor. A smaller number of pro-integrationists, not tainted by military activity and links before and after the referendum, are now back in East Timor. They remain favourable to links with Indonesia but it remains to be seen to what extent they can influence official language policy in favour of Indonesian.

The dramatic blow dealt to Indonesian, in the aftermath of events in East Timor, is of course a boon to Portuguese. The leadership of the CNRT, including Xanana Gusmão, has reiterated on numerous

---

[3]   The impact of the departure of these Indonesian teachers can be gauged by the report in Gunn (1995) that in the early 1990s only one teacher in the whole secondary school system in East Timor was East Timorese in origin.

occasions since the referendum that, in accordance with the Magna Carta, Portuguese and Tetum will become East Timor's official and national languages respectively. Portugal and other Lusophone countries have responded enthusiastically and have become strong supporters of the full reintroduction of Portuguese to East Timor. The CNRT is also committed to full membership of the Community of Portuguese-Speaking Nations (Comunidade dos Paìses de Lingua Portuguesa). The future of Portuguese in East Timor is now guaranteed, although it remains to be seen to what extent Portuguese will re-establish itself in East Timorese society. Presently, according to recent press reports, it is estimated that only 10 per cent of the population is proficient in Portuguese.

Tetum's position is secure, although the precise meaning of its designation as 'national language' remains to be determined at this point. The situation with respect to the other indigenous languages is much less clear. The massive physical dislocation may now have permanently threatened their long-term survival, especially of small languages such as Idate, Waima'a and Naueti. They are also further threatened in the long-term by the active promotion of Tetum in an independent East Timor, if this leads to language shift.

The fate of tiny Maku'a today is completely unknown. All villages in the area where Maku'a was spoken were destroyed. The population was either forcibly removed hundreds of kilometres away to West Timor or fled in large numbers to caves in the region. An additional unknown number were killed in militia rampages that were given television coverage in Australia. Eventually those who were hiding in caves were located by United Nations forces, and allowed to return home. Many of these in West Timor were still in militia-controlled camps in early 2000. The three elderly Maku'a speakers, previously referred to, may simply not have survived events.

REFERENCES

Aubrey, Jim (ed.) 1998. *Free East Timor*. Sydney: Random House.

Baxter, Alan 1990. Notes on the Creole Portuguese of Bidau, East Timor. *Journal of Pidgin and Creole Linguistics* 5: 1-38.

Capell, Arthur 1944. Peoples and Languages of Timor. *Oceania* 14: 191-219, 311-337, 15: 19-48.

_____ 1972. Portuguese Timor, Two More Non-Austronesian Languages. *Oceania Linguistic Monographs* 15: 95-104.

Carey, Peter 1997. From Netherlands Indies to Indonesia - from Portuguese Timor to the Republic of East Timor/Timor Loro Sa'e: Two Paths to Nationhood and Independence. *Indonesia and the Malay World* 71: 3-21.

_____ 1999. The Catholic Church, Religious Revival, and the Nationalist Movement in East Timor, 1975-1998. *Indonesia and the Malay World* 27: 77-95.

Carey, Peter & G. Carter Bentley (eds) 1995. *East Timor at the Crossroads: the Forging of a Nation*. Honolulu: University of Hawai'i Press.

Dardjowidjojo, Soenjono 1998. Strategies for a Successful National Language Policy: the Indonesian Case. *International Journal of the Sociology of Language* 130: 35-47.

Fox, James J. 1997. The Historical Position of Tetun among the Languages of the Timor Area. Ms. Australian National University.

Grade, E. A. 1973. Timor 1973 - Panoramica do ensino. *Revista Militar* 25: 211-252.

Grimes, Barbara F. (ed.) 1996. *Ethnologue*, 13th edition. Dallas: Summer Institute of Linguistics.

Gunn, Geoffrey 1995. Language, Literacy and Political Hegemony in East Timor. In David Myers (ed.) *The Politics of Multiculturalism in the Asia/Pacific*, 117-123. Darwin: Northern Territory University Press.

Hajek, John 1999. A New Language Policy for a New East Timor: Learning from Global Experience, Ms. Melbourne.

Hidalgo, Cesar A. 1998. Language Choice in a Multilingual Society: the case of the Philippines. *International Journal of the Sociology of Language* 130: 23-33.

Laitin, David 1996. Language Planning in the Former Soviet Union: the Case of Estonia. *International Journal of the Sociology of Language* 118: 43-61.

Pinto, Constancio & Mathew Jardine 1997. *East Timor's Unfinished Struggle.* Boston: South End Press.

Sudiartha, I Wayan, Made Denes, I Wayan Tama, & R. B. Suprihanto 1994. *Survei Bahasa dan Sastra di Timor Timur.* Jakarta: Pusat Pembinaan dan Pengembangan Bahasa.

Taylor, John G. 1991. *Indonesia's Forgotten War.* London: Zed Books.

Thomaz, Luis Filipe R., 1974. Timor: Notas Histórico-Linguísticas. *Portugaliae Historica* 2: 167-300.

_____ 1981. The Formation of Tetum-Praça, Vehicular Language of East Timor. In Nigel Phillips & Khaidir Anwar (eds) *Papers on Indonesian Languages and Literatures*, 54-83. Paris: Cahiers d'Archipel 13.

Chapter 14

Steel Tyres or Rubber Tyres — Maintenance or Loss: Pennsylvania German in the "horse and buggy communities" of Ontario

Kate Burridge
La Trobe University

1. INTRODUCTION[1]

The norm for a minority language in a prolonged contact situation is eventually language shift — it might be over a few generations or a few hundred years. In the case of Pennsylvania German, however, shift has not taken place either in Canada or in the US, at least among the Anabaptist communities. Here we have an instance of a non-standard, non-written language of no prestige — associated with rurality, lack of sophistication and with no official recognition (to the extent that it is even banned in the school playground). Yet this is a language that has been holding its own well and truly against English and has been doing so for nearly 400 years. This is one persistent language and the secrets of its survival technique are instructive for helping us to identify the socio-cultural and linguistic conditions under which survival and maintenance are likely to occur.

Let me point out as a note of historical interest that survival was not always the predicted outcome for Pennsylvania German, at least in Ontario. In what is probably the earliest account of Canadian Pennsylvania German, the German linguist Neufeld wrote in 1955 of the decline of the language in Canada — in fact he went so far as to suggest that, at the time he was writing, the Canadian Mennonites had already given up the language and gone exclusively over to English.

---

[1]   To the members of the Mennonite community in Waterloo County I owe a special debt of gratitude for their continued friendship and their time and patience in answering my constant stream of questions. Over the last ten years, they have taught me an enormous amount about their language — and much more. I am also pleased to acknowledge funding from the Australian Research Council (A59803475).

Die oben erwähnte kleine Gruppe pennsylvanischer
Mennoniten sudwestdeutscher Herkunft hat ihre Mundart
bereits aufgegeben und bedient sich heute ausschliesslich des
Englischen.
[The above-mentioned small group of Pennsylvania
Mennonites of southwest German origin [in Waterloo County]
have already given up their dialect and today use exclusively
English.]   (Neufeld 1955: 230, my translation)

One wonders how Neufeld could ever have arrived at such a
conclusion — to overlook the approximately 30,000 Mennonite
people who speak Pennsylvania German in some form and most
importantly the few thousand who use only Pennsylvania German,
except when they have to interact with the non-Pennsylvania German
speaking outside world. While it is true that many of the so-called
"progressive" Mennonites are moving more and more over to
English — and as we will see Pennsylvania German will almost
certainly die within these groups — in no way could this be said of
the religiously more conservative groups. They show absolutely no
sign of giving up their language. For them Pennsylvania German is
alive and thriving, and it looks like continuing to do so for some
time.

2.   THE   PENNSYLVANIA   GERMAN   SPEECH COMMUNITY

Like any speech community, the Pennsylvania Germans do not
represent a totally homogeneous group. What exists is a complex
design of social, cultural and religious diversity which must be taken
into account in any appraisal of the linguistic situation.

The Pennsylvania German speaking group examined here are
Mennonites of Swiss-German origin. The religious and historical
background of these Mennonites, in particular their early persecution
experience, has done much to shape the lively speech community we
find today. These people are Anabaptists and together with the
Amish and the Hutterites form the three major groups of the
Anabaptist religion. Anabaptism originally emerged as a counter
Church movement during the 16th century in Europe, beginning in
Switzerland and later spreading to Holland and Germany. Each of

the three Anabaptist groups mentioned followed different leaders and it is from these they took their respective names — Jacob Hutter (a hatter by trade) was the elected leader of the Hutterites, Jacob Amman of the Amish and Menno Simons (a former Roman Catholic priest) of the Mennonites. The term Anabaptist refers to the practice of rebaptising individuals already baptised as children. Members of these groups argue that infant baptism is not in keeping with their concept of the Church as a voluntary group of believers and accordingly they rebaptise anyone who wishes to join them — adult baptism therefore is a symbol of their faith.

From the beginning, the Anabaptists advocated rigid separation of Church and State and for themselves total separation from the "world". They accepted the Bible as their sole guide of faith and practice. The Bible was their authority — not the Roman Catholic Church and Pope. Not surprisingly, then, they clashed with the Roman Catholic and also the Protestant churches of the time and were severely persecuted. Thousands were imprisoned and burnt at the stake and the strong desire of present-day Mennonites and Amish to maintain a separate existence is not surprising in the light of the what they suffered during this time. Many families today own a copy of *The Martyrs' Mirror*. This huge book, first published in Holland in 1660, offers vivid accounts of all the Anabaptist martyrs of the Post-Reformation. Together with forceful reminders in hymns and sermons, it would certainly have the effect of reinforcing their desire for isolation.

During the 17th century, the Quaker William Penn issued the Anabaptists with an invitation to settle in Pennsylvania. Britain promised that in America they would be given religious freedom and with that many Dutch, German and Swiss immigrated during the 17th and 18th centuries. At the end of the 18th and at the beginning of the 19th century, many resettled in Canada. This was a direct result of the American War of Independence and the anti-German sentiment which followed. Their pacifist principles had already marked them as traitors in the eyes of some of their fellow countrymen, and their situation considerably worsened when the British employed German troops. So they left in their horse drawn buggies, some ending up near the Canadian border but most settling in Waterloo County. It is this group of speakers that is the focus of this current paper.

2.1   Different Subgroups

While I do not intend to go deeply into the social and religious
background of these people, it is important to consider these details
inasmuch as they are relevant to understanding the current linguistic
situation and its development. Religion and way of life are intimately
connected for the Mennonites and govern strongly the attitude of the
people towards their language. For many, language has a deeply
religious significance and this will guarantee its survival, at least for
these groups.

To understand just what the future holds for Pennsylvania German,
we must first consider the complex make-up of the Mennonite Order
since this has important bearing on the progress of shift from
German to English. The order itself comprises over 40,000 members
but this includes many different subgroups.[2] In fact, the Swiss-
German Mennonites of all the Anabaptist groups in North-America
have the largest number of separate congregations. Since the 1870s
they have been experiencing continued factionalism and the result is
a complex pattern of different sub and splinter groups. The major
reason for these schisms is the different degrees to which members
will interpret the scriptural quotation — "And be not conformed to
this world" *[Stellet euch nicht dieser Welt gleich]*. The initial split,
for instance, came about because certain groups were admitting
worldly church practices like Sunday school. They were also more
liberal in their attire. The question of non-conformity poses
enormous problems and has led to great tension and serious splits
within their community. Biblical exactness, as we will see, is an
important factor in maintaining their separate status and close sense
of community, but paradoxically it is also a reason for the continuing
factionalism. To an outsider the situation is complicated and
confusing and it is often difficult to tell the sociological and religious
differences between the groups. Differences can be subtle, such as a
difference in dress styles or buggy technology, or they can involve
more serious issues such as education of the young, or the adoption

---

[2]   This figure of 40,000 includes one-third Russian Mennonites who
speak a form of Low German. These groups originated in Europe but were
later transplanted in Russia and when things did not work out for them
there a number moved to North America and parts of South America; see
Moelleken (1992) who traces the sociolinguistic history of a number of
Russian Mennonite groups. For an excellent account of all these different
Amish-Mennonite congregations in Waterloo County, see Fretz (1989).

of new farming methods. To simplify matters, the Amish-Mennonite Anabaptists are generally divided into two major groups — the Plain and the Non-Plain Folk. This is a gross simplification admittedly, but in terms of the sociolinguistic situation it is a useful distinction to make.

2.1.1 The Plain Groups

The so-called "Plain Folk" are the most conservative Mennonites. Known more colloquially as the "horse and buggy people" (or *Fuhrleit* in German), their separate simple way of life attracts much attention. People often do not understand the theological reasons behind their refusal to accept modern ways, and assume that they are pursuing eccentric behaviour simply in its own right. These Mennonites have a very distinctive style of dress which has changed little over the centuries. They drive only horses and buggies, are opposed to modern conveniences like cars, radios, televisions and telephones and refuse all forms of government aid and insurance.

The Old Order Mennonites are the largest of the plain groups and they are the main focus of this paper. Comprising approximately 12 per cent of the approximately 30,000 Swiss-German Mennonites in Ontario, these people are rural and isolated and alone make up half of the total farming population of Ontario. While the Old Order clearly began as a purely religious group, it now has really become a distinct cultural-ethnic group and contrasts remarkably with mainstream Canadian culture. As Alan Buehler, a former Old Order Mennonite, writes (1977: 96) — "to us there were two kind[s] of people, the Mennonites and the Non-Mennonite[s], the Mennonite or an outsider, or a man of the world". Fishman (1982: 33-35) describes the Old Order Amish in Pennsylvania as a rare example of stable societal biculturism (or what he terms "di-ethnia"). This also aptly describes the Old Order Mennonites in Canada — as in Pennsylvania we see here a stable situation involving two distinct sets of cultural behaviours.

The Old Order want to keep change to a minimum — *ufhalde de alde Wege* [maintain the old ways]. It is true, however, that some accommodations are now being made, for example with respect to electricity and telephones. It seems that both electricity and phones are more readily accepted (at least to certain members of the group) because they are perceived to be less of a threat to community living.

Cars, on the other hand, clearly are a greater threat since they make it possible to travel vast distances, presumably also outside the community, where one would be much more vulnerable to worldly influences. To leave the community means to these people the same as leaving the "true" Church (see also discussion in Bausenhart 1971).

The problem facing these plain groups is that once they start to accommodate to new ways, where is the line to be drawn? Once they start to admit change, the outside culture has a foot in the door and the real fear then is that this contact with the outside will destroy their own sense of community. They have only to look at their more progressive members to see that their fears are well grounded. It is really only groups like the Old Order who have managed to retain this sense of community and remain truly *abgesandert vun die Welt* ["apart from the world"] and these are the ones who hold the key to the survival of Pennsylvania German.

Of course accommodations always mean further fragmentation, with splinter groups wanting stricter discipline, less contact with outsiders and fewer "mod cons" — even rubber tyres became an issue in the early 1900s. Last century in fact saw several new groups emerge from the Old Orders. The earliest and probably the most significant of the break-away groups to establish were the David Martin people, who split off in 1917. This is a very visual group with their noisy steel rim buggies and also a curious group, since they will not associate socially with plain Mennonites outside their group — especially not with the Old Orders. In fact there is a popular saying that whatever the Old Orders object to, the David Martins agree to. They therefore provide a useful comparison with the Old Orders with respect to Pennsylvania German survival.

2.1.2   The Non-Plain Groups
The so-called "Non-Plain Folk" make up the vast majority of the Mennonites and they fall into two distinct groups — the Progressives and the Transitionals. The Progressives are largely urban and represent the modern groups. Generally speaking, they are indistinguishable from those who participate in mainstream Canadian life, and of this group, only the old generation are Pennsylvania German-speaking.

The Transitionals number only about 20 per cent and are almost all rural (although this is changing as more seek employment in the cities and towns). Most of their members come from the large group of Waterloo-Markham Mennonites. This group still follows many of the same beliefs and behaviour patterns as the Old Order Mennonites but have accommodated more to modern ways. For example, although they use the same meeting houses (i.e. their plain churches) as the Old Order, their church services are part English and part German. In addition, black cars now replace the horse and buggy (earning them the nickname the "black bumper Mennonites" — until recently, the chrome on these cars was also painted black). Their dress, like their cars, is plain and without decoration, but not in the same distinctive tradition of the Old Orders (for that reason, they are sometimes referred to as the "Modern Plain"). Although they are associated with the Progressives under this label Non-Plain, sociologically and linguistically, they are actually more closely bound with the Old Orders.

Table 1 provides a summary of the major groups and their most significant sub-divisions:

Table 1:   The major divisions of the Mennonites

THE PLAIN FOLK

Old Order Mennonites — conservative, rural and isolated, few (and for many no) modern conveniences, regular use of German (family, community and work), use of English only with outsiders.

David Martins — conservative, rural and isolated, modern conveniences but for businesses only (not within the home), regular use of German (family, community and work), use of English with outsiders (especially by those running small businesses).

THE NON-PLAIN FOLK

Transitional Mennonites (or "Modern Plain") — modern conveniences, rural and urban, regular use of both German and English.

Progressive Mennonites (modern groups) — indistinguishable from mainstream Canadians, regular use of English, ability to use some German if need arises.

But this is painting a neat picture of what in reality is nowhere near as orderly. There is a mind-boggling array of different sub and splinter groups which can be placed along a continuum — from the ultra-conservative Mennonites (those sub-divisions of the Old Order, for example, with no rubber tyres, no phones and no electricity) to the most progressive. Along this continuum it is also possible to plot the different speakers according to their language skills — from the most competent to those with a passive knowledge only. Basically competence in Pennsylvania German accords with the degree of religious conservatism. It is not of course that religion directly bears on the linguistic abilities of these people, but, as will become apparent, on account of what this religion entails.

The David Martins are an instructive group in this regard. Although described above as plain, they really have a foot at either end of this continuum. Not only do they prefer to associate with outsiders, but they are at the one time both the most conservative and the most progressive of the Mennonite orders. For instance, unlike the Old Orders they still farm with horses and their homes are among the most plain; yet those operating small businesses have fax machines, computers and mobile phones in their workshops! The David Martins are therefore helpful in identifying the factors that have worked most to the detriment of Pennsylvania German continuity within the more modern orders.

3.   THE LINGUISTIC SITUATION

In 1945, a linguist by the name of J.W Frey published a paper on the Amish in Pennsylvania which he entitled "Amish Triple Talk". This study in many ways pre-empts all the recent discussion on diglossia, since it is essentially a triglossic situation that he implies exists for these Amish people. The Old Order Mennonites in Canada are also triglossic — Pennsylvania German, English and High German. To begin with, they are bilingual Pennsylvania German and English. Pennsylvania German (in this schema the L(ow)-variety) is usually only spoken and is the language of home and community. English (the H(igh)-variety) is read and written and is only spoken when dealing with non-Pennsylvania German speaking outsiders.

At the same time, these people also have a knowledge of High German. This is not the same as Modern High German today but is (archaic) Luther German — the language of the Luther Bible, but with influence from their own Pennsylvania German dialect. High German is understandably very important to them and is held in high esteem. As the word of God, everyone must be able to read it and children are taught it by family and at school. It is only ever used for religious purposes, although sermons are now given in the dialect, not in High German as is sometimes thought the case. People do not converse in it, unless to quote from the Bible — like their Pennsylvania relatives, though they are triglossic, they are not trilingual. It is clear, however, that High German is functionally very restricted and in this model would best be described as a classical variety.[3]

This was not always the case, however. At the time of early settlement during the 19th century a diglossic situation existed between High German and Pennsylvania German which was not unlike the situation in Switzerland today (see Costello 1986). High German (then the H-variety) was used in outside-of-home contexts involving education, letter-writing, newspapers, literature, worship etc. Like today, it was acquired through schooling and partly through parents. On the other hand Pennsylvania German (the L-variety) was used in intimate contexts like conversing with family and friends and some folk literature. As it is still today, Pennsylvania German was learned at home as the first language. A number of factors contributed to the demise of High German as the H-variety, but the most important was the simple fact that the German homeland was in Europe and immigration from there was diminishing. This, in addition to the extreme isolation of the Anabaptist groups, meant there was not a productive relationship between Continental German and the form of High German spoken in Canada. It was therefore not a potential source for expressions and terms for new concepts or objects. English, as the national language of North America, was

---

[3]   As a curious aside, there is also influence from English on the High German of the Old Order Mennonites. Since English, **not** Pennsylvania German, is the written language, they quite naturally transfer features of spoken English when reading / quoting from the Bible or singing hymns. In particular, the pronunciation of written "r" in all positions and as a North American retroflex sound makes theirs a particularly distinctive accent of this variety of German.

only too ready to fill those gaps. All this made it hard for High German to remain the H-variety. As it was, the language was difficult for speakers, being morphologically much more complex than their own Pennsylvania German. Not surprisingly then High German became more and more restricted in its domains and English supplanted it as the H-variety. It is not unlike the situation of Latin and the different varieties of Vulgar Latin which eventually gave rise to the Modern Romance languages — the important difference, though, is that Pennsylvania German has never been standardised.

4.   THE SURVIVAL OF PENNSYLVANIA GERMAN

English is not learned by the Old Order children until they go to school at the age of six years. Although there are parents who teach some English at home to make the first school years a little easier, many children know no English before this time. In Canada, school is an "English only environment" which admits *no* Pennsylvania German whatsoever (even during recess in the school yard!) and most Old Order children attend parochial schools taught and run by their own community. School continues until the age of 14 when they return to the farms.

The role of school in the maintenance of minority languages is always difficult to determine. Usually it's a matter of too little too late for first language continuity. In this case, however, these schools are a positive force for maintenance — not for any instruction they receive in Pennsylvania German of course, since there is not a word of Pennsylvania German spoken. It is more the fact that only Old Order children attend these parochial (one or two room) schools and this helps to enhance a feeling of group consciousness and means that the children are insulated from any outside influences. But once again the David Martin group provides an interesting contrast in this regard. As always, they are intent on having no contact with the Old Orders, to the extent that they even send their children to public schools rather than the Mennonite-run parochial schools. Although originally in segregated classes, they are now completely integrated and participate fully in the school curriculum. They are not even adverse to the use of televisions and VCRs. The only class they do not take part in is French and this is because it is felt too difficult for those younger children coming only with Pennsylvania German.

Clearly, for the David Martins school has no role in Pennsylvania German maintenance. For this group there are other factors more crucial within this complex of language, culture, ethnicity and religion.

4.1   Cultural and Religious Factors

The secret of the language's survival must surely lie in its symbolic value. Many linguists have discussed the fact that so-called low-prestige language varieties usually have values for their speakers which are quite different from those associated with the more overtly prestigious varieties (see for example Ryan 1979). This is why they can sometimes show such surprisingly strong resistance against the more powerful standard dialects. One important value has to do with group solidarity. This is clearly a very important dimension here as well. However, in the case of these Mennonites, it is more than just a "sense of identification" within a group.

As I see it, there are three aspects to the Mennonite way of life and religion which contribute most to the continued survival of Pennsylvania German within the plain groups — their separateness, their non-conformity and their humility.

"Be Separated from the World" — Isolation

Iere Glawe is — los uns net involved waere mit em Government, awer los Government un Kaerich separate sei. Los uns e separate Volk sei, wu uns egene Noot un Schulde bezale, un unser God diene so wie mir des Wad verschteen. Se dien als bede far des Government, as God mecht des fiere, so as sie in Friede un e ruhich Leve fiere meche. Awer es das Government un Kaerich separate bleive kenne.
[Their belief is — let us not be involved with the Government but let State and Church be separate. Let us be a separated people, looking after our own needs and obligations, and serving our God in our own way. They always pray for the Government, so that God may guide it in such a way that they may continue to live in peace and quiet. But the Church must stay separated.]   (Buehler 1977: 174, my translation)

Other German-speaking groups, who arrived in various waves during Ontario's history (for example the Roman Catholic and Lutheran communities), have assimilated into mainstream culture and have quickly surrendered their language. As Fretz points out, (1989: 63) these people usually immigrated as individuals, not as organised religions and family groups like the Mennonites and Amish, and this would certainly have accelerated the assimilation process. The Old Order Mennonites, on the other hand, have from the beginning always emphasised rigid separation from the world and through mutual self-help and through economic, social and spiritual self-reliance, they have been able to achieve this (see Fretz 1989 for details). Pennsylvania German has always provided an important barrier to the outside world, allowing not only for insider identification, but most importantly for outsider separation. Its loss would also mean the loss of this separate status and this would be equivalent to losing their faith. And for the David Martin group who has greater involvement with the more progressive orders and outsiders, language is one of their main means of remaining detached and isolated from worldly influences (or *abgesandert vun die Welt*).

4.1.1   *Non-Conformity*

> But ye are a chosen generation, a royal priesthood, an holy nation, a peculiar people   (1 Peter 2:9)

Two linguists, Kloss (1966) and Huffines (1980a), attribute the successful maintenance of Pennsylvania German in Pennsylvania to the fact that any change is per se considered to be sinful by these people. I would argue, however, at least for the Canadian context I am describing, that it is not so much change itself, but rather what change entails. Their doctrine of non-conformity, it is true, means that they keep change to a minimum but I do not believe that new ways are rejected out of hand simply because they are considered necessarily bad things. For example, even though as farmers the Old Order will have little to do with the modernisation of machinery, they are extremely interested and, what is more, well up in the latest techniques and new technologies. These they learn about through reading newspapers and farming magazines (see Bausenhart 1971 and Fretz 1989). It is my experience, that many display considerable interest in what is going on in the rest of the world. They are not opposed to change as such — in fact they are not averse to accommodating changes if they think it will be of some benefit to the community as a whole. It is just that most modern innovations are viewed as unnecessary for a truly Christian discipleship. In order to maintain their old way of life, groups like the conservative Old Order Mennonites realise the importance of keeping their language. Their shared language, their shared dress, their horse and buggy are indispensable — without them their social structure would not continue. Losing these social symbols would be the same as losing essential elements of their faith.

The David Martins clearly embrace more in the way of modern technology, at least when it comes to their businesses. Nonetheless tradition and group influence remain very powerful within this sect — in fact this church has even stricter control of the lives of its members because of the threat of excommunication (or "shunning"). Members who dare to think differently can be made to leave the community and are then completely shunned by the rest of the congregation, and this includes all family members.

4.1.2   Humility and Simplicity
It seems that there are many, both within and outside the community, who view the language as simply a degenerate form of German. For these people, Pennsylvania German has all the negative connotations so often associated with "dialect" or "vernacular". To an outsider like myself, it seems that even the speakers themselves generally hold their language in low esteem and under normal circumstances this would mean almost certain decline and shift to English. But nothing could be further from the truth. In fact here, I believe, lies one of the secrets of the language's success at survival. It has to do with the importance which is placed on the need for humility. As Alan Buehler (1977: 98), once more writing on his Old Order heritage, describes:

> Se brauche des Wad 'Demuut' viel....zu iere duut des Wad mene plaini Gleder. Es Englisch-Deitsch Dictionary saagt des Wad meent "to be humble and meek".
> [They use the word Demuut a lot....to them this word means a plain dress. The English-German dictionary says this word means "to be humble and meek."]

Pennsylvania German, like plain dress, has therefore an important symbolic function within their community. This dialect of German is viewed by the Old Order as a sign of humility and is therefore a good and Godly thing. It is not pride — pride is what they abhor the most — but, if you like, pride almost turned on its head. If High German is the word of God, the language of their Scriptures, then the low status of the dialect variety which they speak is seen as an appropriate symbol of their humility. And as for the David Martins, while their businesses might have the latest technology, as far as the rest of their lives goes the plainer and the more basic, the better. The low status of the language therefore has a positive, even sacred, value for both the Old Order and the David Martin groups.

4.2   Linguistic Factors

There are also several linguistic factors that have an important role to play with respect to the continued survival of the language; namely, diglossia and structural compromise.

4.2.1 Diglossia

Not all bilingualism is stable of course, not all bilingualism is necessarily good news for the continued maintenance of a language. The crucial aspect about Pennsylvania German-English bilingualism within groups like the Old Order Mennonites is diglossia. English and Pennsylvania German have their own quite separate domains of use. There is absolutely no mixing of the languages. Pennsylvania German is only spoken and is the language of home and community. English is read and written and is only spoken when dealing with non-Pennsylvania German speaking outsiders. Indeed, the segregation of the languages is so well defined that no code-switching ever takes place.[4] This sort of strict "compartmentalization" (to use Fishman's 1982 term) seems necessary if languages are to survive alongside one another. As Fishman (1982: 29) has put it, "without compartmentalization of one kind or another ... the flow process from language spread to language shift is an inexorable one".

---

4   The only examples of code-switching I have witnessed among the Old Order Mennonites occur during translation tasks — an artificial situation for them, involving both languages. Of course, it is also highly unusual for them to have someone from the outside speaking Pennsylvania German. My presence necessarily upsets the usual strict compartmentalization. For an excellent account of diglossia among the (US) Old Order Amish, see also Louden (1987).

The segregation of languages is there from the start of the acquisition experience. As mentioned briefly, children acquire the languages successively — Pennsylvania German is well established at home before English is later introduced in the school. Each language has its own distinct functions and no language appears to dominate over the other. Also important in this regard is the fact that the environment in which the Old Order children learn English is a supportive one — something which may seem surprising in a community so inward-looking and so isolationist.[5] In short, all of these acquisition factors — non-mixed input, absence of dominance and a supportive environment — have been shown to be important if linguistic structures are to remain differentiated and resist interference. (See, for example, bilingual studies like McLaughlin 1984.)

What then of the David Martin group? In their workshops and other businesses there is electricity (self generated), fax machines, sophisticated computers, mobile phones — and some English. A few feet away in the house there is no electricity, no phones or fax machines, no carpets, no curtains — and no English. The roles for the languages are still very clearly defined for this group and there is no over-lapping.

4.2.2 *Structural compromise*

For many speakers structural purity of a language and lexical purity in terms of vocabulary are part and parcel of a language's survival. As Nancy Dorian (1994) shows so clearly, this tendency to purism is typically very strong within language revival and revitalisation movements; in particular, there is an unrealistic insistence that the current-day language reflects norms of the past and remains uncontaminated from outside elements. This is not to belittle puristic attitudes — the desire to keep a language pure and free of elements from dominant languages like English is understandable, especially in a situation of potential language shift to the dominant language. Indeed linguistic purism generally appears to be something that is deeply ingrained in the human psyche. But puristic attitudes of

---

5   It is a common misconception that the Amish and Mennonites are totally against any education. This is simply not true — the parents of Old Order children are very supportive of the training given at school. They realise the importance of learning English. After all, successful business with the outside world requires fluency in English, and these people have a keen sense of business.

course can be a real barrier to natural healthy change, change which all languages need if they are to remain viable and versatile tools for a society. And in a language survival context, they can have the disastrous effect of discouraging younger speakers, who feel they don't speak an authentic form of the language if they don't speak the forms that older speakers in the community are insisting on. The result can be that they give up altogether and opt for the dominant language, where they don't experience these same pressures. As Dorian concludes, linguistic straight-jacketing never works, but in the context of language death it can be the kiss of death for a language which is under threat.

Pennsylvania German has been in contact with English for a long time and offers a clear picture of how languages are able to influence each other when they come into contact. And when a language is under threat from another language in this way, especially one which is genetically related to it as in the case of Pennsylvania German and English, its structure can be profoundly affected by this contact. Certainly, the language shows considerable evidence of convergence to English in its structure. The number of lexical borrowings is also enormous and this is commented on frequently by the Mennonites themselves. Typically they are *need* borrowings for new objects and concepts. This is hardly surprising — after all Pennsylvania German has been in North America for nearly 400 years and cannot meet all current communicative needs. As continental German no longer represents a viable source of borrowing, there is no alternative but to borrow from English. But this is what is so striking about the Pennsylvania German-speaking community and indeed another factor which works very positively for the maintenance of the language — speakers are used to linguistic variation and are very tolerant of it. One farmer joked that if you put the language through a winnowing mill and blew all the English words out, there'd be nothing left! But these sorts of comments are never regretful, nor are they ever critical. The Old Orders constantly remark on the variation they see in their language, often commenting: wie *Englisch as mir sin* "how English we are", but I've never heard them say they think this is a bad thing. Despite an isolationist philosophy, this intrusion of English into Pennsylvania German is never criticised or judged harshly. (Of course a "bitzer" language is also an appropriate symbol of *Demuut* or "humility".)

In short, the absence of purist attitudes can mean the language will survive longer — structural compromise is a sign of health and will enhance the chances of a language's survival. The language of the Non-Plain groups is in some respects more conservative, closer to Pennsylvania German in the past, but (as we'll see in the next section) it is disappearing and will most certainly die within these groups.[6]

5.   THE NON-PLAIN FOLK

Not surprisingly, the above factors favouring language maintenance no longer apply in the same way to the so-called "Non-Plain Folk", although of course things are complicated here because this group constitutes quite a broad spectrum of conservatism. All members continue to share many beliefs and behaviour patterns of the Old Order — to a greater or lesser extent depending on how "worldly" they are. The difference is these social customs no longer have the same deeply religious significance and the most noticeable cultural-ethnic traits are being abandoned. It is of course a matter of religious debate, whether or not in giving up these outward symbols they have also given up aspects of their faith, but generally speaking the differences between these Mennonites remain largely sociological rather than theological (see discussion in Fretz 1982, 1989). But what is crucial for the present discussion is that the Non-Plain Folk can no longer be described as one cultural group. They have lost the di-ethnic character of the Old Orders and in the dominant culture in which they are now participating, Pennsylvania German has none of the same values and no real domain.

Certainly, for the Progressives, only fragments remain of the contexts of usage where Pennsylvania German used once to be appropriate; for example, speaking with Old Order members of the community. These people started accommodating in what seemed to be fairly harmless ways and the effect on the community could not have been anticipated. But it was devastating. Once the outside

---

[6]   This outcome is also supported by Lois Huffines' studies of Amish and Mennonite groups in the US. For example, Huffines (1989) confirms that among sectarian groups here the language is less conservative and shows considerable convergence to English. But in these groups the language is, as it is in Ontario, alive and well and thriving.

culture starts to intrude it seems the shift to English swiftly follows. Once they start to accommodate, change accelerates and this destroys the strict "compartmentalization" which is necessary if languages are to survive alongside one another. The more progressive orders show how precarious a situation the survival of the language is. As soon as English is allowed to intrude in what were originally Pennsylvania German domains (for example, church services) the shift to English in all other contexts is swift and complete.

But there are other factors too which have contributed to the demise of *Deitsch*. As earlier discussed, Pennsylvania German can no longer meet the communicative needs of the speakers. Expressions for new concepts and objects, particularly those associated not with Mennonite but mainstream North American life, must come from English. The progressive orders see Pennsylvania German as a "bitzer" language without a standard. It does not have the support of any institution, school or government. It has no written form. All this does much to destroy any feeling of worth on the part of these speakers for their language. And of course, nothing remains of its symbolic value. While its low status has positive repercussions for the Old Order, who see it has an important symbol of their humility, this is clearly not the case with the progressive orders. These people are identifying themselves with dominant culture and the sentimental feelings they display for their Old Order Mennonite heritage and their loyalty is not just enough to keep the language alive. In short, the sort of values held by these progressive groups, namely social and economic advancement, can be via English only.

Huffines (1980a: 52) points to another relevant fact which she argues has contributed to the disappearance of Pennsylvania German in the equivalent non-sectarian groups in Pennsylvania. "The use of Pennsylvania German continues to be associated with having little education". Outsiders perceive the Pennsylvania German people as being against education and Huffines states that her informants in Pennsylvania "expressed the fear that knowing Pennsylvania German might hold their children back in school, that it might confuse them". This also holds true within the Canadian context. It is a popularly held belief that the conservative Mennonites are against education because they refuse to allow their children to attend school beyond the eighth grade. In fact, this is not strictly the case. It is simply that they see higher education as having no value for their way of life.

Nonetheless, the fact remains — there does exist a strong image of the ignorant farmer who speaks an old-fashioned rustic form of German and, what is more, a quaint and curious form of English.[7] As Huffines (1980: 52-53) has observed, many parents in these groups want their children to learn only English in case they acquire a "Dutch" accent and are teased on account of it. In Pennsylvania and Canada alike, there exists a popular perception of the Pennsylvania Germans as speaking a form of mixed English, or what is known colloquially as *Verhoodelt Englisch*. Descriptions of *Verhoodelt Englisch* even appear in reputable publications. For example, Druckenbrod (1981: 10), in the introduction to his teaching grammar of Pennsylvania German, states that

> when the Pennsylvanian German [goes] to speak English (which [is] for him a foreign tongue), he [is] influenced by the German syntax or sentence structure. For some[,] such English as 'Run the steps once up' is largely unintelligible unless you know that it's really the Pennsylvania German 'Schpring mol die Schdeeg nuff'. This is the reason for many of the so-called 'quaint' or 'cute' sayings of the Pennsylvanian German *trying* [my emphasis] to speak English. 'Throw the cow over the fence some hay' is but another example of this process.

In Canada, evidence for this popular view exists in the form of jokes and anecdotes, where these sorts of "quaint" and "cute" sayings abound. The following are some more examples:

> *Throw Father down the stairs his hat once.*
> *It wonders me if it don't gif a storm.*
> *Becky lives the hill just a little up.*
> *Yonnie stung his foot with a bee un it ouches him terrible.*
> *Ve get too soon oldt un too late schmart.*

Clearly, these are examples of stereotyping or popular characterisation and they appear in children's colouring-in books and

---

7   You only have to look at the deterioration of English terms denoting farming people to realise that this attitude is much more widespread than this. For example, *boor(ish); churl(ish), rustic* versus *urbane; villain* etc. All were once neutral terms to refer to people on the land. All have now acquired very negative connotations, reflecting the unfair prejudices of city dwellers towards these people.

on tea towels, beer coasters, serviettes etc. Like most stereotypes, they are stigmatised. And like most stereotypes, they in no way reflect actual usage. There is surprisingly little in the way of German interference in the English of these Pennsylvania German-speakers — certainly there is nothing remotely resembling *Verhoodelt Englisch* (see Burridge 1998 for details).[8] But that is not the point here of course — the perception is they speak it.

Many of the clichéd features of *Verhoodelt Englisch* commonly appear in the English of recent German immigrants to Canada, as you might predict on the basis of a contrastive analysis of German and English. The question is then, why have they come to be identified so closely with Pennsylvania German English? The answer probably lies in history. As described above, up until well into the twentieth century, the diglossic situation which existed in Pennsylvania and Canada resembled that of modern-day Switzerland, with Pennsylvania German as the L-variety and High German as the H-variety — the language of education, worship and (with the exception of some folk literature) all writing. The Pennsylvania Germans were isolated and there was simply no need for them to learn English. One of the prefaces to Horne's nineteenth century elocution manual, for example, describes "their [the Pennsylvania German's] entire ignorance of the English language [which for them] is as much a dead language as Latin and Greek" (Horne 1910: 7) In his manual, Horne suggests drills which exercise precisely those aspects of phonology which have now become fixed in the modern-day characterisations of *Verhoodelt Englisch*. What *Verhoodelt Englisch* does then is provide a historically accurate picture. The curious thing about stereotyping is this tendency towards fossilisation. Despite evidence to the contrary, stereotypes acquire a kind of time-honoured tradition which seem quite immune to change.

The ironic aspect of all this is that is seems to be the Non-Plain Folk, and **not** the sectarian groups who have the strongest interference from Pennsylvania German in their English. With respect to grammar, for example, the English of Old Orders is probably closer to prescriptively "proper" English than the English of many

---

8   Studies from Pennsylvania, like Enninger (1984) and Huffines (1980b, 1984) suggest the same — *Verhoodelt Englisch* has become a modern-day fiction.

mainstream Canadians. This presumably arises out of the way it is acquired in the formal school setting, where there is considerable emphasis on "proper" English (see Enninger 1984 for an account of the Pennsylvania Amish school experience). In addition, their only experience of English is within formal environments — these speakers do not have access to more colloquial varieties heard on radio and television for example. It is actually the Transitional Mennonites who seem to show more interference from German in their English and there are undoubtedly interesting social and psychological factors going on here. These Mennonites are in the process of shifting culturally and linguistically to mainstream Canada, but they are not yet part of the mainstream. These people keep close and continual contact with the Old Orders and identify very strongly with them. While they share many of the same beliefs and behaviour patterns as the Old Orders, however, they have lost the distinctiveness of this group. They no longer have the horse and buggy, nor the extraordinary dress which go to make the Old Orders such a strikingly distinctive group. And now there is every sign that they are also losing Pennsylvania German. For these people then, Pennsylvania German features in their English have a value in signalling their Pennsylvania German ethnicity. As language attitude studies show, ethnic varieties of the dominant language can be "powerful markers of ethnic group belongingness" (see Giles 1979). But for the Old Orders who still maintain "hard linguistic and non-linguistic boundaries" (to use Giles' terminology), Pennsylvania German English has no role in ethnic differentiation and they place no value in it (see also Huffines 1980b, 1984). For those groups, where these boundaries are softening, however, Pennsylvania German features are becoming important ethnic markers.

> The softer the perceived linguistic and non-linguistic boundaries existing between ethnic groups, the more likely speech markers will be adopted in order to accentuate ethnic categorization.   (Giles 1979: 274)

6.   CONCLUSION

In summary then, these different congregations all show different linguistic outcomes of language maintenance and shift and therefore offer us a range of illustrative situations which help to throw light on the socio-cultural and linguistic conditions under which both maintenance and shift are likely to occur.

Among the Non-Plain Folk language proficiency in Pennsylvania German ranges from fully competent speakers to real semi-speakers — a continuum which is directly linked to their degree of religious conservatism. It is not that religion directly bears on the linguistic abilities of these people, but it is on account of what their religion entails. The competent speakers, however, are not supported by diglossia and, as discussed, this implies an unstable situation. It facilitates easy spread and ultimately language shift to English. Among the more progressive groups, the crucial thing is that the children of even the most proficient speakers will most certainly not be teaching their own children Pennsylvania German. For these groups of people language death is inevitable.

For members of the Old Order and conservative splinter groups like the David Martins, however, the future looks more promising. It is their firm belief in the Scriptures and their insistence on biblical exactness which is the crucial factor in the maintenance of their language, by securing for them their humble, separate and "peculiar" existence. For these people the question of formal maintenance efforts does not arise. There is no chance of them ever actively propagating the language. For them it is simple — language and faith are one. One cannot continue without the other. In short where the language-culture-religion network is tight, the future bodes well, even for those groups where some modernisation has taken place.

But here lies the paradox. It is their doctrine of non-conformity and separation from the world that has also been responsible for much of the tension and factionalism. By splitting them into smaller and therefore arguably more vulnerable groups, this has weakened the community and strengthened the foothold of the dominant language, English. And while the threat of excommunication means that the David Martin community remains more or less intact, there are still dangers coming from within this group of disintegration. For one there is plenty of discontent and tension; for example, farmers wonder why they must still use horsepower when their more business-minded brethren have the latest in technology. Theirs is also a very small congregation with membership growing only through adult baptism of members born to the faith. This of course brings with it genetic problems caused through intermarriage (like Maple Syrup Urine Disease and visual/hearing impairments).

But there is more than just religious significance involved here. These groups must maintain their separate status for Pennsylvania German to continue to thrive, but the question is whether they can actually do so. As the twin cities of Kitchener and Waterloo continue to grow and farming land in the region becomes scarce, it forces members to move further and further out, thus causing the community to become more diffuse. The outcome of this could be devastating to the group, as it must weaken community ties and necessarily increase contact with outsiders. One group of Old Orders has moved about 45 miles away to establish themselves in a place called Mt Forest — 45 miles is vast distance in a buggy.

The childhood experience of Mary Anne Horst shows just how precarious the situation is. She recalls here a decision her father made to move a few miles outside the community. This was clearly a crucial factor in bringing about her later decision to leave the order: "When I was almost eight my father made a decision that was going to mean quite a change for his family and would bring to an end our life in the little village. The decision he made somewhat alarmed many of his Old Order Mennonite relatives and friends. He decided that he would buy a farm eight miles north of Floradale in a non-Mennonite English speaking community near the village of Alma. Eight miles by horse and buggy was considered quite a long journey and didn't my father realise, some of his Old Order acquaintance wondered, that the influence of the non-Mennonite English speaking community might cause his children to leave the customs and traditions of Old Order Mennonite life?...Despite the well meaning warnings, my father took us to this farm in this English speaking community. To many of his Old Order friends I am sure it seemed as though he was taking us to the other end of the world" (pp 21-22).[9]

The David Martin situation is slightly different. Their use of horse power means they want smaller farms. These they try to buy close together so they can work the land much like a community (not unlike the Hutterites, they work together, buying in bulk and so on).

---

[9]   Mary Anne Horst has published the memories of her Old Order upbringing in an undated little booklet entitled *My Old Order Heritage.*

And of course many have gone into small businesses, converting their farms into factories and workshops. Their noisy generators are having the additional effect of driving others away, thus geographically bringing the community even more closely together. Nonetheless, the scarcity of land is still a problem for the David Martin group and has forced some to seek land elsewhere. If 45 miles is a vast distance for a buggy with rubber tyres, it is even more significant for a buggy with steel rims such as the David Martins drive. Moving away geographically from the group inevitably weakens community ties and makes them more vulnerable to outside influences.

There is also the tourism factor — the huge influx of visitors to the area also increases the amount of contact with "English" culture. Tourism of course means greater prosperity for the group, but also the threat of increased assimilation. And here too, the current emphasis on multiculturalism comes as a "mixed blessing". While it does bring with it greater tolerance of and respect for distinct cultural minority groups like the Old Order Mennonites, it arguably also endangers the community by greatly increasing the popular interest in the horse and buggy community and their language. (And this is of course my one niggling fear — namely, to draw attention to the successful maintenance of Pennsylvania German, as I have done here, is also somehow to cause trouble. After all, one key to this language's survival technique is surely to be left alone!)

So who really knows what the future holds for Ontario's "peculiar people"? If they are able to maintain their isolation and limit their interaction with the outside world, there is probably no reason to assume that the language, like the other symbols of their faith, could not continue for generations to come. Certainly, recent trends in globalisation suggest a more promising future for such communities than might previously have been forecast. They indicate that there are two distinct effects of the global village — while there is definitely a general levelling of difference going on at the international level, local diversity continues to thrive. If early indications of these predictions hold true, we should expect to see horses and buggies along the "superhighway" for some time to come.

REFERENCES

Bausenhart, William 1971. *The Terminology of Agronomy of the Pennsylvania German Dialect of Waterloo County, Ontario.* MA thesis, University of Waterloo.

_____ 1977. Deutsch in Ontario 1: Toronto und Ottawa; Deutsch bei den Mennoniten. In L. Auburger, H. Kloss & H. Rupp (eds) *Deutsch als Muttersprache in Kanada.* Wiesbaden: Franz Steiner Verlag.

Buehler, Allan 1977. *The Pennsylvania German Dialect and the Life of an Old Order Mennonite.* Kitchener: The Pennsylvania Folklore Society of Ontario.

Burridge, Kate 1998. Throw the baby from the window a cookie: English and Pennsylvania German in contact. In Anna Siewierska & Jae Jung Song (eds) *Case, Typology and Grammar* (Essays in Honor of Barry J. Blake), 71-94. Amsterdam: John Benjamins.

Burridge, Kate & Enninger, Werner 1992. *Diachronic Studies on the Languages of the Anabaptists.* Bochum: Universitätsverlag Brockmeyer.

Costello, John R. 1986. Diglossia at twilight: German and Pennsylvania "Dutch" in the mid-nineteenth century. In W. Enninger (ed.), 1-14.

Dorian, Nancy 1994. Purism vs. compromise in language revitalization and language revival. *Language in Society* 23: 479-494.

Druckenbrod, Richard 1981. *Mir lanne Deitsch.* R. Druckenbrod: Allentown, PA.

Enninger, Werner et al. 1984. The English of the Old Order Amish of Delaware: phonological, morpho-syntactical and lexical variation of English in the language contact situation of a trilingual speech community *English World Wide* 5/1: 1-24.

Enninger, Werner (ed.) 1986. *Studies on the Languages and the Verbal Behaviour of the Pennsylvania Germans 1.* Stuttgart: Franz Steiner Verlag.

Fishman, Joshua A. 1967. Bilingualism with and without diglossia; diglossia with and without bilingualism. *Journal of Social Issues* 23: 29-38.

_____ 1982. Bilingualism and biculturalism as individual and as societal phenomena. In Joshua A. Fishman & G.D. Keller (eds) *Bilingual Education for Hispanic Students in the United States*, 23-36. New York: Teachers College Press.

Fretz, Winfield 1982. *The Mennonites in Ontario.* Waterloo: The Mennonite Historical Society of Ontario.

_____ 1989. *The Waterloo Mennonites: A community in paradox.* Waterloo: Wilfrid Laurier University Press.

Frey, J. William 1945. Amish triple talk. *American Speech.* 20: 85-98.

Giles, Howard 1979. Ethnicity markers in speech. In K.R Scherer & H. Giles (ed.) *Social Markers in Speech*, 251-289. Cambridge: Cambridge University Press.

Horne, A.R. 1910. *Pennsylvania German Manual* (third edition). Allentown, PA: T.K Horne Publishers.

Horst, Mary Anne (n.d.) *My Old Order Mennonite Heritage.* Kitchener: Pennsylvania Dutch Craft Shop.

Huffines, Lois 1980a. Pennsylvania German: maintenance and shift. *International Journal of the Sociology of Language.* 25: 43-57.

_____ 1980b. English in contact with Pennsylvania German. *The German Quarterly* 54: 352-366.

_____ 1984. The English of the Pennsylvania Germans: a reflection of ethnic affiliation. *The German Quarterly* 57: 173-82 .

Kloss, Heinz 1966. German-American language maintenance efforts. In Joshua A. Fishman (ed.) *Language Loyalty in the United States*, 206-252. The Hague: Mouton.

Louden, Mark L. 1987. Bilingualism and diglossia: the case of Pennsylvania German *Leuvense Bijdragen* 76: 17-36.

McLaughlin, Brian 1984. *Second-Language Acquisition in Childhood.* Hillfield, NJ: Lawrence Erlbaum Associates.

Moelleken, Wolfgang W. 1992. The development of the linguistic repertoire of the Mennonites from Russia. In Kate Burridge & Werner Enninger (eds), 164-193.

Neufeld, N. J. 1955. Sprechen die Mennoniten in Kanada noch Deutsch? *Muttersprache.* 65: 229-231.

Ryan, Ellen Bouchard 1979. Why do low prestige language varieties persist. In Howard Giles & Robert St Clair (eds) *Language and Social Psychology*, 145-157. Oxford: Basil Blackwell.

Chapter 15

Language Maintenance at the Micro Level: Hmong ex-refugee communities[1]
Christina Eira
University of Melbourne

1.   INTRODUCTION

The concept of language endangerment can be approached in terms of the existence of a language per se, or in terms of its viability in a given speech community. This is by now a familiar idea, considered often in terms of whether a language can be said to be endangered if there is some location in the world in which it is not apparently at risk.[2]

In this paper, on the basis of the language situation of ex-refugee Hmong and their families, I explore the issue of language endangerment from the perspective of speech communities rather than languages. According to this approach, a language is endangered if it is at risk of loss in the speech community under consideration. In this way, the question becomes, not *whether* a language is endangered, but *who* is at risk of language loss. As a starting point for this new question then, it is necessary to have a means of delineating who the speech community comprises. I take the position that a functional delineation must take into account any and all factors which serve to differentiate subgroups of 'speakers of the same language' in such a way as to affect their being able to maintain their heritage language. Hmong people now living in the west face different levels and types of difficulty in the task of actively maintaining their language, reflecting their differentiation into subgroups by such factors as dialect, area of residence, sociopolitical positioning, orthodoxy of beliefs and attitude to

---

1   Much of the information in this article was generously passed on by my teachers Lee Yang, Lee Long, Nao Shoua and other members of the 벼ᄐ ᄇ ᄭᄀᄒ ᄭᄒᄒ ᄂᄒᄒ ᄒᄒᄒ ᄭᄒ ᄂᄒᄝ ᄀᄝ Hmong Language Institute. Responsibility for any errors in representing or analysing this information of course remains with myself.
2   See for instance Verma (1994).

different scripts. This paper sets out to show how the identifying factors of the speech community at a micro level serve to effect different language endangerment and maintenance concerns.

1.1 Language maintenance at the micro level

As implied above, the approach taken in language maintenance work will depend crucially on how the speech community is defined in relation to the assessment of language endangerment. At the macro level, the speech community could be considered to comprise all speakers of the language world wide: a working definition which allows the position that a language is not endangered if it flourishes in any part of this speech community. At intermediate levels, the speech community could be considered to comprise, for instance, a set of speakers sharing an area of residence and hence communication environments: this would facilitate the position that language endangerment should be assessed on the basis of country or a smaller geographical unit. For speakers of some languages, religion serves to restrict interaction and thereby distinguish speech communities: this scenario may give rise in some contexts to different kinds of language education needs between one subgroup and another. At the most detailed levels, relevant factors will be all those which are instrumental in differentiating speakers into subgroups with different language maintenance needs.

The micro levels of assessment do not present a theoretical basis which can be worked out in advance and overlaid on any language endangerment/maintenance situation as it arises. Rather, they require an approach from the opposite direction, assessing language maintenance needs from the inside out. *Who* has optimal access to maintenance strategies and materials? Whose access is restricted? even though it may appear from the outside that such strategies and materials are readily available. Defining membership of a speech community in terms of similar kinds of restrictions on language maintenance access is a starting point to practically redressing language endangerment within this community.

1. 2 Hmong ex-refugee communities

Before I discuss the status of Hmong speech communities in the west, I will briefly give the context in which this topic has arisen.

Hmong people started arriving in America, Australia and some other western countries during the seventies, escaping from the aftermath of the war in Laos, often after long periods spent in refugee camps in Thailand.[3] Almost all the Hmong now living in the west are ex-refugees and their families. This situation gives rise to a particular set of circumstances in regard to language status, including an accelerated phase of standardisation (see section 2. 1 and following). All speak Hmong as L1, and many adults, particularly men, also speak and are literate in Lao, then English, and some also in Thai and French. Young people are generally fluent in Hmong and English. Since Hmong has only been being established as a language of literacy since the late sixties, a significant proportion of Hmong have low literacy skills in their first language.[4] This is particularly the case for women.

I started meeting with a subgroup of the Hmong community in Melbourne[5] about four years ago when they were looking for assistance in establishing their chosen writing system — ə̃ǩ ñ̄Ɪ ᵇE *Phaj hauj Hmoob*—for their language.[6] Some of this work, they felt,

---

[3]   For a comprehensive account of this period presenting as far as possible a Hmong perspective, see Hamilton-Merritt (1993).

[4]   To qualify: several scripts have in fact been proposed and to some extent implemented for Hmong before this time; but none became well established, with the possible exception of the Pollard scripts within China. For a description of major scripts proposed for Hmong see Smalley, Vang & Yang (1990), or for a more sociolinguistic discussion see Eira (1998). More detailed information on specific scripts can be found in Enwall (1994) (Pollard script) and Wimuttikosol & Smalley (1998) (Sayaboury script).

[5]   Specifically, I meet with representatives of the group promoting the ə̃ǩ ñ̄Ɪ *Phaj hauj* script in Melbourne. The people involved most regularly in our meetings are ᵒꞮ ə̃Ɪ, ᵒꞮ ᵇꞮꞮ, Ɪᵤ ꞹꞮꞮ, Ɪᵤ ᵒꞮ ə̃Ɪ (Lee Yang, Lee Long, Nao Shoua, Nao Lee Long) and initially ꞮꞀ ə̃Ɪ (Chia Yang)—also, less formally, ꞮꞀꞀ ꞱꞮꞀ ꞱꞀꞀ (Pa Shoua Moua) and ꞱꞮꞱꞀ ꞮꞀ, the mother of ᵒꞮ ə̃Ɪ (Lee Yang).

[6]   Two Hmong orthographies appear in this paper for Hmong words (see section 2.3 for explanation of this situation). Where I refer to ə̃ǩ ñ̄Ɪ ᵇE *Phaj hauj Hmoob*, I usually use both this script and the roman script. The font I am using for ə̃ǩ ñ̄Ɪ *Phaj hauj* is *naadaa*, developed by the ᵇE ᵇ ꞀꞮꞀ

had to be accomplished before overt language maintenance work could begin. The first task was to make a font for the script, as the concept of technological access was very important to the group. We also set up a web page for the purposes of releasing a ə̃ӄ n̄ᴦ *Phaj hauj* font. Next, in collaboration with a sister group in California,[7] we began making a dictionary—the California group working on a monolingual dictionary and the Melbourne group a bilingual, with a large degree of overlap of material. These and other related groups have now taken on the joint name ษⅡ̃ ฝ ∩ᴦ ∩n̂ ʋ́ʋ́ n̄ᴦ n̈ ʋ̃ᴧ̃ ᴧᵛ *Hmoob koom haum txhawb nqa moj kuab txuj ci* (Hmong Language Institute), by which they are officially known and occasionally release books, tapes etc.[8]

∩n̂ ʋ́ʋ́ n̄ᴦ n̈ ʋ̃ᴧ̃ ᴧᵛ Hmong Language Institute; and I use the orthography (set of conventions for implementation of a script) current in Melbourne.

The roman script used is the Roman Popular Alphabet (RPA). Words in RPA are differentiated from standard English equivalents by italicisation. For detailed information on pronunciation of Hmong and its representation in RPA, see any of Heimbach (1979), McKibben (1994), or Ratliff (1996). A brief description of key features appears in section 2.3. For an approximate reading, the most important thing to note is that word-final consonant graphemes are not pronounced as consonants, as they are tone markers. Unless otherwise stated, all examples and other Hmong words are in *Hmoob Dawb*, being the primary dialect of my teachers.

7   Another associated group in St Paul, Minnesota, is also consulted to a degree.

8   The current status of the various projects is as follows:

•   a first edition of the bilingual dictionary is nearing completion

•   a Melbourne-based website is on line introducing the ə̃ӄ n̄ᴦ *Phaj hauj* and providing fonts for downloading. This font has also been supplied to Unicode towards the inclusion of ə̃ӄ n̄ᴦ *Phaj hauj* in their project (see section 3. 3).

•   a revised font is nearly ready in Melbourne conforming to new standards

•   work is continuing on the bilingual dictionary

•   a weekend school is running in Melbourne with about sixty students, teaching Hmong literacy in ə̃ӄ n̄ᴦ *Phaj hauj*

•   plans are under way in Melbourne for the production of several dozen books starting in the year 2000.

The particular situation of this subgroup of Hmong distinguishes them from other Hmong groups in terms of language status. They are delineated by a specific configuration which includes country of residence, dialect, script, sociopolitical allegiance, religious beliefs, and sources of authority.[9] This delineation has ramifications for the resources available to them for language maintenance, including teaching materials, accessible literature in their language, technology access and involvement in the international discussions current among Hmong in the west on language standardisation.

These kinds of divisions in various forms are evident throughout the Hmong community, so that language standardisation, education, or maintenance projects established for one group are often less than optimal for use by another. As is often the case, Hmong people are not usefully seen as a single group but as many groups with complex connection structures.[10] In the next section, I describe at an intermediate level the sorts of factors delineating subgroups among the Hmong which in turn give rise to specific language maintenance needs.

2.   SPEECH COMMUNITIES (I): INTERMEDIATE LEVEL

On a global level, Hmong as an active L1 language is certainly in no immediate danger of disappearance. There are estimated to be over six million Hmong speakers in the PRC,[11] up to one million more in Laos and other parts of Asia, and many thousands in other parts of the world. The language situation is very different, however, for different groups of Hmong people; the most readily apparent differentiating factors being area of residence, dialect, and script of literacy.

---

9   For a detailed analysis of kinds of authority sources, focussing on Hmong orthography selection, see Eira (1998).
10   For other discussions on the problems of presumed homogeneity, see Gates (1986) and Riley (1988), amongst others.
11   Or Western Hmongic. The PRC census includes speakers of other related langages, such as A-Hmao, in the same category.

2.1   Area of residence

In terms of language status, Hmong who live in Asia and those who have migrated to western countries have come to form two very distinct speech communities. Within Asian countries, Hmong would not generally be considered to be a language at risk. In the west however, in the first place the numbers of Hmong speakers living within reasonable proximity of each other are very small, and the established community of origin is scattered between states and even continents. The rising generation are thoroughly acculturated to the mainstream in the countries in which they now live. In contrast, the traditional pattern in Laos and other parts of Asia[12] is for Hmong people to live in mostly-Hmong villages, some travelling for purposes of study (in the official language of the region) but otherwise remaining in the village to participate in a largely subsistence economy. So although the Hmong are classifiable as a minority group wherever they live, it is only in the west that the bulk of daily interactions must be carried out in a non-Hmong speaking environment. Furthermore, since there is now only sporadic contact between expatriate Hmong and those 'back home', a condition of ongoing language vitality in Laos or Thailand has little bearing on the language competence of Hmong children growing up in Australia or America.

Secondly, since this mass migration during the late seventies and eighties, and in some senses because of it, the Hmong language in the west is undergoing a concentrated standardisation effort which is not parallelled in Asia. In part, this is due to a sense of urgency about language and cultural identity maintenance,[13] as well as the greater focus necessary on maintaining connections between families and clans. The move to the west has also served to heighten the sense that many have of the need for Hmong to become fully established as a language of literacy in order for it to compete equally with other

---

[12]   Although the majority of the world's Hmong live in China, it is appropriate here to focus on Laos and to a degree Thailand, as these are the former home countries of the Hmong in the west.

[13]   This is evidenced most frequently in the form of concern expressed both by parents (about children) and by young adults (about themselves) at the loss of traditional knowledge and an associated language attrition.

languages and nations of the world.[14] The resultant impetus for concentrated standardisation work has been facilitated by greater freedom of minority language use and education in the new countries of residence, and improved access to publication and communications technology. So the Hmong language is being developed in Australia and America, in terms of code elaboration, script choice and details of orthographic conventions, decisions about word class identification and phonemic status of the various tones etc—in ways which highlight and are gradually increasing the distance between Hmong and its status in the west, and the varieties spoken in Laos and Thailand.

My focus for the remainder of this paper will be the language situation of Hmong in the west, as these are the people for whom language endangerment and maintenance are at issue.

2.2   Dialect

Speakers of two major dialects have migrated to the west: *Hmoob Dawb* (Hmong Daw or 'White Hmong') and *Moob Ntsuab* (Mong Njua or 'Green Mong').[15] The two dialects are mutually intelligible, distinguished primarily by some predictable phonetic alternations and a small degree of lexical variation.

Most adults identify strongly with one or the other dialect but have native-speaker competency in both.[16] Now that the community of Hmong speakers is more dispersed and interwoven with an English-speaking society however, it is becoming clear that young people are no longer acquiring fluency in both dialects. Pronunciation, phrases

---

[14]   This is a very longstanding concern of the Hmong, reflected in traditional stories about loss of a Hmong script and the expectation of a messiah figure who brings and teaches it again, along with moral and spiritual teaching which ultimately results in the establishment of Hmong lands and autonomous rule. It is a theme represented also in traditional stories of neighbouring peoples in Laos and Thailand such as the Karen. For a thorough examination of this theme in Hmong literature see Tapp (1989).

[15]   Some sources use the term *Moob Lees* (Mong Leng) interchangeably with *Moob Ntsuab*.

[16]   Or at least this is the perception of my Hmong teachers.

and individual lexical items which for the parent generation had been automatically assimilated are beginning to pose a problem in both conversation and literacy settings for the rising generation. Added to this is the fact that, now that Hmong is being overtly standardised, and particularly since this is being undertaken for the first time by the speakers themselves, it has become more critical for Hmong people to assess what is the appropriate official place and treatment of the two dialects. Postings through Hmong LG, a prominent Hmong email network, have discussed questions including the preferred spelling of the word *Hmoob/Moob* and its anglicised equivalent(s), and the recognition or otherwise of the minority dialect, *Moob Ntsuab* in standardisation and education tools such as dictionaries.[17] (Notably, the more vocal group on these matters self-identify as *Moob Ntsuab* speakers.)

Table 1: Examples of distinguishing phonetic features of *Hmoob Dawb* and *Moob Ntsuab*

Hmoob Dawb	sample word	*Moob Ntsuab*	sample word	gloss
[a]	*dabtsi*	[ã:]	*dlaabtsi*	'what'
[ia]	*niam*	[a]	*nam*	'mother'
[d]	*sawvdaws*	[tˡ]	*suavdlaws*	'everyone'
[m̥]	*Hmoob*	[m]	*Moob*	'Hmong'

It can be seen then, on the basis of both speaker competence and the issues around selection of standard variety, that dialect is emerging as a more significant focal point of group differentiation among the Hmong now than it has been previously.

2.3   Script

Literacy is a crucial aspect of language maintenance for the Hmong in the west. This has already been hinted at in terms of (i) the need to use various forms of long-distance communication, including email where possible, in order to retain connections with family, clan and

---

17   For details, archives etc, see Hmong LG home page at <http://www.geocities.com/Tokyo/4908/>.

other Hmong; and (ii) the need to be able to use Hmong in all spheres, in a world of languages of literacy. At least as important is the fact that young Hmong who grow up in an environment where not only English language, but also western education and communication norms are dominant, are heavily reliant on literacy as a tool of language education.

In this light, a critical factor that impinges directly on language maintenance efforts is that there are two Hmong scripts current in the west—Roman Popular Alphabet (RPA) and ꓜꓹ ꓠꓲꓼ ꓧꓱ̃ *Phaj hauj Hmoob* (or 'Pahawh Hmong').These scripts reflect two major streams of cultural allegiance among Hmong speakers, so that language materials for one stream are largely inaccessible to the other, partly because they are not readable, but also because they may be unacceptable for sociopolitical reasons.

The RPA is, as the name suggests, a roman alphabet, devised by three missionary-linguists (including William Smalley). It is now the most widely-known orthography for Hmong, being the standard script in western countries, in use by non-Hmong academics, and also by Hmong in some parts of Asia. It is essentially a featural orthography, representing complex consonants as clusters, and tone by means of a set of consonant graphemes written syllable-finally.

Table 2:   RPA samples[18]

RPA	IPA	gloss	notes
hnub	$[\underset{.}{n}u^{55}]$	'sun'	
ntshai	$[^{n}t\int^{h}ai^{33}]$	'afraid'	This tone has zero representation.
rooj	$[t\bar{o}{:}^{51}]$	'table'	A doubled vowel denotes both lengthening and nasalisation.
rian	$[nia^{31}]$	'mother'	Some tones have additional features specified.

Various proponents of RPA speak of their preference in terms of:[19]

---

[18]   Tones are represented using the 1 (low pitch) to 5 (high pitch) scale, so for example a $[^{33}]$ tone is mid level.

fulfilment of a historic long-held hope for the establishment of a writing system for Hmong

the status quo of the RPA as a major recognised writing system for Hmong—an investigation of other possible systems at this stage is seen as losing valuable time needed to move forward in the process of standardisation and establishment of Hmong as a literary language

concern about accessibility of communications technology—a roman-based orthography is effectively already installed on any computer in the west[20]

accessibility to people already familiar with/literate in other roman-based literacies, in particular English.

The ə̄ẍ n̄ɪ̈ *Phaj hauj* is a messianic script[21] received and then developed to the current version by a Hmong man ԿƖ̈ Ͳʟɒ ə̄ʊ̈ *Soob Lwj Yaj* (Shong Lue Yang).[22] It is in use by a significant interconnected minority in western countries, Thailand and possibly Laos. The ə̄ẍ n̄ɪ̈ *Phaj hauj* system uses a single grapheme unit (i.e. basic grapheme plus diacritic) to represent consonants, and another unit to represent the vowel-tone complex. Its most unusual feature is that each $(C)V^t$ syllable is written in the order $V^t(C)$, as shown in Table 3 below.[23]

Various proponents of ə̄ẍ n̄ɪ̈ *Phaj hauj* explain their preference in terms of:

religious imperative—the ə̄ẍ n̄ɪ̈ *Phaj hauj* is considered to be a more genuine candidate for identity as the traditional long-

---

[19] Hmong LG.

[20]   Pao Saykao, personal communication.

[21]   Divine intervention is not uncommonly associated with scripts. See also Cooper (1991).

[22]   The history of this event is available in Smalley, Vang & Yang (1990).

[23]   I use the superscript <t> for convenience to represent tone as a suprasegmental.

awaited script, since a) it is a received script, and b) it eventuated through a Hmong person

national origins—the ә̇Ӿ ñ̈ſ *Phaj hauj* 'is Hmong'[24]

reflection of cultural heritage—this is considered conducive to maintenance of a sense of community identity, particularly for those growing up outside of their country of origin

superior phonological representation—meaning that the single grapheme units used to represent consonant and vowel-tone complex are seen as more closely reflecting the $(C)V^t$ structure of Hmong, as in Table 3.

Table 3:   ә̇Ӿ ñ̈ſ *Phaj hauj* examples

ә̇Ӿ ñ̈ſ *Phaj hauj*	IPA	gloss	notes
ᴜ̇ѧ	$[ŋ̥u^{55}]$	'sun'	Zero diacritics occur in both consonant and tone specification.
ꙍ̇ѧ̈	$[{}^{n}tõ{:}^{33}]$	'tree'	Consonant diacritics have no featural meaning (compare ᴜ̇ѧ).
Ӡʊ	$[tõ{:}^{51}]$	'table'	There are two basic vowel graphemes for each vowel phoneme, selected according to tone (compare ꙍ̇ѧ̈).
Ԃʊ	$[tõ{:}^{55}]$	'mountain'	Tone is represented by a combination of vowel grapheme and diacritic. It is not predictably represented by a given diacritic (compare ᴜ̇ѧ).

Some of the concerns of both factions arise from very similar bases. Both accept a longstanding need for a script in Hmong, whether this need is associated with a traditional or religious basis or simply seen

---

[24]   A comment I have heard frequently from ә̇Ӿ ñ̈ſ *Phaj hauj* proponents and RPA-users alike.

as a necessity for linguistic/cultural survival. Both are concerned for the maintenance of a specifically Hmong identity, but differ in their judgement of what are the essential markers of this identity. Both are concerned for practical application, some prioritising technological convenience and others focussing more on linguistic features. However, it should be noted that technological application is also very important to ȧk̄ n̈r *Phaj hauj* proponents, who have gone to great lengths to establish readily-available fonts for their chosen script; while intuitively meaningful representation of the form of the language is also very important to RPA proponents, many of whom are engaged in revising spelling conventions as part of the standardisation drive (see section 3.2 below).

Most people literate in Hmong have at least a working knowledge of RPA. However, ȧk̄ n̈r *Phaj hauj* proponents are motivated enough about establishing ȧk̄ n̈r *Phaj hauj* in their communities to refuse to make any use of materials written in RPA for language education work. Many RPA-using Hmong, on the other hand, express interest in ȧk̄ n̈r *Phaj hauj* because its uniqueness and the fact of its origination from within the Hmong ethnic group mean that it symbolically embodies Hmong identity. Consequently it is acknowledged here and there within primarily RPA spheres of literacy by, for instance, a series of newspaper columns giving simple phrases, clan names and other basic terms in ȧk̄ n̈r *Phaj hauj*.[25] A small number are also interested for reasons of phonological representation—notably Tzexa Cherta Lee, who views the graphemes of this script as being relatively untied to specific phones and therefore in theory useable to represent more than one dialect without compromise to variant pronunciations.[26] The principle is that it is easier to read, say, <Ē> as [m̩] or [m] than to read the RPA equivalent <hm> as [m] or vice versa.

---

[25]   Hmong Tribune, St Paul, early 1999 editions.

[26]   Lee's work is based on a reconstruction of Proto-Hmong. Taking the phonemes in this language as underlying those in the present-day dialects, he proposes representing each proto-phoneme with a single grapheme unit, to be realised in pronunciation as appropriate to the current surface dialectal form (see for example Lee, TC 1995).

Table 4: Representation of variant pronunciations in ᴂᴋ ᴎᴦ *Phaj hauj*

ᴂᴋ ᴎᴦ *Phaj hauj* (written order)	ᴂᴌ ᴧᴋ	ᴌᴜ	ᴂ
ordered as pronounced	ᴌ ᴂ ᴋ ᴧ	ᴧ ᴌ	ᴂ ᴂ
ᴂ ᴧᴌ *Hmoob Dawb*	d a^{55} tʃ i^{33}	n ia^{31}	m̩ ʒ^{55}
ᴂᴦ ᴧᴋ *Moob Ntsuab*	t^{1} ã:^{55} tʃ i^{33}	n a^{31}	m ʒ^{55}
gloss	'what'	'mother'	'Hmong'

The primary focus of the majority of Hmong, however, is Hmong literacy per se, and so the accessibility of RPA is generally accepted as more important in the end. Moreover, as part of its status as a messianic script, the ᴂᴋ ᴎᴦ *Phaj hauj* has strong associations with a particular sect who were active as guerilla fighters during the war in Laos.[27] Although there is disagreement about the relevance of this, it is certainly still the case that the strong proponents of this script link its teaching with a particular quasi-religious orientation which derives from that time. This sociopolitical loading of the script thus rules it out as a viable alternative for many Hmong, while at the same time ensuring its ongoing significance amongst others. On the other side of the fence, the RPA is associated for some Hmong with the image of modernity and progress, as against the image of the ᴂᴋ ᴎᴦ *Phaj hauj* as a more conservative or nativistic movement. The choice of one or the other script, then, reflects a deeper division in the community.

Script is clearly an important factor in assessing language maintenance status and needs for Hmong. Since materials in one script are effectively unusable by users of the other script, there is a need for the development of a body of educational and other

---

27   See Smalley, Vang & Yang (1990) for details.

literature in both.[28] The developing language skills of young people in particular will be affected by the availability of language materials in their community script. So here again it is evident that an assessment of language vitality needs to take into account the specific delineation of the communities in which people are using and learning Hmong.

3.   SPEECH COMMUNITIES (II): MICRO LEVEL

I have described above an intermediate level of categories which must be taken into account for an assessment of Hmong language status to be useful in ex-refugee migrant communities. In the following section I will look deeper into some factors demarcating subgroups of Hmong, towards a more detailed level of understanding of the specific location(s) of the risk of language loss, and of what sorts of strategies are therefore needed to counter it.

3.1 Area of residence

Because of the circumstances surrounding Hmong arrival in the west, the wave of migration has been rapid and not always under the control of the people migrating. The refugee period and its aftermath have resulted in the dispersion of communities and families throughout Australia, and America in particular. This gives rise to two sociolinguistic conditions of divergence:

1.   The Hmong language has begun to undergo transition in response to its new environments. For one thing, as has been discussed, it is in the process of becoming established as a language of literacy. Another significant process is extension of the lexicon, occurring firstly as a natural process of everyday use in a culture with different bases and norms to the culture of origin, and secondly as part of an overt language planning effort. Because people are now living in

---

[28]   These need not be entirely separate. For instance, a program written by Nick Nicholas now allows for automatic transliteration from RPA to ə̃ʌ ñ̈ır *Phaj hauj*—although not vice versa.

areas far removed from each other, this process of code elaboration is developing in different directions.[29]

2. People in different areas are living under different conditions of minority language policy, finances, education, and lifestyle choices. This has an effect on how much time, money and energy is available towards language maintenance efforts.

By way of illustration of the second point, the kinds of resources available for heritage language education vary widely depending on place of residence. In Minnesota, a government school provides limited bilingual education to many disadvantaged NESB children, including a large proportion of children of Hmong refugees.[30] In California, however, a bill was passed in 1998 which prohibits bilingual education in regular schools throughout the state. As regards ᖃᗷ ᑎᒥ *Phaj hauj* -based teaching, there are several community-run schools in the USA set up primarily for this purpose, but the ᖃᗷ ᑎᒥ ᕼᘿ *Phaj hauj Hmoob* website[31] gets many inquiries from Hmong in America who are interested in learning the script but have no school within reasonable distance. Here in Melbourne, weekend community language schools are common amongst many minority language groups, and there are at least two running for Hmong children. I have occasionally visited the ᕼᘿ ᕼᒥ ᑎᒥ ᑎᕐᖆ ᖘᖘ ᑎᒥ ᕼᕝ ᐱᗷ ᑎᗷ ᕘᕟ ᑯᕟ (Hmong Language Institute of Australia—HLIA) school: it operates on very limited funding which only covers hall rental, and consequently runs on the bare minimum of resources. Part of the problem here is that the ᕼᘿ ᕼᒥ ᑎᒥ ᑎᕐᖆ ᖘᖘ ᑎᒥ ᕼᕝ ᐱᗷ ᑎᗷ ᕘᕟ ᑯᕟ HLIA are reluctant to apply for funding in competition with other Hmong groups.

Further information on the sorts of situations in which Hmong ex-refugee families are living is readily available: see for example Falk 1994, Lee, GY 1984, and Rice 1994 (about Australia), or Bliatout et

---

29   See also Fainberg (1983) on the process of code elaboration in Hebrew.

30   Namely, the Saturn School, home of the Saturn School Hmong Talking Dictionary,
 <http://www.saturn.stpaul.k12.mn.us/hmong/sathmong.html>.

31   <http://www.linguistics.unimelb.edu.au/research/hmong/>.

al 1988, Hmong Youth Cultural Awareness Project 1994, and Vang & Lewis 1990 (about America).

In regard to the first point, much discussion on lexical extension is carried out over the internet, so that people do at least have access to what is happening elsewhere to the degree that they have access to the net. What is evident in these discussions, however, is that people in different areas are developing independent lexical strategies for dealing with newly foregrounded concepts such as western reckoning of the calendar, different forms of transport, the language of technology, and western medical practices. Likewise, the new wave of dictionaries being developed and published for Hmong in the west, as distinct from those previously produced largely by and for missionary work in Asia, demonstrate a wide divergence of new terms for the same concepts, varying according to the Hmong compilers or language consultants involved.[32]

Lexical extension is a topic which is guaranteed to attract a large number of responses on the email networks whenever it is brought up—recent concepts discussed in Hmong LG include 'computer', 'garbage' 'left' and 'right'.[33] The degree of variation involved is not simply that of a natural richness of synonyms and closely related terms; the variation includes basic terms for which there would normally only be one term in common use. For example, Table 5 lists just a few of the paradigms for days of the week which have been suggested or reported.

The parallel usage of totally distinct paradigms for concepts such as days of the week shows how the need for lexical extension is beginning to result in a slight or emerging divergence of variety based on area or regular contact environment. I find that my Hmong teachers often reject terms I come across in sources such as Hmong dictionaries, sometimes preferring a different term and sometimes not understanding them at all.

---

[32]   See for example McKibben (1994), Thompson & Yang (1999) or Thao (1981).

[33]   <http://www.geocities.com/Tokyo/4908/>.

Table 5: Days of the week: proposed terms and terms in use

	Pahawh	RPA proposed	Terms in use	
Monday	ꗁꗵ ꗊꗠ	zwj hli	hnub ib ('day one')	nubhli
Tuesday	ꗁꗵ ꗘꗵꗵ	zwj quag	hnub ob ('day two')	nubci
Wednesday	ꗁꗵ ꗜꗧ	zwj feej	hnub peb	nubtswv
Thursday	ꗁꗵ ꗜꗠ	zwj teeb	hnub plaub	nubntuj
Friday	ꗁꗵ ꗡꗢ	zwj kuab	hnub tsib	nubhnlub
Saturday	ꗁꗵ ꗢꗧ	zwj cag	hnub rau	nubtso
Sunday	ꗁꗵ ꗢꗊ	zwj hnub	hnub xya	nubkaaj
Source	ꗁꗥ ꗁ ꗊꗢ ꗊꗢ ꗢꗢ	Saturn School		Hmong
	ꗊꗢ ꗢ ꗢꗧ ꗊꗧ ꗢꗣ	Hmong Talking		LG[34]
	ꗢꗠ ꗣꗤ (HLIA)	Dictionary		

3.2   Script (i): RPA

As part of the standardisation process, there are now two current working versions of the RPA system. As observed above, the RPA is essentially a featural system, overtly marking the following:

(i)   basic consonant
(ii)   start and end points of affricates
(iii)   prenasalisation
(iv)   preaspiration/devoicing
(v)   postaspiration
(vi)   lateral release
(vii)   basic vowel—monophthong
(viii) vowel plus length and nasalisation
(ix)   start and end points of diphthongs
(x)   tone

Many of the possible combinations of this list do occur, so that although the syllable structure is $(C)V^t$, it can take up to seven letters to spell a monosyllabic word, as shown in Table 6 below.

---

[34]   Note that this set is in *Moob Ntsuab*, recognisable by the voicing on the initial consonant of 'day' (spelt without an <h>). These terms have been designed on a loose analogy with English terms: *nubhli* 'day of the moon', *nubntuj* 'day of the sky' and so on.

Table 6: **Featural representation in RPA**

ntseeg   [^{n}tʃ^{h}ẹ̃^{11}]   'believe'
(features: iii, ii, viii, x)

nplhaib   [^{m}p^{h}lai^{55}]   '(finger-)ring'
(features: iii, i, vi, v, ix, x)

A common criticism of the RPA is that the number of letters taken to spell perceptually single sounds is unwieldy. Furthermore, although the system originally worked out is phonetically adequate as a broad featural representation, it fails to reflect native speaker perception of the sound produced. Prenasalisation of consonants in particular comes into this category. In the first place, prenasalisation is always represented with <n> in RPA, although in surface pronunciation it always occurs at the place of articulation of the following consonant. Secondly, it is perceived by many speakers not as prenasalisation but as a voicing contrast. This is shown in Table 7 below.[35]

Table 7: **Perception and notation of prenasalised consonants**

RPA	transcription	common perception of sounds	gloss
Npis	[^{m}pi^{22}]	[bi^{33}]	'Bee (personal name)'
nkaub	[^{ŋ}kau^{55}]	[gau^{55}]	'egg yolk'

The response of some has been to work on revision of this system, while others prefer to continue with the orthography as taught initially. Major proposed changes, now in use by a significant minority, are as shown in Table 8 below.[36]

---

[35] Whether this perception is influenced by transfer from English I have not yet determined—such a question may require investigation of speaker perceptions in Laos and/or assessment as to whether a new phonology is emerging amongst speakers in the west.

[36] It is worth noting also that the distinction between glottal initial (marked with zero) and zero initial (marked with ') included in the RPA

Table 8:   ·Revision of RPA system[37]

nk	>	g	hl	>	lh	g	>	ng
np	>	b	hm	>	mh			
nplh	>	blh	hn	>	nh			
nts	>	j						
ntsh	>	jh	(in line with					
			<nqh>, <nplh> etc.					
ntxh	>	jxh						

Sample
Cov tub hlaus ntxhais hluas Hmoob ua neeg ntse
Cov tub lhaus jxhais lhuas Mhoob ua neeg je
'The Hmong young people are becoming intelligent (educated)'

Furthermore, speakers of the two different dialects also use different orthographic systems, as indicated in Table 1 above. These systems are different enough so that *Moob Ntsuab* speakers complain that public notices, letters from official bodies etc. which tend to be written in *Hmoob Dawb*, are difficult to read.[38] Discussion is also under way as to the best representation of compounds—should they be written as separated words, hyphenated, conjoined, or some combination of these?[39]

The concurrent use of such strongly distinctive orthographic systems poses problems for literacy acquisition. Unless one version, perhaps a compromise position, is eventually settled on as the standard version, it is likely that up to four streams of conventions will be informally established—a conservative and a revised version for each of *Hmoob Dawb* and *Moob Ntsuab*. Which version or versions

---

has effectively disappeared. Overt marking of this distinction has also been eliminated in one version of ə̃к̃ ñ̈ſ *Phaj hauj*, although it is still indirectly marked in all versions.

[37]   Thanks to *Ntxawg Lis Yaj* .

[38]   Hmong LG.

[39]   For discussion of compound types and options for their representation, see Eira (1999).

people learn will depend on their dialect, access to overt language and literacy education, and social contact groups. So here we see that even if we restrict our consideration to the dominant script, people may be literate in Hmong, but such an assessment can disguise the specific limitations of such literacy in a situation where several orthographies are in use.

3. 3   Script (ii): әK̇ ñ̈r *Phaj hauj*

In a similar way, factions of conservatism and progressivism are operative amongst әK̇ ñ̈r *Phaj hauj* users. In this case, however, it is more accurate to speak of degrees of orthodoxy, since the motivations of the conservative element are directly related to the ethos of maintaining the script as originally given, in its purest form. The Hmong term used to talk about this is ▽K *tseem* 'pure, unmixed' (used also of pure metals as distinct from alloys).

The degrees of orthodoxy are seen in different groups of users in a number of forms: selection of version of script, tone representation, dialect, and variability of grapheme forms. In the most widely available monograph on the subject, *Mother of Writing* (Smalley, Vang & Yang 1990), four versions of the әK̈ ñ̈r *Phaj hauj* are described, distinguished primarily by a progressive degree of regularisation of vowel and tone representation. The version deemed to be in use by the group who assisted in the writing of that book is Version Three. However, all the organised groups using and teaching the script now employ Version Two exclusively. These groups see Version Two as the one intended to be used, while they see Version Three as rlm *cuav* 'impure/mixed'; the idea of just a few people, at odds with the wider community belief. In the example below, the degree of diacritic variation (which, in combination with basic grapheme choice, indicates tone) between the two versions is clearly apparent: notice also that occasional variation in basic grapheme choice occurs in words with tone [35] (see ɷr/ñ̄r *hauv*).

Table 9: **Comparison of Versions Two and Three**

Version 3 ꗉ ꕴ ꔲ ꗂ ꕴ ꖧ ꔞ ꕴ ꖦ ꗃ ꕵ ꘃ ꖐ ꗂ ꖨ ꘃ ꗌ. ꕵ ꖨ ꗀ ꕵ.

Version 2 ꗉ ꖧ ꔲ ꗂ ꕴ ꖧ ꔞ ꕵ ꖦ ꗃ ꕵ ꘃ ꖐ ꗂ ꖨ ꘃ ꗌ. ꕵ ꖨ ꗀ ꕵ.

Nws yog Vaj Leej Txi tso kom nqis los Theej Kaj thiab cev lus rau noob neej hauv lub Ntiaj teb.

'He said that he was commissioned by God his father to bring a message to people and to be the saviour on earth.'

Vang, Yang & Smalley 1990

The ꖳ ꕵ ꖐ ꖦ ꕴ ꖦ ꕴ ꗃ ꕧ Hmong Language Institute in Melbourne (HLIA) emphasise a higher level of orthodoxy than does their sister group in California (ꖳ ꕵ ꖐ ꖦ ꕴ ꖦ ꕴ ꗃ ꕧ HLI—Fresno). A contentious issue among ꕴ ꖐ *Phaj hauj* users is that Version Two only recognises seven of the eight phonological tones in Hmong—on the basis that tone [:[13]] is a (mostly) predictable variant of tone [~[31]] (a perception supported also by comments from RPA-using Hmong).[40] The ꖳ ꕵ ꖐ ꖦ ꕴ ꖦ ꕴ ꗃ ꕧ HLI (Fresno) has decided on a compromise solution, incorporating separate representation of the marginal tone with an otherwise straightforward use of Version Two. For the ꖳ ꕵ ꖐ ꖦ ꕴ ꖦ ꕴ ꗃ ꕧ ꕴ ꗃ ꔲ ꖦ HLIA, however, this is not acceptable. When I first got to know them, four years ago or so, they were writing this tone in the same way as tone [~[31]] — i.e. the tone of which it is a variant—for any given vowel. Now they have shifted to writing it in the same way as tone [[35]] on the basis of phonetic similarity (i.e. these are the only two rising tones).

---

40 Where a tone with an associated feature is notated without a contextualising vowel, the associated feature is included with the tone symbol.

Table 10: Tone representation in ə̀Ɑ Ꞑɪ *Phaj hauj*

Tone	California	Melbourne early stage	Melbourne current	RPA	gloss
[:¹³]	ꞐꞲ	ꞐꞲ	ꞐꞲ	*ntawd* 'there'
[~³¹]	ꞐꞲ	ꞐꞲ	ꞐꞲ	*ntawm* 'that one there'
[³⁵]	ꞐꞲ	ꞐꞲ	ꞐꞲ	*ntawv* 'paper'

Dialect is also an issue among the ə̀Ɑ Ꞑɪ Phaj hauj users. Despite the theoretical possibilities of using the script pan-dialectally, in practice the focus has been almost entirely on representation of ꓭ Ꙅ Ꞑ꙳ Hmoob Dawb. Some specifically ꓭɪ ꙳ꓭ Moob Ntsuab sounds were included in the versions described in Smalley, Vang & Yang 1990, but even these are no longer included in all ꓭ Ꙅ Ꞑɪ Ꞑ꙳ ꙶꙶ Ꞑꞈɪ ꙳ ꙶꙶꙶ ꓥꓦ HLI fonts. Some people independent of the ꓭ Ꙅ Ꞑɪ Ꞑ꙳ ꙶꙶ Ꞑꞈɪ ꙳ ꙶꙶꙶ ꓥꓦ HLI, however, have introduced some additional characters targeted to ꓭɪ ꙳ꓭ ꓵꙶꙶꞐ ꞷ⳯ꞐꞐ speakers: notably at Cwjmem Homepage.[41]

Finally, differences of opinion on the basic forms of graphemes used are resulting in a series of different fonts being made for use by different groups. A few graphemes are distinct enough so that variants are not easily interchangeable, for instance the consonant *mau*: Ꞑ (ꓭ Ꙅ Ꞑɪ Ꞑ꙳ ꙶꙶ Ꞑꞈɪ ꙳ ꙶꙶꙶ ꓥꓦ HLI) and ʀ (in Smalley, Vang & Yang 1990). Although the latter grapheme set is no longer in active use, several publications have used it and it is being included in the Unicode set.[42] Current work on new fonts in Melbourne is differentiated from that in California by what appears to an outsider to be only minor details of style—the new ꓭ Ꙅ Ꞑɪ Ꞑ꙳ ꙶꙶ Ꞑꞈɪ ꙳ ꙶꙶꙶ ꓥꓦ Ꞑ꙳ ꙶꙶꙶꙶ ꙅ꙳ HLIA fonts are characterised by a plain and square appearance with no decorative variants, as distinct from a slimmer and slightly more florid or cursive style in California, with a wide

---

41   <http://www.geocities.com/SiliconValley/Pines/5884>.
42   This is a long term project towards availability of the scripts of most world languages in standard computing. For the current status of the ə̀Ɑ Ꞑɪ *Phaj hauj* proposal under development by Michael Everson, see <http://www.indigo.ie/egt/standards/iso10646/pdf/hmong.pdf>.

range of decorative fonts available.[43] However, despite the apparent similarity of these fonts, what functionally distinguishes them is the requirement by the Melbourne group that only the plain, square style be used. This is due to the sacred nature of the script: it represents a new beginning for the Hmong and as such must be clear and straightforward to encourage positive developments for their future. The fine tuning of the font style is reflected also in a parallel shift in writing style used and taught by the recognised authorities in the group. Consequently, in this respect as well as because of differences in tone representation, the ᕼᕦ ᕨ ᓂᒥ ᓂᒫ ᑌᑌ ᓅᒥ ᗷ ᑌᒫ ᛚᐁ ᓂᐱ ᑌᔐ ᔑᒪ HLIA are beginning to need their own printed resources for teaching purposes; for ease of readability for learners, and for reasons of group-internal official sanction.

The differences between versions of the ᔑᒫ ᓂᒥ *Phaj hauj* in current use may appear to be minor, but because of the motivating factors behind their divergence, because of what those fine differences symbolise, they reflect subgroups becoming steadily more distinct, to the point where language materials targeted to one are likely to become unsuitable for another.

4.   CONCLUSION

Factors of large scope such as dialect, country of residence and script of literacy are relatively easy to understand as affecting different groups of speakers with different language status configurations and language maintenance needs. I have endeavoured to show in this paper how less easily discernible factors can have the same effect. The ramifications of all this are that language maintenance efforts and materials appropriate to one subgroup of Hmong people bear no guarantee of language maintenance benefits in another group.

There are of course other possible criteria for delineation of speech communities in the sense I am interested in. Implied in this paper has been the factor of generation, which for the Hmong is linked with

---

[43]   I regret that no examples can be given as yet as the new ᕼᕦ ᕨ ᓂᒥ ᓂᒫ ᑌᑌ ᓅᒥ ᗷ ᑌᒫ ᛚᐁ ᓂᐱ ᑌᔐ ᔑᒪ HLIA font has not been released to the public at the time of writing.

place of birth or growing up. The difference between language status among men and women, which is linked with literacy and second language acquisition, is also implicated, raising some fairly complex issues which there is not the space to discuss here.

The question which logically ensues from this discussion is what sorts of language maintenance strategies and materials are useful, given the range of speech communities which are evident. In a phase of rapid change in the standardisation process this is not a simple question: the immediate need for maintenance efforts vies with the need to establish scripts and produce materials which will have longlasting use in the community. The involvement of many Hmong and non-Hmong academics in web publishing is interesting as a solution to this: materials published on the web have the major advantage of being amenable to revision without wastage of books and money or inconvenience to the people referring to them.

At a global level, the Hmong language is certainly not an endangered species. However, such observations have no relevance to relatively isolated groups of Hmong seeking to maintain communication and cultural memory across generations. For genuinely useful programmes then, the needs of each group must be considered individually.

REFERENCES

Bliatout, Bruce Thowpaou, Bruce T. Downing, Judy Lewis & Dao Yang 1988. *Handbook for Teaching Hmong-speaking Students.* Folsom, CA: Folsom Cordova Unified School District, Southeast Asia Community Resource Center.

Cooper, Robert 1991, Dreams of scripts: Writing systems as gifts of God. In Robert Cooper & Bernard Spolsky (eds) *TheIinfluence of Language on Culture and Thought: Essays in honour of Joshua A Fishman's 65th birthday*, 219–26. Berlin and New York: Mouton de Gruyter.

Cwjmem Homepage, 1998. Hmong Script Software. <http://www.geocities.com/SiliconValley/Pines/5884>.

Eira, Christina 1998. Authority and discourse: towards a model for orthography selection. *Written Language and Literacy* 1/2: 171-224.

_____ 1999. Compound types and representation in Hmong. *Melbourne Papers in Linguistics* 18: 19–34, Melbourne: Department of Linguistics & Applied Linguistics, University of Melbourne.

Enwall, Joachim 1994. *A Myth Become Reality: The history and development of the Miao written language.* Vols I and II. Stockholm: Stockholm University, Institute of Oriental Languages.

Fainberg, Yaffa Allony 1983 Linguistic and sociodemographic factors influencing the acceptance of Hebrew neologisms. *IJSL* 41: 9-40.

Falk, Cathy 1994. The Hmong in Australia. <http://minyos.its.mit.edu.au/~s914382/hmong/hmelb.htm>

Gates, Henry Louis Jr 1986 [1985]. *"Race", Writing and Difference.* Chicago: University of Chicago Press.

Hamilton-Merritt, Jane 1993. *Tragic Mountains: The Hmong, the Americans, and the secret wars for Laos, 1942–1992.* Bloomington and Indianapolis: Indiana University Press

Heimbach, Ernest 1979. *White Hmong–English Dictionary.* Linguistic Series IV, Data Paper No. 75. Ithaca, NY: Southeast Asia Program, Cornell University.

Hmong LG homepage <http://www.geocities.com/Tokyo/4908/>.

Hmong Tribune, 1999. St Paul <HmongPaper@aol.com>.

Hmong Youth Cultural Awareness Project 1994. *A Free People: Our stories, our voices, our dreams*. Minneapolis: Hmong Youth Cultural Awareness Project.

Lee, Gary Yia, 1984, Culture and adaptation: Hmong refugees in Australia 1976-83. Special Supplement, Hmong Newsletter 6/1: 13-22.

Lee, Tzexa Cherta 1995. Which is the true Hmong writing system? Paper presented at Hmong national conference, April 6–8, St Paul.

McKibben, Brian 1994 [1992]. *English–White Hmong Dictionary/Phau txhais lus Askiv–Hmoob Dawb*. Brian McKibben: Provo, Utah.

Ratliff, Martha 1996. The Pahawh Hmong script. In Peter Daniels & William Bright (eds) *The World's Writing Systems*, 619–24. New York and Oxford: Oxford University Press.

Rice, Pranee L. 1994. When I had my baby here! In Pranee L. Rice, (ed.) *Asian mothers, Australian Birth — pregnancy, childbirth and childrearing: the Asian experience in an English-speaking country*, 117-132. Melbourne: Ausmed Publications.

Riley, Denise 1988. *Am I That Name? Feminism and the category of 'Women' in history*. London: Macmillan.

Smalley, William, Chia Koua Vang & Gnia Yee Yang 1990 *Mother of Writing*. Chicago: University of Chicago Press.

Tapp, Nicholas 1989. *Sovereignty and Rebellion: the White Hmong of Northern Thailand*. Oxford: Oxford University Press.

Thao, Cheu 1981. *English-Hmong Phrasebook with useful wordlist (for Hmong speakers)*. Washington, DC: Refugee Service Center, Center for Applied Linguistics.

Thompson, Mark, & Yee Yang 1999 [1997]. *Saturn School Hmong Talking Dictionary*.
<http:ww2.saturn.stpaul.k12.mn.us/hmong/sathmong.html>.

Vang, Chia Koua, Gnia Yee Yang & William Smalley 1990. *The Life of Shong Lue Yang: Hmong 'Mother of Writing'/Keeb kwm Soob Lwj Yaj: Hmoob 'Niam Ntawv'ꝓ* ꞇ ꞗꞯꞟ ꞇꞁ ꞅꞟ: ꞗꞗ̂ ꞟꞟ ꞟꞝ̂.[44] Trans. Mitt Moua and Yang See. Southeast Asian Refugee Studies Occasional Papers No. 9. Minneapolis: Center for Urban and Regional Affairs, University of Minnesota.

Vang, Lue & Judy Lewis 1990. *Grandmother's Path, Grandfather's Way/Poj rhawv kab, Yawg rhawv kev: Oral lore, generation to generation*. Rancho Cordova, CA: Vang and Lewis [Zellerbach Family Fund].

Verma, Mahendra K. 1994. Ethnic minority languages in Scotland: a sociolinguistic appraisal. In J. Derrick McClure (ed.) *Scottish Language (Proceedings of the Fourth International Conference on the Languages of Scotland and Ulster*, 118-133.. Sabhal Mòr Ostaig, Isle of Skye: Association for Scottish Literary Studies 14/15 (August).

Wimuttikosol, Nina, & William Smalley 1998. Another Hmong Messianic script and its texts. *Written Language and Literacy* 1/1: 103-128.

---

[44]   Note that this title is in ꞵꞗ̂ ꞟꞟ *Phaj hauj* Version Three, as used by this book.

Chapter 16

Community Initiatives towards Language Renewal among Moluccan Migrants in the Netherlands

Margaret Florey
Monash University

1. INTRODUCTION[1]

This paper addresses the issue of language endangerment among the languages of the Central Maluku region of eastern Indonesia and discusses aspirations for language renewal or language maintenance among the population of Moluccans which has grown from those who migrated to the Netherlands in the 1950s and 1960s. The linguistic situation in this community is very unusual because of the opportunities it provides to document and support in a migrant setting the retention of a substantial number of languages which are severely endangered in their homeland.

I first outline the linguistic situation in Central Maluku before reviewing the circumstances which led to the migration of Moluccans to the Netherlands. The linguistic economy of the migrant community is detailed, focusing on the existence of a substantial

[1]   This paper reports on two components of a project, *Language shift in indigenous and immigrant settings: a study of endangered Moluccan languages in Maluku and the Netherlands*, which is being undertaken in collaboration with Dr. Aone van Engelenhoven (Leiden University). We are very grateful for the assistance we have received in the Netherlands from Mr. Wim Manuhutu at the Moluks Historisch Museum, Utrecht, and Mr. Victor Josef at the community radio programme, *Suara Maluku*. The author thanks participants at the Eastern Indonesian workshop, held 1 December 1998 at the International Institute for Asian Studies (IIAS), Leiden University, the Netherlands, and at the 3rd Annual Conference of the Victorian Southeast Asian Linguistics Society, held 1-2 July 1999 at the University of Melbourne, for their interest and feedback. The project is funded by the Australian Research Council (A59803475) and UNESCO's Endangered Languages Fund. Florey's fieldwork in the Netherlands from November - December 1998 was carried out under the auspices of a Visiting Fellowship at the IIAS, Leiden University, the Netherlands.

number of indigenous Moluccan languages, the presence of which has only emerged in recent years following a resurgence of interest in linguistic heritage. Finally, I discuss the language-related activities which are taking place among remaining speakers and descendants of the Amahai and Haruku language communities.

2.   LANGUAGE ENDANGERMENT IN CENTRAL MALUKU

The languages of Maluku are largely Austronesian,[2] and are subgrouped within the Central-Eastern-Malayo-Polynesian branch of the Austronesian language family. Following Blust (1983/84, 1993), at a lower level the languages spoken in Central and South Maluku are subgrouped within the Central-Malayo-Polynesian branch while the Austronesian languages of north Maluku are subgrouped within the South Halmahera-West-New Guinea branch of Eastern-Malayo-Polynesian.

It has been noted that the eastern Austronesian region is marked by greater linguistic diversity and smaller speaker populations per language than the western Austronesian region (see Tryon 1994). This is indeed the case in Maluku, where there are approximately 130 languages with speaker populations most commonly averaging several hundred to a thousand people dwelling in a few villages. In the case of a number of larger languages (such as the Alune and Wemale languages of western Seram island), speaker populations may reach twenty to thirty thousand speakers.

Yet behind this picture of rich linguistic diversity, Maluku could reasonably be assessed as the most severely endangered linguistic region in Indonesia. This area has been subject to centuries of contact with non-indigenous peoples, the impetus for which was the spice trade in nutmeg and clove. Although Central Maluku was not important as a spice-growing region until the seventeenth century, Ambon, Seram, and the smaller adjoining islands provided ports along the routes taken by the Javanese, Malay, Arab and Chinese

---

[2]   The exceptions are a few Papuan languages which are found in North Maluku on the islands of Halmahera, Makian, Tidore, and Ternate.

traders (van Fraassen 1983). Perhaps more influential was the trade relationship with the sultanates of Ternate and Tidore in North Maluku. Before the arrival of the colonial authorities in the sixteenth century, Ambon and the so-called Lease islands of Saparua, Haruku, and Nusalaut were part of the North Moluccan sultanate of Ternate. With the arrival of the Portuguese and later the Dutch colonial authorities, garrisons were successively stationed on Ambon and the Lease islands to break Ternate's control of the area. The redistribution of political power resulted in Central Moluccan Muslim villages aligning with Ternate, and Christian villages aligning with the Dutch. Closer ties with the Dutch provided Christian villages with greater access to education and to employment in various branches of government.

Ambon Bay and the southern side of Ambon island became the centre of colonial activity. Thus the most intense influence from colonial authorities and traders has been experienced by ethnolinguistic groups which were located in this area of Ambon island, on the neighbouring Lease islands, and on or near the coast of Seram island. Collins (1983) notes that in these regions a number of languages have become extinct, including Batumerah, Tenga-tenga and Liliboi on Ambon Island, and Awaiya on Seram Island. A large number of languages are moving rapidly towards obsolescence, including Laha, Allang and Tulehu on Ambon Island, Naka'ela, Loun, and Hulung on the north coast of Seram Island, Piru, West Littoral,[3] Kamarian-Rumakai, Paulohi, and Amahai on the south coast of Seram, and Nusalaut on Nusalaut Island (ibid.).

Language shift is occurring primarily towards the regional creole, Ambonese Malay, which has been used as a lingua franca from early in the colonial era. Use of this Malay variant has predominated among Christian Moluccans, and linguists working in Central Maluku have noted that languages in Christian villages in Maluku are becoming obsolescent at a much faster rate than languages spoken in Muslim villages (see Florey 1991, 1997, B.D. Grimes 1991). Thus languages in ethnolinguistic groups which have entirely

---

[3]   West Littoral comprises four dialects spoken in villages of Hatusua, Waesamu, Eti, and Kaibobo (Collins 1983: 81).

converted to Christianity, such as Amahai, are in greater danger of obsolescence in their homeland than those, such as Haruku, in which the population in some villages converted to Christianity while other villages converted to Islam. Very few ethnolinguistic groups have resisted conversion from their ancestral religion to either Christianity or Islam. However, villages in which ancestral religious practices have been retained, such as the Nuaulu of central Seram, are marked by language maintenance and greater retention of traditional ritual practices (see Bolton 1990, Florey and Bolton 1997). Alongside Ambonese Malay, the national language, Indonesian, is now also clearly impacting on the linguistic economy through the status it acquires in its public role as the language of education, the media, and government.

Given the high level of language endangerment in Central Maluku and a lack of written materials for most of the languages, the task of documentation is critical. Although speaker numbers for moribund languages in Maluku are very small, the opportunity for documentation is enhanced by drawing upon remaining speakers of these languages in the migrant Moluccan community in the Netherlands.

3.　　HISTORY OF MIGRATION TO THE NETHERLANDS

The presence of a large migrant population of Moluccans in the Netherlands can be traced to events following the proclamation of the Republic of Indonesia by Indonesian nationalists in 1945. The Dutch government finally acceded to the independence of its former colony in 1949. In that year, the colonial army, the KNIL,[4] was sent home to await independence (Chauvel 1990: 398). When the army was disbanded in 1950, the Dutch Court of Justice disallowed any involuntary demobilisation on Indonesian territory. As a result, in 1951 the Dutch government transported to the Netherlands 12,500 Moluccan soldiers who had either not yet resigned or refused to go over to the Indonesian army.

---

[4]　　*The Koninklijk Nederlands Indische Leger* (Royal Netherlands Indies Army).

Moluccan members of the government of the former state of East Indonesia continued to resist inclusion within the Republic of Indonesia. On the evening of 24th April 1950, an independent Republic of the South Moluccas - *Republik Maluku Selatan* (RMS) - was proclaimed on Ambon Island by Mr. J.H. Manuhutu, who became the first Prime Minister. Dr. Ch. Soumokil, a co-founder of the RMS who became a key figure in its government, left Ambon in July 1950 to establish on Seram Island an emergency government which could continue to press for independence in the event that Ambon was occupied by Indonesian forces (ibid.: 375). The occupation of Ambon took several months but had succeeded by December 1950. The guerrilla war then continued to be fought on Seram between the Indonesian military (TNI[5]) and RMS guerrillas throughout the 1950s. Soumokil was finally arrested by the TNI in 1962 and was tried and executed in 1966.

The RMS rebellion was suppressed in Maluku by 1963 yet the struggle for an independent Republic of the South Moluccas has continued to thrive in the Netherlands among the former KNIL soldiers, their families and dscendants (see Steijlen 1996). It is estimated that up to 50,000 Moluccans live in the Netherlands today. Van Engelenhoven (2000: 2) observes that 76 per cent of the migrant population originated from Central Maluku (*Maluku Tengah*) and the remaining 24 per cent from Southeast Maluku (*Maluku Tenggara*). The majority of Central Moluccan members of the armed forces were drawn from Christian villages in Ambon, Saparua, Haruku, and Nusalaut. 97 per cent of the Central Moluccan migrants are Christian and the remaining 3 per cent Muslim (ibid.).

4. MOLUCCAN LANGUAGES IN THE NETHERLANDS

For much of the past five decades it has been considered unlikely that any indigenous languages were represented among the migrant Moluccan community in the Netherlands. Malay was widely spoken among the soldiers and has retained an important position as a lingua franca in the Moluccan community. It has great symbolic value in the

---

[5]   *Tentara Negara Indonesia.*

RMS and its use has been encouraged by the RMS government. For several decades, the politics of this government in exile led to a focus on unity among the migrants rather than the diversity which could have emerged through a focus on separate ethnolinguistic identities. One outcome of this policy has been that the reality of the extent of linguistic diversity in Maluku has been reduced through folk belief among second- and third-generation migrants to one language. This unified Central Moluccan *bahasa tanah* (literally, 'language of the land') is held to originate on Nunusaku, a mountain in Moluccan mythology from which all life is said to derive. Nunusaku is believed to be located in western Seram, the region which for these generations holds growing symbolic power as the heartland of Moluccan identity. It also appears that some younger Moluccans are creating a mixed language incorporating components of several *bahasa tanah* in order to claim or develop a link to the interior of Seram.

This perception that the linguistic economy of migrant Moluccans comprises Malay and Dutch has been perpetuated among linguists in the Netherlands. For example, Broeder et al. (1995) investigated the criteria which are used to identify ethnic minority groups in various nations and argued for the criterion of home language rather than that of country of birth of the respondent and her or his parents. They undertook a pilot study of home language use among school children in 31 primary schools in Den Bosch. Five larger ethnic groups were identified in this population: Moroccans, Turks, Surinamese, Antilleans, and Moluccans. Broeder et al. state "It is obvious that the criterion of home language use traces ethnic minority children which are outside the scope of identification through origin. This applies in particular to the Moluccans. Of all the groups under discussion, Moluccans have the longest migration history in the Netherlands" (1995: 126). Their discussion indicates that Broeder et al. assume that Malay alone is the language other than Dutch which may be spoken in the home of migrant Moluccans.

During the past decade there has been a strong revival of interest in ethnolinguistic identity which has been driven largely by the second generation of Moluccans in the Netherlands. This is a particularly interesting development in a community in which Malay has served not only as a lingua franca but also as a language of separate identity from the broader Dutch community. It suggests that younger people are narrowing their identity within the immigrant community from "Moluccan" to a more specific ethnolinguistic identity. The accompanying interest in *bahasa tanah* has encouraged elderly members of the first generation to reveal their residual knowledge of Moluccan languages - in many cases for the first time since migration.

The first generation of Moluccan migrants to the Netherlands included speakers of *bahasa tanah* who predominantly originated from the islands of southeast and southwest Maluku, including the Kei, Tanimbar, Aru and Babar island groups. However the first generation also included some speakers of *bahasa tanah* originating from the islands of Central Maluku - Ambon, Haruku, Nusalaut, Seram, and Buru. Our research indicates that perhaps twenty-five *bahasa tanah* are represented within the migrant community. From the Central Moluccan islands we have confirmed the presence of speakers of Allang, Amahai, and Haruku and have reports of speakers of Alune, Buru, Hila, Hitu, Kamarian and Tulehu. From the Southeast Moluccan islands we have confirmed the presence of speakers of Ewaw and Fordate and have reports of speakers of Dobo, Selaru, Selwasa and Yamdena. From the Southwest Maluku region we have confirmed the presence of speakers of Kotalama, Central Marsela, Meher, Nila, Oirata, Serua and Wetan and have reports of speakers of Southeast Babar, Imroing and Tela.

Eight of the twelve languages which we have confirmed are represented by speakers in the Netherlands are moribund in their homeland. Speakers and their dscendants in the Netherlands have begun the work of documenting languages and increasing their status in the community. The presence of remaining speakers of indigenous Moluccan languages not only enables documentation to proceed but also provides an opportunity to address sociolinguistic issues concerning language attitudes and language behaviour. Longer term research will also include examining and comparing the process of language shift within a language (Amahai) which is spoken in both its homeland and a migrant location, and which is nearing obsolescence in both sites.

5.   COMMUNITY INITIATIVES IN LANGUAGE RENEWAL

Among different ethnolinguistic groups in the migrant Moluccan community, we note a range of aspirations relating to *bahasa tanah*. The activities which are now taking place vary according to interest, access to speakers, and access to written materials. Some people are eager to become speakers while others wish to learn about the languages and cultures of their parents and ancestors and perhaps incorporate a few words into their speech as markers of identity. All of the language activities have been initiated by members of the community, some of whom have subsequently sought support from the linguists undertaking this project. Here I focus on two contrasting cases - Amahai, which is moribund in its homeland on Seram Island and is represented by only one elderly speaker in the Netherlands, and Haruku, which is maintained in Muslim villages in its homeland and is represented by four speakers in the Netherlands.

5.1   Amahai or Bahasa Koako

Although the revival of interest in *bahasa tanah* has been driven largely by the second generation, there are cases in which language revival is led by elderly speakers in the first generation who promote the importance of *bahasa tanah* and the value of language learning. One such case concerns the Amahai language - one of the languages which is nearing obsolescence in its homeland.

Amahai, as this language has been known in the literature, is located on south central Seram on the eastern coast of Elpaputi Bay and is subgrouped within Proto-East Central Maluku as an East Piru Bay language (Collins 1983: 102). Its closest relative is the Nusalaut language spoken on Nusalaut Island. A 1987 SIL survey found 50 speakers (B.F. Grimes 1996) while Collins (1983: 99) asserts that Amahai is near extinction. One speaker of Amahai has been located in the Netherlands.

Mr. Dirk (Dede) Tamaela, was born in 1932 in Soahuku village on Seram island. At age fifteen, Mr. Tamaela left Soahuku to join the merchant navy. He travelled throughout Indonesia with the navy before settling in Irian Jaya. In 1964, Mr. Tamaela migrated with his family to the Netherlands. Although Mr. Tamaela was a young man when he left his village, he has retained good communicative competence and a passionate interest in the language he terms Bahasa Koako. His interest includes transmitting the language to future generations. To further this goal, in February 1998 Mr. Tamaela produced a guide to learning Bahasa Koako, which he notes is spoken in four villages in Seram: Amahai, Makariki, Ruta, and Soahuku.

The language learning material incorporates wordlists of numerals, kin terms, pronouns, adjectives, interrogatives, and frequently used verbs and nouns. A number of short dialogues are aimed at assisting young people in learning the language. The sketch grammar provides rules for the placement of adjectives and intensifiers and describes possessive constructions. The wordlists are given trilingually in Bahasa Koako, Malay and Dutch. Grammatical explanations are written in Dutch, which indicates that they are aimed at younger (third- and some second-generation) Moluccans who are not fluent in Malay. However the introduction is written in Malay, as is the concluding section which discusses traditional law (*adat*).

The book is aimed at the dscendants of Mr. Tamaela's language group who now reside in the Netherlands. A secondary aim is to provide language material for members of the broader migrant Moluccan community. Mr. Tamaela notes in the introduction (1998: i):

Beta harap buku ini mau djadi satu djembatan par katong pung anak-tjutju atau generasi mendatang jang rindu mau tau/kenal dia pung bahasa pusaka peninggalan mojang-mojang-nya.[6]

Mr. Tamaela's attitude to language is further exemplified in the following advice which he provides to young members of the community (1998:15).

---

[6] "I hope that this book will be a bridge for our children and grandchildren and the generations to come who may yearn to know or become familiar with the language of their ancestors."

Njong-njong deng nona-nona ale dong djangan lupa kio!!!; bahwa:
a.   *Bahasa itu suatu utjapan djiwa!*
b.   *Kalu tau bahasa sandiri berarti itu berarti: lebe lagi mangarti dan kenal katong pung adat-istiadat sandiri!*
c.   *Bangsa sandiri itu lebe lagi membakar dan mengkuatkan katong samua pung semangat kebangsaan!*
d.   *Bangsa jang besar itu adalah bangsa itu jang djundjung dong punja adat-istiadat dan bahasa sandiri!*[7]

5.2   Haruku

The Haruku community typifies those cases in which the revival of interest in *bahasa tanah* has been driven by the second generation and is supported by elderly speakers in the first generation. Haruku is spoken on Haruku Island, to the east of Ambon Island in Central Maluku. Haruku is subgrouped within Proto-East Central Maluku as an East Piru Bay language (Collins 1983: 100). Its closest relatives are the languages spoken on the neighbouring Lease islands of Saparua and Nusalaut, and the Amahai language, spoken on Seram Island. This language follows the pattern noted earlier, of language maintenance in Muslim villages and obsolescence in Christian villages. Collins notes that Haruku is still spoken in the northwestern villages of Rohomoni, Kabau, and Kailolo, and the northern villages of Pelau, Kariu and Hulaliu but is "apparently extinct" in the southern villages (ibid.).[8] SIL (B.F.Grimes 1996) suggests extensive dialect differentiation but this has not been supported by research.

In October 1997, a radio interview with the author was broadcast on the Moluccan community radio programme *Suara Maluku.*

---

[7]   "Young men and young women you must not forget!!! That;
a. Language is an utterance from the soul!
b. If you know your own language that means you will even more understand and be familiar with our own traditions!
c. Language by itself can even more arouse and strengthen all of our national spirit!
d. The nation which is great is the nation which holds in high esteem its own traditions and language!"
[8]   Collins' fieldwork was undertaken in the northwest coastal village of Kailolo.

Following the programme, a number of people contacted the researchers to seek assistance in working with their language or to express interest in participating in language workshops. Among those who contacted us were two second-generation members of the Haruku community, aged approximately 40 years.

Unlike Amahai, a reasonable amount of archival material exists for the Haruku language and culture.[9] The men had already undertaken library searches and had read whatever material they could find. They were now seeking assistance in taking their study of the language further. In 1998 the men arranged meetings between the author and four first-generation migrants who have varied histories and levels of fluency in the Haruku language.

Two of the first-generation men were born in the 1920s in Aboru, a Christian village on Haruku Island. They attended elementary school in their village and both joined the Dutch colonial army (KNIL) in the 1940s. In 1951, the men moved to the Netherlands with the first wave of migration. Although these two speakers had lived for twenty years in Aboru village, they noted that in their early years they spoke only (Ambonese) Malay and would reply in Malay even when addressed in Haruku by older people, including parents and grandparents. Their observations about their early language use accords with other observations about the process of language shift which was discussed earlier and which is most noticeable in Christian villages. Yet despite the doubts they voiced about their language ability, work with these two speakers indicated a reasonable fluency in Haruku. They were able to undertake a translation task and had little problem with lexical recall.

This picture contrasts with the two other speakers - brothers whose father also originated from Aboru village. The brothers were born in other parts of Indonesia while their father was a serving member of the military. They were educated in Dutch and speak standard Malay rather than Ambonese Malay. The men lived away from Haruku until the Japanese occupation in 1942, at which time they were sent back to their village where they remained until 1946. During that four year

---

9   See van Hoëvell 1877, Stokhof 1982.

period the men gained some competence in Haruku. Like the other Haruku speakers, they moved to the Netherlands with the first wave of migration in 1951. Because of their history, the receptive abilities of these brothers exceed their productive skills.

Each of these four men demonstrated an intense commitment to their ancestral language and culture, and willingness to work with younger members of the community to assist them in language learning. Their children and grandchildren have a range of interests in the Haruku language. One of the second-generation men who first contacted the author yearns to become a speaker of Haruku and had spent some time in his ancestral village trying to learn about the pre-Christian culture. He would like to see the production of a Haruku dictionary and language learning materials. He is also keen to learn how to undertake linguistic work with elderly speakers so that he can continue to document the language.

In contrast, his brother does not want to become a speaker of the language yet is deeply interested in Haruku culture. He sees his growing knowledge about his linguistic heritage as a key to his history and identity. A third Haruku member of the second-generation is drawn to the sounds of her ancestral language. Ms. Monika Akihary is a professional jazz singer who incorporates Haruku into her song texts with the assistance of speakers of the language. Ms. Akihary first composes a preliminary text in English. This text is then translated into Malay and the speakers provide a Haruku translation from the Malay. Ms. Akihary also does not aim to become a speaker of Haruku and focuses on the feeling which the sounds evoke in her music rather than the accuracy of the translations. Like a number of other second-generation migrants, Ms. Akihary also draws on historical sources about other ethnolinguistic groups in Maluku and incorporates cultural concepts and elements of myths in her songs.

6.   CONCLUSION

The migrant community of Moluccans in the Netherlands represents a very complex sociopolitical and linguistic situation in which there are exciting opportunities to document and support languages which are moribund in their homeland. The first phase of this project involved delineating the status of *bahasa tanah* in the Netherlands and the linguistic economy of various generations of the Moluccan migrant community. This phase revealed a wealth of linguistic resources, a high level of interest in various language-related activities, and a range of aspirations in regard to *bahasa tanah*.

In recent years, the changing political scenario in both Indonesia and the Netherlands has enabled Dutch Moluccans to return to Maluku for short periods of time. This, together with changing sociopolitical attitudes within the migrant community, has triggered a resurgence in interest in linguistic heritage. However, this resurgence exists alongside a range of folk beliefs which have developed among second- and third-generation migrants concerning *bahasa tanah*. The second phase of the project therefore involves increasing language awareness among second- and third-generation members of the community.

In order to address community needs and desires for language awareness programmes, a number of seminars have been held, mostly under the sponsorship of the Moluks Historisch Museum, Utrecht, which has as one of its functions serving as an information centre for the migrant community. The seminars have served two primary purposes: younger Moluccans are gaining knowledge about the linguistic situation in Maluku and the Netherlands, and community aspirations for language-related projects are becoming clarified.

During this phase of the project, a number of language workshops which will be run in conjunction with the Moluks Historisch Museum and community groups (*kumpulan*). The workshops have been planned in response to the expressed wishes of members of the second and third generation who would like to gain the linguistic skills required to maintain, renew, or revitalise their languages. Students will be taught basic linguistic skills such as elicitation and recording techniques, phonetic transcription, basic issues in analysing morpho-syntactic structures, selecting an appropriate orthography, and literature production. We hope that these workshops will continue to strengthen the position of minority Moluccan languages and support aspirations for language renewal.

REFERENCES

Blust, Robert A. 1983/84 More on the position of the languages of eastern Indonesia. *Oceanic Linguistics* 22/23: 1-28.

_____ 1993. Central and Central-Eastern Malayo-Polynesian. *Oceanic Linguistics* 32: 241-293.

Bolton, Rosemary A. 1990. *A preliminary description of Nuaulu phonology and grammar*. MA thesis, University of Texas at Arlington.

Broeder, Peter; Guus Extra & Roeland van Hout 1995. Language-related criteria as determinants of ethnicity: goals and results of a feasibility study in the Netherlands. In Willem Fase, Koen Jaspaert & Sjaak Kroon (eds) *The state of minority languages: International perspectives on survival and decline*, 113-134. Lisse: Swets and Zeitlinger.

Chauvel, Richard 1990. *Nationals, soldiers and separatists: The Ambonese islands from colonialism to revolt 1880-1950*. Leiden: KITLV Press.

Collins, James T. 1983. *The historical relationships of the languages of Central Maluku, Indonesia*. Pacific Linguistics D-47. Canberra: Department of Linguistics RSPAS, ANU.

Engelenhoven, Aone van 2000. *Concealment, Maintenance and Renaissance: Language and Ethnicity in the Moluccan Community in the Netherlands*. In this volume.

Florey, Margaret J. 1991. Shifting patterns of language allegiance: a generational perspective from eastern Indonesia. In Hein Steinhauer (ed.) *Papers in Austronesian Linguistics*, No.1. Pacific Linguistics A-81, 39-47. Canberra: Department of Linguistics RSPAS, ANU.

_____ 1997. Skewed performance and structural variation in the process of language obsolescence. In Cecilia Ode & Wim Stokhof (eds) *Proceedings of the Seventh International Conference on Austronesian Linguistics*, 639-660. Amsterdam/Atlanta: Editions Rodophi B.V.

_____ & Rosemary A. Bolton 1997. Personal names, lexical replacement, and language shift in eastern Indonesia. *Cakalele: Maluku Research Journal* 8: 27-58.

Fraassen, Chris F. van 1983 Historical introduction. In K. Polman (ed.) *The Central Moluccas: an annotated bibliography*, 1-59. Leiden: Koninklijke Instituut voor Taal-, Land-, en Volkenkunde.

Grimes, Barbara Dix 1991. The development and use of Ambonese Malay. In Hein Steinhauer (ed.) *Papers in Austronesian linguistics, No. 1*. Pacific Linguistics A-81, 83-123. Canberra: Department of Linguistics RSPAS, ANU.

Grimes, Barbara Fox (ed.) 1996. *Ethnologue: Languages of the world*, 13th edition. Dallas: Summer Institute of Linguistics.

Hoëvell, G.W.W.C. van 1877. Iets over de vijf voornaamste dialecten der Ambonsche landtaal (*bahasa tanah*). *Bijdragen tot de Taal-, Land- en Volkenkunde* 4/1: 1-136.

Steijlen, Godefridus I.J. 1996. *RMS: van ideaal tot symbool. Moluks nationalisme in Nederland, 1951-1994*. Amsterdam: Het Spinhuis.

Stokhof, W.A.L. (ed.) 1982. *Holle lists: vocabularies in languages of Indonesia. Volume 3/3: Central Moluccas: Seram (111), Haruku, Banda, Ambon (1)*. Pacific Linguistics D-49. Canberra: Department of Linguistics RSPAS, ANU.

Tamaela, Dirk 1998 *"Komo oe?" Bahasa Koako, Pulau Seram*. Unpublished manuscript.

Tryon, Darrell T. 1994. The Austronesian languages. In Darrell T. Tryon (ed.) *Comparative Austronesian Dictionary: An introduction to Austronesian studies*. Part 1: Fascicle 1: 5-44. Berlin: Mouton de Gruyter.

Chapter 17

Concealment, Maintenance and Renaissance: language and ethnicity in the Moluccan community in the Netherlands[1]

Aone van Engelenhoven

Leiden University

1. INTRODUCTION

1.1 Geographical location and concise ethnolinguistic sketch of the Moluccas

The Moluccas comprise about 1300 islands, which nowadays form the Province of Maluku in the East of the Republic of Indonesia. The islands are grouped into four major subdistricts: *Maluku Utara* and *Halmahera Tengah* in the North, comprising the island of Halmahera and surrounding islands,[2] *Maluku Tengah* ('Central Maluku') in the middle, comprising the island of Seram and surrounding islands, and in the

1   The research underlying the present paper has been executed in the framework of funding by the Australian Research Council (A59803475). Financial support has also been granted by the Ambon Studies Fund (Utrecht), Yar Nain Foundation (Zwolle) and the Saniri Overleg-/Adviesorgaan SOA (Krimpen aan de IJssel). I want to thank the following persons: my colleagues Margaret Florey, Betty Litamahuputty, Wim Manuhutu and Hans Straver; the working-group Berdikari (SOA, Krimpen aan de IJssel), Mr H. van Hernen (Malr@ organisation), Mrs N. Klein-Katipana (Noha-Rai, foundation of SW Moluccans in the Netherlands); Mr S. Pormes (Letra Natu, the Serua association in the Netherlands); Mr W. Rahayaan, the late Mrs 'C. Surmiasa' (2); Mr B. and N. Ubro and Ms N. Rahayaan (Yar-Nain, foundation of Keiese in Zwolle). Special thanks to Ms Monica Akihary for her enthusiastic and candid information. For their input and comments I would like to thank the participants of the Colloque de la langue native, Université Denis Diderot/Paris-7 (March 19-20 1999), the Language Contact Colloquium at the University of Amsterdam (20 April 1999), and the symposium.

2   The two northern subdistricts, Maluku Utara and Halmahera Tengah, have now become a separate province.

South *Maluku Tenggara* ('Southeast Maluku') to which belongs the string of islands that stretches from the Aru Archipelago off the coast of New Guinea to the island of Wetar off the tip of East Timor. No information to date is available on the number of languages found in Maluku. On the basis of recent research by the Summer Institute of Linguistics, the *Atlas bahasa tanah Maluku* mentions a total of 117 definitely identified different languages.[3]

From a comparative linguistic point of view, the islands can be regrouped into four ethnolinguistic zones, according to the mutual genetic relationships of the indigenous languages. The northern two subdistricts form one ethnolinguistic zone, where languages are either Austronesian (the South Halmaheran-West New-Guinean branch, Blust 1978) or non-Austronesian isolates (Voorhoeve 1987). The present paper focuses on languages found in the remaining three zones. Except for the non-Austronesian Oirata isolect on Kisar (SW Maluku), they all belong to an early off-branch of Proto-Austronesian, labelled Central Malayo-Polynesian (Blust 1993).

Maluku Tengah forms one ethnolinguistic zone whose languages descended from Proto-Central Maluku, one of the daughter proto-languages of Proto-Central Malayo-Polynesian (Collins 1983). Before the 16th century these islands were part of the North Moluccan sultanate of Ternate. Attracted by its economic interest, the European powers of that time, Portugal and the Netherlands, successively stationed garrisons on Ambon and the Lease Islands to break Ternate's control of the area. The redistribution of political power resulted in the establishment of Moslem villages in favour of Ternate, and Christian villages in favour of the Dutch. On Ambon and the Lease Islands the indigenous languages partly survived in the Moslem villages, whereas in the Christian villages they were fully replaced by (Ambonese) Malay, the contact vernacular of the colonisers. Only a few Christian villages managed to maintain their indigenous language, albeit under heavy pressure from local Malay (Collins 1980).

---

[3]   The reliability of this number, however, remains questionable; cf. van Engelenhoven's (1997b) review of Taber et al. (1996).

Maluku Tenggara comprises two ethnolinguistic zones. The five indigenous vernaculars of the Tanimbar and Kei archipelagos are direct descendants of Proto-Southeast Maluku (Collins 1981). The Aru archipelago off the coast of New Guinea features fourteen languages in different stages of endangerment, which independently are linked directly to Proto-Central Malayo-Polynesian (Hughes 1987:103). Together they form one ethnolinguistic zone under the dominance of Ewaw (Kei Archipelago) and Fordate (Northern Tanimbar). The other ethnolinguistic zone comprises the islands in the Southwest. They either directly or indirectly descended from Proto-Timor (Taber 1993). The non-Austronesian isolate of Oirata has been identified as a member of the Trans New Guinea Phylum (Stokhof 1975). The position of the Babar languages remains unclear thus far. Ongoing research seems to support van Engelenhoven's (1988) suggestion that Babar forms a borderland between the Timor and Southeast Maluku regions. Many words in Marsela, for example, indicate significant lexical influence from Tanimbarese languages. Its morphophonology on the other hand inclines toward the Luangic languages west of Babar (van Dijk & van Engelenhoven In progress).

1.2   History of the Moluccan exiles in the Netherlands

Shortly after the Japanese capitulation in 1945 Indonesian nationalists proclaimed the Republic of Indonesia on the island of Java. It took till 1949 before the Dutch government accepted the independence of its former colony as the United States of Indonesia. The Republic of Indonesia made up one of the fifteen states in this federation. Its easternmost state was East Indonesia to which the Moluccan islands belonged. The original proclamation, however, aimed at a unitary state, because of which the Republic of Indonesia sought to include all states of the federation. Already in the following year, the government of East Indonesia acceded into the Republic of Indonesia (Steijlen 1996: 36ff).

As a reaction, Moluccan members of the former East Indonesian government proclaimed an independent Republic of the South Moluccas, *Republik Maluku Selatan* (RMS) on Ambon Island, on 24 April 1950. When, a few months later, the Dutch government disbanded its colonial army, the KNIL,[4] the Dutch Court of Justice disallowed any involuntary demobilisation on Indonesian territory. As a result, in 1951 the Dutch government transported 12,500 Moluccan soldiers to the Netherlands who had either not yet resigned or who refused to go over to the Indonesian army (Manuhutu 1996).

1.3   Language policy in exile

Thus far there is no solid information about the ethnic composition of the Moluccan group. On the basis of the figures in Wittermans (1991),[5] 24 per cent of its members originated from the region which is now called *Maluku Tenggara*. They will in the remaining part of this chapter be referred to as Tenggara people, or as Tenggara Moluccans.

Figure 1a:

Ethnolinguistic composition of Moluccans in the Netherlands

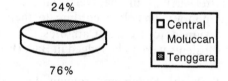

---

4   *Koninklijk Nederlandsch-Indisch Leger*, Royal Netherlands-Indies Army.

5   Wittermans (1991) provides no source for his figures. Thus his calculations need to be used with caution (van der Hoek 1994: 6, note 22). Since his absolute numbers refer to the number of soldiers, I have perceived them as representing the initial exile households, supposing that each soldier lived separately, either with or without a family.

Figure 1b:

Religious composition of Central Moluccans in the Netherlands

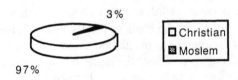

Figure 1a above shows that most Moluccans in the Netherlands are of Central Moluccan origin. Among the Central Moluccans and the Tenggara people there are respectively a minority of Moslems from Ambon (Figure 1b) and Roman Catholics from Kei Kecil and Tanimbar (Figure 1c). After arrival in the Netherlands, the migrants were regrouped in temporary hostels according to their religion. Special hostels were assigned to Roman-Catholics, for example Geleen (Limburg); the Moslems were to be lodged in Balk (Friesland).

In the early 1960s the Dutch government decided to relocate the Moluccan families into permanent quarters in order to facilitate their acculturation into Dutch society. Nevertheless, religious distinctions remained. The Moslems moved to Ridderkerk (South Holland) and Waalwijk (North Brabant); the Roman Catholic Tenggara Moluccans resided for example in Echt (Limburg) and Nistelrode (North Brabant).

Figure 1c:
Religious and ethnolinguistic composition of Tenggara Moluccans in the Netherlands

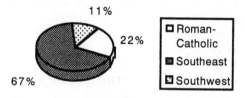

Initially, it was planned to provide education for Moluccan children exclusively in the hostels. In some hostels, however, the formation of special 'camp schools' was not feasible, due to a very small number of children. Very soon most Moluccan children went to Protestant or Roman Catholic schools in nearby places, depending on their respective religious conviction.[6] In most Moluccan households at that time Malay was still the first language among parents and children (see 2 and 3 below). Therefore, the school teachers were soon confronted with the fact that most Moluccan children spoke Malay rather than Dutch. At the outset, instruction for Moluccan children implied 'remedial teaching' to enhance their fluency in Dutch (*Molukkers in Nederland* 1997). In this period, life in the hostel was dominated by the idea of a temporary stay. Boys were advised to learn all kinds of craftsmanship with which they could build up their country after its liberation from Indonesia. This view explains the enthusiasm for Dutch instruction, because it was perceived as the gateway to better education.

---

6   The Moslem children joined the secular state primary school in Balk.

The so-called 'second generation' - the children of the original migrants - was thus 'immersed' into Dutch culture. At the end of the 1970s and the beginning of the 1980s the awareness of the permanency of their exile grew among the members of the 'second generation'. In this period, the idea of OETC[7] evolved, which was initially meant for Frisian bilinguals and children of Turkish and Moroccan workers. When among 'second generation' members it was suggested to apply OETC in the Moluccan community too, this was immediately adopted by the Department of Education. It was not clear, however, what the 'Own Language' of the Moluccans was.

Around the turn of the century, the Dutch colonial government set up a school system throughout the entire archipelago, which endorsed Malay as the principal vehicle of instruction. This system was maintained up to 1950, when the Moluccan separationist struggle began. The extemporaneousness of the RMS is corroborated in A.J. Manusama's (1953) prison diary. Nowhere in the official documents a reference is made to a national language. The fact that the proclamation is in Malay[8] suggests its anticipated function as the national language of the Moluccan Republic. However, the official representative of the Moluccan community, the IWM,[9] perceived Modern Indonesian Malay as the 'language of the enemy' and advised people not to use it for educational purposes. The vernacular of instruction had to be a different type of Malay, 'Moluccan Malay'.

> Moluccan Malay is an 'umbrella term', which covers different language variants like Riau Malay (underlying the national languages of Indonesia and Malaysia, AvE), Church Malay (the vehicle of sermons in Moluccan Protestant churches, AvE), Ambonese Malay, Barracks Malay and *Melaju Sini* (the Malay

---

7   *Onderwijs in Eigen Taal en Cultuur*, 'Instruction in one's Own Language about one's Own Culture'.

8   In fact, it was contemporary Indonesian.

9   *Inspraakorgaan Welzijn Molukkers* 'Participatory Organisation for Moluccan Care'.

variant spoken by Moluccan youth in the Netherlands, AvE). In other words, it refers to all variants brought along by the first generation of Moluccans, shaped into an individual language by the second and third generations.   (Tahitu 1993:25).

This definition implies that there was no clear-cut native tongue available for Moluccans, unlike other minority groups. The *Landelijk Steunpunt Edukatie Molukkers* (National Support Centre for Moluccan Education, LSEM), who are responsible for the development of teaching materials for Moluccan education, therefore regularly needed to propose and refine definitions of Moluccan Malay in their publications (Perspectieven 1994:15).

2.   LETI (SW MOLUCCAS): CONCEALMENT AND OBLIVION

Language profile:
Leti is an early off-shoot of the Luangic-Kisaric branch of Proto-Timor, which is spoken on the island with the same name off the tip of East Timor. It has a Subject-Verb-Object word order, predicate-initial negation, postpositions and subject agreement on all verbs and predicatively used adjectives. Possession is marked by suffixes on the noun. Plurality is indicated on definite human nouns by means of a suffix and on non-human nouns by means of reduplication. Leti has very complex phonotactics and morphophonology with metathesis, the inversion of vowels and consonants on and across morpheme boundaries, as its most salient feature. The main functions of metathesis are marking phrase membership, 'definiteness' of predicate constituents and subordination. Leti has a complex deictic system of nine definite markers with spatial, endophoric and empathic reference. There is no passive voice. (van Engelenhoven 1995a, 1995b)

11 per cent of all Tenggara families are estimated to be of Southwest Moluccan origin,[10] representing three ethnolinguistic groups: TNS,[11]

---

[10]   Based on information kindly provided by Mr Ch. Katipana (Noha-Rai

the Babar archipelago and the islands of Kisar, Leti, Roma and Damar, usually referred to as the Leti-Kisar group.

Figure 2:
Ethnolinguistic composition of SW Moluccan migrant groups

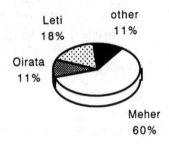

Leti-Kisar group

Fn) and Mr S .Pormes (Letra Natu), Leha 1989.
11   TNS stands for the initial characters of the islands Teun, Nila and Serua, which form a separate district, nowadays on the southcoast of Seram. As far as I have been able to check, there are no migrants from Teun in the Netherlands.

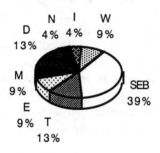

Babar group[12]

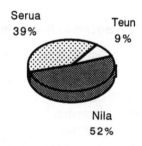

TNS group

Rinsampessy (1992) notes that most Moluccan families are based on mixed marriages. This observation adequately applies to most Southwest Moluccan families, where the husband married a wife from either the Ambon-Lease Islands (Central Moluccas) or from Java. Only in a few

---

12 Legend: D: Dawlor-Dawra, E: Emplawas, I: Imroing, M: Marsela, N: North Babar, SEB: Southeast Babar, T: Tela, W: Wetan.

cases a marriage was contracted with a mestizo or Dutch wife. Consequently, the vernacular used by the spouses was Malay rather than a language indigenous to the Southwest Moluccan islands. Another feature, typical for Southwest Moluccan culture and without any doubt influencing the language behaviour of this group, is the phenomenon of 'culture concealment' once one is outside the home region permanently (cf. van Engelenhoven 1998a). This is illustrated below by analysing the migrant history and the corresponding language behaviour of the Surmiasa family,[13] who is of Leti origin.

On 24 April 1951 the Surmiasa family disembarked from HM 'Castel Bianco' in Rotterdam. At that moment the family was composed of a husband, a wife and six children. Both partners were born on Leti island. The two oldest children (A and B) were born in a previous marriage of Mr Surmiasa to a Kisarese. The oldest boy (D) is an adopted nephew of Mr Surmiasa.

Table 1:   Movements of the Surmiasa family

year	place	hostel type	population
1951	Geleen	barracks	SE Moluccan
1952	Groesbeek	barracks	Central Moluccan
1954	Barneveld	mansion	Central Moluccan
1955	Barneveld	barracks	Central Moluccan
1964	Nijverdal	village quarter	Central Moluccan

The chronology of the Surmiasa family's movements (Table 1) exemplifies the chaos of the housing of the Moluccan migrants. The ongoing movements of this particular family were for different reasons:

The first transfer was motivated by government planning to assign the same residential location to families with similar religious convictions (Akihary 1991). Most families initially located at Geleen were Roman Catholic Southeast Moluccans. Notwithstanding its ethnic background,

---

13   For reasons of privacy, the name of this family has been changed.

the Protestant Surmiasa needed to be relocated to an available location, Groesbeek. Here, the majority originated from the Central Moluccas[14] and law and order was maintained by the CRAMS.[15] As elaborated by Steijlen (1996: 65-98), this committee had constituted itself as the official and rightful agent of the guerilla government on Seram. It had set itself the task to prepare all exiles for a regularised return to a free Republic of the South Moluccas. As such, it fanatically advocated the ethnic oneness of the Moluccan people. In this view, the ethnolinguistic divergence of the SW Moluccan Surmiasa family - whether or not manifested on purpose - was perceived as a constant offence and violation to the Republic's cause. In 1954 the Surmiasas once again moved, to Barneveld. Barneveld accommodated two locations, which lodged mostly Central Moluccan families. Around the turn of the decade especially the second location, De Biezen, had evolved into a centre of political power. With the traumatic experiences in Groesbeek in mind, Mr and Mrs Surmiasa managed to raise their children to conform to the expectations of the Central Moluccan majority. As such a reasonably agreeable life for the entire family was guaranteed. Three children were born here (Table 2). However, in 1964 the Indonesian army managed to eliminate the final resistance on Seram, which created a vacuum of political power in the Moluccan locations in the Netherlands (Steijlen 1996: 241). Being an ardent adherent of the armed resistance, Mr Surmiasa and his family fled to Nijverdal, one of the centres of the incoming contra-president General I. Tamaela.

---

[14]   Van der Hoek, however, specifically mentions Groesbeek as a 'Keiese camp' (van der Hoek 1994:106, note 13).

[15]   *Commissie voor de Rechtspositie van Ambonese Militairen en Schepelingen,* 'Committee for the Legal Status of Ambonese Military and Naval Soldiers'.

Table 2:
Composition and linguistic repertoire of the Surmiasa family

household member		year/place of birth	origin of spouse	linguistic repertoire[16]			
				Leti	Meher	Malay	Dutch
husband		1912 Leti	Leti	1	0	2	4
wife		1921 Leti	Leti	1	4	2	3
A	F[17]	1935 Timor	SW[18]	0	1	2	3
B	F	1937 Timor	SE	0	2	1	3
C	F	1940 C Java	Dutch	4	0	1	2
D	M	1942 Leti	SW	4	4	1	2
E	F	1947 Jakarta	CM	0	0	3	1
F	M	1950 W Java	Dutch	0	0	3	1
G	M	1953 Groesbeek	-	0	0	3	1
H	M	1955 Barneveld	Dutch	0	0	3	1
I	F	1957 Barneveld	Dutch	0	0	3	1
J	F	1960 Barneveld	CM	0	0	3	1

Table 2 shows the linguistic repertoire of each member of the family. As can be seen, the family is composed of three different groups as far as their linguistic repertoire is concerned. Mr and Ms Surmiasa and the two oldest daughters are clearly bilinguals having an indigenous language, Leti or Meher, as first language (L1) and Malay as a second language (L2). The Meher fluency of A and B in Meher can be explained since they are children from an earlier marriage of Mr Surmiasa to a Kisarese wife. Because of the early death of their mother, they were brought to Kisar rather than being raised in the barracks with their father. They were picked up together with their cousin D, shortly before the family's

---

16   0: unknown, 1: first language, 2: second language, 3: elementary knowledge, 4: rudimentary knowledge.

17   F= female; M= male

18   SW= Southwest Moluccan; SE = Southeast Moluccan; CM = Central Moluccan. Marrying a Meher man, Ms. A founded the third 'unmixed' marriage within the SW Moluccan group.

transfer to the Netherlands. The repertoires of the daughters, however, appear to be reversed. Whereas A's L1 is Meher, Malay is the first language for B. A possible explanation may be the marriage of A to a fellow-speaker of Meher, because of which she was able to maintain her L1 fluency. B, however, married a Keiese with whom she could only speak Malay. She depended on contacts with her sister A and other Kisarese to practice her Meher skill.

Mr and Mrs Surmiasa display the typical linguistic repertoire of the 'first generation'. This term is used in the Moluccan community to refer to the soldiers and their wives coming to the Netherlands in the early 1950s. Mrs C and Mr D are typical examples of the 'second generation', which refers to the children of the soldiers. The ones born in the East Indies are generally referred to in the community as the '*bung* and *usi* generation', using the Malay address terms 'brother' and 'sister', respectively. As can be seen from Table 2, they only have two languages available, Malay (L1) and Dutch (L2). The first was taught at school in the Netherlands Indies and the latter in the residential areas of Moluccan groups in the Netherlands. They only have a rudimentary knowledge of Leti, which they heard their parents speak with guests in the army and in the residential areas. D's residence on Kisar before his arrival in the Netherlands explains his rudimentary knowledge of Meher. The Malay speech of Mrs C, however, is noticeably different from that of her older sisters and her younger siblings. It features extensive lexical borrowings from other Indonesian languages like Javanese; and the grammatical structures that are produced often feature pidgin characteristics (van Engelenhoven In progress). It is hypothesised for the time being that her speech is an exponent of *Melayu Tangsi* or 'Barracks-Malay', the speech of the KNIL-soldiers (Tahitu 1993: 18).

The definition of 'second generation' given above includes the children born in the Netherlands too. From a sociolinguistic point of view, however, they are a separate generation. Their language behaviour and speech correspond in general outline with the Malay produced by the grandchildren of the migrant soldiers, the so-called 'third generation'. In his analysis, Tahitu (1989) describes this particular Malay variant of

Dutch-Moluccan youths, dubbed *Melaju Sini*,[19] as a mix of lexical and grammatical elements from Malay and Dutch. The fact of E's and F's young age at their arrival in the Netherlands explains the similarity of their linguistic repertoire to those of their younger siblings born in the Netherlands.

As elaborated elsewhere (van Engelenhoven 1998a, In press), languages in the Southwest Moluccas are easily exchanged for another more suitable language. It therefore does not come as a surprise that already in the barracks in the East Indies both Mr and Mrs Surmiasa decided to speak Leti only at home, either to each other or to visiting fellow Letinese. To their children they only spoke Malay.

Although four other Leti soldiers and their families came to the Netherlands, only Mr Surmiasa had a Leti spouse. In practice this meant that the Sumiasas could only speak Leti with others at certain family gatherings like baptisms or professions of faith and later, in the 1970s and 1980s, weddings and funerals. Since public discussion between men and women was at that time still very unusual, perhaps even culturally restricted, Leti speech was implicitly confined to Mr Surmiasa and the other husbands. Mrs Surmiasa could only speak Leti to her husband at home.[20]

The CRAMS decree mentioned above made all family members very wary not to display 'un-Moluccan' behaviour. The children encouraged their father especially to refrain from any behaviour that manifested their ethnolinguistic divergence from the Moluccan ideal (see section 5 below). For the spouses, Leti became a secret language to be used when they did not want the children to understand. In some instances it functioned as a taboo language, in which dangerous topics like witchcraft, caste and guilt were discussed. The chants in *Lirasniara*, the

---

19   Meaning 'Malay Here' as opposed to the Indonesian variants labelled 'Malay There'.

20   There was some communication in Leti with wives from Wetan and Tela (Babar), whose mother tongues were closely related to hers. How far there was real communication remains unclear.

'singing language' used on most SW Moluccan islands (van Engelenhoven In press) were felt to be especially embarrassing. The only public Leti performance allowed in the presence of the children appeared to be the incantations for which both Mr and Mrs Surmiasa were often consulted by the other residents in the areas and later in the quarter.

When both parents had died, in 1979 and 1986 respectively, none of the children had any knowledge of their native tongue, while they were only slightly acquainted with the cultural framework of their home island. Through the years, Mrs C, Mr D and Mrs E were to be perceived by the other siblings — without their agreement — as family authorities on Leti language and culture.

3. EWAW (SE MOLUCCAS): REJECTION AND MAINTENANCE

Language profile:
Ewaw is a descendant of Proto-Southeast Maluku, which is mainly spoken, either as mother tongue or as contact language, in the Kei archipelago off the west coast of New Guinea (Irian Jaya). It comprises two dialects, Kei Kecil and Kei Besar which mainly differ in phonological make-up. It has a Subject-Verb-Object word order, clause-final negation and postpositions. Verbs, but not adjectives, feature subject agreement when used predicatively. Possessive marking is encoded by means of pronominal suffixes on inalienable nouns or by means of pronominal particles preceding alienable nouns. Plurality is indicated on nouns by means of reduplication. Ewaw features only apposition. There is no passive voice. Ewaw has a very complex deictic system which is elaborated by means of directional verbs according to the North-South axis of Kei-Besar (Hughes 1987, van Engelenhoven Forthcoming)

The majority of the Southeast Moluccan soldiers who came to the Netherlands are of Keiese origin. From an ethnolinguistic point of view, the Keiese culture differs significantly from those found in the Central Moluccas. Between these groups there exists an almost traditional feeling of resentment. Although of little influence in the colonial army, these sentiments underlie the many clashes between Keiese and Central Moluccans in their residential areas in the 1950s. Many Keiese remained neutral towards the Republic of the South Moluccas, which was perceived as a specific Central Moluccan cause. In the 1970s many Roman-Catholic Keiese adopted Indonesian nationality. The Keiese wish not to identify with the Central Moluccan majority resulted among other things in a separate social-political association, the KRPPT,[21] which explicitly looked after the interests of the Southeast Moluccans (Steijlen 1996: 78). A the end of the 1950s, a separate Tenggara church, the GMPT,[22] seceded from the RMS-oriented GIM[23] on similar grounds (van der Hoek 1994: 106-14).

The violence which sometimes accompanied the clashes between Central Moluccans and Tenggara people forced the CAZ[24] to assign special locations to Keiese families in order to maintain peace and order among the exiles. When in the early 1960s the Department of Home Affairs evacuated the temporary locations and relodged the Moluccan families in permanent quarters, the Keiese regrouped themselves according to social and cultural descent. The families from Kei Kecil[25] mostly moved to cities in the South of the Netherlands. The Kei Besar people moved to Rijssen and Zwolle.

The Keiese segregation on the social and political plane also affected their language, Ewaw. Both Southwest and Central Moluccan languages underwent language loss and shift (respectively section 2 and section 4). Ewaw, on the contrary, appears still to be very much used in the

---

21 *Kepentingan Rajat Pulau-Pulau Terselatan* 'The Interests of the People from the Southernmost Islands'.

22 *Gereja Protestan Maluku Tenggara* 'Southeast Moluccan Protestant Church'.

23 *Gereja Injili Maluku* 'Moluccan Evangelic Church'.

24 *Commisariaat voor Ambonezenzorg* 'Ambonese Care Directorate'.

25 The toponym Kei Kecil ('Small Kei') refers to Roa Island and the surrounding smaller islets. Kei Besar ('Big Kei') refers to the island of Yuut.

several Keiese quarters. In the next paragraph I elaborate on this phenomenon by focusing on the community in Zwolle.

The Moluccan community in Zwolle at the moment comprises 138 households. The Keiese component in the community is significant: 70 per cent (96 households) are ethnic Keiese. Only 14 per cent (20 households) are of other Moluccan origin, whereas the remaining 16 per cent (22 households) are Dutch or Dutch-Keiese marriages. According to these figures, this specific quarter may safely be dubbed a Malay *Sprachinsel* or 'linguistic enclave' (Clyne 1991:266), since 84 per cent of the households have Malay as first language.

The position of Zwolle in comparison with other Tenggara quarters is unique because of the social cohesion of its population. Most families belong to the *Mel-mel*, the highest class in the traditional Keiese community. This implies that it would be very difficult for these families to find marriage candidates with a matching social status in other Tenggara quarters. Consequently, the eldest sons were very much encouraged to look for a partner on Kei Besar instead. As a result of this marriage policy 30 of the 96 Keiese households in Zwolle consist of 'second generation' men married to an Indonesian wife (Figure 4).

Figure 3:[26]
Ethnic composition of households in the Zwolle community

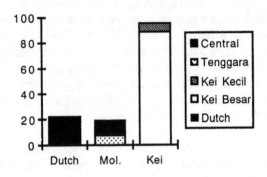

Figure 4:[27]
Generational composition of Keiese households

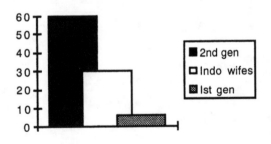

---

26   Mol. = Moluccan.

27   Indo wives = Indonesian wives; 1st gen = first generation; 2nd gen = second generation.

The Indonesian wives control an integral part of social life in the quarter. Like the Southwest Moluccan children (Table 2), the 'second generation' speakers in Zwolle are bilinguals whose actual first language is Dutch rather than Malay. Keiese informants paint a picture of language behaviour in the barracks in the East Indies which is similar to the one described for the Southwest Moluccan soldiers (see section 2 above). Ewaw was confined to Keiese visitors and between the spouses, whereas Malay was the vernacular of their children. However, in the locations in the Netherlands, these children were exposed to Dutch education and were 'immersed' in the Dutch language (Tahitu 1993: 19). They became therefore bilingual speakers whose first language was Dutch, whereas Malay became their second language for speech at home. The figures above show that the 'first generation' is now outnumbered by the 'second generation' (and consequently by their children, forming the 'third generation'). In practice this scenario implies that the indigenous language would shift to the background and finally be lost, just as happened with Leti in the Southwest Moluccan subcommunity (section 2 above). Ewaw was acknowledged as the language of the 'first generation'. The 'first generation', as the initial link to the indigenous society overseas, was perceived as the source of traditional knowledge. Consequently, Ewaw was assigned to those domains that were connected to traditional knowledge: clan histories, marital law and the village alliances. The Indonesian wives, being the only ones in the 'second generation' to understand Ewaw, started to function as intermediaries between the two generations in the above mentioned domains.

Above I briefly touched upon the GMPT church as an exponent of the Keiese wish to distinguish themselves inside the Moluccan community. The church still plays a central role in the daily life of the Zwolle community. This does not come as a surprise, because a significant part of its families had come from the Laarbrug Hostel in Ommen, where they were either directly or indirectly involved in the secession out of the Evangelic Moluccan Church. Since Malay is still preferred in church, the natural fluency in (Indonesian) Malay of the Indonesian wives proved to be an asset in the preparations of the services.

The Ewaw speech of the Indonesian wives nearly completely mirrors the account of Ewaw by Geurtjens (1921). Recent research in Zwolle suggests the beginning of a process of simplification. As shown in Table 4, only three of the fourteen numeral classifiers mentioned by Geurtjens (1921: 15) were recognised: *u* for boats, *watu* for globular objects and the neutral *ain*. Only *ain*, however, was actually used by my informants.

Table 3:   Ewaw classifiers

Geurtjens (1921)	gloss	Zwolle variant
wat tomat ru	'two women'	*wat ain ru*
rubi waan ru	'two Guilders'	*rubi ain ru*
mo 'u[28] *wur ru*	'two bananas'	*di'in ain ru*
mantilur watu ru	'two eggs'	*mantilur ain ru*

The informants could recognise all complex deictic verbal constructions found in Geurtjens' (1924) texts. Nevertheless they did not appear in daily speech or in elicitation. The absence of deictics referring to height and sea may very well be based on environment rather than language simplification. Unlike the Keiese environment, where these are intrinsic landmarks, there is no sea or mountains in the Zwolle geography (van Engelenhoven 1998b).

Keiese society has a principally patriarchal and patrilineal tradition where social life tends to be separate for men and women. Whereas in other Keiese quarters like Distelrode, Ewaw is still considered to be a first generation language, in Zwolle it is increasingly seen as a vernacular for women. As such, all male respondents in Zwolle denied any knowledge of Ewaw, which was generally explained by its function as a secret language between parents. However, several instances of Ewaw sentences in otherwise Malay discourse between Indonesian wives and 'second generation' speech partners have been attested

---

28   This is actually the word for 'banana' in the Kei Kecil dialect on which Geurtjens (1921) is based. The Ewaw speech in Zwolle is in the Kei Besar dialect.

throughout the entire fieldwork period.[29] Awaiting decisive results from future research, this phenomenon is hypothesised as an exponent of the failure to distinguish Ewaw from Malay. Notwithstanding the differences in phonological make-up, their respective grammars are very much alike.[30] Said differently; the 'second generation' members are aware that Dutch is their first language. They acknowledge Malay, with which they are also acquainted, as their second language. In their cognition 'second language' stands for 'non-Dutch'. Their term 'Malay' or *Melayu*, therefore, refers to L2 features and 'non-Dutch' features of Malay speech. It equally applies to Ewaw, which they cannot distinguish from Malay. Because of the exclusive character of Keiese oral and musical traditions, the 'second generation' can distinguish Ewaw from Malay, when it is either sung or chanted. Extensive *Ngel-ngel*, classic poetry consisting of parallel lines, has been reported still to be performed at weddings and funerals to an exclusively Keiese audience. Modern Ewaw music from Kei, for example by *Black Mama*, is very much appreciated by the third generation as a token of their own Keiese identity.

---

[29]   In one instance, it was attested that a young man of 'the third generation' immediately closed the door when his mother - one of the Indonesian wives - asked him to do so in Ewaw. How far this was an exponent of real Ewaw discourse is a topic for further research. My informants emphasised the use of Ewaw clichés like *Fel be?* 'How (are you)?' and *Ya'au!* '(It's) me!' as shibboleths of Keiese identity on Ambon and in the Netherlands. The above mentioned case may also be a Keiese equivalent of the Malay clichés for small commands used by Moluccan parents and grandparents in an otherwise Dutch discourse to their children or grandchildren. In the latter scenario one only needs to 'understand' the pragmatics of the command, not its semantics.

[30]   Ewaw differs notably from Malay in its postclausal negator and its postpositions, which are preverbal and prepositions in Malay.

4.   HARUKU (CENTRAL MOLUCCAS): ACQUIESCENCE AND RENAISSANCE

Language profile:
Haruku is an early off-shoot of the Hatuhaha branch of Proto-Central Maluku through Proto-Nunusaku. It is spoken in Moslem villages on Haruku island and on the southwest coast of Seram. It has a Subject-Verb-Object word order, predicate-initial negation and postpositions. It lacks subject agreement. Possession is marked by a particle between the possessor and possessed nouns. Inalienable possession is no longer marked. No information is available yet on plural marking on nouns. It is unclear whether a landward-seaward opposition is still maintained in the deictic system. There is no passive voice. Like all Ambon-Lease languages, Haruku features extensive language erosion due to heavy grammatical and lexical influence from local Malay. On Haruku it is on the edge of extinction. (Collins 1983, Florey 1998b).

Most Moluccan soldiers and their families originated from the Ambon and the so-called Lease Islands: Haruku, Saparua and Nusa Laut. Here, the indigenous languages are under severe pressure from local Malay. Nowadays they are reported to be spoken exclusively in Moslem villages. According to Collins (1980), in most languages only the lexicon is retained, whereas the original grammatical patterns are replaced by new ones from local Malay.

Local Malay covers most domains in daily life. Throughout the Moluccas indigenous languages display a special register for traditional affairs like lawsuits and marriages. In the Southeast and Southwest Moluccas this register features extensive lexical parallelism, the pairing of words and subsequent sentences (van Engelenhoven 1997a). Similar phenomena have been attested in the verbal arts of the Alune in the highlands of West Seram. Florey (1998a) reports how, notwithstanding the ongoing language loss in this community, a small core of incantations is being maintained among younger Alune. On the Ambon-Lease Islands the indigenous languages, dubbed *bahasa tanah* 'language of the land' in local Malay, now function as special vernaculars for traditional affairs. Memorised traditional songs - called *kapata* -

document the local histories and the alliances among the Central Moluccan villages. Although these *kapata* are still highly appreciated in Central Moluccan society, their archaic word choice obscures their actual meaning for young people (Straver 1997: 5).

Indigenous languages that have been located in the Central Moluccan subcommunity in the Netherlands are Allang and possibly Tulehu (Ambon); also Haruku and Amahei (Southwest Seram). As among the Southwest Moluccans, most Central Moluccan families contain mixed marriages, even if both spouses were of Central Moluccan origin. As explained in section 2, mixed marriages obstruct the transmission of indigenous language knowledge to another generation. Another influencing factor was the fact that in the respective backgrounds of most spouses the 'language of the land' had been assigned to the transmission of cultural and historical knowledge. Teaching indigenous vernacular therefore implied teaching sacred cultural knowledge. Most soldiers were still teenagers when they enlisted and as such had little experience with traditional knowledge. They were acquainted with the ethical security measures linked to traditional knowledge, paraphrased in the exile community as *Jangan sembarang* 'No indifference!' (van Engelenhoven 1998a). Consequently they were not encouraged to perform any speech act in their 'language of the land'.

During the colonial period Central Moluccans built up a name as good musicians. *Kroncong*, an originally Portuguese music style, was promoted in Indonesia and in the Netherlands by famous artists like George de Fretes and Ming Luhulima. In the early 1970s music by Moluccan youth was still devoted to the RMS. In the early 1980s Moluccan musicians tended to a more international range in which ethnic identity prevailed over the political cause. Sessions on traditional drums, *tifa*, and Malay songs, as for example by Massada, were intended to demonstrate the Moluccan identity. Only recently a CD was released containing Central Moluccan music in indigenous language.[31] The

---

31   The music performed on this particular CD is in the New Age Style, which is at present very fashionable in the Netherlands. It is unclear whether this kind of music will remain popular.

music itself, however, was traditional and not newly composed. New compositions in indigenous language required somebody who was able to detach himself from the traditional self-restriction.

This requirement seems to have been met by Ms Monica Akihary, a professional jazz singer of Aboru origin, who incorporates Haruku into her song texts. Aboru is the only Christian village on Haruku where the indigenous language is still spoken. Although it is not known how many families from Aboru live in the Netherlands, they are perceived in the Moluccan community as a closed and distinct group. Florey (1998b) found only four native speakers of Haruku, all males whose respective fluency differed from 'reasonable' to 'very little'. None of these speakers spoke Haruku on a regular basis, which is clearly connected to the mixed marriages mentioned above.

The open-mindedness of Ms Akihary to the 'language of the land' may be connected to her age. Being born in 1965, she actually stands between the prudent 'second generation' of military children born either in Indonesia or in the hostels and the 'third generation' of grandchildren born in the Netherlands. Unlike the former, the latter fully experienced the 'immersion process' in the Dutch language and culture. The fact that her father too was educated in Dutch — which is reflected by his Dutch fluency — suggests, that the effects of the 'immersion' are inherent to this particular family. In a 1998 interview on the Dutch radio she explained her perception of and attitude to 'languages of the land' as follows:

> A part of them (the texts, AvE) are in English. Another part is in - what is called 'the ancestral language of the Moluccas'. In this case (the Boiakih CD, AvE) ... I used the old, dead languages from Seram and from Haruku where my father comes from.

When the interviewer asked her why she used this language for her texts, she elaborated:

> ... I liked its sounds. ... That African language, that Pygmy language looks very much like the ancestral language of the

Moluccas. For me, that too are beautiful sounds. I thought, ..., why do I not use it? It is something extra I can add to my music.

These words demonstrate how in fact the separate indigenous languages found in the region are considered to be exponents of one and the same native tongue, the ancestral language of the Moluccas. This is indeed the common perception on the Ambon-Lease Islands, where the inhabitants trace their origin on the 'mother island' of Seram.

In this interview Ms Akihary elaborates how her texts are created in consultation with her informants. First she composes a preliminary text in English, which she translates into Malay. Her variant of Malay she explicitly defines as 'Moluccan Malay' (see 1 above), probably to distinguish it from the variant she learned during her study leave in Indonesia. Her informants then try to provide a Haruku translation, of which she observes in the same interview:

It was really a continuous search for the right words. A word in Dutch has about ten different meanings, which makes it easier to describe one's intention. That is absolutely not so in this language! It is more like: Well, here are the words and there is no more...

In several of our meetings, Ms Akihary emphasised that the texts were not just translated. As becomes apparent from her remarks in the interview above, it was often impossible for her informants to provide accurate translations of the initial texts. Therefore she modified the texts in such a way that both her intentions and the meanings of the Haruku words converged. This is exemplified in the following song:

Tenaga gaib	Mystical Force
Sima-Sima, pusaka dari ina,	Sima-Sima, inheritance of a woman,
Bidadari, nama Tapalasewa.	A nymph called Tapalasewa.
Koto kihy ama ina e,	Cut loose from the fatherland,
Nusa kohy, lahirlah.	Small island, come forth.
Tenaga gaib, seit Sima.	A mystical force is the knife Sima.

Telah mengubahkan dunia.	It has changed the world.
<u>*Koto kihy ama ina e.*</u>	Cut loose from the fatherland,
<u>*Nusa kohy,*</u> *lahirlah.*	Small island, come forth.

(Akihary 1997)

This text is composed of 28 words. The 12 underlined words are Haruku, whereas the rest is in Malay. The names Sima-Sima, Tapalasewa and Sima are Wemale (Seram). The song relates to the Central Moluccan origin myth where an exiled princess[32] cuts off the Lease Islands from the 'mother island' of Seram by means of a magical knife, called Sima-Sima. The source for Ms Akihary must have been the voluminous books of Jensen (1948) and Jensen & Niggemeyer (1939) on the Wemale in Seram, which are widely read among Moluccan youth. The Haruku words *ama* 'father' and *ina* 'mother' are combined in order to reflect the meaning of 'fatherland'. The combination of *ama ina* literally reads 'father and mother'. Its use clearly rests on the notion of 'origin' or 'source' embedded in both 'father' and 'mother'. Similarly, *ina* reflects the notion 'woman' in the first line.

This procedure matches the one described for the 'Singing Language', the traditional contact language that is sung among the islands of the Southwest Moluccas. This register contains only about a hundred words whose meanings are homonymically extended, because of the many sound mergers. Rather than seeing it as a genuine language as in the view of the islanders, van Engelenhoven (In press) perceives this highly endangered type of verbal art as a register in the individual indigenous languages.

The acceptability of a song in 'Singing Language' to an audience, however, depends greatly on the quality of certain required compositional techniques as for example lexical parallelism. In the Central Moluccan scenario, especially among the migrants, this last

---

32   Named Boi Ratan. The first part of her name makes up the first part of the music group, Boiakih. The second part relates to the family name of the singer, Akihary.

feature does not apply. The use of non-Malay terms sufficiently determines somebody's text or speech as 'original' or 'native' as has been convincingly shown in Florey's (1991) account of language allegiance among Alune youth on Seram.

In both settings, the Central Moluccan islands and the Netherlands, simple words from an indigenous language in an otherwise Dutch or Malay conversation corroborates the ethnic identity of the speaker.[33] Although Ms Akihary herself has no need to identify herself as a Harukunese, this particular element in her language behaviour is a phenomenon emerging among Moluccan youth on the search of their ethnic roots.

5.   THE ALIFURU CONCEPT: MOLUCCAN LINGUISTIC DIVERSITY REDEFINED

On the brink of a new era, the Moluccan exile in the Netherlands has lasted for almost fifty years. As time went by, the community experienced considerable changes. The Netherlands were still recovering from the effects of the Second World War when the Moluccan soldiers and their families arrived. In these circumstances their presence was unforeseen and unwanted. The initial organisation of their lodging was chaotic. In the first years of their stay, the Moluccan families were located wherever possible. Former convents, empty mansions and even former concentration camps of the German occupation period functioned as the initial residences. In the eyes of the exiles this situation confirmed the temporariness of their stay.

---

[33]   I am continuously confronted with this phenomenon. During a public lecture, which I gave in the Moluccan community in Krimpen aan de IJssel, for example, a 'first generation' man from Nusa Laut defined it as 'expanding one's (traditional) knowledge'. Nowadays, on Nusa Laut remnants of indigenous language may only be found in the speech of the oldest inhabitants of the Moslem village of Titawai (Taber et al. 1996: 40). It remains to be studied how far this language is actually spoken or is confined to a special register within the local Malay lexicon.

The anticipated return to a liberated Republic of the South Moluccas dominated daily life in the hostels. Parents encouraged their sons to learn crafts with which they could help to build their country. In this situation the political and religious leaders emphasised the need for unity in the Moluccan group. To stress the mutual 'sameness' of the families, the RMS ideology developed in the hostels emphasised the centrality of Seram as the 'mother' of all Moluccan islands (section 4). The Seramese mountain tribes, dubbed *Alifuru* ('Mountain Children'), were perceived as the prototypical inhabitant of the Moluccan motherland. Descriptions of the Wemale and Alune in Jensen (1939) and in Jensen & Niggemeyer (1948) functioned as models for a unitary Moluccan culture. In Indonesia, on the other hand, *Alifuru* had become a denigrating term referring to retardedness and ignorance.

The concealment of the Southwest Moluccan identity can only be appreciated in the light of the Alifuru concept. The complex ethnolinguistic composition of this group and its numerical insignificance made it impossible to uphold an identity of its own within the Moluccan community (section 2). Thanks to their large number, the Keiese could easily maintain a distinctive identity. Their cultural disagreement with the Alifuru concept was strengthened by the grouping of the residences according to religious conviction. The Roman Catholics of Kei Kecil were assembled in exclusive 'Keiese' or 'Tenggara' camps. This allowed for the collective Indonesian naturalisation of Tenggara people during the 1970s, which firstly has to be perceived as a public disassociation from the RMS cause.

In an attempt to accelerate the integration of the Moluccan community into Dutch society, the families were relocated into permanent quarters in the municipalities. This was generally felt to be the conclusive Dutch betrayal. It was clear that the Netherlands would never support the Moluccan cause. Especially among the 'second generation' this resulted in a feeling of disappointment, of which the occupation of the Indonesian embassy in 1970 was a first expression. The independence of Surinam, the other major colony of the Netherlands, in 1975 and the government's family reunion policy for foreign labourers diverted the attention of the Dutch government from the Moluccan cause. The Dutch public, and consequently the government, started to focus on the increasing flow of immigrants from Surinam and the countries of origin of the foreign labourers. In comparison with them, the Moluccan community numerically declined among the other minorities (Willems 1996). This provoked a radicalisation of Moluccan youth that culminated in the notorious train hijackings of 1975 and 1977.[34] Together with the secession of the Tenggara churches, these events contributed to the social isolation of the Keiese community that underlies the unexpected maintenance of Ewaw in Zwolle (section 3 above).

Rinsampessy (1992:121) emphasises the importance assigned to language in the Moluccan community. I quote one of his informants here:

> We find it important for our children to speak their own language. (...) Malay is necessary for a good understanding of your parents, but the language is even more important for one's own identity and concern with the Moluccan community. (Rinsampessy 1992:52).

It was a known fact within the community that Malay was not the original mother tongue for everybody. Also within the Central Moluccan majority there were families where an indigenous language was still remembered, albeit fragmentarily. The ethnolinguistic diversity of the area of origin undermined the unitary perception of the Moluccas ideology of the RMS. Parallel to the favourite Malay proverb *Lain padang, lain belalang*,[35] different languages implied different cultures. The Moluccan ethnolinguistic diversity therefore needed to be redefined. The camp of the contra-president, General I. Tamaela, elaborated the idea of a shared origin by comparing the respective island cultures. The

---

[34] Notwithstanding the disagreement within the Moluccan community, its members collectively refrained from comment. The occupation of an entire primary school in 1978, however, was strongly denounced by both the community and the government in exile.

[35] Free translation: 'In another field you'll find different grasshoppers'.

many alliances between villages and islands which were found around the Keiese islands were perceived as a token of one original Moluccan culture. This phenomenon was dubbed *Siwa-Lima* ('Nine-Five'), after the indigenous term that referred to the organisation of the allied villages. At a 1988 symposium in Barneveld, an authoritative member of the 'first generation' explained it as follows:

> *Siwa Lima* is a historical expression stating 'the chain of brotherhood' for us, the society of the Moluccan people. ... authentic Moluccan literature asserts that *Siwa Lima* originates from Nunusaku in the western part of the 'Mother Island' ... (Behoekoe Nam Radja et al. 1993: 23).

In this philosophy, the perceived differences in the 'languages of the land' were only superficial:

> ... In the beginning there only was S*ou Esa, Sou Ina Tuny*, or One Language, the Genuine Mother Tongue in Maluku. Then, after Moriale (the mythical reign of origin located at West-Seram, AvE) broke up and became many *Hena*,[36] *Sou Ina Tuny*, or the Alifuru Tongue split up too into many local and regional languages, almost as many as (there are) villages. On Seram thirteen regional languages are found beside Alune and Wemale. All contain features of Alune and Wemale. Furthermore, all the names of the villages and the names of the clan houses of the inhabitants of Ambon, the Lease Islands, Manipa, Kelang, Boano and the others still contain (words from) the Alifuru Tongue. Therefore, although our *Sou Ina Tuny* scattered all over our archipelago, it is nevertheless *Siwa Lima*, our Social Principle, that shows that Maluku is One People ... (Behoekoe Nam Radja et al. 1993: 105)

Those who were born in the hostels upheld the strivings for one Moluccan culture up to the 1980s. The *Balai Pusat* ('The Central

---

36   Nagarees, village-states.

House')[37] made it its task to propagate Malay as the native tongue of the Moluccans. The Malay variants spoken in the Moluccan community were consequently renamed *Bahasa Maluku* 'Moluccan Language' in opposition with *Bahasa Indonesia*, the language of the enemy (section 1). One of the instruments with which the Balai Pusat tried to differentiate Moluccan Malay from Indonesian Malay was the promotion and popularisation of indigenous words among Moluccan speakers (Tamaela 1986, Supusepa 1998).

After almost fifty years the RMS ideal still exists. Steijlen (1996) points out, however, that its intentions have changed. In an interview in *Marinjo*, the community's major magazine, the Moluccan anthropologist E. Rinsampessy observed that the RMS cause had become a 'drawing-room struggle' that had ceased to be the community's focal point. In a reaction to the alarming events in Maluku in January 1999, a representative of the Moluccan government in exile explained on television that liberation no longer was the main goal. Rather, they focused on the economic and social well-being of the fellow-Moluccans in Indonesia. The new strategy of the RMS government was already announced a month earlier, when an official letter from the RMS government circulated in the Moluccan community, which was written in modern Indonesian spelling.

Notwithstanding its efforts, the *Balai Pusat* did not succeed. The language allegiance of Moluccan youth has shifted to Dutch. In the 1980s the Dutch government started the *Nederlander-Medelander*[38] campaign against xenophobia which emphasised the multicultural composition of the Dutch society. People were encouraged on the radio and television to declare their ethnic backgrounds and explain them to their fellow-citizens. In this context it is understandable that the ideological ban on Moluccan ethnolinguistic diversity was lifted. Not

---

[37]   This term is obviously modelled after the *Pusat Bahasa*, the 'Language Centre', the official organisation for the development of the National Language in Indonesia and Malaysia.

[38]   Translatable as 'Dutch Citizen — Fellow Citizen'

only the music group Boiakih started to express its linguistic roots. Courses in indigenous languages like Allang (Ambon) and Fordate (Tanimbar) were set up for the benefit of those who wanted to get acquainted with their ethnolinguistic background. Even in Moluccan poetry, which is meant for performance rather than reading (Perspectieven 1994), 'language of the land' is being used (for example by Franky Berhitu). Knowledge of *bahasa tanah*, the 'languages of the land', is no longer seen as dangerous. Instead, they are perceived as a means for a better understanding of one's own ethnic and cultural identity (see also note 32).

REFERENCES

Akihary, Huib 1991. Van Almere tot de Zwaluwenberg. Molukse woonoorden in Nederland [From Almere to Zwaluwenberg. Moluccan hostels in the Netherlands]. In W. Manuhutu & H. Smeets (eds) *Tijdelijk verblijf, de opvang van Molukkers in Nederland, 1951,* 40-73. Amsterdam: De Bataafsche Leeuw.

Akihary, Monica 1997. Tenaga gaib. Sound track 4 on Boi Akih: *Boi Akih,* CD, Amsterdam: Invitation Records/EMI.

_____ 1998. Radio interview in the 'Schuim en As' programme, NCRV Radio, 10/7/1998.

Bartels, Dieter 1994. *In de schaduw van de berg Nunusaku* [In the Shadow of Mount Nunusaku]. Utrecht: Landelijk Steunpunt Edukatie Molukkers.

Behoekoe Nam Radja, Billy, Pieter Thenu & Agus Manuhutu 1993. *Siwa Lima. De alfoer in ons geweten* [Siwa Lima. The Alifuru in Our Conscience]. Utrecht: Sg. Tjandu.

Blust, Robert 1978. Eastern Malayo-Polynesian, a subgrouping argument. In S.A. Wurm & Lois Carrington (eds) *Papers from the Second International Conference on Austronesian Linguistics:*

Proceedings, vol. 1, pp. 181-234, Canberra: Department of Linguistics, RSPS, ANU.

_____ 1993. Central and Central-Eastern Malayo-Polynesian. *Oceanic Linguistics* 32: 241-293.

Clyne, Michael G. 1991. *Community Languages: the Australian experience*. Melbourne: Cambridge University Press

Collins, James T. 1980. Laha, a language of Central Maluku. Indonesia Circle 23: 3-20.

_____ 1981. Linguistic research in Maluku: a report of recent fieldwork. *Oceanic Linguistics* 21: 73-146.

_____ 1983. *The Historical Relationships of the Languages of Central Maluku, Indonesia*. Pacific Linguistics D-47, Canberra: Department of Linguistics, RSPS, ANU.

Dijk, Toos van & Aone van Engelenhoven. In progress. Marsela; its ethnographic and ethnolinguistic position in Maluku Tenggara.

Engelenhoven, Aone van. 1988. De *bahasa tanah* van de Centraal- en Zuid-Molukken [The *Bahasa Tanah* of the Central and South Moluccas]. *Daja Upaja II, taalachtergronden*, 10-18. Assen: Samenwerkingsverband Bikultureel Onderwijs.

_____ 1995a. *A Description of the Leti Language (as spoken in Tutukei)*. PhD Thesis, Leiden University.

_____ 1995b. Van Proto Malayo-Polynesisch naar Proto Luangisch-Kisarisch [From Proto Malayo-Polynesian to Proto Luangic-Kisaric]. In Connie Baak et al. (eds) *Tales from a Concave World, Liber amicorum Bert Voorhoeve*, 246-264. Leiden: Projects Division, Department of Languages and Cultures of SE Asia and Oceania, Leiden University.

_____ 1997a. Words and expressions: notes on parallelism in Leti. *Cakalele Maluku Research Journal* 8: 1-25.

_____ 1997b. Review of Taber et al. (1996), *Cakalele Maluku Research Journal* 8: 91-4.

_____ 1998a. Epithets and epitomes: management and loss of narrative knowledge in Southwest Maluku (East-Indonesia). *Journal of Interdisciplinary and Cultural Studies* 1: 29-41, available http://www.geocities.com /Athens /Parthenon /7867/n1ae.html.

_____ 1998b. *Ewaw in Zwolle, a preliminary research report.*. Paper presented at the East-Indonesian Linguistics workshop held at the International Institute of Asian Studies, Leiden, 1/12/1998.

_____ In press. Lirasniara, the sung language of Southwest Maluku. In James T.Collins, Mohammed Hj Salleh & Hein Steinhauer (eds.) *The Study of Endangered Languages and Literatures of Southeast Asia.* Leiden: KITLV Press.

_____ Forthcoming. *Geurtjens ni tom Ewaw, een grammaticale schets plus woordenlijst van het Keiees aan de hand van teksten van Pater Geurtjens* [Geurtjens ni tom Ewaw, a grammatical outline and wordlist of Keiese by means of texts of Father Geurtjens].

_____ In progress. This here apple now. Deictics in the Malay speech of Southwest Moluccans in the Netherlands (a clue in the search for Tangsi Malay?).

Florey, Margaret J. 1991. Shifting patterns of language allegiance: a generational perspective from eastern Indonesia. In H. Steinhauer (ed.) *Papers in Austronesian Linguistics, No.17,* 39-47. Pacific Linguistics A-81, Canberra: Department of Linguistics, RSPS, ANU.

_____ 1998a. Alune incantations: continuity or discontinuity in verbal art? *Journal of Sociolinguistics* 2/2: 205-321.

_____ 1998b. *Haruku in the Netherlands: a preliminary research report.* Paper presented at the East-Indonesian Linguistics workshop held at the International Institute of Asian Studies, Leiden, 1/12/1998.

Geurtjens, H. 1921. *Spraakleer der Keieesche taal* [Grammar of the Keiese Language]. Verhandelingen van het Bataviaasch Genootschap LXIII, The Hague: M. Nijhoff, Weltevreden: Albrecht & Co.

_____ 1924. *Keieesche legenden* [Keiese Legends]. Verhandelingen van het Bataviaasch Genootschap LXV, The Hague: M. Nijhoff, Weltevreden: Albrecht & Co.

Hoek, Antje van der 1994. *Religie in ballingschap. Institutionalisering en leiderschap onder christelijke en islamitische Molukkers in Nederland* [Religion in Exile. Institutionalisation and Leadership among Christian and Islamic Moluccans in the Netherlands]. PhD Thesis, Leiden University.

Hughes, Jock 1987. The Languages of Kei, Tanimbar and Aru: a lexicostatistic clasification. In Soenjono Dardjowidjojo (ed.) *Miscellaneous Studies of Indonesian and Other Languages in Indonesia, Part IX,* 71-111. NUSA 27. Jakarta: Badan Penyelenggara Seri NUSA, Universitas Katolik Indonesia Atma Jaya.

Jensen, Ad.E. 1948. *Die drei Ströme: Züge aus dem geistigen und religiösen Leben der Wemale, einem Primitiv-Volk in den Molukken* [The Three Flows: Characteristics of the Psychological and Religious Life of the Wemale, a Primitive People in the Moluccas]. Leipzig: Hassarowitz.

Jensen, Ad.E. & H. Niggemeyer. 1939. *Hainuwele, Volkserzählungen von der Molukken-Insel Ceram* [Hainuwele, Folktales from the Moluccan Island of Ceram]. Frankfurt am Main: Klostermann.

Leha, Obed L. 1989. *Daftar warga-2 Babar yang berdiam di Negeri Belanda* [List of Babar Families in the Netherlands]. Vaassen: ms.

Manuhutu, Wim Chr. 1996. *Politieke achtergronden rondom de proclamatie van de RMS* [Political Background about the Proclamation of the RMS]. Originally published in Mena Muria 0, 25/4/1996. <http://www.dlm.org/geschiedenis/RMS>.

Manusama, J.A. 1953. *Om recht en vrijheid. De strijd om de onafhankelijkheid der Zuid-Molukken* [For Justice and Freedom. The

Struggle for Independence of the South Moluccas]. Utrecht: Libertas N.V.

Molukkers in Nederland [Moluccans in the Netherlands] 1997. Djangan Lupa Maluku website. <http://www.dlm.org/geschiedenis>.

Perspektieven voor het Moluks Maleis in Nederland: een diskussienota [Perspectives for Moluccan Malay in the Netherlands: a Working Paper]. 1994. Alasan 10, Utrecht: Landelijk Steunpunt Edukatie Molukkers.

Rinsampessy, Elias 1992. *Saudara Bersaudara, Molukse identiteit in processen van cultuurverandering* [Saudara Bersaudara, Moluccan Identity within Processes of Cultural Change]. Assen/Maastricht: Van Gorcum, Wychen: Pattimura.

Steijlen, Godefridus I.J. 1996. *RMS: van ideaal tot symbool. Moluks nationalisme in Nederland, 1951-1994* [RMS: from Ideal to Symbol. Moluccan Nationalism in the Netherlands, 1951-1994]. Amsterdam: Het Spinhuis.

Stokhof, W.A.L. 1975. *Preliminary Notes on the Alor and Pantar Languages*, Pacific Linguistics B-43, Canberra: Department of Linguistics, RSPS, ANU.

Straver, Hans 1993. *De zee van verhalen. De wereld van Molukse vertellers* [The Sea of Stories. The World of Moluccan Storytellers]. Utrecht: Landelijk Steunpunt Educatie Molukkers.

_____ 1997. Introduction to Suleman Latukau, *Lani Nusa, Lani Lisa, Kapata dari Morela/ Zangen uit Morela* [Lani Nusa, Lani Lisa, Songs from Morela], SUMBER, Utrecht: Landelijk Steunpunt Educatie Molukkers.

Supusepa, Edi F.M. 1998. *Woordenlijst Nederlands-Moluks-Saparuaans* [Dutch-Moluccan-Saparuan Wordlist]. Acquoy: Sg. Honimoa-Nederland.

Taber, Mark 1993. Towards a better understanding of the indigenous languages of Southwestern Maluku. *Oceanic Linguistics* 32: 389-441.

Taber, Mark et al. (eds) 1996. *Atlas bahasa tanah Maluku* [Moluccan Languages Atlas]. Ambon: Pusat Pengkajian dan Pengembangan Maluku, Universitas Pattimura, Summer Institute of Linguistics.

Tahitu, Egbert 1989. *Melaju Sini, het Maleis van Molukse jongeren in Nederland* [Melaju Sini, the Malay of Moluccan Youth in the Netherlands]. PhD Thesis, Leiden University.

_____ 1993. *Studieschrift Moluks Maleis, achtergronden* [Moluccan Malay Working Paper, Background]. Alasan 7, Utrecht: Landelijk Steunpunt Edukatie Molukkers.

Tamaela, Dede 1986. *Bahasa Maluku* [The Moluccan Language]. Lecture given at the Language Symposium at Paparisa, The Hague.

Voorhoeve, C.L. 1987. The non-Austronesian languages in the North Moluccas, In E.K.M. Masinambow (ed.) *Halmahera dan Raja Empat sebagai kesatuan yang majemuk: studi-studi terhadap suatu daerah transisi*, 479-529, LEKNAS Bulletin 2, Jakarta: LEKNAS.

Willems, Wim 1996. Koloniaal en etnisch. Molukkers, Hindostanen en Indische Nederlanders vergeleken [Colonial and Ethnic. Moluccans, Hindustani and Indian Dutch Compared]. In Marjolein 't Hart, Jan Lucassen & Henk Schmal (eds) *Nieuwe Nederlanders. Vestiging van migranten door de eeuwen heen*, 187-202. Amsterdam: Stichting beheer IISG/SISWO/Instituut voor Maatschappij wetenschappen.

Wittermans, T.W. 1991. *Social Organization among Ambonese Refugees in Holland*. Amsterdam: Het Spinhuis.

Chapter 18

Extinction in Whose Terms?
Which parts of a language constitute a target for language maintenance programmes?

Nicholas Thieberger
University of Melbourne

Structural linguistics has a particular view of the integrity of language which may be detrimental to the construction of appropriate language maintenance programmes for small indigenous languages. In this paper I outline ways in which 'affective' use of language may be the most useful target of language programmes in some situations. Fluency in a language may not be the achievable outcome of a language course for a number of reasons, not least among them being the enormity of the task perceived by learners of the language. For languages with few or no speakers we should be able to construct language programmes in which the use of a small number of terms in the target language, for purposes of identity, is a sufficient and realistic outcome.

While we need to talk about language extinction to motivate speakers of the languages and funding agencies into action, we also need to be sensitive to the fact that languages can be in various stages of endangerment, or extinction, but still be claimed as 'the language' of a group of people.

This leads to a fundamental question for language maintenance efforts, and for notions of 'ecolinguistics'. Which parts of a language are the ones which are necessary to keep in order that extinction can be said not to have occurred? And so where is the 'difference' that is claimed to exist by the language endangerment movement between one language and another? If, for example, a language with an extensive noun class system touted as being the genius of the language loses that system but still continues to be spoken, is it still worthy of language maintenance efforts? Do different varieties of English constitute endangered varieties if they are not being spoken by young people in their community?

Clearly what linguists want from language maintenance programmes can be quite different to what speakers or their descendants want. What is used to mark identity can shift quickly depending on circumstances. There are serious political consequences for arguments that value the intact and traditional over the so-called tainted and modern. We don't want to devalue what people do with what little they may have left of their language, but at the same time we need to argue for the recording and support of as much of an endangered language as we can.

Often it is precisely those features of a language which are completely opaque to its speakers which generate the most interest among linguists and which linguists then claim as the major reason for 'saving' the language. Conversely, the features focussed on by speakers of a language that is no longer used everyday may be at the level of phonology and a highly restricted part of the lexicon or at the level of 'communicative conventions', as Gumperz & Gumperz point out: "Even where the original native language is lost .. discourse conventions tend to persist and to be taken over into the group's use of the majority language. In fact these conventions come to reflect the identity of the group itself ..." (Gumperz & Gumperz 1982: 6). This observation was confirmed in work by Diana Eades with Aboriginal English in Queensland (Eades 1983), where she demonstrated that Aboriginal ways of talking English showed a number of features associated with Aboriginal ways of talking Aboriginal languages.

What informs such work as that of Eades is the important understanding that identity is flexible and adapts to the needs of the moment. Speaking a particular language may be part of one's identity, but you do not lose your identity when that language is no longer spoken. You may refocus on other identity-forming issues and decide to use whatever parts of the language are still available to you for identity purposes. Woodbury (1998) addresses Eades' work, and agrees with her findings, while cautioning that the notion that not all is lost when a language is no longer spoken can be a "salve to the colonial conscience, happy instead to support an emergent, newly 'nativized' variety of English ..." (Woodbury 1998: 238). In this paper I want to tread the delicate line between 'salving the colonial conscience' and empowering the colonised through recognition of their linguistic heritage.

The only Aboriginal PhD linguist to date, Eve Fesl, quoted in National Languages and Literacy Institute of Australia (nd: 83), says: "The many decades of linguistic persecution which persisted until the present time only adds to the desire of the Indigenous Australian individual and community to regain and claim whatever they are able. In the case of language this may be only a few words or sentences, but these are cherished far beyond what most non-Indigenous Australians are able to comprehend." Yet she also (Fesl 1993: 164) criticises programmes that concentrate on words with no appreciation of the complexity of the traditional language.

How then does the philosophy of language maintenance deal with situations in which people no longer use the language in question as an everyday medium of communication? What are people asking for when they say they want a language taught to their children? This situation is normally regarded as requiring a linguistic 'revival', with courses designed to ensure there will be speakers of the language in the future. This type of revival (of which Hebrew or Cornish are typical examples) is rarely practical in the Australian context and in this paper I will argue that it is not necessarily what is being asked for by the client group, speakers or descendants of speakers of the language.

Our usual definition of language in the Australian context allows neat divisions into living and dead languages, traditional and non-traditional languages, divisions which belie the continued use of Aboriginal languages or aspects of Aboriginal languages (depending on one's theoretical approach) today. This is fine if we are attempting to write a grammatical description of a language, or to do comparative work, after all comparisons are difficult if you don't have discrete objects to compare. We tailor our definition of the object of study, language, to suit the situation that we encounter. But linguists do not have a monopoly on language study, and the resurgence of interest in Aboriginal languages by Aboriginal people means that another discourse is being heard in discussions of what, for want of a better term, is called language maintenance. This discourse situates language quite differently from the position of the academic linguist. As we shall see, efforts to preserve languages that rely solely on the linguists' definition of 'language' are more likely to fail than those that are a result of understanding what is actually asked for by the client group.

If there is a spectrum of approaches to language maintenance, with bilingual education at one end and second language teaching at the other, then revival is at a point close to second-language teaching. It is useful to think of the definition of language changing at that point to become what Eastman & Reece (1980) call "associated language". It is often this associated language that is in demand for language revival in Australia, and a practical approach based on this different perception of 'language' is outlined below.

Eastman & Reece (1980) talk of the identity forming role of a language that we associate with a chosen heritage, "regardless of whether the language is actually spoken by those claiming it or not. This 'associated' language is distinguished from a) the structuralist definition of language, and b) the 'emblematic' use of language. The former typically sees language as a system of shared meaning (langue) used for communication by individuals whose parole is a product of their own experiences, and of the moment of production. The latter is the use of parts of a language (words, fixed expressions) for purely emblematic reasons, not as a means of everyday communication. "An associated language is neither langue nor parole nor is it emblem - but it may be both or each of these forms" (Eastman & Reece 1980: 110).

I would go further and suggest that the relationship of minority groups to the dominant society is an intrinsic part of the definition of identity and language. It is in identity formation, and in resistance to the dominant society that the group's language has value. This is the context that is crucial to an understanding of the role of minority languages in the future. Attempts at language maintenance that insist on dealing with a structuralist model of language may fail to appreciate the rich possibilities for recreation of nonstandard forms (in either the target language or the mainstream language).

The Aboriginal people that I have worked with have often taken for granted the inter-relationship between traditional values and language. When talking about their own language and bringing words back to mind, the first topics of conversation often include kin-terms, or hunting terms, or (depending on the context) swearwords. Using these words is an important way of showing not only that there is a difference between the cultural history of these Aboriginal people and the non-Aboriginal people around them, but also between different groups of Aboriginal people.

Language plays a role in Australian Aboriginal society that is different to the role of English for the dominant society. Sutton (1982: 193) talks of the use of naming in confrontation, Ellis (1985: 53) talks of the power of songs in healing or inflicting injury, Strehlow notes that songs were thought to "contain those magic virtues which gave power over Nature and environment in the locality where they had originated - a power capable both of creation and destruction" (Strehlow 1971: 126). Language itself is seen as effecting changes in the physical world.

An oral culture obviously places great importance on language, for ritual purposes, for story telling, for its location in history. My experience with Aboriginal people who no longer use their ancestral language as their main means of communication leads me to suspect that the role of language and the value placed on traditional languages has carried through changing physical circumstances, becoming even more of a marker of identity as the everyday use of the traditional language declines and it becomes seen as a link with an idealised harmonious past.

The claims made for traditional languages by the people I have worked with initially appear to be quite fantastic. It is not unusual to be told that, if only language can be relearned, then the traditional order will be returned. The order of parental authority and rule by elders is lost by losing the language that conveyed instructions and discipline. The coordinator of a childcare centre in Perth who was trying to run a language programme for Nyungars (local Aboriginal people) emphasised the need for 'respect' words to be included in the first lessons of the language course that was being planned. Further topics to be included were "strict moral aspects of the language, discipline", and greetings and farewells. "I'd like to see more promotion (of language). At the moment the kids are in limbo because they don't really identify with it. ... if they get into crisis it causes real problems because they can't identify with one or the other. ... If we would establish something like this, they can see where they fit in, and therefore they're moving forward with the technology" (Middle-aged Nyungar woman, Perth 1986).

It is most common when discussing language and language maintenance for the following topics to be raised;

'olden days' rituals involving increase ceremonies, bush skills, healing, medicine, spirits, (often, but not necessarily, including the use of ritual language).

importance of protecting local significant sites or preparing for land claims by reviving interest in the language associated with a part of the country. One group in WA has been reasserting its tribal affiliation with some country which is also being claimed by a rival group. As part of the reidentification with the land in question the group have been engaged in collection of wordlists and stories in the traditional language.

general confidence: "I think it worries the government that if we do bring up the maintenance on Aboriginal languages, they may get worried that Aboriginals are becoming more independent... teaching their own languages, that's what they need, because then their incentive might come for an enterprise development" (Middle-aged Nyungar man, Perth 1986).

On a trip in the bush with some Aboriginal people from Roebourne, two middle-aged men, two 16 year-old boys and myself, the topic of conversation was the goanna that we were looking for, I was asked if I knew the language name for goanna. I used the Yindjibarndi word *kurrumanthu* which I had heard all four members of the party using earlier. I was told I was wrong by one of the men who asked the boys for the correct (Ngarluma) name. One of the boys called it *birkala* and was corrected by his questioner who said the "right language" was *birrikarlira*. The boy replied with "It's a word isn't it?" The boy's concern was that he had a language word, not whether it was the appropriate language in a town where there are two main languages and numerous other languages are represented; 'language' in opposition to English.

From all of the above examples it is clear that the language being referred to is not the language of the descriptive linguist. 'Language' can refer to parts of what a descriptive linguist thinks of as language; words, sentences, stories, meetings. This is not surprising when we consider that Aboriginal languages generally have one word that means word, language, way of talking, and discussion.

It is important for contemporary speakers or descendants of speakers of Aboriginal languages to define directions for language work themselves, hence their need for information that linguists can provide, and hence the need for linguists to recognise the aims involved in Aboriginal calls for language maintenance, revival or reintroduction. Aboriginal participation in the process is essential both for the success of the project itself, for the development of skills involved in collecting stories, words and associated information, as well as for the more amorphous idea of empowerment.

By starting from a person's knowledge of the language there is not as great an implication that their contemporary usage is a degenerate form of the 'old language' as there would be in a typical language revival programme. By involvement as researchers into their own language situation the participants become more aware of their own usage and how it differs from the dominant society. They may use a pidgin or creole or speak Aboriginal English and it is a thin line to tread between attempting to revalue 'traditional' Aboriginal languages and devaluing contemporary Aboriginal usage (especially Kriol). The emphasis on traditional languages in maintenance programmes, can fall into the trap of portrayal of indigenous culture as either traditional (= true) or non-traditional (= degenerate).

The process of revival described here is a way of valuing minority languages and dialects and has implications for education and for confidence in dealing with speakers of other dialects. Discussing models of such revival work, and determining what sort of language to use, are extremely productive forms of language awareness activities and satisfy the need for information about cultural heritage.

It is politically unwise, given the imbalance in the power relationship of the dominant society and Aboriginal society, for the linguist who is developing a language course to attempt to use forms that the present population rejects, be they in the spelling system, the lexicon or syntax. The course materials may be rejected because the orthography contains, for example, a voiced rather than a voiceless symbol, or entire programmes may be shelved because of a disagreement about the phonemic status of one sound. Russo and Baldauf (1986: 310) discuss the case of Elcho Island and Garden Point where the language of instruction for a bilingual programme was chosen after too brief a period of consultation. In the first case a minority language was chosen, and in the second case the language (Tiwi) was undergoing rapid changes, resulting in a form of everyday language quite different from the 'classical' style adopted by the language programme. Involvement of speakers of the language, in the second case, as designers of the course may have ensured a more appropriate and so more successful language course.

Language revival programmes typically rely on recorded sources, and on the knowledge of remaining speakers who have been unable to pass their knowledge on to the present generation. Both sources will provide only partial information about the language; in the absence of a speech community it can be assumed that there will be attrition in the discourse styles and syntactic structures of remaining 'semispeakers' (Dorian 1977). Even if historical written records of Aboriginal languages are immediately usable, which in my experience is rarely the case, there is not always going to be the type of information recorded that is required in revival programmes (see Barlow & Triffett 1987: 92). Thus the forms that will be used in this type of programme will have to be reconstructed or drawn from similar languages. The question then will be, what language is actually being revived?

If a revival programme is requested, we can assume that there is an interest in the community in learning the language, and that there is a group of people who will undertake the course and will engage in finding out about the language. 'Revival' programmes deal with a language that is still used or still remembered. Typical among the revival programmes discussed in the literature are Gaelic in Ireland (Benton 1986), Hobbema in Alberta, Canada (Kent-Gooderham 1975) Same, in Scandinavia (Paulston 1976) and, in Australia, Kaurna (Varcoe 1994), Awabakal (Heath 1982), Ngarrindjeri (Kirke 1987), and Wangkamara (ALA Newsletter April/ May 1985). Wurm (1986: 535) observes that it is "not uncommon" for a language to be successfully revived "if economic and status advantages result to the speech community". He goes on to suggest that "such instances have occurred in Australian Aboriginal groups", unfortunately without references. In fact there is no documented case of the revival of everyday use of an Australian Aboriginal language.

The methods used in these courses vary, depending on resources available, but usually language revival relies on recorded sources and on a linguist who can interpret the recorded information. An example of this type of revival is Cornish, whose last monolingual speaker died in the late eighteenth century (although it may have been spoken for up to a century after that (Shield 1984)). A movement to resurrect the language began in the seventeenth century, but the revival of the 1950s resulted in approximately 1000 people attending classes, of whom only 50 were subsequently capable of holding a conversation in Cornish (although undoubtedly a different type of Cornish to that originally spoken in Cornwall). Similarly, Mithun & Chafe (1979) describe a Mohawk revival course planned and developed with Mohawk teachers over several years. The language is taught from kindergarten through to sixth grade and only Mohawk is spoken in the classes. It is a programmed approach roughly following the order of a child's acquisition of Mohawk, aiming at communicative competence in the language. The authors consider a key factor in the success of the programme to be community attitudes and assistance in devising the course. At the same time there were objections to the programme from Mohawk people who had been punished for using the language in their youth and who now considered the language to be 'backward' (Mithun & Chafe 1979: 29). This type of programme benefits from having a large population of potential users, and this is one reason that such a course is rarely practical in the Australian context. In the cases where it is possible, the materials devised for Ngarrindjeri (Kirke et al. nd) or Wangkamara are a good example.

Where there is not the time or dedication on the part of potential users to learn all the complexities of the traditional language, another approach may be more useful.

Powell (1973) discusses the type of language programme designed with Quileute people in the USA. Powell had designed a course of instruction assuming that the goal was student fluency in Quileute, i.e. to resuscitate it as an everyday spoken tongue. The programme failed in a very short time. The complexity of the language is such that the class had "neither the time nor the interest to master a system so different to English". "The Quileute wished to know their language

1) as a means of cultural identity,
2) as a link with their heritage

1) as a means of cultural identity,
2) as a link with their heritage
3) as a symbol of group identity, and
4) as a portable proof of Quileuteness that could be
brandished before whites or other Indians.

Interestingly, none of these goals required native fluency or even reasonable virtuosity." (Powell 1973: 6).

The Hobbema Curriculum Project in Alberta, Canada similarly found that, while it was to teach Cree language to primary school children, "at no time did the Hobbema Curriculum Committee identify the development of fluency in the Cree language as one of the objectives of their project." (Kent-Gooderham 1975: 52)

My experience in writing introductory lessons for Paakantji (Western NSW) (Thieberger 1983) is similar to that described by Powell. The lessons follow a second- language teaching approach, and assume (implicitly) that the goal of the user is proficiency in the second language. The course material has not been used to my knowledge, and there have been no requests for further lessons to be written. The materials fail to address the needs initially expressed by the users. A major reason for this is the lack of involvement of the users in the design of the material.

Powell goes on to discuss the type of language (which he characterises as a pidgin) that was used in the course as he redesigned it. He reasons that it is best to start with the known language, English in the case he describes, and to use Quileute vocabulary that is known to the students as the starting point for the exercise. He gives the following example;

Give me half that candy,
Give me half that łape',
Hes me half sa' łape',
Hes me tala'a sa' łape'   (Powell 1973: 6)

The final version retains the English word order with Quileute words.

Sandefur (1983) uses the term 'relexification' rather than 'pidginisation' for the process Powell advocates. He gives examples of the process in Ngandi (Northern Territory), where the known language, Kriol, is used as a base and relexified with Ngandi words. At the risk of aiding in a proliferation of terms, I suggest that Aboriginal people in their efforts at reviving a language are actually recreating the language. The process of recreation, rather than revival, best describes the way in which language is reified and interpreted in the situations described in this paper.

Kirke (1987) describes a similar programme for Ngarrindjeri, and notes that there is tension in the relationship of 'young fellers' (who had gone to the School of Australian Linguistics to work out how to approach the language) with the older people who are the authorities on the language and consider that they should be consulted before any work is done with the language. A group in Bunbury (Western Australia) avoided this problem by involving older people as teachers in the course. They set about learning Nyungar, a generic name for the languages of the South-west of Western Australia. They had a sketch grammar and numerous vocabularies, and the class included two older people who remember some Nyungar. When faced with the morphological complexity of the language as presented in historical sources, the group reconsidered their aims. They drew a timeline, with 'Old Nyungar' on one end, and English at the other end. They chose a form of language that they considered would be located somewhere along the timeline closer to the English end than to the Old Nyungar end. The use of the timeline illustrates their identification of their own vernacular as related to the traditional language, however distantly. While they produced some literature in their neo-Nyungar, deciding what form of language to use, and conducting fieldwork with their grandparents was a worthwhile process in itself. They have continued to work on this recreation of Nyungar and will soon produce a kit that will be used in schools. The project has been a result of the efforts of Nyungars, and its success must, in part, be seen as resulting from their informed consent for the choice of language used.

There is a large number of Aboriginal languages in Australia whose 'last speakers' (cf. Evans forthcoming) have been dying, and their children have not been learning more than a few words. Language death studies show the attrition in knowledge of aspects of a language that accompanies language death or decline. Languages usually do not just disappear, but they undergo a series of structural and functional changes ending up in shift to the dominant language. It is the product of this attrition that will be the input into the language programme that is discussed here. Hence there is a cline of possible inputs to the language programme, depending on how much of the language is left to work with.

Some typical examples of the way that the Aboriginal students I have worked with have re-created the traditional language are given below. This re-creation is based on the products of attrition, that is, the students' knowledge may have been gained from 'rememberers' of the language so that their input has been subject to the process described in studies of language shift or language death.

Phonological: A collapse of distinctions in the recreated language that are not made in the dominant language (e.g. palatal, interdental, retroflex points of articulation collapsed to alveolar), the use of the stop d/t in place of the trilled rr (Wajarri (Gascoyne, WA) *yirra -> ita, *marnkurr -> mangkut).

Morphological: Regular citation form involving some suffix which is now regarded as part of the stem. Paakantji (NSW) use of the present participle ending -ana, or Nyungar (South-West) use of -iny, present continuous, on all remembered verb forms regardless of actual tense/aspect required.

Semantic: Narrowing, widening or shifting of meaning of words of the traditional language, use of one word in a semantic field as a hyponym for the field, e.g. the word for 'silver bream' becoming the contemporary word for 'fish' (Ngarluma).

Word order: General use of English word order except for some fixed expressions, which students referred to as 'back to front' (e.g. Nyungar: *kart wara* = 'head-sick', or *twangka purt* = 'ear-bad').

Donaldson (1985: 137) discusses similar changes undergone in Ngiyampaa, and points out that older speakers do not chide or correct younger people for using a form that "may not seem to be speaking properly when judged by outside standards (those of the older Ngiyampaa speakers) [but] is in a sense proper (and intimate) for those people within their age-group." However, the Ngiyampaa story-books produced by Donaldson still had to be written, at the request of older speakers, in the oldest speakers' language. The fact that there was no objection to this on the part of younger people Donaldson ascribes to respect for the elders.

While the current understanding of the language should be the input for a language course, the principle of community involvement must also be paramount in any course design. Donaldson does not provide further information about the story-books, but one suspects that they may become tangible tokens of the 'old language', and while useful, may not have the same appeal to younger speakers as would an approach which related more closely to their own understanding of Ngiyampaa (compare the use of 'classics' of literature in European society as a guide to 'proper' usage, both written and spoken).

Factors in the Australian context that favour language programmes of the kind advocated here.

1) Not enough resources are allocated even for bilingual programmes (which make sense in the type of economic analysis used by most funding bodies) hence there is no great prospect of funding for the usual types of revival programmes whose rationale is almost exclusively based on sentiment, not often a successful basis for government funding.

2) The small numbers of people interested in language work in a community which is itself very small militate against attempts at reviving a language.

3) There are too few linguists available to work in the existing programmes.

The type of programme advocated here:

1) does not require the amount of resources that would be used by a revival programme. The process involved in the discovery of the 'old language' and in awareness of Aboriginal ways of speaking requires classwork but not the elaborate literature and material support that a revival programme would require.

2) is suited to small groups of people doing their own fieldwork in their own community.

3) requires only a part-time advisory linguist, a role suited to language centres, who could also make available the work of previous researchers in the area.

Problems with using the model of associated language:

'Mixed-up' language may be rejected by members of the community who want either the old language or English and nothing else in between. In Jigalong Martu Wangka is the language used in school, made up of the different Western Desert languages that were brought into Jigalong, however there is criticism by some people there that the language is not pure Kartujarra or Manjiljarra or Putijarra. In places where less of the language is remembered by young people than at Jigalong however it is more likely that older people will welcome any knowledge of the language, even if it is not exactly how they remember the language to have been.

The ownership or custodianship of knowledge in Aboriginal society means that certain people will have to be consulted, even though they may not actually know the particular information that we are after, because they are widely recognised as authorities.

There is a danger that the form of language used in this course will be taken as evidence of the simplicity of Aboriginal languages. Obviously students will have to be aware of the complexity of the traditional language. In the example of Nyungar and Quileute we saw that it is precisely because of the complexity of the language that students chose to recreate the language in a more familiar form. Once students have understood the recreated pidgin or relexified version of their language they may want to go on with more research into the complexities of the language as it once was.

CONCLUSION

It is necessary to provide assistance in the form of linguistic advice to those groups of Aboriginal people who are asking for revival programmes in their languages or the languages of their ancestors.

I have suggested that language revival need not be an 'all or nothing' venture. Revival in the sense of Hebrew, for example, requires huge resources, a committed population of potential speakers, and then will develop a form of language which might bear great resemblance to a hypothesised, once-spoken language, but which is nevertheless a new form of the language. The approach advocated here is not intended for languages that are still spoken and have adequate resources supporting their use. Language recreation is ideally suited to situations where older people still remember something of the ancestral language, and where younger people have a core of words.

Positive outcomes for language recreation programmes are most likely when students can begin with their own knowledge of the language, and create forms that conform with that knowledge. It is this process which is of value, and any other outcomes must be seen as bonuses.

REFERENCES

Aboriginal Languages Association 1985. Wangkamara *Aboriginal Languages Association Newsletter* April/May.

Barlow, Alex & GeraldineTriffitt 1987. Aboriginal Languages in Education. *Australian Aboriginal Studies* 1987/2: 90-92.

Benton, Richard A. 1986. Schools as agents for language revival in Ireland and New Zealand. In Bernard Spolsky (ed.) *Language and Education in Multilingual Settings*, 53-76. Clevedon: Multilingual Matters.

Chafe, Wallace L. (ed.) 1976. *American Indian Languages and American Linguistics*. Lisse: Peter de Ridder.

Donaldson, Tamsin 1985. From speaking Ngiyampaa to speaking English. *Aboriginal History* 9/2: 126-147.

Dorian, Nancy C. 1977. The Problem of the Semi-Speaker in Language Death. *International Journal of the Sociology of Language* 12: 23-32.

Eades, Diana 1983. English as an Aboriginal language in southeast Queensland. PhD Thesis, University of Queensland.

Eastman, Carol M. & T.C. Reece 1980. Associated language: How language and ethnic identity are related. *General Linguistics* 21/2: 109-116.

Ellis, Catherine J. 1985. *Aboriginal Music, Education for Living: cross-cultural experiences from South Australia*. St Lucia: University of Queensland Press.

Evans, Nicholas Forthcoming. The last speaker is dead – long live the last speaker! In Paul Newman & Martha Ratliff (eds) *Linguistic Fieldwork*. Cambridge: Cambridge University Press.

Fesl, Eve Mumewa D. 1993. *Conned!* St Lucia: University of Queensland Press.

Gumperz, John J. & Jenny Cook Gumperz 1982. Introduction: language and the communication of social identity. In John J. Gumperz (ed.) *Language and Social* Identity, 1-21. Cambridge: Cambridge University Press.

Heath, Jeffrey 1982. The Awabakal Aboriginal Co-operative. In J. Bell (ed.) *Workshop to Develop Aboriginal Leadership in Language Planning*, 124-126. Alice Springs: Institute for Aboriginal Development and Aboriginal Languages Association.

Kent-Gooderham, G. 1975. Bilingual Education for Indians and Inuit: The Canadian Experience. In Rudy C. Troike & N. Modiano (eds) *Proceedings of the First Inter-American Conference on Bilingual Education*, 43. Arlington, VA: Center for Applied Linguistics.

Kirke, B. 1987 [letter to Toby Metcalfe]

Kirke, B. et al. nd. Ngarrindjeri comic book

Michaels, E. 1985. Constraints on Knowledge in an Economy of Oral Information. *Current Anthropology* 26/4: 505-510.

Mithun, Marianne & Wallace L. Chafe 1979. Recapturing the Mohawk language. In Timothy Shopen (ed.) *Languages and their Status*, 3-33. Cambridge, MA: Winthrop.

National Languages and Literacy Institute of Australia. nd. *Backing Australian Languages: Review of the Aboriginal and Torres Strait Islander languages initiatives program.* Canberra: NLLIA.

Paulston, K.G. 1976. Ethnic Revival and Educational Conflict in Swedish Lappland. *Comparative Education Review* June: 179-192.

Powell, J.V. 1973. Raising Pidgins for fun and profit: a new departure in language teaching. Paper presented at the Canadian Sociology and Anthropology Association Conference, Kingston, Ontario.

Russo, C. & Richard B. Baldauf 1986. Language Development without planning: A case study of tribal Aborigines in the Northern Territory,

Australia. *Journal of Multilingual and Multicultural Development* 7/4: 301-317.

Sandefur, John 1983. The Quileute approach to language revival programs. *The Aboriginal Child at School* 11/5: 3-16.

Shield, L.E. 1984. Unified Cornish-Fiction or Fact? An examination of the death and resurrection of the Cornish2 language. *Journal of Multilingual and Multicultural Development* 5/3-4: 329-337.

Strehlow, Theodor G.H. 1971. *Songs of Central Australia.* Sydney: Angus and Robertson.

Sutton, Peter 1982. Personal power, kin classification and speech etiquette in Aboriginal Australia. In Jeffrey Heath, Francesca Merlan & Alan Rumsey (eds) *Languages of Kinship in Aboriginal Australia*, 182-200. Sydney: Oceania Linguistic Monographs No.24.

Thieberger, Nicholas 1983. An introduction to Paakantji. Ms.

Trigger, D. 1986. Blackfella and Whitefellas: The concept of Domain and Social Closure in the Analysis of Race Relations. *Mankind* 16/2: 99-117.

Varcoe, Nelson 1994. Nunga languages at Kaurna Plains school. In D. Hartman & J. Henderson (eds) *Aboriginal Languages in Education*, 33-39. Alice Springs: IAD Press.

Woodbury, Anthony C. 1998. Documenting rhetorical, aesthetic, and expressive loss in language shift. In Lenore A. Grenoble & Lindsay J. Whaley (eds) *Endangered languages: language loss and community response*, 234-258. Cambridge: Cambridge University Press.

Wurm, Stephen A. 1986. Remarks on a Case of Language Decay and Revival. In Joshua A. Fishman, Andrée Tabouret-Keller, Michael G. Clyne, Bh. Krishnamurti & Mohamed Abdulaziz (eds) *The Fergusonian Impact*, 2: 533-541. Berlin: Mouton de Gruyter.

Chapter 19

Dictionaries and Endangered Languages
Miriam Corris, Christopher Manning, Susan Poetsch, Jane Simpson
University of Sydney and Stanford University

A good dictionary is one in which you can find the thing you are looking for preferably in the very first place you look

(Haas 1962: 48)

1. INTRODUCTION[1]

Linguists have seen creating dictionaries of endangered languages as a key activity in language maintenance and revival work. However, like any approach to language engineering, there are concerns to address. The first is the tension between language documentation and language maintenance[2]. The second is the role of literacy. A lot of effort has been put into vernacular literacy, on the assumption that it assists language maintenance, as well as language documentation. In some respects this is a dubious assumption, because writing a language does not necessarily lead to speaking it or maintaining the

[1]   Earlier version presented at 1999 Perth Congress of the Applied Linguistics Association of Australia, 26-29 September 1999. We thank many people for their help: Mary Laughren for access to the *Warlpiri Dictionary*, Robert Hoogenraad, Jenny Green and Myf Turpin for arranging Miriam Corris's work in Central Australia; Mark Donohue, Lipiyus Biniluk and Johnson Haan for help with Corris's work on Lani and Adang; Denise Angelo and Margaret Sharpe for arranging Susan Poetsch's work; Carmel O'Shannessy, Elizabeth Ross Nungarrayi, Margaret Carew, Marija Tabain and Robin Hardiman for help with Jane Simpson's work; Margaret Florey, Kevin Jansz, David Nash, Peter Oram and the audiences at the Central Australian Linguistics Circle, the Applied Linguistics Association of Australia's Annual Congress, the University of Sydney Linguistics Postgraduate Seminar, and the symposium participants. The work was funded in part by Australian Research Council small grants to Manning and Simpson in 1998 and 1999.

[2]   The term 'preservation' is often used in discussion of language endangerment. However, it is used ambiguously between preserving a language for science in the future by documenting it, and preserving it for the speakers as a living language by helping them maintain it.

language. Moreover, in some cases putting effort into writing the language can detract from efforts to encourage learners to speak the language. It is certain that much more effort should be put into oral language development.

In this chapter, however, we focus on the structural issues arising from this relation between language documentation and maintenance, discussing literacy to the extent that varying levels of literacy result in different abilities to use dictionaries, as well as uses of, and attitudes towards dictionaries.

Historically, dictionaries for endangered languages have been mainly concerned with the task of preserving the languages for future study or revival. The major audience for these dictionaries was felt to be other people from literate traditions, such as linguists and researchers (Schebeck 1983). To this end most of the literature on the subject deals with the problems of representing the particular language as exhaustively as possible in a written form (Corris 1999). Such 'documentation dictionaries' are, in principle, vast and encyclopaedic as they attempt to capture most of what the lexicographer thinks a speaker knows, if they know the meaning of a given word and can use it.

Another use for dictionaries has been providing evidence for the speakers and others of the status of the minority language as a 'real' language, one that is recognised as an equal of the language of wider communication (LWC). We could call this the 'symbolic' function of the dictionary.

Documentation is still very much an issue for speakers of some languages. However, emerging literacy among speakers of the endangered languages creates a new range of users and uses for dictionaries. We will call these the 'maintenance dictionaries' (although their range can include language renewal). The structure of these is the focus of this paper.

When designing a dictionary for an endangered language (EL), we have to consider first the uses that the speakers may want to make of the dictionary, and then the useability of the dictionary for such users. In the first part of the paper we discuss uses by looking at the views on potential dictionary organisation of some speakers of endangered languages. In the second part of the paper we summarise some of our findings on useability of dictionaries of Australian Aboriginal languages.

Generally speaking, dictionaries for endangered languages have similar macrostructures, and differ mostly in the amount of information in certain parts of the microstructure.

1.1 Macrostructure

EL dictionaries are almost always bilingual, because the makers are usually not speakers. The main body is usually arranged as EL-LWC. Occasionally, such dictionaries have LWC-EL finderlists, sometimes separated into semantic domains. The EL-LWC direction is important for two reasons.

(i)   This arrangement is typically most useful for speakers of LWC (including the lexicographer) trying to learn, understand or explicate the EL, in other words for decoding EL.

(ii)   It can also be put down to the symbolic function of the dictionary. Speakers sometimes feel that EL-LWC is the only direction that could truly be described as a dictionary of the EL. Having the EL first gives it a kind of primacy.

1.2 Microstructure

The microstructure of EL dictionaries differs according to how big the dictionaries are. Most of the bigger ones include vernacular definitions and example sentences for some words; these are useful because they can contain cultural and grammatical information. This information is also useful for further study and documentation as well as for speakers maintaining the language. Actual definitional practice varies from one or two LWC glosses, to structured entries. Part of speech information is usually included.

Many of these properties of the macro- and microstructure have been taken for granted by lexicographers. Now, the emerging literacy among EL speakers means that these properties now have to be reconsidered.

Linguists and lexicographers hope that EL dictionaries can free learners (both of language and of literacy) from dependence on teachers, allowing them to learn independently. To some extent this view is shared by literate speakers of indigenous languages. It seems that EL speakers often agree that documentation and maintenance are important functions of a dictionary (Carroll 1999). There is also anecdotal evidence to suggest that the dictionary is important in the minds of speakers as symbolic of the status of the language. But there is little record of negotiations between speakers of endangered languages and dictionary makers, in particular of speakers' views on dictionary structure (perhaps because in some cases the speakers were not previously aware of dictionaries) (but see McConvell et al. 1983, Carroll To appear and Stebbins 1999).[3]

2. SPEAKERS' ATTITUDES TOWARDS, AND REQUIREMENTS OF, DICTIONARIES

We started to realise the importance of understanding speakers' attitudes towards, and requirements of, dictionaries as a consequence of testing an electronic interface to a dictionary of Warlpiri (Laughren et al. In preparation), and looking at the useability and uses made of dictionaries of two other Australian Aboriginal languages (Sharpe 1999, Simpson In preparation). The computer interface is described further in Jansz et al. (1999), and our testing is further described in Corris et al. (In preparation). We felt it might give additional context if we expanded the study to speakers of ELs who had prior experience with bilingual dictionaries (of English/Indonesian).

Corris then interviewed speakers of two Trans New Guinea Phylum languages, Lani (spoken in the highlands of West Papua) and Adang (spoken on the island of Alor), about their wishlists for dictionaries of their languages. Subsequently she has been working with Lipiyus Biniluk and Mark Donohue to put some of the ideas into practice in a Lani dictionary (Biniluk 1999).

---

[3] Dictionaries made by speakers themselves need further investigation. Margaret Florey (personal communication) reports two wordlists made by speakers, one with the order LWC-EL, and the other with the order EL-LWC. Both are trilingual with just single word definitions in each language. Supusepa (1998) is a professionally published sketch grammar and wordlist for the language of Saparua Island, central Maluku. The wordlist order is Dutch - Malay (Melayu Sini, the Dutch Malay variant) - Saparuan. Tamaela (1998) is a typed manuscript sketch grammar and wordlist for the Amahai language of Seram Island, central Maluku. The wordlist order is Amahai - Malay - Dutch.

For both Adang and Lani the language of wider communication is Indonesian. Neither language has a widely used dictionary at the moment[4]. The two speakers who Corris worked with (LB, Lipiyus Biniluk, the Lani speaker, and JH, John Haan, the Adang speaker), are literate in Indonesian and English and have frequently used dictionaries in both these languages.

The main questions Corris asked were: What do you see as the uses of a dictionary for your language? What do you think it should look like? We discuss the answers for each language in turn.

2.1　Lani

The[5] *Ethnologue* (Grimes et al. 1996-99) lists about 180,000 Lani speakers, (also known as Western Dani) in the 1993 Church registries census, and an additional 97,500 speaking closely related languages with orthographies based on the Lani one. There may now be as many as 300,000 Lani speakers in Irian Jaya.[6] There has been a strong missionary presence among the Lani for more than thirty years. As a result of early Bible translation[7] there is an established orthography, based on Indonesian letter values, with some characters having special values. On the initiative of Lani educators basic Lani literacy is taught in the lower classes of primary school, but Indonesian is the primary language of instruction. About 10 per cent of Lani speakers are semiliterate in Indonesian (Grimes et al. 1996-99); there are no figures for Lani literacy, but LB says that only a few people (mostly with religious training) are likely to have Lani literacy skills. LB feels that Lani people would use a Lani dictionary because they want to learn Indonesian and English. That is, he wants an **LWC learner** dictionary.

---

[4]　　There is said to be a Lani-Dutch dictionary, but LB says it is not used at all, and we have not traced it. There is also an unpublished Lani-English dictionary (Dale 1993), describing a dialect different from LB's. The introduction notes its use for decoding bible translations.

[5]　　We thank Mark Donohue and Lipiyus Biniluk for most of the information in this paragraph.

[6]　　This estimate takes into consideration the use of Lani as a lingua franca in central and northern Irian Jaya, the number of Lani people living in cities, and the population increase due to improved health care and diet.

[7]　　Bible portions have been translated since 1966, and the New Testament appeared in 1981 (Grimes et al. 1996).

This should have repercussions for the macrostructure, since the most common kind of existing learner dictionary is a decoding dictionary, that allows you to decode texts or speech from the target language. Implementing LB's desire for an LWC learner dictionary would require LWC-EL directionality. However, the main LWC decoding capabilities of traditional EL dictionaries are usually the finderlists.

LB is not particularly interested in a decoding dictionary for English or Indonesian (that is, a dictionary with Lani definitions of English or Indonesian words). He is adamant that the direction be Lani-Indonesian-English. This seems to be part of the symbolic importance of the dictionary; an English-Lani or Indonesian-Lani dictionary is not a Lani dictionary. So here there is a tension between the symbolic function of an EL dictionary and its usefulness as an LWC Learner Dictionary. A way to resolve this tension is to put more effort into an LWC-EL finderlist for such a dictionary, and to make it as accessible as possible.

2.1.1 Microstructure

LB does not see the need for vernacular definitions, because learning about Lani is not the primary use he envisages for the dictionary. He does not recognise Lani as an endangered language, saying with confidence that Lani people know Lani language and culture. He accepts that for non-Lani speakers vernacular definitions would be useful, but for the most part he is interested in a dictionary that tells Lani speakers about English and Indonesian.

2.2   Adang

Adang is spoken by about 5-10,000 people (Haan personal communication[8]). It is spoken as a first language by children, but Indonesian rapidly takes over at school. Most adults can speak Adang but their Indonesian is stronger. As yet Adang has no established orthography (but see Haan In preparation). There is no written support of the language in schools. 80 per cent of Adang speakers are literate in Indonesian (Haan personal communication).

---

[8]   The *Ethnologue* (Grimes et al. 1996-99) classes, with reservations, Adang as a dialect of Kabola, and notes that the number of speakers of Kabola is doubtful, perhaps 10,000. Haan does not consider Adang as a dialect of Kabola.

JH feels that preserving Adang language and culture is the main reason to have a dictionary. That is, he wants a **documentation** and **maintenance** dictionary. He is happy with the EL-LWC directionality of traditional EL dictionaries, but he is also interested in having a monolingual dictionary, as English has. Because he is worried about the loss of cultural and linguistic information due to the encroachment of Indonesian, he is keen to have explanations of Adang words in Adang language, as well as example sentences,

The interviews with LB and JH suggest a division of EL dictionaries into several types.

Documentation dictionaries

The normal EL-LWC format is appropriate for these, since such a dictionary is in effect an historical record that must remain interpretable in the absence of native speakers. Reversals and abridged versions of the documentation dictionary can be created later if future revival movements need them.

Maintenance dictionaries

These maintain the EL among speakers and their descendants. They may take different forms depending on the users and on what use they will make of the dictionaries. These include:

(i) providing resources for EL speakers to learn the LWC, such as LWC-EL learner dictionaries.

(ii) providing resources for EL speakers wanting to maintain the EL, such as monolingual EL dictionaries with substantial definitions.

(iii) providing resources for descendants of EL speakers wanting to learn the EL, such as learner dictionaries , both decoding (EL-LWC) and encoding (LWC-EL).

Thus, in creating EL dictionaries, the lexicographer needs to consider what uses people think they will make of dictionaries (McKay 1983:58-9), what uses they actually make of dictionaries, and how dictionaries can be made more useable to support these different uses. We turn now to the uses that we observed speakers and learners of Australian Aboriginal languages making of dictionaries of their languages, and the useability of these dictionaries.

3.   USE AND USEABILITY OF DICTIONARIES OF AUSTRALIAN ABORIGINAL LANGUAGES

In Central and Northern Australia we investigated dictionary use among seventy-two people affiliated with indigenous languages. As in many EL situations, the only dictionaries available were documentation dictionaries. The important properties distinguishing these users and the uses they made of these dictionaries were:

> level of knowledge of the indigenous language
> level of attainment of literacy in the indigenous language
> level of attainment of English literacy
> familiarity with dictionaries
> job-related uses of literacy in the indigenous language
> level of knowledge of the indigenous language in the community, both of the spoken language and of the written language

The first five properties relate to individual competence, while the last describes the environment that users find themselves in, which conditions their dictionary practice. We expand on the last point.

3.1   Background
Table 1 provides basic information on the situations of speakers, and descendants of speakers, of the three languages that we investigated. We discuss each language group in turn.

Table 1: **Situation of speakers and descendants of speakers**

Language	Community	Type of Dictionary	Language requiring...	Bilingual programme[9]
Alawa	Minyerri	paper	revitalisation[10]	no, LOTE
Warumungu	Tennant Creek	paper	revitalisation	no
Wakirti Warlpiri	Tennant Creek	paper	revitalisation	no
Warlpiri	Alice Springs Yuendumu Willowra Lajamanu	paper and electronic	maintenance	yes

3.1.1 Alawa

Alawa is a language which some speakers and descendants of speakers are trying to revitalise. They have never had bilingual education programmes. Only elderly people are competent speakers. However they are unlikely to be able to read or write their language competently. Children and young adults do not speak Alawa as their first language, and nor do they write it. The language that people aged six to fifty were most likely to be literate in is English; they were less likely to be literate in Kriol;[11] and they were unlikely to be literate in Alawa.

3.1.2 Warlpiri (Lajamanu, Willowra, Yuendumu)

Warlpiri is the first language of the community in all three places. People of all ages speak Warlpiri, although at Lajamanu children and young adults speak Kriol and English, and language shift appears to be in progress. At Willowra and Yuendumu the English spoken is closer to standard English. As a result of bilingual education

---

[9] Lack of bilingual programme means that no one has much chance to write the indigenous language, let alone have any literacy reinforcement, through for example, newsletters and public notices.

[10] 'Revitalisation' in this context means that children do not speak the indigenous language.

[11] Kriol is the name given to the creole spoken over large areas of the northern part of Australia.

programmes in all three communities, many people write Warlpiri as well as English, but inevitably literacy skills differ according to age; most old people are illiterate. Young to middle age adults who are literate in Warlpiri are likely to be comparably literate in English as well. There is Warlpiri literacy reinforcement through the presence of the school, newsletters, and some public notices.

3.1.3   *Eastern Warlpiri and Warumungu*

Eastern (Wakirti) Warlpiri and Warumungu in the Tennant Creek area are in similar positions. Both are languages which some speakers and descendants of speakers are trying to revitalise. Only middle-aged and elderly people are competent speakers. They have never had bilingual education programmes. A few can read or write Wakirti Warlpiri and Warumungu as a result of adult education courses. The language that people aged six to thirty are most likely to be literate in is English; they are less likely to be literate in Wakirti Warlpiri and Warumungu. There has been no attempt to provide Kriol literacy. With respect to speaking skills, they are likely to be most proficient in Kriol, less proficient in English and least proficient in Wakirti Warlpiri and Warumungu.

3.2   Actual uses

Unlike LB, the main use that all the Australian Aboriginal people we worked with had for dictionaries of their language was for maintaining and learning the EL, their languages. They had many other ways of learning English, the LWC. The seventy two people fell roughly into two types: speakers who needed maintenance dictionaries, and descendants of speakers who needed learner maintenance dictionaries. Within these two rough categories, people had different uses for dictionaries, and different problems in using dictionaries.

We observed their use of dictionaries, both when they were shown them for the first time, and in literacy courses, where dictionaries were lying around. We also got some of them to carry out tasks using dictionaries. We discussed dictionaries with many of them.

At the moment, the lack of availability of dictionaries of indigenous languages and the low levels of vernacular literacy restrict the uses of dictionaries by speakers and their descendants. We saw no systematic use of paper dictionaries of indigenous languages in school classrooms, whether LOTE or bilingual. The few instances of natural uses we have observed include:

1) people doing translation jobs and documenting paintings used the paper Warlpiri dictionary for decoding, to find out meanings for Warlpiri words now used only by older speakers.

2) people used the dictionary for encoding the EL in two main ways, making materials for school language programmes, and checking spelling in literacy classes.

3) when people were given dictionaries they browsed them, often stopping to check unfamiliar words or to find out how familiar words are represented in the dictionary.

In general, the indigenous people most able to use dictionaries and most keen to have them were those who had been through adult education courses in linguistics and indigenous language literacy.

Potentially, dictionaries of indigenous languages can play a role in classroom and non-classroom acquisition of language (McKay 1983:58-9), (allowing for our earlier remarks about the dangers of relying too heavily on a literacy-based programme). However, most people were not aware of this potential. Poetsch observed a telling example of Alawa people's lack of consciousness of the dictionary as a port of call for meaning. She engaged in two two-hour sessions with three young women on different activities with the dictionary. She then proposed that they should find the Alawa words for different kinds of kangaroo. They wrote down a handful of Kriol terms for kinds of kangaroo. They then said that they would go home (350 kilometres away), and ask the old people for the Alawa equivalents. It apparently did not occur to them to look them up in the dictionary which was there in front of them. That is, the speakers did not yet see the dictionary as a language learning tool.

Of course, asking a speaker for a word has several advantages over looking it up in a dictionary. First, you don't have to know how to write the word (whether in English or the indigenous language). Second, you can hear the sound of the word. Third, speakers may be seen as more reliable sources of information than a dictionary prepared by a lexicographer who is not a native speaker of the language. Finally, people may appreciate the excuse to talk about language with a speaker (Margaret Carew personal communication).

To conclude this section, a serious problem with all potential uses is that currently, people in the communities do not have good access to dictionaries, do not use dictionaries and typically are not aware of their potential In turn this affects the actual uses people make of dictionaries.

3.3   Useability

A key factor conditioning the actual uses of dictionaries is the fact that many potential users do not necessarily have all of the literacy and reference skills required to use the dictionary. Our major finding was that people's skills at using dictionaries were not developed, and thus it took them far too long to carry out tasks. Thus, for our study Poetsch designed thirteen task-based activities, assuming low levels of spoken and written competency in Alawa. In the event, she was only able to carry out the first four tasks with the users, because the time taken to complete each task was so great. For example, a crossword requiring twelve lookups took users some forty-five to sixty minutes. Simpson incorporated dictionary tasks as part of literacy and linguistics training courses, e.g. getting a literacy worker to proofread her traditional song text by looking up words in the Warlpiri electronic dictionary. Looking up twenty-six words with discussion took about two hours. When participants went through the long process of finally locating the sought EL word, they often found that they couldn't read it, because they didn't know how to pronounce the sounds nor did they know where the stress falls.

Actual uses of dictionaries are tightly constrained by the accessibility of the dictionary, how useable it is for different purposes. Creating an accessible dictionary is subject to four competing pressures on lexicographers:

> attitudes of users and makers to dictionaries (Corris 1999)
> exhaustiveness
> functionality
> practical considerations

We have discussed the importance of ascertaining user attitudes, and noted how they may conflict with makers' attitudes, in the first part of this paper. In what follows we concentrate on the exhaustiveness and functionality points, commenting on the practical considerations in passing.

3.3.1. Exhaustiveness

People wanting to make documentation dictionaries tend to want to include as much information as is known, in terms of number of entries, kinds of words, amount and kind of information about each word. But this wealth of information can be counterproductive for users needing maintenance dictionaries.

At the macrostructure level, users are put off finding words in huge dictionaries, because they are intimidated by the size of the volume. On the other hand they are put off by not finding an uncommon word they want in a small dictionary. This is a problem common to standard modern learners' dictionaries - they have the word for *water*, but not the word for *chutzpah*.

At the microstructure level, the amount and kind of information about each word is important. Users with low levels of literacy were intimidated by long entries. They found it difficult to ignore unnecessary/unwanted information. They found overcrowding of information confusing.

To sum up, there is a tension between the linguist/lexicographer's desire for exhaustiveness, which is essential for documentation dictionaries, and the user's need for accessible dictionaries, that is, for maintenance dictionaries.

3.3.2. Functionality

If indigenous Australian users are familiar with dictionaries, they are familiar with the structure of English dictionaries. Thus it makes sense to use people's skills in using LWC dictionaries as a springboard, and serious thought should be given before creating a macrostructure or microstructure which is radically different from what they have learned from English dictionaries. For example, this argues for using the same alphabetical order as the LWC, English in this case, rather than separately ordering accented letters or digraphs (Goddard and Thieberger 1997).

For proficient speakers of languages like Adang and Lani, the order should be Language-LWC, and this is useful for proficient speakers of Australian indigenous languages. But Alawa and Wakirti Warlpiri semi-speakers and descendants of speakers used the English finderlist section of the dictionary in preference to the indigenous language section. The English-Indigenous language section is very valuable for indigenous language learners with good English literacy skills, as well as for those who want to improve their English literacy (see also Zorc 1983). It is the most likely to be used and needs to be the most user-friendly. Of course this goes against the symbolic value of EL-English order, which is also the order in most dictionaries of Australian indigenous languages (Goddard & Thieberger 1997).

Many issues of design and convention cropped up in our investigation. They are discussed in detail in Corris et al (in prep.). However, we briefly list here some of the more important:

Design issues

Dense text and small font size was a difficulty for users with low levels of literacy, as well as those users with eye-sight problems. However, practical considerations prevent printing with large fonts dictionaries with large numbers of entries.

Locating the relevant section of the dictionary proved difficult for some users. We suggest coloured dividers as a possible solution.

In three-way dictionaries, such as the Alawa-Kriol-English dictionary (Sharpe 1999), users were able to find the Alawa forms which were in bold typeface, but had trouble distinguishing Kriol and English forms because the typefaces were too similar.

Dictionary conventions

Dictionary conventions were foreign to users. These include part of speech abbreviations and grammatical descriptions, as well as cryptic abbreviations such as SYN, ANT, or symbols, such as arrows. They also had trouble with definitional conventions, such as *kangaroo, plains*, since they did not realise that these are read in the reverse order, 'plains kangaroo'.

Some participants found the idea of a citation form of verbs hard to grasp. They were disappointed when they couldn't find inflected forms of verbs in the dictionary, and they couldn't remove the necessary inflections to find citation forms. They wanted inflected forms of verbs in the dictionary.

Lengthy, detailed entries were very hard for users not familiar with dictionaries. For example, some Alawa users had trouble recognising a definition that went on to a second line. They also became distracted where there were a lot of subentries. They would not look beyond the first one.

Many of these problems can be solved by using electronic dictionaries (Corris et al, in prep.). First, an electronic dictionary can resolve the tension between exhaustiveness and functionality by allowing different levels of interface, ranging from a simple word-definition list in large font suitable for a learner, to an encyclopaedic entry suitable for a specialist. Second, they also allow in principle solutions to the problems of space restrictions. Third, they allow access by a variety of means, by typing words, clicking on them, as well as using alphabetical order. Finally, they also allow for digital sound, thus solving the problem of representing pronunciation phonetically.

In first world countries like Australia, where schools have computers, electronic interfaces are starting to be useful to speakers. Even so, users still want paper dictionaries that they can take away into the dust of the camp. In situations where computers are not readily accessible, such as in parts of Indonesia, electronic interfaces will be out of reach of EL speakers for many years to come.

4. CONCLUSION

To conclude, of the four competing demands placed on a lexicographer, the first, speakers' attitudes, is essential for designing a dictionary, be it documentation or maintenance. The second, exhaustiveness, is essential for a documentation dictionary. However it conflicts with the third demand, functionality, the key property of a maintenance dictionary. whether for speakers or for learners. In turn practical considerations affect the end product. Lack of time, lack of money, lack of computer expertise among the lexicographers, all have effects on the eventual outcomes.

Some of the structural considerations are related to the fact that maintaining a language means recording the language in a way that is useful to the speakers and their descendants **now.** In most of these situations, however, lack of resources means that one dictionary often has to fulfil all of the above roles.

This is where importance must be placed on the design of the dictionary database. Everything the lexicographer finds out about a word can be stored in the database, thus creating the 'documentation dictionary'. However it should also be designed so that material can be printed out in whatever forms are most useful to the speakers, thus creating 'maintenance dictionaries', or LWC learner dictionaries. These will usually be smaller dictionaries of simpler structure. Some will resemble learners' dictionaries. Others will resemble children's dictionaries, or topical picture dictionaries, or very simple wordlists. While a dictionary extensively hand-edited with a particular purpose in mind will always produce the best results, even in places where electronic dictionaries cannot be regularly used, considerable value can be achieved by being able to produce good quality dictionaries customised for different user groups automatically from a single computer dictionary database. The essential ingredient for being able to do this is a syntactically and semantically well-structured database.

We have focused on redesigning the dictionary as one part of the solution. Doing this well requires community consultation, investigation of actual and potential uses, and checking useability. The other part of the solution involves training the users. Community wide dictionary skills training should be an essential part of creating EL dictionaries.

Dictionaries provide status to a language and are a means of documenting dying languages with decreasing numbers of speakers. They can be made more useful for maintenance purposes, when users, uses and useability are taken into consideration in the design of such dictionaries. However, dictionaries alone will not revitalise or maintain a language; they are but one tool in the task.

REFERENCES

Atkins, Beryl T. S. & F. E. Knowles 1990. Interim report on the EURALEX/AILA research project into dictionary use. In T. Magay & J. Zigany (eds) *Proceedings of BudaLex '88*, 381-392. Budapest: Akadémiai Kiadó.

Atkins, Beryl T. S. & Krista Varantola 1997. Monitoring dictionary use. *International Journal of Lexicography* 10/1: 1-45.

Austin, Peter K. (ed.) 1983. *Papers in Australian Linguistics No.15: Australian Aboriginal lexicography.* Pacific Linguistics A-66. Canberra: Department of Linguistics RSPAS, ANU.

Baker, Brett & Christopher D. Manning 1998. A dictionary database template for Australian languages. In *Proceedings of Australex 1998*, <http://www.anu.edu.au/linguistics/alex/a98/>

Béjoint, Henri 1981. The foreign student's use of monolingual English dictionaries: a study of language needs and reference skills. *Applied linguistics* 2/3: 207-222.

_____ 1994. *Tradition and innovation in modern English dictionaries.* Oxford: Clarendon Press.

Biniluk, Lipiyus 1999. *Lani-Indonesian-English Dictionary.* Ms. Sydney: Department of Linguistics, University of Sydney.

Carroll, Peter To appear. User friendly dictionaries for native speakers of Australian indigenous languages. Submitted to *Dictionaries,* the Journal of the Dictionary Society of North America. [Paper presented at the Australian Linguistics Society Annual meeting, Perth.]

Corris, Miriam 1999. *Dictionary use and useability.* BA Honours thesis, Department of Linguistics, University of Sydney.

_____, Christopher Manning, Susan Poetsch & Jane Simpson In preparation. Using dictionaries of Australian Aboriginal languages. Submitted to *International Journal of Lexicography.*

Dale, Wesley 1993. *Lani Dictionary.* R.B.M.U. International. October 1993. [incorporating Gordon Larson's material]

Goddard, Cliff & Nick Thieberger 1997. Lexicographic research on Australian Aboriginal languages, 1969-1993. In Darrell T. Tryon &

Michael Walsh (eds) *Boundary rider: essays in honour of Geoffrey O'Grady*, 175-208. Pacific Linguistics C-36. Canberra: Department of Linguistics RSPAS, ANU.

Grimes, Barbara F., Richard S. Pittman & Joseph E. Grimes 1996-99. *Ethnologue: languages of the world.* 13th Edition. Dallas, Texas: SIL International. <http://www.sil.org/ethnologue/>

Haan, Johnson In preparation. *Adang grammar.* PhD dissertation, University of Sydney.

Haas, Mary R. 1962. What belongs in a bilingual dictionary? In Fred W. Householder & Sol Saporta (eds) *Problems in Lexicography*, 45-50. Mouton & Co.: Bloomington, Indiana.

Hartmann, R.R.K. 1989. Sociology of the dictionary user. In F.-J. Hausmann, O. Reichmann, H. E. Wiegand & L. Zgusta (eds) *Wörterbücher, Dictionaries, Dictionnaires, An international encyclopaedia of lexicography*, 102-112. Berlin: Mouton de Gruyter.

Hatherall, Glyn 1984. Studying dictionary use: some findings and proposals. In R.R.K. Hartmann (ed.) *LEXeter '83 Proceedings*, 183-189. Lexicographica Series Maior No.1. Tübingen: Niemeyer.

Jansz, Kevin 1998. *Intelligent processing, storing and visualisation of dictionary information.* BA Honours thesis, Department of Computer Science, University of Sydney. <http://www.sultry.arts.usyd.edu.au/kjansz/thesis/>

_____, Christopher D. Manning, & Nitin Indurkhya 1999. Kirrkirr: Interactive visualisation and multimedia from a structured Warlpiri dictionary. Proceedings of Ausweb99, the Fifth Australian World Wide Web Conference, 302-316.

Laughren, Mary, Ken Hale & Robert Hoogenraad In preparation. *Warlpiri Dictionary.* St Lucia: Department of English, University of Queensland.

McConvell, Patrick, Ron Day, & Paul Black 1983. Making a Meriam Mir dictionary. In Austin (ed.) 19-30.

McKay, Graham 1983. Lexicography and Ndjebbana (Kunibidji) bilingual education program. In Austin (ed.) 57-70.

Schebeck, Bernhard 1983. Dictionaries for Australian languages: some general remarks. In Austin (ed.) 41-55.

Sharpe, Margaret 1999. *Alawa Wanggaya: Alawa-Kriol-English Dictionary.* Katherine: Diwurruwurru-Jaru.

Simpson, Jane In preparation. *Warumungu Dictionary.* Tennant Creek: Papulu Apparr-kari and Sydney: Department of Linguistics, University of Sydney.

Stebbins, Tonya 1999. Tsimshian contributions to the design of the Sm'algyax Dictionary. Paper presented at AUSTRALEX meeting, Canberra, 30/10/99.

Supusepa, Edi F.M. 1998. *Woordenlijst Nederlands - Moluks - Saparuaans.* Holland: Honimoa Reeks.

Tamaela, Wate Dede 1998. *"Komo oe" Bahasa Koako, Pulau Seram.* Ms.

Zorc, R. David 1983. A Yolngu-Matha dictionary: plans and proposals. In Austin (ed.) 31-40.

Chapter 20

Conclusion: Resources for Language Maintenance[1]

David Bradley & Maya Bradley
La Trobe University

As the preceding papers have shown, the prospects and needs for language maintenance (LM) for endangered languages (ELs) differ greatly between communities. Institutional and other resources available also differ widely: from full government support and massive funding, as for Irish in Ireland (Ahlqvist), to nothing available (most Yi in China, Bradley and Bradley; Tai in Assam, Morey) or even desired (Anabaptist German, Burridge) from outside the community, to active government attempts to suppress ELs and assimilate their speakers (until quite recently Sm'algyax, Stebbins; and most Australian Aboriginal languages, Blake, Thieberger). Such practices are fortunately now a thing of the past in most of the developed world, but the aftereffects of assimilationist policies have created an ecolinguistic disaster for most minority indigenous and migrant languages there. In the developing world, minority LM understandably has a lower priority than nation-building, education, health and so on; so language shift continues to accelerate.

There are various academic organisations which support practical work in EL communities. The Foundation for Endangered Languages of the UK is also active in publicity and political pressure for LM and language rights. In the USA there are the the Society for the Study of Indigenous Languages of the Americas, the Endangered Languages and Their Preservation Committee of the Linguistic Society of America, the Endangered Languages Fund and Terralingua. There is also the Gesellschaft für bedrohte Sprachen of Germany. Internet access information is given below.

More practical work has been carried out for many years by individuals and groups in various parts of the world. Some notable

---

[1] The authors are very pleased to acknowledge the symposium presentation by David Nash, which provided various details on internet and other resources discussed here; he is of course not responsible for our discussion and comments.

centres where scholars are working with communities for LM while also carrying our research include Yamamoto and many others in the American Indian Languages Development Institute (see Watahomigie and Yamamoto 1992) and Krauss and his coworkers in the Alaska Native Language Center in the USA, among many other places. In Australia there have been the research-oriented Australian Institute of Aboriginal and Islander Studies in Canberra; the School of Australian Languages at Batchelor providing practical training, and the Institute for Aboriginal Development at Alice Springs working with communities on various types of projects including LM, along with a large number of regional language centres, language projects involving particular groups, and individual teacher linguists in schools. Outrageously, some of these initiatives in Australia have recently been downgraded; few politicians or bureaucrats share our concern for LM. In most developing and underdeveloped countries there is even less support available for indigenous languages, particularly those of minorities.

The United Nations and a variety of its component organisations, as well as other NGOs, prepared and signed the Universal Declaration of Linguistic Rights after meeting from 6 to 9 June 1996 in Barcelona. This treats language rights as a basic component of human rights.

Within the UN, UNESCO has identified work on ELs as a priority, on a par with other aspects of the maintenance of humanity's cultural heritage; it has also convened a number of international conferences on this topic: part of the International Congress of Linguists at Québec in August 1992 (Robins and Uhlenbeck 1991) and a special conference to inaugurate the International Clearing House for Endangered Languages in November 1995 (Matsumura 1998). UNESCO has been directly funding work in this area since formally launching its 'Endangered Language Project' in November 1993. It has already published Wurm (1996) and supported a wide variety of other projects and publications, and its Linguapax project is preparing a world languages report.

A new major funding initiative is from the Volkswagen-Stiftung of Germany, which is now supporting a resource centre in Cologne and a large number of projects on specific languages. Another proposed initiative is to subsidise the establishment of a new journal on ELs, to be published by Mouton de Gruyter.

The Tokyo clearing house established in 1995 has been one major Japanese initiative. In 1999 the Ministry of Education of Japan identified ELs as a Priority Area for research and provided a large multi-year grant to a team of 72 scholars from Japan and a number of overseas collaborators including some from Australia, Estonia, the Philippines and Russia to undertake a total of 34 related projects under the overall title 'Endangered Languages of the Pacific Rim'. One of their initial activities is a public symposium at Kyoto in November 2000.

Apart from the UNESCO-sponsored conferences noted above, there has been an increasing number of meetings on this topic in the last few years. There have been annual conferences on stabilising indigenous languages in the western hemisphere since 1994. The Foundation for Endangered Languages has held annual conferences since 1997, each with a specific LM-related topic: FEL2 at Edinburgh in September 1998 was on 'What role for the specialist?', FEL3 at Maynooth, Ireland in September 1999 was on 'Endangered languages and education' and FEL4 at Charlotte, North Carolina in September 2000 on 'Endangered languages and literacy'. Proceedings of FEL2 onwards are available from Dr Nicholas Ostler, the President of FEL. These have been particularly stimulating and energising for those who participated, because they tackle practical issues and real situations, with active participation by members of communities speaking ELs. Other conferences with both theoretical and practical goals have included one held at Dartmouth College in the USA in February 1995 (Grenoble and Whaley 1998) and this symposium. More recently, there was a conference at Bonn in February 2000 funded by Volkswagen-Stiftung, which will soon produce a major theoretical volume edited by Brenzinger which will also attempt to set priorities for work on ELs.

Of course there are frequent more localised conferences and meetings in many countries, such as the workshop at the Australian Linguistic Institute at La Trobe University in July 1994, 'Language shift and maintenance in the Asia Pacific Region', supported by the Wenner-Gren Foundation; the symposium on minority languages of the north held at Osaka in November 1994 (Shoji and Janhunen

1997); the 1995 symposium on language loss and public policy at the University of New Mexico, during which Terralingua was set up; and the 'minority languages in context' conference held in Chur, Switzerland in September 1998, which enabled LM workers from across Europe to meet and discuss progress in their work (Dazzi Gross and Mondada 1999), and the symposium at La Trobe University in November 1999 on which the present volume is based.

In addition to these institutional and published resources, there are various web and listserv sites available; some of these are listed below, and others can readily be found through these or with any search engine. Of course, we need to be aware that very few speakers of ELs outside the developed world have computers or internet access. It must also be noted that nearly all the references given are to work in English, with just a few in other major European languages. This is a reflection of sociolinguistic reality: English is the world's most dangerous language!

As Krauss (1992: 10) has pointed out,

> Obviously we must do some serious rethinking of our priorities, lest linguistics go down in history as the only science that presided obliviously over the disappearance of 90% of the very field to which it is dedicated.

This formerly widespread obliviousness has now been replaced by much greater interest within the community of professional linguists; but a great deal of work is needed. More listservs, web sites and conferences may help to bring additional linguists into the area, but perhaps not necessarily assist in LM, especially if some continue "hit and run" fieldwork: collect the data, get out, publish with academic publishers in a first-world language, get an academic job and leave the speakers of "their" EL to their own devices.

One clear need is for more outreach: letting communities who may want to do something about their language know that we are here, able and willing to help. Few communities with an EL have access to computers or the internet, most cannot and would not want to read our theoretical outpourings in English, and almost none can come to our conferences. So the outreach needs to be in forms that are really accessible: through a language known to the community with an EL and in a form that will interest them: video or audio tapes, attractive written materials with pictures containing appropriate traditional material, and so on. A major component of this outreach should be the training of skilled and enthusiastic insiders, who can continue the LM work when the outsiders cannot be in the community.

Another essential is ethical use of data: not just for developed-world "science", but for undeveloped-world LM: to maintain whatever the communities want – even if that is not what we might think they should want, as Thieberger has pointed out above – and to be ready when what they want changes.

INTERNET RESOURCES

Endangered Languages Fund (Whalen)
<http://www.ling.yale.edu/~elf/>

Endangered Languages List (Listserv)
<http://carmen.murdoch.edu.au/lists/endangered-languages-l/>

Ethnologue (Grimes)
<http://www.sil.org/ethnologue/ethnologue.html>

Gesellschaft für bedrohte Sprachen (Sasse)
<http://www.uni-koeln.de/gbs/e_index.html>

Foundation for Endangered Languages (Ostler)
<http://www.bris.ac.uk/Depts/Philosophy/CTLL/FEL/>

International Clearinghouse of Endangered Languages (Tsunoda)
<http://www.tooyoo.l.u-tokyo.ac.jp/ichel-j.html>

Linguistic Society of America Committee on Endangered Languages and their Preservation
<http://www.linguistlist.org/el-page/>

Terralingua
<http://cougar.ucdavis.edu/nas/terralin/home.html>

UNESCO World Languages Report
<http://www.unescoeh.org>

Universal Declaration of Linguistic Rights
<http://www.indigo.ie/egt/udhr.html>

REFERENCES

Brenzinger, Matthias (ed.) forthcoming. *Language Diversity Endangered.* Berlin: Mouton de Gruyter.

Dazzi Gross, Anna-Alice & Lorenza Mondada (eds) 1999. Les langues minoritaires en contexte. *Bulletin Suisse de Linguistique Appliquée* 69/1-2.

Grenoble, Lenore A. & Lindsay J. Whaley (eds) 1998. *Endangered Languages.* Cambridge: Cambridge University Press.

Krauss, Michael 1992. The world's languages in crisis. *Language* 68/1: 4-10

Matsumura, Kazuto (ed.) 1998. *Studies in Endangered Languages. Papers from the International Symposium on Endangered Languages. Tokyo November 18-20, 1995.* Tokyo: Hituzi Syobo.

Ostler, Nicholas (ed.) 1998. *Endangered Languages: What Role for the Specialist?* Bath: Foundation for Endangered Languages.

_____ (ed.) 1999. *Endangered Languages and Education.* Bath: Foundation for Endangered Languages.

Robins, Robert H. & E. M. Uhlenbeck (eds) 1991. *Endangered Languages.* Oxford: Berg.

Shoji, Hiroshi & Juha Janhunen (eds) 1997. *Northern Minority Languages: Problems of Survival.* Osaka: National Museum of Ethnology.

Watahomigie, Lucille J. & Akira Y. Yamamoto 1992. Local reactions to perceived language decline. *Language* 68/1: 10-17

Wurm, Stephen A. (ed.) 1996. *Atlas of the World's Languages in Danger of Disappearing.* Paris: UNESCO Publishing and Canberra: Pacific Linguistics. Second edition, revised and expanded 2001.

Contributors

Dr David Bradley (AB Columbia, PhD University of London) is Reader in Linguistics at La Trobe University. He has done research on various languages in China, Thailand, Burma and India, and has published very widely on descriptive, historical, geolinguistic and sociolinguistic issues.

Dr Maya Bradley is a Research Fellow in Linguistics at La Trobe University. Her BA is from Tel-Aviv, with MA and PhD from Monash. She has published a variety of studies on Hebrew grammar, Australian and Asian Englishes, and on minority languages of China.

Dr Anders Ahlqvist is Professor of Irish at the National University of Ireland (Galway), where he has been since 1977. After undergraduate study in Finland, he completed a PhD at Edinburgh in 1974. He has published on Irish historical morphosyntax, history of linguistics and sociolinguistics, and edited early Irish texts.

Dr Alexandra Aikhenvald (PhD Moscow) is Professor of Linguistics at La Trobe University; formerly at USSR Academy of Sciences, Santa Catarina in Brazil, and Australian National University. Her research is on typology, with a recent Oxford University Press book on classifiers, and on Arawak and Afroasiatic languages.

Dr Barry Blake is Foundation Professor of Linguistics at La Trobe University. His work on a number of Australian Aboriginal languages has provided materials for several language revival programmes. He has also published very extensively on typology and theoretical morphology and syntax.

Dr John Bowden is now a Research Fellow in Linguistics, RSPAS, Australian National University. After studying at Auckland and Melbourne, he was a Post-Doctoral Fellow at Max-Planck Institute for Psycholinguistics. He has done research on a number of Austronesian languages.

Dr Kate Burridge is Associate Professor of Linguistics at La Trobe University. After study at the University of Western Australia, she completed her PhD at the University of London in 1983. Her main areas of research are grammatical change in Germanic languages; Pennsylvania German; linguistic taboo; and English.

Miriam Corris wrote an Honours thesis on dictionary use and useability in 1999 at the University of Sydney. She is currently involved in a dictionary and literacy materials project for Lani (Western Dani; West Papua).

Christina Eira is currently completing her PhD at the University of Melbourne on Foucaultian discourse analysis of standardisation in Hmong. She is assisting local ex-refugee Hmong on a dictionary project using the ə̄к̄ n̄ᴦ (Pahawh) script. Previously she worked in medieval music paleography.

Dr Aone van Engelenhoven (Drs and PhD Leiden) is Senior Lecturer in Austronesian Linguistics at Leiden University. His research areas are comparative and descriptive linguistics and oral traditions of East Indonesia and East Timor, especially Maluku Tenggara and the Moluccan community in the Netherlands.

Dr Margaret Florey is Lecturer in Linguistics at Monash University. Her research has focused on the study of endangered languages, including work on Australian Aboriginal languages and the languages of the Maluku region of eastern Indonesia (in Indonesia and among migrants in the Netherlands).

Dr John Hajek is Senior Lecturer in the School of Languages, University of Melbourne; formerly Research Fellow at Oxford and at Melbourne. Educated at the University of Melbourne (BA Hons), Florence, Padua and Oxford (DPhil 1992). Principal research areas are phonetics/phonology, typology, Southeast Asian linguistics and East Timor.

Christopher Manning is an Assistant Professor of Computer Science and Linguistics at Stanford University. While on the staff of the University of Sydney, he developed an interest in making better use of computer software for assembling and visualising lexical information.

Stephen Morey is a postgraduate student and tutor at Monash University, Melbourne. He graduated with a BA (Hons) in 1998 after completing a dissertation on manuscript sources of the languages of Victoria. He is presently doing research for a dissertation on the Tai Languages of Assam.

Dr Peter Mühlhäusler (BA Hons Stellenbosch, MPhil Reading, PhD ANU) is Foundation Professor of Linguistics at Adelaide University; he has formerly taught at the Technical University of Berlin and at Oxford. His research is concerned with pidgins and creoles, language maintenance and ecolinguistics.

Susan Poetsch has been an adult ESL and literacy/numeracy teacher for ten years in the Torres Strait, China, Korea and Sydney. During 1999 she worked at Diwurruwurru-jaru, the Katherine Region Aboriginal Language Centre in the Northern Territory.

Dr Jane Simpson teaches linguistics at the University of Sydney. She has been studying the Warumungu and Warlpiri languages since 1979. Her interest in lexical semantics has led her to work on dictionaries for both languages.

Dr Tonya Stebbins (PhD University of Melbourne 1999) s currently a Postdoctoral Fellow at the Research Centre for Linguistic Typology, La Trobe University. She has worked for years on the Northwest Coast of British Columbia, supporting language maintenance efforts including a dictionary. She is now working on the description of a endangered languages in Papua New Guinea.

Nicholas Thieberger is a PhD student at the University of Melbourne University and has worked at the Pilbara Aboriginal Language Centre and at the Australian Institute of Aboriginal and Torres Strait Islander Studies. His current research is on a language from Vanuatu.

Dr Stephen Wurm was Professor Emeritus of Linguistics, RSPAS, Australian National University. He published extensively on Pacific, Turkic, Pacific and Asian Pidgin and contact languages; also on language endangerment and language atlases (Pacific, China), and was founding editor of the *Pacific Linguistics* series.

CPSIA information can be obtained
at www.ICGtesting.com
Printed in the USA
FFHW02n0349190918
48365850-52206FF